Community and Clergy

Community and Clergy

Bristol and the Reformation
c.1530–c.1570

MARTHA C. SKEETERS

CLARENDON PRESS · OXFORD
1993

Oxford University Press, Walton Street, Oxford OX2 6DP
Oxford New York Toronto
Delhi Bombay Calcutta Madras Karachi
Petaling Jaya Singapore Hong Kong Tokyo
Nairobi Dar es Salaam Cape Town
Melbourne Auckland
and associated companies in
Berlin Ibadan

Oxford is a trade mark of Oxford University Press

Published in the United States
by Oxford University Press, New York

British Library Cataloguing in Publication Data
Data available

Library of Congress Cataloging in Publication Data
Skeeters, Martha Clayton. Community and Clergy: Bristol and the Reformation
c.1530–c.1570/Martha C. Skeeters.
p. cm.
Includes bibliographical references and index.
1. Clergy—England—Bristol—History—16th century. 2. Bristol
(England)—Church history—16th century. I. Title.
BR742.S54 1993
262'14'0942393—dc2092-28430
ISBN 0-19-820181-8

Typeset by Hope Services (Abingdon) Ltd.
Printed and bound in
Great Britain by Biddles Ltd.,
Guildford and King's Lynn

Acknowledgements

LONG before this book was conceived the debts incurred in writing it began to accumulate. Historians and mentors Bill Painter and Ed Coomes of the University of North Texas and Michael Baylor of Lehigh University contributed more than they realize in numerous conversations. At the University of Texas at Austin Janet Meisel and Guy Lytle offered useful criticism at an early stage, and Myron Gutmann made discerning comments on early drafts. Brian Levack directed my dissertation there and continued as a supportive critic through the successive revisions which made the dissertation a book. The comments of Conrad Russell, Carole Levin, Michael Rogers, and David Levy on the manuscript in its later stages were perceptive and useful.

While doing the research for this work in England, I received advice and assistance from a number of people. I am particularly grateful to Patrick McGrath, formerly of Bristol University, for his guidance and encouragement and for the benefit of his knowledge of the history of Bristol. His comments on the manuscript were insightful and helpful. At the Bristol Archives Office I received invaluable aid from former city archivists, Elizabeth Ralph and Mary Williams, and more recently from City Archivist John Williams and Assistant Archivist Margaret McGregor. I am especially grateful to Miss Ralph for her aid in regard to the archives of the parish of St Mary Redcliffe. I also am indebted to the archivists of the Public Record Office, the Hereford and Worcester Record Office, and the Somerset Record Office. Derek Shorrocks of the Somerset Record Office was particularly helpful in identifying ecclesiastical records of the diocese of Bath and Wells. A second visit to English archives was supported by a grant from the National Endowment for the Humanities. At the Instructional Services Center of the University of Oklahoma Greg Mittmeyer contributed the maps and Margaret Smith advised on graphics.

Two anonymous reviewers, historians of late medieval and Tudor England respectively, made wise criticisms and saved me from many mistakes. Editors at Oxford University Press have also helped to make the book much better than it might have been. The errors that remain are, of course, my own.

The book could not have been undertaken without the support of my parents Laborn and Ellein Tullos Skeeters, nor completed without the sustenance and confidence of my husband João Rego Cruz and my daughter Amy Skeeters-Behrens.

Spelling, punctuation, and capitalization of fifteenth- and sixteenth-century documents have been modernized in quotations, but not in the titles of early printed books. Dates are given in New Style.

M.C.S.

Contents

List of Tables

Abbreviations

APC	J. R. Dasent (ed.), *Acts of the Privy Council of England*, NS (London: HMSO, 1890–3)
B&GAS	Bristol and Gloucestershire Archaeological Society
B&W	Bath and Wells
BAO	Bristol Archives Office, Bristol
BIHR	*Bulletin of the Institute of Historical Research*
BL	British Library
BRS	Bristol Record Society
BRUC	A. B. Emden, *A Biographical Register of the University of Cambridge to 1500* (Cambridge: Cambridge University Press, 1963)
BRUO	A. B. Emden, *A Biographical Register of the University of Oxford to A.D. 1500* (Oxford: Oxford University Press, 1957–9)
BRUO 1501–1540	A. B. Emden, *A Biographical Register of the University of Oxford, A.D. 1501–1540* (Oxford: Clarendon Press, 1974)
CPR	*Calendar of Patent Rolls* (Henry VIII, Edward VI, Philip & Mary, Elizabeth), (London: HMSO)
CSPD	*Calendars of State Papers Domestic* (Elizabeth), (London: HMSO, 1900)
DNB	*Dictionary of National Biography*
EETS	Early English Text Society
EHR	*English Historical Review*
EHS	Ecclesiastical History Society
Foster	Joseph Foster, *Alumni Oxonienses*, 4 vols. (Oxford and London: Parker, 1888–91)
GRB	E. W. W. Veale (ed.), *The Great Red Book of Bristol* (Bristol: BRS, 1933–53)
GWB	Elizabeth Ralph (ed.), *Great White Book* (Gloucester: Bristol Record Society, 1979)
H&WRO	Hereford and Worcester Record Office, Worcester
HJ	*Historical Journal*
JBS	*Journal of British Studies*
JEH	*Journal of Ecclesiastical History*

LP	J. S. Brewer, James Gairdner, and R. H. Brodie (eds.), *Letters and Papers Foreign and Domestic of the Reign of Henry VIII*, 36 vols. (London: Longman, Green, Longman, & Roberts, 1862–1932)
LRB	F. B. Bickley (ed.), *The Little Red Book of Bristol* (Bristol: W. C. Hemmons, 1900)
Mayor's Kalendar	*The Maire of Bristowe is Kalendar, by Robert Ricart, Town Clerk of Bristol, 18 Edward IV*, ed. Lucy Toulmin Smith (Westminster: Camden Society, 1872)
P&P	*Past and Present*
PCC	Prerogative Court of Canterbury
PRO	Public Record Office, London
Regs. B&W	Henry Maxwell-Lyte (ed.), *Registers of the Bishops of Bath and Wells, 1518–1559* (SRS 55; London: Somerset Record Society, 1940)
RHS	Royal Historical Society
SCH	Studies in Church History
SRO	Somerset Record Office, Taunton
SRS	Somerset Record Society
STC	W. A. Jackson, F. J. Ferguson, and K. F. Pantzer (eds.), *A Short-Title Catalogue of Books Printed in England, Scotland and Ireland, and of English Books Printed Abroad, 1475–1640*, 2 vols. (London: Bibliographical Society, 1976, 1986)
Trans. B&GAS	*Transactions of the Bristol and Gloucestershire Archaeological Society*
TRHS	*Transactions of the Royal Historical Society*
VCH	*Victoria County Histories*
Venn	J. Venn and J. A. Venn, *Alumni Cantabrigienses*, 4 vols. (Cambridge: Cambridge University Press, 1922–7)

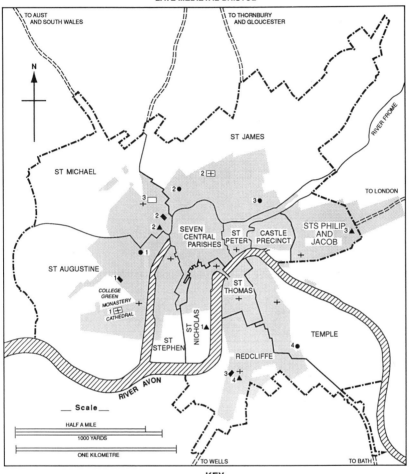

LATE MEDIEVAL BRISTOL

TO AUST
AND SOUTH WALES

TO THORNBURY
AND GLOUCESTER

N

RIVER FROME

ST JAMES

ST MICHAEL

2 ⊞

2 ●

TO LONDON

3 +   3 ▢

3 ●

2 ▲

2 ▲

SEVEN
CENTRAL
PARISHES

ST
PETER

CASTLE
PRECINCT

STS PHILIP
AND
JACOB

3 ▲

● 1

+

+

ST AUGUSTINE

1 ▬

COLLEGE
GREEN
MONASTERY

1 ⊞
CATHEDRAL

+

ST
THOMAS

+

+

ST
NICHOLAS

1 ▲

TEMPLE

4 ●

ST
STEPHEN

REDCLIFFE

3 ●
4 ▲

RIVER AVON

__ Scale __

HALF A MILE

1000 YARDS

ONE KILOMETRE

TO WELLS

TO BATH

KEY

● Friaries
1. Carmelite
2. Franciscan
3. Dominican
4. Augustinian

▬ Hospitals
1. St Mark or Gaunts
2. St Bartholomew
3. St John

▲ Chapels
1. St Clement
2. Three Kings
3. Holy Trinity
4. Holy Spirit

▢ Monastic Institutions
1. Monastery of
   St Augustine
2. Priory of St. James
3. Priory or Nunnery of
   St Mary Magdalen

+ Parish Churches

Parish boundaries: ———
from Ashmead's map, 1828

Shaded area houses, gardens and orchards
depicted on Millerd's map,
1673 (about 300 acres)

City boundary: ━ ∙ ━ ∙ ━ ∙
from Ashmead's map, 1828

MAP 1. Late medieval Bristol

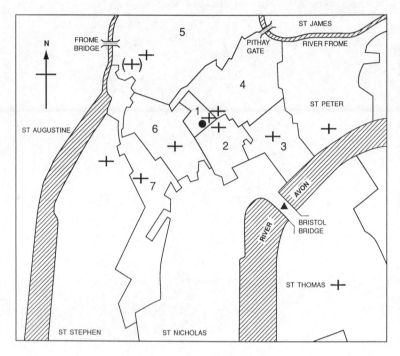

Key to the Central City Parishes

1. St Ewen
2. All Saints
3. St Mary-le-Porte
4. Christ Church
▲ Chapel of the Assumption
   on Bristol Bridge

5. St John
6. St Werburgh
7. St Leonard
● Chapel of St. George in the
   Guildhouse
+ Parish Churches including
   St Lawrence (+)

MAP 2. The central city parishes

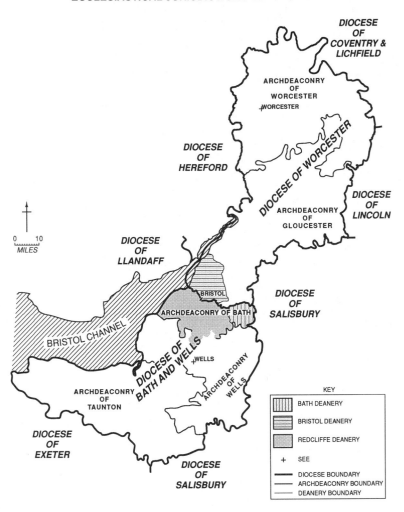

MAP 3. Ecclesiastical jurisdictions before 1541

I

Introduction

THE Reformation period in Bristol brought dramatic changes in the city's ecclesiastical institutions, in the number and character of its clergy, and in relationships between clergy and laity. The examination of these changes is the purpose of this study. English towns and cities experienced the Reformation differently from the rest of the primarily rural nation because of the presence of municipal authorities and large concentrations of clergy, both concerned with preserving their own power and privileges. The towns and cities may not have been typical of the rest of the country, as H. G. Owen rightly said of London, but their stories can still contribute something more to our understanding of the Reformation than exceptions which contrast with the typical.[1] If common denominators of the urban Reformation can be found, the experiences of the towns and cities may be viewed as a part of the whole nation's experience rather than a contrast to it. The urban experience can provide another facet in our understanding of the Reformation, which may change the appearance of the whole.

In addition, a closer look at the urban ecclesiastical and religious picture adds a needed dimension to our understanding of early modern towns and cities. Although I do not propose here to examine in detail the relationship between changes in religion and ecclesiastical structures and those in other areas of life in Bristol, I do suggest broad connections between religious and ecclesiastical change and changing political and social structures. Thus I hope that this study can contribute not only to our understanding of urban ecclesiastical history but also to its integration into the whole of urban history.

Until other urban ecclesiastical studies in the period are conducted in depth, we cannot know how representative Bristol and its experience of the Reformation were. In the sixteenth century Bristol ranked with some half dozen cities as provincial capitals, none of which compared to London in size or national importance. With a population of around 9,500 to 10,000, it ranked second to Norwich in both population and wealth and was wealthier and more populous than Exeter, Salisbury,

Coventry, or York.[2] It was the largest port outside London. Unlike these cities, Bristol was not a see and thus did not have a cathedral or the traditional title of city until 1542. It was not an ecclesiastical centre. Moreover, Bristol was unique in being split between two dioceses. The city north and west of the Avon River was in the diocese of Worcester; to the south and east three parish churches, one friary, and one hospital lay in the diocese of Bath and Wells.

Even in those cities which were sees, however, the local importance of the bishop could vary widely. Salisbury, for example, was still under the lordship of the bishop, who was thus supremely important in local affairs.[3] Exeter's largely non-resident bishops clearly did not see themselves as local figures though they sometimes impeded the authority of the local government.[4] York's archbishop was a national and international figure who was hardly, if at all, connected to the local scene.[5] The organization of diocesan administration and the configuration of cathedral clergy could also influence civic and ecclesiastical relationships as well as relationships within the city's clerical community.[6] While there may be no typical example of these relationships, knowledge of the differences and their meanings should provide insights into the nature of early modern English towns and cities as well as their experiences of the Reformation.

Bristol's multiple parish structure was similar to that of many other cities and towns. The number of parishes was important because it influenced the size of the local clerical population, it had an impact on the value of the parish clergy's livings, and in some places it may have affected the pace of religious change.[7] Claire Cross, however, warns against the notion of a typical urban parish structure in the sixteenth century. She distinguishes between older towns, which had inherited a large number of parishes from the early Middle Ages, and the new towns of the High Middle Ages wherein the boundaries of the township and a single parish often coincided. She also notes the overlapping of urban and rural communities in various circumstances within the same parish.[8] Bristol, like York, Norwich, Lincoln, Stamford, Worcester, and Winchester, was an older town with many parishes. Gloucester and Exeter also fell into this category. Even within this group, however, there were significant variations. York and Norwich, for example, had forty to fifty parishes while Bristol and Exeter had fewer than twenty. Generally, the more parishes, the poorer the livings.[9] We will see some of the consequences of this in the discussion of Bristol's parish clergy in Chapter 6.

Like some other provincial capitals and lesser towns, Bristol had a significant population of monks and friars.[10] The size and influence of religious communities in and around towns and cities was an important dimension of urban life. While their challenges to municipal governments' authority and their conflicts with each other and the parish clergy have often been noted, little attention has been given to the meaning of their demise to the local church, the local clerical community, and thus, the local community as a whole.[11] These matters require further exploration and it is hoped that the examination undertaken here will encourage further work.

Whether or not Bristol proves 'typical', this study asks new questions which I hope will be carried over to studies of other early modern English towns and cities. The answers should lead us not only to a more holistic knowledge of individual urban realities but also to a plateau from which the outlines of the urban landscape as a whole and its relation to the nation are clearer.

The focus of this study, however, is not only a place; it is the clergy of that place. Most previous studies of the English clergy in the sixteenth and seventeenth centuries have not recognized the significant distinction between urban and rural areas. This lacuna in clerical studies has grown out of the questions posed, the sources used, and the desire to undertake work which will have broad application either for typification or comparison and which will include a complete picture of the nation's clergy. Studies of the clergy of the sixteenth and seventeenth centuries have centred on the competency of the clergy to perform their duties, the lay perception of that competency, and the social status of the clergy. This focus has caused most scholars to limit their studies to the beneficed parish clergy, who were throughout the period the church's primary link to the laity. Investigations of the educational attainments and income of the parish clergy as well as of the problems of pluralism and non-residence generally make no distinctions between the rural clergy and their urban counterparts. Occasionally an offhand statement or brief disclaimer will note the exceptional poverty of urban livings, but usually no distinction is made between the realities of the urban and rural churches and clergies.[12] This limitation has in turn obscured the importance of the urban church and clergy, which underwent their most dramatic change during the Reformation. For in the urban church there were important connections between the religious, the friars, the chantry priests (all of whom disappeared as such by the mid-sixteenth century), and parish incumbents and curates. In an urban setting, the parish clergy cannot be isolated.[13]

Although my focus on the urban clergy represents a new direction in studies of the clergy, a number of valuable works have provided a foundation for the endeavour. In a very successful effort to give a full picture of the nation's parochial clergy just before the Reformation, Peter Heath uses evidence from many English dioceses. D. M. Barratt's study of the parish clergy from the Reformation to 1660 also employs evidence from a number of dioceses, particularly Oxford, Worcester and Gloucester.[14] The work of Margaret Bowker on the pre-Reformation secular clergy in Lincoln diocese deals with diocesan clergy and administration as well as parish clergy, extending the question of clerical competency to include the role of ecclesiastical authorities in maintaining it.[15]

The Lincoln archives have also been mined for a study of the Leicestershire parochial clergy in the later Stuart period and for three brief studies of the sixteenth-century parochial clergy, drawing especially upon wills.[16] Only Hoskins's study of the 'country' parson, however, distinguishes urban and rural clergy. D. M. Owen, in her study of the medieval church in Lincoln diocese, stresses the importance of the friars to the towns and cities and their conflicts with the parish clergy, but does not connect this material to questions of the parish clergy's competence.[17]

Philip Tyler's article on the Elizabethan parish clergy draws on evidence from the dioceses of York, Lincoln, and Oxford and blames the clergy's poverty on monastic appropriations, but he misses completely the urban–rural distinction which is also important in considerations of clerical poverty.[18] Claire Cross has addressed urban clerical poverty in one of the very few works with an urban focus. Her extremely valuable contribution, however, is not to distinguish rural and urban livings, but rather to show variations within the urban context.[19] Until recently the study of urban clergy has been limited to London, certainly a crucial setting and useful as a contrast to the rest of the country.[20] Contrasting London and the rest of the nation as a whole, however, diminishes the distinction between the provincial urban clergy and the rural.

Rosemary O'Day has examined the clergy from 1558 through 1642, primarily using her research on the diocese of Coventry and Lichfield.[21] Although she emphasizes that circumstances varied in different parts of the country, she too draws no distinctions between urban and rural clergy except to note Seaver's work on corporations' lectureships.[22] This is a curious omission since she acknowledges that the existence of preachers or lecturers alongside parochial incumbents created a peculiar clerical career structure which was 'an odd mix of the medieval and the reformed'.[23] A closer look at the urban scene, which was characterized by the presence of lecturers in the late sixteenth and early seventeenth centuries, might offer further contradictions to her thesis that the post-Reformation clergy followed a career pattern aimed at gaining a benefice where resident pastoral work could be done.[24]

While Michael Zell's work on the church and gentry in the county of Kent during the Reformation does not include an urban study, it transcends the limitations suggested by diocesan sources and by concentration on the parish clergy. Zell uses the ecclesiastical records of the dioceses of Canterbury and Rochester, into whose jurisdictions the county was divided. Moreover, he integrates the religious with the parochial clergy and does not limit his examination of the latter to the beneficed clergy. Inasmuch as the stipendiary clergy were an important element in the ecclesiastical service of the laity, Zell's inclusion of them as a group distinct from both the elite pluralists and the beneficed parish clergy who served their cures represents an important insight.[25] He does not, however, investigate the experience of an urban clergy as such.

Historians are, of course, dependent upon and guided by their sources, and the primary sources for studies of the clergy are ecclesiastical and arranged by dioceses. They do not forbid, but at the same time do not encourage, urban–rural distinctions. The ecclesiastical historian who concentrates on the parish clergy is certain to find it inconvenient and inefficient to cultivate intimacy with, and comb through, local sources in order to flesh out the suggestions in diocesan records that urban parish clergy were different. The small numbers of urban clergy reassure the historian that whatever the distinctions, they do not seriously skew the broad picture of the clergy.[26]

While the present work represents a departure from the studies conducted heretofore, it does take up some of the same questions with which scholars have been concerned. Questions of clerical competence and anticlericalism are important in any setting during the sixteenth and seventeenth centuries. So are those of clerical education, income, and social status, which I examine in the context of the magisterial and popular reformations. Finally, I relate the condition of the clergy to changes in local ecclesiastical institutions and popular religious beliefs and consider the changed character of the clerical community in relation both to its various parts and to the lay community.

The evolution of this work has depended greatly on the sources available: the loss of some important ecclesiastical records is, of course, always lamentable, but the limitations thus imposed in this case led me from plans to study the parish clergy to a more far-reaching work. The most important sources of the period which are lost are the episcopal registers and visitation records for the diocese of Bristol and the ecclesiastical court records before 1556. The registers are important for institutions (which identify incumbents), letters dimissory (which indicate clergy from outside the diocese), and ordination lists (which suggest the numbers of clergy recruited and available for service). The visitation records usually contain clerical lists which also help identify clergy, show the number of parish clergy at a given time, and often give the number of pluralists and non-residents. Such records may also include reports of disciplinary action taken against the clergy, suggesting areas in which the clergy failed to meet their responsibilities. The loss of ecclesiastical court records before 1556 reduces greatly the information about tithe disputes, cases of clerical immorality, the decay of chancels and parsonages, or other indications of clerical behaviour which might have provoked anticlericalism.[27]

Determination of clerical income also presents problems: although the rural deanery of Bristol is included in the *Valor ecclesiasticus* of 1535, the city parishes are omitted.[28] For all its faults, this document is still the basis for determining the values of parish livings in the sixteenth century. The subsidy list of 1540 from Worcester diocesan records and entries in the Crown composition books provide an alternative means for ascertaining the value of local livings, but they still do not supply the very important information regarding the source of income.[29] To what extent were the parish clergy dependent upon personal tithes and to what degree did they enjoy glebe of lands or rental property and predial tithes? Without this information, which the *Valor* usually specified, the picture has to remain incomplete.

The small number of wills for the parish clergy during the period affords little relief in regard to the question of income or to questions about housing, households, and marriage. The most interesting information about the parish clergy comes from research on individuals, particularly in university records, which reported a greater number of BA degrees among the parish clergy than did ecclesiastical sources.

In spite of the difficulties presented by the lack of records, those documents that survive create a picture of the parish clergy that is sometimes surprising in its detail. Both the evidence which exists and that which does not, however, suggest that it would be desirable to include all the city's clergy in a single study and to set them solidly within the context of the period. The available sources make this possible. Before 1542 records from the dioceses of Worcester and Bath and Wells and Crown records offer a great deal of information. Episcopal registers and visitation records are extant from both dioceses; commissary court records, from Bath and Wells.[30] The royal composition books help to identify clergy after 1534 as do wills of the laity.[31] State and other Crown papers record the disputes involving clergy and laity in the 1530s and offer information about the clergy and ecclesiastical institutions in Bristol throughout the period.[32]

In Bristol, parish accounts, cathedral chapter accounts, local calendars, the mayors' audits, and miscellaneous ecclesiastical documents give some information about the clergy throughout the period.[33] The most valuable local ecclesiastical records are those of the consistory court, which begin with a series of acts and depositions for 1556 and then with only a few exceptions, include only the acts of the court.[34] Mixed in with the judicial records after 1558, however, are some documents usually found in episcopal registers, such as letters dimissory, commissions, notices of convocations of the city or deanery clergy, and of elections of proctors to the national convocation. The inclusion of these documents sometimes related to the work of the court but may also have occurred because the head judge of the court administered the diocese both during vacancy of the see and when the bishop of Gloucester held it *in commendam*.

Bristol's peculiar diocesan history, which is discussed below, and the loss of ecclesiastical documents for the sixteenth century make it difficult for the historian to determine the state of the parish clergy or the way the diocese was administered. One cannot create an ecclesiastical model here. One can, however, catch glimpses of the clergy and of the church in one of England's largest cities at a time of tremendous ecclesiastical change. With similar changes occurring in all England's towns and cities, this work addresses questions about

urban realities and experiences. It suggests that the urban experience
was a facet of the Reformation which must be added to the list of
categories which make up our perception of that national experience. It
also directs our attention to national changes in religion and
ecclesiastical institutions which directed and coloured the urban
experience.

REFORMATION CHANGES: A SUMMARY

The first of the following chapters introduces the church and clerical
community as they appeared on the eve of the Reformation, a complex
collection of clergy belonging to numerous institutions whose leaders
formed a clerical elite. The period from around 1530 to 1570 saw the
devastation of Bristol's late medieval church, and the transformation of
its diverse clerical community into a simple configuration comprising
the cathedral elite and the much-weakened clergy of the parishes.
Both the status of the clergy and their capacity to serve the city's laity
were severely diminished.

The shock of the Reformation, both magisterial and religious, is the
focus of Chapters 3 and 4. In these chapters we see two continuing
themes which help to explain why the laity of Bristol were willing to
accept a diminished church and clergy: the vulnerability of the city to
outside forces through its church and the disorder brought by religious
conflict. For the local authorities, who had to deal not only with local
clergy and populace but also with two sets of ecclesiastical officials and
the Crown, the threat to order and their own authority became
palpable in the 1530s. While they may not have sought a simpler,
weaker church and clergy, there was ample reason for them to accept
this development, even to welcome it. Chapter 3 also highlights the
clergy's dilemma when faced with conflict which threatened church
and city; their loyalties were divided and they had to choose. Chapter 4
focuses on continuing religious strife in the city's streets and churches,
which divided both clergy and laity and, along with protestantization,
contributed to the decline in the clergy's status.

Chapters 5, 6 and 7 focus on institutional changes in the city's
church, which had dramatic effects on the clergy and the laity. The
dissolution and surrender of religious houses in the 1530s was a
turning point for the church and clergy, and thus, the city. These
institutions had been fundamental to clerical independence from the
local laity and to the diversity which gave the laity some choice in

religious expression. All of this was lost by the end of 1539 and would never be regained. The eradication of chantries was a further step in the erosion of a pluralistic church and clerical community, and it struck even closer to the heart of lay involvement in the church. Chapter 5 explicates these losses and connects them to the laity's acceptance of even a diminished parish clergy. Why invest in institutions which were prey to the Crown?

The deterioration of the parish clergy, which is the subject of Chapter 6, was not simply the result of religious conflict and change or royal ravaging of local institutions, although these certainly had an effect. Structural factors such as the relatively poor livings, based as they were for the most part in personal tithes, and rampant inflation would have brought a crisis of lesser dimensions even without the Reformation. That the advowsons of the livings were private property would have made the crisis difficult to deal with regardless; the religious crisis and the plundering of the Crown made it virtually impossible. The result was a weakened parish clergy, under the control, for the most part, of parish laity, but unqualified to serve them well. These clerics, no longer part of a coherent clerical community or even part of a well-educated, tenured parish clergy, were dependent upon the parish laity, their employers, who could both hire and fire them. They thus were tied more closely to the laity whose approval they sought than to each other.

But what are we to make of the creation of Bristol diocese and the establishment of a cathedral in 1542? Surely this lay outside the theme of ecclesiastical degradation. It would appear so, but the appearance is false. As Chapter 7 relates, this diocese was so poorly endowed and led that from its beginning it was weak and under threat of eradication. Thus its clergy were dependent upon the local secular elite, and the initial role these clergy played in the city was not to strengthen the local church but to extend the influence of the lay elite. The ecclesiastical authorities, who were closely identified with the cathedral chapter, regulated the parish clergy and were an instrument of social control of the laity as well.

The diverse and independent clerical community of the late Middle Ages had become by the accession of Elizabeth I a simple configuration with the cathedral clergy (the chapter and the diocesan authorities) at its centre and individual, competing parish clerics at its perimeter. The city's lay elite, whose own configuration was narrowing in the sixteenth century, dominated the cathedral clergy, who in turn

exercised control over the parish clergy and laity. The parish vestries
governed the much-diminished parish clergy. But only the lay elite
gained in this transfiguration. The clergy at both levels were weaker
and more vulnerable than the pre-Reformation clergy to the laity.
They no longer enjoyed a clerical community and its benefits. The
laity of the parishes also lost. Greater control over clerics whose
qualifications did not compare to their predecessors' can hardly be
termed a gain.

In the late sixteenth and early seventeenth centuries these developments went further when the local government established its
own lectureship. Money to pay for the Corporation's lecturer came
from the parishes, removing resources which might have provided for
parish laity. Nor could these resources be used to supplement
the impoverished livings within the church. Thus the crisis within
the church and the local community, which was embodied in the
replacement of the late medieval clerical community with a low-paid,
ill-qualified parish clergy and a cathedral elite heavily influenced by
the Corporation, was to lie unresolved.

The crisis, which developed between *c.*1530 and *c.*1570 and which
the city and its clergy endured for many decades longer can perhaps be
simply summarized, but it was not a simple development. Let us begin
to unravel the complexities of its creation by examining the city's
church and clergy on the eve of the Reformation.

2

The Late Medieval Church and Clergy

THE church was at the heart of life in late medieval Bristol as in other large towns and cities. One of the benefits of urban life for both laity and clergy was the diversity of religious institutions. For the laity it meant varieties of religious expression, and perhaps experience, as one moved from mass and a sermon at one's own parish church to offer at another, to an outdoor sermon at a friary or on St Augustine's Green or at Redcliffe Cross. In the city merely the glimpse of a church's interior through an open door on a busy way could excite a religious emotion or invite the passer-by to worship. One imagines the many visitors to the monastery church at St Augustine's when the Corporation's representatives, the Mayor and Council, worshipped there on Easter and the Monday after. And undoubtedly many extra-parochial worshippers joined the Mayor and Council when they heard a sermon at St Mary Redcliffe on Whitsunday. The very existence of eighteen parish churches within the city offered opportunity not only for variety but for the exercise of preference in choosing preachers, priests, and choirs, and the clamour of bells served as a constant reminder. For the urban laity there were choices which the villager never knew.

For the urban clergy, the matter of choice depended upon position. The parish incumbent, the monk, the friar, the endowed chantry priest, each had professional responsibilities to meet within the confines of his own institutions. If the clerical proletariat which a city like Bristol attracted had more choice about worship and more diversity, they also had less security in regard to occupation, picking up work at a funeral here, an obit there, providing masses under a short-term chantry endowment, becoming an assistant curate or even filling in for the rush of Easter confessions. But regardless of the kind of work which engaged a cleric, Bristol, like other cities, offered him a priceless perquisite—a clerical community, a concentration of people with similar concerns and experiences and lifestyles.

On the eve of the Reformation Bristol's clerical community was a
diverse collection of monks, friars, parish incumbents and stipendiaries,
chantry priests, hospital masters, and guild and other chaplains. The
heads of the various religious houses were relatively independent of lay
influence because of their economic position, education, status as
heads of houses, and perhaps also because of clerical contacts outside
the city.[1] Some parish parsons shared most of these characteristics,
and most of the incumbents in parish livings were distinguished by
their high educational achievements. They undoubtedly had an
elevated status, even though the livings of most did not allow them the
independence enjoyed by other clerical leaders.[2] There can be little
doubt that the status of all the city's clergy reflected that of their elite.

There were more than 140 clergy in Bristol around 1530. It seems
that the religious were fewer in number than they had been at earlier
periods and dwindled even more during the decade before the
dissolutions of religious houses. There were two monastic institutions
in Bristol, the monastery of St Augustine outside the city to the west
and the priory of St James, a cell of the Benedictines of Tewkesbury,
to the north-east. In 1353 St Augustine's housed eighteen monks; at
its peak in 1498, an abbot and twenty-four canons; in 1534, eighteen
canons; in 1535 only fourteen; and at the dissolution in 1539, eleven.[3]
The priory of St James, attached to the parish church of the same
name, was of course much smaller, the monks fewer. There may have
been three present in 1534, and no more than three or four at the
official dissolution in 1540, including the prior.[4] The four orders of
friars were represented in the city, their friaries helping to form the
ecclesiastical ring around the original walled city. The only estimate of
their numbers near 1530, however, comes at the dissolution and they
had been reduced to some extent during the decade: the Augustinians
numbered seven; the Franciscans, six; the Dominicans, five; the
Carmelites, four.[5] One of three hospitals, that called Gaunts or St
Mark's, was a house whose members lived under the Benedictine rule.
Originally an almonry of the adjacent monastery of St. Augustine, it
later resembled a college which fed and perhaps housed some poor.
Five men were brothers of the house in 1534, and the master and four
brothers were present at its dissolution in 1539.[6] The priory of St
Mary Magdalen, which was very poor, had only a prioress and a novice
at its dissolution in 1536. Founded for Augustinian canonesses, it later
became a priory housing men and women. After the dissolution,
however, it was referred to as a house for nuns.[7] The figures given

suggest that the religious in Bristol around 1530 numbered some fifty-five or more.

The secular clergy outnumbered the religious. The parish clergy of the city's fifteen parishes in Worcester diocese appeared in a subsidy list of 1534 and included nine rectors, five vicars, one perpetual curate, three curates, twenty-two chantry priests (including the prior and three brothers of the Kalendars' Guild), and fourteen stipendiaries. Other sources suggest that in the three city parishes of Bath and Wells diocese across the Avon were one vicar, two perpetual curates, ten or eleven chantry priests, and at least six stipendiaries.[8] Thus in the early 1530s there were at least seventy-three parish clergy in Bristol. This number does not include clerks and sextons who served the churches and who may have been in minor orders.[9]

The masters of two local hospitals, which ostensibly served the poor, should also be included among the secular clergy of the city. In 1532 St Bartholomew's outside Frome Gate housed a master and an unknown number of brothers and sisters, presumably lay devotees, when the city acquired it for use as a grammar school.[10] The Hospital of St John near the parish church of St Mary Redcliffe seems always to have had a priest as master, although at various times lay women as well as men staffed it. When the hospital was dissolved in 1544, only the master and two others were present.[11]

In addition to these clergy, there were at least a few men serving in small chapels; ten medieval almshouses and eight chapels have been traced in Bristol, but it is impossible to say precisely how many survived to 1530.[12] Among those which still existed in 1530 were two supported by the Corporation. A fraternity closely related, perhaps identical, to the Corporation supported the chaplain of its Chapel of the Assumption of the Virgin Mary on Bristol Bridge.[13] The Corporation also supported a chaplain in the chapel of St George in the Guildhouse.[14] The chapel of the Three Kings of Cologne, attached to Foster's Almshouse in the parish of St Michael, probably had a chaplain who both prayed for the souls of the founder and his family and served the inhabitants there.[15] Holy Trinity chapel also was joined to an almshouse, while St Clement's chapel just outside the town wall near the Marsh Street gate may have had a chaplain to serve the mariners who lived in the associated almshouse.[16] A chapel on Brandon Hill, just north of the abbey of St Augustine, housed a hermit, probably as early as 1184 and still in 1480. It is doubtful, however, that the hermit served as a chaplain.[17] Evidence of private chaplains in the city, scattered for the fifteenth and early sixteenth centuries, shows that apparently wealthy women, and possibly one man, employed priests.[18] The provincial capital also would have attracted unemployed clergy seeking employment in the elaborate burial services and obits which characterized the wealthy merchant culture.[19]

While there was no cathedral in the city, there were some representatives of episcopal and archiepiscopal authority there for administration of justice and probate. Medieval wills suggest the regular presence of ecclesiastical officials from the dioceses of Worcester and Bath and Wells and the archdiocese of Canterbury, and in the 1530s a commissary for the bishop of Worcester lived in the city.[20] The city's secular clergy in the 1530s from all these sources cannot have been fewer than eighty-three, and probably their numbers exceeded that figure by a significant margin. Thus at the beginning of the Reformation Bristol's clerical population included at least 140 men and probably a good many more. The clergy represented about 1.5 per cent of Bristol's total population, estimated at around 9,500 to 10,000.[21]

This collection of clergy was diverse, but it formed a single clerical community which was manifested in several ways. First, the community resided in the network of personal and professional relationships the clergy established among themselves. Second, both laity and clergy perceived all the clergy as a separate professional caste which engaged in distinctive activities. This clerical community existed in contrast to and in relationship with the laity. Finally, the city's clergy embodied the Church as an institution which complemented the secular government, completing the body politic. The organic city was unthinkable without this local manifestation of the Church.[22]

The extent to which the clergy can be characterized a community on the basis of their personal and professional associations is problematic because few clerical wills, the best evidence, are extant.[23] Only four from the late fifteenth century, two from the early sixteenth century, and three _c._ 1530–40 have been found.[24] Nevertheless these combined with other evidence suggest that professional and personal relationships were important among the clergy, even across institutional lines. Gifts and bequests from one cleric to another included books, money, equipment for church and home, and clothes.[25]

The will of Nicholas Pittes, vicar of St Mary Redcliffe from at least 1468 to nearly the end of the century, included a bequest to his serving man, John Pittes, of his 'estate from the master of St. John Bristol'. Whatever the extent of this estate, the initial bequest indicated friendship between two clerics.[26] In 1486 Thomas Hawkyssocke, who had served one of Canynges' chantries since its creation in 1466, made his will. He made bequests to both clergy and laity. To three unidentified clergy he left his breviary and two service books, a pair of vestments of amber, and a surplice. To Thomas Meryfeld, then also chaplain of one of Canynges' chantries, he also left a surplice and to William Carpenter, stipendiary of St Nicholas in 1498, he left his silver bowl. He left money to the priests and clerks of St Mary Redcliffe who attended his exequies and mass and left the residue of his goods and chattels to be used for the health of his soul.[27] When John Mason, vicar of Temple, died in 1489, he left the residue to his executors, his four brothers, one of whom was a cleric, apparently serving in the parish. He left a black gown to another cleric in the parish, Thomas Golway, and three books to the parish church for all the parish clergy to read in the future. To an undenfied cleric who witnessed the will Mason left his breviary.[28]

In 1495 Thomas Sywarde, rector of St Ewen, left £11 to the hospital of St Mark's (the Gaunts) for candlesticks, a goblet to serve the brethren, and all the ornaments and utensils of the chamber in which he lived. He also made bequests to the master and brothers, and the master, Thomas Tiler, was executor of the will.[29] John Griffith, the priest of St Augustine-the-Less, a parish church which was near the hospital, left a gown to 'the young priest called Sir Thomas' of the Gaunts, and the master of the house, John Kedall, was a witness to his will of 1506.[30] Both priests also made bequests to the four orders of friars.[31]

John Colman, who was master of the Gaunts at its dissolution, gave John Bradley, chantry priest of St Mary Redcliffe, on the other side of the city, a book. It was an octavo volume in Latin, written in the fifteenth century in England and containing 'An exhortation to virtuous living' and 'Albertus Magnus de virtutibus animae'. Two other clergy from widely separated parishes apparently also had a close relationship. In 1510 Thomas Tofte, parson of St John the Baptist, witnessed the will of Robert Fychett, priest of Eborard le Frensch's chantry in St Mary Redcliffe. Tofte's role as a witness was unusual given that these two priests came from parishes divided by the city centre and the river.[32] The priest of Frensch's chantry in the closer parish church of St Nicholas also witnessed the will along with an unidentified priest, Edward Canwall, who received a bequest of clothing.

In 1533 Edmonde Dauncer, chantry priest of the parish church of St Mary Redcliffe, made bequests to priests from two churches. To Thomas Atwell of St Mary Redcliffe, he left 'my black chamblett coat'; to Hugh Jenkenson, chantry priest of the same church, 'one coif'; and to Lewis Morgan, also a chantry priest there, 'my short gown'. He bequeathed to William Cowper, chantry priest of St Nicholas, 'my tipped furred black coney' (rabbit fur). To John Beche, clerk of St Thomas, and to other unnamed clergy of St Mary Redcliffe and St Nicholas went small sums for dirge and mass and the month's mind. The only bequest to a lay person was 'my cupboard standing in my parlor' to Jone Bygges, daughter to Margret Bennett. The total worth of Dauncer's goods was £5. 13s. 8d. ob.[33]

Two years later William Sturges, a chantry priest in the parish church of St Thomas, bequeathed his belongings in a similar fashion. His 'best gown' went to Thomas Atwell of St Mary Redcliffe and his 'frieze (ffryce) gowne' to John Sherman, a priest of the parish church of Temple. Thomas Carter, a stipendiary priest with a chamber in the church of St Thomas, received 8d., while Richard Betty, an unidentified priest, received 8d. and 'a book called ludolophus' ('Vita Jesu' by Ludolphus de Saxonia). Sturges left 6d. to John Clarke and 8d. to William Sexton, possibly men in minor orders. To 'Alice that keepeth me' he left a 'red mantle and a pair of hose'.[34]

The will of John Floke, prior of the guild of Kalendars in All Saints, in 1540 was extremely abbreviated, making a layman executor and a cleric overseer. To the clerical overseer, John Geffreys, he left a gown. The two had been friends for over a decade. They had known each other in the late 1520s when Floke had been vicar of All Saints and Jeffreys had been a priest in the parish. In 1533 Floke had become vicar of St Mary Redcliffe, returning to All Saints in 1535 as prior of the guild of Kalendars. Jeffreys had become a chantry priest in the parish of St John by 1534 and remained in the parish in 1540. On 22 December 1534, Jeffreys had been proxy for Floke's admission as subdeacon and vicar in Westbury College, near Bristol.[35]

These clerical wills suggest personal and professional interaction and relationships among clergy of various institutions, parochial and non-parochial. That parish incumbents made bequests to the friars is especially important, for the rivalry of these groups is virtually a cliché. These wills indicate that at least in some cases it no longer existed.

This also seems to have been the case in Norwich. In discussing relations among the late medieval clergy there, Norman Tanner concludes that 'the fact that a significant proportion of the secular clergy entrusted their burial to friars or to other religious orders shows that relations between the secular and the regular clergy were not altogether strained'. Moreover the secular clergy 'were as keen as the laity in giving [in their wills] to the regular clergy as well as to hermits and anchorites'.[36]

Initially opposition to the founding of friaries had come from monastic appropriators of local livings who saw the friars as a potential threat to vicars' incomes, and sometimes when friaries were established prolonged and bitter disputes occurred. Rights of burial and confession, important sources of incomes for all parish clergy, were most often at issue. In Bristol the only known conflict involving friars came around 1230 when the Benedictine monks of St James objected to the establishment of the Franciscan friary and the Bishop of Worcester supported the friars.[37] In the fifteenth and sixteenth centuries the resolution of conflict over burial rights in Bristol seems to have been manifested in bequests to parishes and parish incumbents when testators requested burial by the friars.[38] A grammatical miscellany compiled by a secular cleric of Bristol between 1427 and 1465 did advise confession to a secular priest rather than to a friar.[39] However, this was written from the perspective of the clerical outsider, one not in a parish position, who hoped for employment at Easter, the only time each year that most of the laity confessed.

The early dispute in Bristol, its resolution by an ecclesiastical authority and the lack of evidence of further conflict reflects a broad pattern. In the centuries following the friars' arrival in English towns most disputes were settled by agreement or regulation, they diminished in number as time passed, and the bitterness they engendered dissipated. This pattern is reflected in the information about friars given in some eighteen volumes of the *VCH*.[40] Conflicts were recorded in twelve places in the thirteenth century; in ten places in the first half of the fourteenth; in eight places in the second half of the fourteenth; in four places in the first half of the fifteenth, and only two in the second half. Most of the conflicts were resolved by ecclesiastical authorities such as the bishop, archbishop, or even the Pope. After the thirteenth century not all disputes were even between groups of clergy or individual clerics; rather some involved the Crown, local authorities, or other local groups in disputes with the friars.[41]

Once disputes among clergies were regulated, mutual professional concerns could grow. In Exeter conflict over burial and confession between secular clergy and friars ended before the close of the fourteenth century. Friars from both the city's friaries preached in the cathedral, which was a place for training local clergy, who moved up a ladder from chorister to parish priest. Whether Exeter's parish clergy were qualified to preach through formal education or learned from listening to the friars is unknown, but undoubtedly there was interaction among members of both groups in the cathedral when some of the parish clergy were very young. The large numbers of preachers among Bristol's educated parish clergy must also have shared professional concerns with the preaching friars, even as they eyed each others' successes.[42] So the regulation of disputes, the passage of time, and the growth of mutual professional concerns all contributed to the alleviation of rivalry among the various groups of clergy.

The existence of Lollardy in Bristol also had implications for conflict among the clergy. In fifteenth-century London the friars took the Wycliffite view against tithes, a position which threatened both parish incumbents and monastic impropriators of livings. Even London's Corporation attempted to protect inhabitants against personal tithes. Since no judicial records are extant for Bristol before the Reformation, there is no evidence of the tithe disputes which undoubtedly did occur from time to time. It does not seem likely, however, that in Bristol, where the mayor continued to swear an oath to fight Lollardy, friars would have risked positioning themselves on the Wycliffite side of the tithing issue. Moreover, the English Dominicans and Carmelites strenuously opposed Lollardy from the beginning of the fifteenth century, and there were fairly frequent exhortations to the prompt and cheerful payment of tithes in printed sermons of the Dominicans in the sixteenth century.[43] When the anticlerical and antisacramental sentiments of the Lollards are added to these considerations, the sum indicates that the Lollards' presence in Bristol would have united rather than divided the city's clergy.

An amiable relationship between parish clergy and friars is also suggested by cases where friars worked in or for parish churches. In 1498 the parish of All Saints began paying two friars to bear the shrine holding the sacrament in their contingent of the Corpus Christi Day procession. Thus the two friars joined some four to six parish clergy, the parish clerk, and a number of boys who held the clergy's copes, the bell, censers, and candlesticks and who sang. This practice continued until the surrender of the friaries in 1538. For the period 1510 to 1515 the parish also paid two friars to carry the sacrament in procession on Palm Sunday. While undoubtedly the labouring role of the friars in carrying the shrine indicated humility not considered appropriate for the parish clergy, the participation of the clergies together in the processions clearly indicates an absence of uncompromising hostility and might even show a certain mutual goodwill. Undoubtedly they shared the bottle of wine provided them by the parish to be enjoyed in the marsh or commons after the procession.[44]

Other parishes also hosted friars. John Masday, prior of Bristol's Carmelites in 1529, had been priest of Chepe's Chantry in the parish church of St Thomas before 1524 and chantry priest in St John the Baptist for most of the 1530s.[45] The Austin friar Robert Geffrey was probably the man of that name who in 1537 was referred to as 'late clerk of Christ Church'. He was still a friar when the Austins surrendered in 1538.[46] Interaction between friars and the parishes also is evident from occasional entries in churchwardens' accounts. In 1454–5 the parish of St Ewen paid a friar 6*d*. for some unnamed service on Ascension Day and in 1527 the parish of All Saints paid 2*d*. for the fetching of a ladder at the White Friars.[47]

The presence of friars at funerals and anniversaries of deaths in parish churches was also a regular occurrence which brought them into contact with both parish clergy and laity. In 1473 William Coder left bequests to the four orders of friars, each curate of the city, each chantry (*annuellere*) priest, and every parish clerk if present on the day of burial. John Shypward, the elder, left similar legacies in the same year. In 1494 William Spenser gave specific instructions for his funeral and obits. The vicar and twenty-four chaplains would be present along with the four orders of friars, who would accompany the body to the grave. The chaplains who had cure of souls or were celebrating in his parish of St Nicholas would receive 16*d*. while the others and the clerks of the church would receive only 8*d*. More common were wills such as those of Robert Hynde, goldsmith, and Hugh John, brewer, from 1476 and 1505 respectively, which included the four orders of friars (often with one order given special favour) and the clergy of the testator's parish. Hynde also left bequests to all the parish churches of the city in Worcester diocese. In 1512 Symon Pasheley, soapmaker, left bequests to the four orders of friars and to fourteen priests to be present at his burial, month's mind, and year's mind.[48] That friars and secular clergy interacted on a regular basis is undeniable.

The monks of St Augustine and St James also had connections to the secular clergy. A conflict between the abbot of St Augustine and the vicar of St Nicholas occurred in 1304. In that year the bishop of Worcester issued a commission for investigation into allegations against his own commissary general by Adam, vicar of St Nicholas, regarding a recent case before the commissary between the vicar and the abbot and convent of St Augustine. This conflict remains a mystery, but in 1399 the monastery appropriated the living.[49] In fact the monastery appropriated four of the city's fifteen livings before the Reformation. These appropriations gained resources for the abbey at the expense of the secular clergy, but they may also have represented another means of regulating conflict among the various clergies in the city.[50] In 1452 relations between the monastery and the vicar of All Saints were more congenial, with the abbot and convent (through their representative, the vicar of St Augustine-the-Less) joining the vicar and parish in approving the establishment of the Halleway Chantry.[51] The monks of St James were charged with providing a curate for the parish church of St James, and their paths must frequently have crossed the curate's since the church was part of the priory complex. Their mother house at Tewkesbury was patron of six livings in the city, one of which was appropriated. We know very little of the local monks' relationships with local secular clergy, but an indenture between the abbot of Tewkesbury and the parson of St John the Baptist suggests some interaction.[52] The indenture, concerning burials, was listed, though not transcribed, in an inventory in the parish Church Book. It suggests that even where a living was not appropriated the patron asserted some long-term rights over the incumbent. The indenture may have involved the patron's initial claims on income or a restriction protecting another living in the abbot's patronage. It may have represented the resolution of a conflict. Whatever the indenture's exact meaning, it is likely that the monks of St James monitored the parson's compliance for their abbot. We know too little about relations between monastic patrons and their Bristol livings to estimate their overall character. What we do know, however, indicates a web of contacts and relationships between monks and secular clergy that could entail conflict requiring formal resolution and also at least a modicum of co-operation.

Interaction between religious and secular priests could also occur in the monastery. In 1353 when the canons divided over the election of a new abbot, the ecclesiastical authority in Worcester sent the rural dean of Bristol, always the incumbent of a local parish, to investigate and report. The conflict settled, the new abbot was installed by the prior of St James.[53] The relationship of the monks of the abbey to the secular clergy is also suggested by the appearance of the priest John Honybrigge in the abbey's accounts of 1506–7. The monastery fed him for eleven weeks and classified him as 'conversi [sic]' or visitor. Was he sick, unemployed, or temporarily working at the monastery? Perhaps he was a part of the floating clerical population, the clerical proletariat, who eventually gained steady employment. Between 1509 and 1534 he rented a chamber in Redcliffe Street from the trustees of Canynges chantries.[54]

Kinship also could bind parish priest and monk. In 1446 the Bishop of Worcester ordained John Arffos, MA, deacon. At the same time he ordained 'friar' William Arffos, canon of the monastery of St Augustine in Bristol, priest. John Arffos became vicar of the parish of St Nicholas in Bristol within a year. It is difficult to imagine that these men were unrelated and did not maintain contact.[55] Members of the monastic community did venture into the parishes on occasion. In 1515 the parish of All Saints paid 9*d.* to 'Brother Toby' for the mending of the great organs. In 1479 the parish had paid 20*d.* to the 'singer of St Austins' for the same task. This function was not, however, limited to those associated with the monastery; in 1490 the parish paid William, the clerk of St Nicholas, 20*d.* for the work.[56]

We are able only to glimpse the web of personal and professional relationships which added to the richness of urban clerical life, but it was an important part of the clergy's experience there.[57] When a cleric worked in Bristol he became part of a clerical community, which gave him not only a recognized and valued place in the larger community but also at least the chance of association and even friendship with a variety of other clergy. Secular clergy, friars, and monks encountered each other regularly; they shared many concerns and experiences even as their institutions emphasized differently their roles of prayer, preaching, and pastoring. In a city like Bristol these roles overlapped as did the lives of the clergy who lived them.[58]

A second facet of the clerical community, in Bristol or any comparable city, was its relationship to (and with) the laity. Whether White Friar, Black Friar, Franciscan, Austin, Benedictine or Augustinian, parish, chantry, or hospital priest, the clergy were perceived as a distinct professional caste upon whom the laity depended. A cleric stood out on a city street, in a shop, in a parish vestry's meeting, as well as in church. For the most part they dressed and lived differently from the laity. They did not marry and lived without families, often in groups. As a whole they were known and undoubtedly respected for their education. There were university graduates among the religious, friars and parochial clergy; and monks, friars and chantry priests ran the city's schools. As celebrants of the mass, they held a unique and privileged position; many of them were involved either directly or indirectly in the care of souls, with their offerings of masses, prayers, or words. And that the clergy's offerings were both different from and necessary to those of the laity, was made plain by ordination, ritual, dress, and lifestyle. The clergy were a distinct community, recognized by the laity and by each other.

If they were distinct from the laity, however, they also were intertwined with them, the distinctions blurring when rank and kinship were manifested. There are indications that the clerical elite shared status with the lay elite as leaders within the community. In 1533 for example, the abbot of St Augustine's sat with four former mayors on an investigatory commission, and the parish incumbents were assailed along with members of the lay elite by religious radicals in 1537.[59] In the parishes incumbents had duties peculiar to their station, but they also shared leadership of parish vestries with the churchwardens. Clerical and lay leaders thus had some common concerns and status which perhaps in some ways bonded them as much to each other as to their respective clerical or lay subordinates.

Occasional lay bequests of clothing to clergy represent these bonds between elite laity and clergy and probably helped further to blur the unmistakable distinction between the two groups. In 1430 and 1473 the vicar of St Nicholas received testators' second-best gowns, in both cases 'scarlet' and 'furred'. In 1475 the rector of St Werberg received a gown furred with beaver ('penulat' cu' bever') and in 1518 a murrey (purplish black) gown ingrained (i.e. of fabric made of dyed yarn, or of yarn made with dyed fibre) and also furred. In the latter year fellow unidentified clerics Master John Brym and Hugh Carner received a crimson gown furred with 'foynes[?]' and 'a violet gown grained lined with tawny sarsenet in the four quarters and sleeves, and the hinder quarters with buckram', respectively. In 1508 the parson of St Ewen received a violet gown ingrained from his brother; in 1509 the vicar of All Saints received a 'violet gown ingrained, lined afore with black camlet'; and in 1540 the vicar of All Saints bequeathed a 'gown of mustard villis [wool] furred with black lamb' to Sir John Geffreyes, a fellow priest.[60] These items of clothing were both valuable and personal, indicating both common rank and common bond between layman and cleric and distinguishing them from those of lesser rank. It may be, however, that the items of clothing also represented the laity's dependence on their clerics; what better would keep the deceased in the priest's mind, and, it may have been hoped, his prayers?

Kinship also bridged the distinction between clergy and laity. While we know little about the social and geographical origins of local clergy, there is evidence that local laity had clergy or nuns among their kin, outside as well as inside the city. Seven testators between 1397 and 1512 mentioned five sons, two brothers, one nephew, and one other relative who were clerics or had plans to be, but were not identified with local institutions.[61] In addition the early sixteenth-century wills of two wealthy and prominent women indicate daughters in the abbeys of Shaftesbury and Lacock.[62]

More kin can be identified within the city. In the fifteenth century three testators had relatives, two of whom were sons, who were canons in the local monastery of St Augustine.[63] There also were clergy kin in Bristol's parishes. In 1387 a chaplain of the Kalendars Guild in the parish of All Saints was the kinsman of burgess Thomas Sampson's wife. When the Halleway Chantry was created in the same parish in 1449, the first priest was a member of the Halleway family. In 1461–2 the parish of St Ewen received 4*d.* from a local cleric for the hire of the best cross for the burial of his mother.[64] In 1508 testator Thomas Pernant, grocer of the parish of All Saints, made bequests to his brother John Pernant, parson of the local parish of St Ewen.[65] In 1514 William Muriell, merchant of the parish of St Nicholas, made a bequest to John Muryell, priest, apparently of the Halleway chantry in the parish of All Saints, and undoubtedly a relative.[66] In 1521 John Carleon, stipendiary priest in the parish of St Leonard, paid 3*s.* 4*d* to the parish of All Saints for his father's grave.[67] Some parish clergy who became canons in the cathedral, such as Thomas Sylke, John Williams, and Christopher Pacy, also came from local families or had local relatives.[68] The city's inhabitants must have had sons and daughters, sisters and brothers, aunts and uncles, nieces, nephews, cousins, and friends who became priests, friars, monks, or nuns. Without doubt some of the clergy had grown up in Bristol; they had not always been clerics; they had been someone's child and someone's playmate. Ordination created a gulf between clergy and laity but not a chasm without bridges. They lived in contrast to, and in relationship with, the laity.

Undoubtedly the clergy were judged as men and as professionals by the quality of their relationships with the laity. This was, of course, particularly true of the parish clergy whether incumbent, chantry priest, or stipendiary. The extant sources do not make it easy, however, to gauge these relationships. The numbers of parochial clergy and the numbers of communicants or housling people in each parish show that the ratio between clergy and parishioners could vary widely. In the parish of St Ewen the ratio was 1 : 28; in St Michael, 1 : 252. The median ratio of parish clergy to communicants was 1 : 86, the mean, 1 : 99, and these figures suggest that personal contact between priests and parishioners varied greatly from parish to parish.[69] The contact of the parson with the chief men of the parish, who served as churchwardens (proctors) and who signed parish accounts, and with parish benefactors (including women) was undoubtedly greater than with other parishioners. Confession, which could have provided some intimacy between parson and parishioner, occurred for most laity only before the Easter communion and was heard not only by the parson or vicar but also by stipendiaries and chantry priests.[70] Nevertheless lengthy tenure, which was the norm for Bristol's rectors and vicars at the beginning of the Reformation, abetted the relationships of incumbents and parishioners; we know less about the length of time served by priests in other positions, but priests of endowed chantries also seem to have been fairly stable.[71] While there is really no way to determine the quality of parish clergy's relationships with their parishioners, charitable giving to religious uses before the Reformation suggests a positive attitude to the church and its clergy, at least among those who had something to give. Almost one half of all benefactions went to religious uses, primarily to chantries and church buildings, and this percentage was rising.[72]

One measure of the parish incumbents was how well they met their responsibilities. Were they resident? Did they maintain hospitality and keep chancel and parsonage in good repair? Their role in the mass may have remained paramount, but in a city where friars had been preaching for centuries, the parish incumbents no doubt were also expected to preach. We have little evidence of how well the parsons kept chancels and houses or what kind of hospitality they kept, but there is good reason to believe that most were resident and were able to preach. Over 40 per cent and perhaps more than 80 per cent of the incumbents in 1534 were graduates, some with more than one degree.[73] Those who were educated and could preach were a part of the city's clerical elite, and presumably they had more direct verbal contact with all their parishioners collectively than did the non-preaching clergy individually. None the less all regularly provided the sacraments, an activity which at once distinguished and joined priest and laity.

It is likely, given the multifarious duties of chantry priests, that they, too, were in frequent contact with the parish laity. With their vestments, vessels, and books, they contributed much to parochial liturgical practice. Many not only offered daily masses (beyond the high mass offered by the incumbent) but also presented themselves in the choir for high mass and for the keeping of canonical hours. They provided polyphonic music and taught parishioners' children; these activities may in fact have been the vocational focus for many chantry priests who nevertheless realized the importance of the intercessory duties which gave them their incomes. Undoubtedly many assisted parish incumbents with the cure of souls. Beyond the concrete contributions made by the chantry priests, the chantry foundations also symbolized the parish community of clergy and laity, both before and after death, and their special emphasis on the founders kept the merchant tradition of the city before its populace. The continued founding of chantries in the sixteenth century and the care parish churchwardens gave to chantry accounts indicate their lasting importance to the laity.[74]

If the parish clergy related to the laity on a more frequent and regular basis than the rest of the clerical population, there nevertheless were strong connections between the non-parochial clergy and the lay community. The community of Augustinian canons, unlike cloistered monks, enjoyed a pastoral mission. Throughout Europe they had a reputation as practical men and those in Bristol were probably no different.[75] The abbot's complaint against royal restrictions in the 1530s suggests that he was a familiar figure riding and walking about the area on business.[76] His appointment to a royal investigatory commission along with several former mayors of the city in 1533 indicated his elite position in the community.[77] Perhaps because the monastery was appropriator of the living, the abbot also had contact with the laity of the parish of All Saints. In the mid-fifteenth century he delivered certifications to them from the Bishop of Worcester regarding the establishment of a chantry, and the parish accounts for 1525

recorded payment of 16*d.* for a gallon of muscatel to 'my lord of
St Austin's and the company at John Hoper's house'.[78] Conflicts in the
late fifteenth and early sixteenth centuries between the Corporation
and the abbey suggest that the abbey's leadership was taking initiatives
to meet the problem of declining revenues.[79]

Although the monastery of St Augustine was the religious establishment most independent of city authorities, it was well integrated into
civic life. The parishes participated in a communal procession to the
monastery in the spring, probably at Easter.[80] The Corporation paid
for preachers when they worshipped at the monastery on Easter
Sunday and Monday, and surely many of the community's laity visited
the monastery church throughout the year.[81]

The Benedictine monks of St James also had close connections to
the laity. Their priory was connected to the parish church and they
provided a curate, and other clergy as well, to serve there.[82] The monks
associated with extra-parochial laity when the Mayor and other
officials attended the church to supervise two chantries and when
collecting profits from the fair of St James.[83] They may also have been
involved in the patronage which the mother house of Tewkesbury
exercised in seven city parishes. The priory itself had extensive
property holdings which lent prestige to the monks and projected their
presence in the community.[84]

As preachers, the friars were an important part of the city's life, and
it is likely that they preached outdoors as well as to visiting
congregations in the friaries.[85] The friars maintained chantries and
attended funerals, obits, and anniversaries in parish churches as well
as their own.[86] Friars appeared in processions on Corpus Christi Day
and perhaps other occasions, while the corporation attended the
houses of the Dominicans and Franciscans twice each to hear sermons
during Advent.[87] If a single parishioner saw more of his own parochial
clergy, all the city's population knew and mingled with the friars,
whose activities crossed parish boundaries.

The clergy of the hospital of St Mark also were known and
respected by the laity. Traditionally the function of the house was the
feeding of the poor, but in the early sixteenth century its clergy also
administered several local endowments.[88] One of the five brothers at
the hospital's dissolution was the brother-in-law of a Bristol merchant,
and at least two of them obtained parish posts of one kind or another
after the dissolution of their house.[89] The house also supported sixteen
men and children, servants, and choristers ('queresters').[90] The master

was a prominent member of the clergy, riding about the area on business and presiding over his lodging with hall, buttery, pantry, and kitchen, the churchyard with its orchards, gardens, ponds, and waters, and a little close with a dovecote.[91]

The masters of the other two prominent hospitals, St Bartholomew and St John, probably also oversaw the properties attached to their sinecures and in 1530 both probably held graduate degrees. The master of St Bartholomew, George Croft, was a pluralist and may not have resided in Bristol, but he probably was present on St Clement's Eve and Day when the Mayor and Aldermen worshipped there.[92] The master of St John, Richard Bromfield, appeared as a witness and overseer in local wills and was more closely identified with the community. Formerly the vicar of the local parish of All Saints, he had held the living in conjunction with the mastership of the hospital for some four years. Around the time he vacated the living he gave the parish 20s. and having left, he contributed tiles to the reparations of the church. One of the wills which he witnessed as master of the hospital suggests his position in the community; it was also witnessed by the recorder of the city, the rural dean of Bristol, and two parish incumbents.[93]

It may be significant, however, that these two parish incumbents, including Bromfield's successor at All Saints, were among the clergy who became involved in a conflict with the Corporation in 1533, and in 1535 Bromfield was at odds with Nicholas Thorne, a member of the lay elite, over timber for a ship Thorne was building for Cromwell.[94] Although the patronage of the mastership was in the Mayor's hands, it appears that the Crown had great influence over it, and the master probably was a part of the elite clergy who had extra-urban loyalties.[95] Nevertheless he and the other non-parochial clergy were a visible part of the city's clerical community and an integral part of the Church in the laity's perception even if personal contact was limited.

Thus the clerical community was both distinct from the laity and intertwined with it. While ordination brought a distinctive and powerful role and the clergy lived differently from the laity, the distance between the two groups was bridged in many ways. Distinctions of rank within the two groups encouraged bonds between the elites, while kinship and friendship revealed the common humanity of all. Parish clergy, the religious, and the friars interacted regularly with the laity in a number of ways, forming associations or intermingling in churches and schools, businesses, streets and homes, for funerals and obits, education, processions, negotiations, and visiting.

For all its diversity, the visible clerical community represented a single body, the Church. The variegated clerical community at this third, symbolic level, was represented as a whole in the procession on Corpus Christi Day occurring annually in the eighth week following Easter. The procession in Bristol appears to have been primarily ecclesiastical although some guilds may have participated as in London and Exeter.[96] The host itself was carried by friars, accompanied by clergy from the parish of All Saints whose patronage was in the hands of the monks of St Augustine's abbey. The friars probably led the procession, followed by the monks or at least their leaders, and then the clergy of the parishes, ending with those of All Saints and friars accompanying the host.[97] The city's parishes sponsored contingents with bearers carrying the parish banner and cross and sometimes torches and censers, clergy wearing copes borne up by boys, and sometimes children with candles, and singers.[98]

It makes sense that a public showing of ecclesiastical unity would have developed out of the conflicts occurring when friars first settled in an urban setting.[99] Such a procession would have encouraged the resolution of conflict, provided for the continued negotiation of status within the clerical community, and presented the laity with an image of a church unified by the body of Christ, even if its parts might occasionally bicker. That the laity also participated in the body of Christ through the sacrament of the Eucharist would also have been implied, whether or not they participated in the procession itself. Thus, even though the Corpus Christi procession in Bristol was not a 'civic' occasion in that it was not sponsored by the municipal authorities, it did represent the local church, pulling the city's diverse ecclesiastical institutions together and implicitly, through the sacrament, uniting them with the laity.

While 'communitas', or the overcoming of social and institutional divisions among clergy and between clergy and laity, may have been the goal of parading the host, the powerful symbol of wholeness, there were other implications in the situation, highlighted by the absence of the civic authorities.[100] Mervyn James argues that cities such as Exeter and London, which had strong oligarchies unthreatened by powerful craft guilds, saw no need to develop Corpus Christi processions and dramas in order to negotiate social status and overcome social divisions. This also describes Bristol and undoubtedly helps to explain the absence of civic sponsorship there. Given an annual procession of such magnitude, however, one would think Bristol's secular elite would have been tempted to take advantage of association with this powerful symbol even if they did not consider it absolutely necessary. They may have chosen to absent themselves from the Corpus Christi procession because participation risked a reading or reception of the procession by observers that was not to the corporate elite's advantage.

Even as the Corpus Christi implied union of all the city's inhabitants, clergy and laity alike, the procession made clear the clergy's closer relationship to the host and the laity's dependence upon the clergy. Only the clergy could create the body of Christ and only the clergy could touch it; the host was a reminder of power which the clergy had and the laity did not. Even though the traditional processional position of mayors next to the host was the position of honour and associated them with its power, it was a position mediated by the clergy. Emphasis upon the host potentially emphasized that the power of even the lowliest cleric in the procession contradicted the Mayor's headship of the civic body. Perhaps this was less noticeable when the procession was extremely elaborate and the procession of craft guilds demonstrated gradations of power leading up to the Mayor, but it was an unavoidable reality. In Bristol, where dealing successfully with powerful guilds was not necessary, it must have seemed wiser to allow the diverse ecclesiastical institutions to show their unity and ultimate power without civic participation. What would civic authority have gained by revealing its impotence in regard to the sacrament?

The clergy also could have chosen not to unite in a procession, for there were potential disadvantages as well as advantages for them, too. The challenge for the clergy was to demonstrate their position as powerful sacramental mediators who were a fundamental part of the urban microcosm, without calling too much attention to the fact that as priests they also were outsiders, inhabitants with loyalties to supra-urban institutions. For them, the advantages of displaying jointly their power over and their union with the laity in the Corpus Christi procession far outweighed the potential disadvantage of a different reading which might see them as outsiders. The sponsorship of parish clergy by the laity of their parishes made it unlikely that the clergy's position as outsiders would be emphasized; the absence of the civic authorities, on the other hand, invited such a perception.

Could the local civic élite have been unaware that the Church was both a necesssary part of the local community and also an alien institution, that the clergy were essential inhabitants but were not citizens?[101] The task of the city's secular leadership was to integrate the local church into the civic community by encouraging civic loyalty among the clergy. They needed to do this in ways that would preserve their own centralized political power and superordinate social position, without starkly displaying the unavoidable tension between the powers of local church and state or encouraging co-operation among clergy which might enhance their power *vis-à-vis* the local civic authorities. Thus they avoided the Corpus Christi procession and chose instead a round of civic ritual which drew the city's ecclesiastical institutions into the civic whole one by one rather than all together. Through these rituals the civic authorities placed themselves at the centre of civic life and identity. While recognizing the Church's role and its importance to the city, they nevertheless attempted to dilute its significance and lessen the inhabitants' awareness by segmenting it. Nevertheless they unintentionally created a web which displayed the ecclesiastical community over time just as the Corpus Christi procession demonstrated it in concentrated form. The yearly round of civic ceremony was a perpetual reminder that the clergies of various institutions were parts of one civic Church and that ecclesiastical and secular elements of Bristol were part of a single entity, the city.

The annual round of civic ritual began on the first day of the civic year, Michaelmas, 29 September. The old and new mayors, new city officials, and the council (all of which formed the Corporation) walked to the parish church of St Michael to offer.[102] After a month's break, All Saints' Day (1 November) signalled a very busy period of ceremonial activity. The officials gathered at the Tolsey before walking to All Saints parish church to offer. Afterwards they gathered at the Mayor's house for refreshment before returning to their own parishes for evensong. The following day, All Souls', brought the Mayor and a smaller group to the parish church of St Mary Redcliffe to audit the two chantries of William Canynge. (They would go again in winter and summer to attend the two obits.) The chapel of St Clement, within the hospital of St Bartholomew, was the site for the Corporation's attendance at evensong on St Clement's Eve, 22 November. On St Clement's Day they heard mass and offered there. Worship with the Weavers' Guild was the object of the group's visit to St Katherine's chapel in Temple church on the eve of that saint's day, 24 November. After evensong all went to St Katherine's Hall for refreshment. Then the Mayor and Council returned home to receive St Katherine's players at their doors. The following morning they gathered at Temple church again and walked about before attending mass and offering there.[103]

Within two weeks of the celebrations at St Katherine's came the festival of the boy bishop at the parish church of St Nicholas.[104] Roles were turned upside down when the city's leaders listened to the sermon of a boy who played the bishop. On the eve of St Nicholas Day, 5 December, the Corporation walked to the parish church to hear evensong and the next morning to hear mass, offer, and hear the 'bishop's' sermon and receive his blessing. After dinner on the same day the group awaited the coming of the bishop at the Mayor's counter, playing at dice while they waited. Again, the leaders took a subordinate and, this time, a youthful, playful role. After the 'bishop' arrived, his 'chapel' sang, he offered his blessing, and he and his chapel were served with bread and wine. Then the group returned to the parish church to hear the 'bishop's' evensong. Overlapping with these rituals in late November and December were sermons at the friars. On the four Sundays of Advent the Mayor and Sheriff and their brethren walked alternately to the convents of the Dominicans and the Franciscans to hear sermons.

In the spring civic ritual turned to the town's most prominent churches, culminating in the most important communal religious processions of the year. On Easter and the Monday after the Mayor and Council worshipped at the monastery of St Augustine, returning for a sermon on Wednesday.[105] On Whitsunday, seven weeks after Easter, they went to St Mary Redcliffe to hear an invited preacher, who dined afterwards with the Mayor.[106] On these occasions they passed through town gates and crossed bridges to reach their destinations.

The cycle wound steadily from Michaelmas through Advent and again from Easter to Whitsuntide. There may even have been other civic occasions, however, for which evidence is lost. (It is only by chance that we know the Mayor and Sheriff were present during a sermon at the Carmelite friary on Lady Day (25 March) 1534.[107]) There are also occasional references in parish accounts to un-named processions and in a few years to a procession on St George's Day.[108] The chapel of St George was in the Guild Hall and the *Mayor's Kalendar* indicates that the Mayor received two torches for St George's 'fest' from the bailliffs. Surely these are clues to a procession which may sometimes or always have involved the Corporation and at least the city's parishes.[109] In 1463–4 and 1468–9 the parish of All Saints paid for bearing banners in Whitsun Week and in 1525 the parish paid for ringing at the procession at the commandment of the King for taking of the French king.[110] In 1545 the parish of Christ Church paid 2*s*. 2*d*. to 'ringers and children that bear the copes and candlesticks and to them that bear the copes to the minster when the procession was commanded for the King'. Clearly the cycle of ritual was supplemented when the need arose and could be extended to express the city's place in the commonwealth.[111]

In addition to the cycle of civic ceremony which tied local church and state together, on the fourth day of Michaelmas the Mayor also called before him some fourteen chantry priests enrolled in the Little Red Book and compelled them to take an oath to carry out their duties. Further, the Mayor and other officials were overseers of a number of chantries and attended several of their services to see that the benefactor's instructions were being followed.[112] In addition, while there is no specific evidence making it a formal civic occasion, it is hard to believe that the Mayor, who was patron of the Kalendars' Guild, with its chantry priests at All Saints, would have missed the guild's two endowed sermons. The schedule for the visits to chantries is unknown, but they were part of the yearly cycle of some thirty ceremonial occasions bringing local state and church together.

Thus, the civic elite preferred to integrate the church into the city piece by piece, occasion by occasion. The cycle of rituals, however, symbolized the union of ecclesiastical and secular elements in the civic community's identity and pointed towards the city's clerical community as representatives of the civic church even as civic officials sought to define it in their own way by segmenting it. Moreover, the clergy put it back together again in the Corpus Christi procession, dramatically displaying the ideal of a comprehensive church which implicitly included all the city's clergy and laity, but emphasized a unified clerical community.

The clerical community, then, was a complex phenomenon, intricately woven of the clergy's own professional and personal relationships, the laity's perceptions of and relationships with the clergy, and symbol. It is significant that it did not have an episcopal focal point. For a city of its size, Bristol was unique in not being a see, not having a bishop, and of course, in the traditional sense, not being a city at all. This circumstance left the clergy without an ecclesiastical centre, but it added rather than detracted from the civic and personal levels of clerical community. Without a single leader there were broader opportunities for clerical leadership, and clerical relationships were bound to have stretched outward across institutional lines as well as upward. There were a multiplicity of hierarchies which gave more strength to all the lower clergy within them than a hierarchical arrangement under a bishop might have given. As a consequence of this arrangement the clergy may have drawn closer to the city, away from the universal Church. That is, without a bishop, whose purview went beyond the city and whose loyalty was to the Church, or a centralized cathedral clergy who might have distinguished themselves from the rest of the city's clergy, the clergy were more likely to see themselves as part of a city-wide community of clergy which was an integral part of the urban community.

The integration of the clerical community into the civic community was intact right up to the time that the Reformation burst upon the city in 1533 with the preaching of Hugh Latimer.[113] There is no reason to think that the clergy were not respected. There is no evidence of anticlericalism other than Lollard antipathy in any of the surviving documents, and the parish records are monuments to the Church's vitality and continuity.[114] Yet there were weaknesses in the body politic and in the clerical community, vulnerable points that would give way when the kind of pressure that the 1530s brought was placed upon them.

3
Community and Conflict: The 1530s

WHEN religious controversy erupted in Bristol in 1533, incited by the preaching of reformist Hugh Latimer, little did the participants know what dramatic changes in the Church and the clerical community it signalled. Latimer's preaching turned out to be not a passing challenge to the *status quo* but one element among several that would decimate the local church and fragment the clerical community. Conflict in the 1530s demonstrated interaction among the various groups involved—the municipal authorities, the local clergy, the populace, the diocesan authorities, and the Crown—and placed the Corporation at the centre of events. The difficulties the local government had in dealing with religious conflict and the exacerbation of these difficulties by the independent action of some local clergy help to explain the lay elite's response to the clerical crisis which developed during the Reformation. Struggling to assert their authority and to maintain order, they did little to stem the disintegration of the clerical community or the decline of the parish clergy.

How could Bristol's vital and cohesive late medieval Church be disturbed so suddenly and with such a far-reaching impact? While the Church was sound and firmly rooted in local society, there were weaknesses in it and in its relationship to the community which would give way when the kind of pressure that the 1530s brought was placed upon them. The Church's first vulnerable point lay in weak ecclesiastical authority, which stemmed from the city's division between two dioceses and its lack of episcopal oversight. Ecclesiastical jurisdiction was distributed among an assortment of officials representing the dioceses of Worcester and Bath and Wells. In Worcester diocese the Commissary General, Sequestrator General, the Dean of Bristol, parish parsons, and others acting as commissaries held probate courts, and other resident commissaries and the archdeacon of Gloucester or his official probably heard other cases.[1] In Bath and Wells diocese commissaries, who included the Archdeacon of Bath, also held courts.[2] The rural deans of Bristol in Worcester diocese and of

Redcliffe in Bath and Wells diocese were the diocesan officials who advised local clergy concerning episcopal injunctions and could be commissioned to hold courts, admit and institute clergy, hear confessions, and engage in a number of other activities. The office rotated among parish incumbents or curates in both deaneries, but there is little evidence of their work.[3]

The dilution of ecclesiastical authority which divided jurisdiction brought was compounded by the distance of the city from both sees and the usual absence of the early sixteenth-century bishops from both dioceses.[4] Furthermore, as early as the thirteenth century, the Archbishop of Canterbury had decreed that no citizen of Bristol could be tried in ecclesiastical courts outside the city.[5] This meant that all dealings with the ecclesiastical authorities would occur under the watchful eyes of the city's municipal governors. Undoubtedly the city's secular authorities felt comfortable with this subordination of ecclesiastical power. Ironically, however, when religious conflict became a problem for the municipal authorities in the 1530s, the divided and distant ecclesiastical authorities made matters more confused and difficult.[6]

Another major consequence of this weak ecclesiastical authority was that it created a haven for Lollards, heretics who could cross diocesan boundaries within a busy city to avoid apprehension and prosecution by the ecclesiastical authorities. It is only with hindsight that we can see the importance of Lollardy to the Reformation and thus as an important counterpoint to medieval religious consonance. In the early sixteenth century the activities of this group were firmly underground in Bristol as the result of prosecutions in the diocese of Bath and Wells. Without the infusion of Lutheran activism in the 1520s their importance, even to religious change and conflict, would have been limited. And as we shall see, without the King's great matter, the much desired divorce, even the amalgamation of Lollards and Lutherans in Bristol would have amounted to little. As it turned out, however, this activism was at the forefront of religious conflict and change, and an understanding of it is helpful in comprehending how Bristol's medieval underpinnings came undone, how its church was virtually destroyed, and its clerical community disintegrated.

The heretical Lollard movement, which stemmed at least partially from the theology of John Wycliffe, had spread to Bristol before the end of the fourteenth century, and continued as a minor inconvenience to the authorities thereafter. The oath which every new mayor took provided that he would give his utmost effort to destroying 'all manner heresies and errours, clepid openly lollardies, within my bailly' and would assist the ordinaries and commissaries of the church 'in all rightful causes' when required by them.[7] As late as 1512 Lollards were reported in the trans-Avon parishes of the city, where a number had been prosecuted in 1499 by the bishop of Bath and Wells.[8]

Lollardy cannot be characterized by a particular set of beliefs common to all in the movement, but J. A. F. Thomson has identified some of the movement's central attitudes and beliefs.[9] A negative attitude towards ecclesiastical authority and the clergy was widespread among Lollards, taking different forms at different times and places. Some believed that a priest in a state of sin had no power to consecrate the elements of the Eucharist or to hear confession and grant penance, while others held that the clergy had no special powers of consecration or at least no more than the laity. Denial of transubstantiation was a common belief; some held that the sacrament of the Eucharist was a commemoration as well. Denial of or reservations about the need for sacraments or their efficacy bred hostility to a clergy whose position rested on those tenets. Anticlericalism may also have developed in response to the fees which clerics often charged for christenings, weddings, and burials.

Lollards also disavowed images and pilgrimages, the former connected to the idea that prayer should not be offered to saints or to anyone but God. Some also disavowed fasting and saints' days. Lollards were also known for their ownership of books in English, particularly the Scripture. They condemned religious doctrines and practices not mentioned in the Bible. Many held that anyone could preach the Gospel; women teachers, and perhaps even priests, were among the dissidents.[10] Testimony in 1512 from Lollards with Bristol connections revealed the primary tenets of the Bristol community to have been hostility to pilgrimages and to veneration of images and denial of transubstantiation.[11] The sermons Latimer preached in Bristol in 1533 were influenced by Lutheran doctrines, but they had a great appeal to those with Lollard tendencies.[12]

Bristol's Lollards, whose numbers are unknown, almost certainly became part of a reform movement in the city, joining Lutherans in the 1520s to distribute heretical books.[13] Weak ecclesiastical authority in the city provided a suitable environment for underground religious dissidence, whether Lollard, Lutheran, or a combination of both. Not a great deal is known about the spread of Lutheran doctrine in Bristol, but the presence in the area during the 1520s of three very important early Lutheran reformers indicates the existence of a significant reform movement there. William Tyndale, tutor to a family of Chipping Sodbury, Gloucestershire, in the early 1520s, preached on St Augustine's Green in Bristol. At that time an Erasmian reformer, he was not welcomed by some local clergy whose ignorance he scorned, and their opposition to the 'new learning' may have helped to keep reform ideas firmly underground.[14]

The Austin friar, Robert Barnes, who was a well-known Lutheran, also was involved in reform activity in Bristol in the 1520s. Tried for heresy in the spring of 1526 as the result of a Cambridge sermon, he had to do penance in Bristol as well as at St Paul's. It was during the following house arrest in London that he sold Tyndale's New Testament to Lollards from Steeple Bumstead. There is no indication that he ever returned to Bristol, and in 1540 he and other heretics, including Thomas Garret, were burned in London.[15] In 1528, if not earlier, Garret, too, had been in Bristol where he undoubtedly had direct links to Lollard dissidents. He made his way from Oxford after ecclesiastical authorities accused him of distributing Lutheran books and was captured just a mile outside Bristol in Bedminster, which bordered the area in Bristol, Redcliffe, where Lollards lived.[16] Here there were contacts for the distribution of proscribed books, an activity which connected Garret to Lollards in London and Essex as well.[17]

The distribution of heretical literature in Bristol was well known. Sometime between 26 October 1529 and 16 May 1532, Richard Webbe, identified variously as a local bookseller and the rector of West Kingston, appeared before Sir Thomas More accused of distributing proscribed books in the city.[18] Other heretics who had come before More said Webbe had sold and continued to sell many heretical books. Other 'good and honeste' men had informed him that in Bristol where Webbe lived the proscribed books were 'thrown in the street and left at men's doors by night that where they durst no offer their poison to sell they would of their charity poison men for naught'.[19]

More had given a commission to trusted Bristolians to attach Webbe and take sureties for his appearance before the Chancellor in London. Webbe, arriving in the city early for his appointment, met with another notorious bookseller, Robert Necton, with whom he agreed to keep the meeting secret. Necton, however, probably previously in trouble with the authorities over his connections with Lollards in Lincolnshire, feared that Webbe would reveal their meeting and its contents and went to More first with the information. More caught Webbe in lies about his relationships not only with Necton but also with one Sir Nicholas, a priest to whom Webbe had sold books in Bristol and had seen in London within the last six weeks.[20]

In 1535 a Richard Webbe appeared in the will of David Hutton, a reformist member of the Common Council, the city's governing body. Hutton forgave Webbe a debt of £20.[21] This is particularly intriguing because in 1499 a Robert Hutton was accused of heresy along with other Bristol Lollards at the visitation of the Bishop of Bath and Wells. Inquiries were made about his having previously abjured in London, but he was dismissed from court when nothing could be proved against him.[22] If Hutton's loan to Webbe were to support the distribution of proscribed books, it points to a reformist network similar to, though perhaps less sophisticated than, that of the Christian Brethren in London.[23] The evidence for a reform movement which brought Lollards and Lutherans together in Bristol is circumstantial, but given the secrecy necessary to their enterprise, the evidence which survives is strong, and it corresponds to what has been uncovered in other places.[24]

The existence of this reformist network was important to the Reformation in Bristol and the changing circumstances of the clergy. Not only did it spread ideas which radically challenged the clergy's role, but it also helped to create a receptive audience for Hugh Latimer when he preached in the city in 1533, introducing reformist ideas publicly, perhaps for the first time since Tyndale had preached some ten years before, and emphasizing concepts familiar to Bristol's Lollards. This receptivity was countered, of course, by traditionalists, and the result was the first episode of the religious conflict which characterized the Reformation in the city.

THE LATIMER AFFAIR

The first of the decade's controversies took the local authorities by surprise. In March 1533, Hugh Latimer, beneficed in not-too-distant West Kingston, Wiltshire, preached in Bristol at the invitation of local clergy. His preaching was well received by laity and clergy alike, and Mayor Clement Base invited him to return and preach before the Corporation at Easter.[25] During the week following his visit, however, opposition to Latimer developed, led by some of the same clergy who initially had invited and accepted him.

Why the clergy invited Latimer and then turned against him is puzzling. They surely knew the direction of his preaching, which had an implicit anticlerical bent, for Convocation had only the year before instructed him not to preach against images, pilgrimages, and purgatory.[26] Were the Bristol clergy really surprised when he defied his instructions in Bristol? Perhaps, given that many of them were university graduates, they simply wanted the pleasure of hearing him for themselves. Perhaps they wanted to dispel their doubts before condemning him as Convocation had done. Or perhaps their purpose was more devious—possibly the local clergy had set a trap for Latimer. On 26 March only about two weeks after he had preached in Bristol, Convocation began proceedings against him for ignoring the previous year's prohibition.[27]

Equally puzzling is why the Mayor then invited Latimer to return and preach before him and the rest of the Corporation at Easter. It is possible that the Mayor supported his ideas.[28] There were a few reformists in the town council, but we do not know how great their influence was nor whether they would have courted open controversy. Most members of the local government would not have wanted to stir up trouble. Of course, no one knew about the clerical opposition to Latimer when the invitation was given. Apart from the religious motivations, there were political considerations. Because Latimer was a supporter of the royal divorce, he was a favourite at court. This in itself merited consideration by most members of the council that he was worth hearing and honouring as their preacher at Easter.[29]

This, however, was not to be. The clerical opposition in Bristol persuaded the Chancellor of Worcester diocese, Thomas Bagard, to prohibit all unlicensed preaching in the diocese and thus to prevent Latimer's return at Easter.[30] While the success of the clergy in banning Latimer's preaching was, in a sense, a challenge to the Corporation's authority, it was not a confrontation. By going to the diocesan authority, they had gotten another power to ban Latimer. But they did not leave the matter with the prohibition. Apparently moved by the Crown's attack on the Church and by Latimer's anticlericalism, they proceeded to bring well-known outsiders to town to preach against Latimer. For Easter they imported William Hubberdine, a flamboyant speaker, who according to Foxe, later died of injuries sustained while dancing during a sermon. On Easter Eve, 12 April, Hubberdine preached in St Thomas and on Easter Day in St Nicholas.[31] A more prestigious preacher, the theologian Edward Powell, prebendary of

Bedminster and Redcliffe in Salisbury Cathedral, preached on St Mark's Day and the Sunday following, 25 and 27 April.[32] After Hubberdine preached at Easter the strife worsened when those who favoured Latimer's new manner of preaching and those who favoured Hubberdine's old manner became even more ardent.[33]

The Corporation, stung by the prohibition of Latimer's preaching and the public denunciations of him from local pulpits, counter-attacked. Their main weapon was the conversion of one of Latimer's opponents to their camp. John Hilsey, the local prior of the Dominicans, had been among the clergy who first invited Latimer to preach and then preached against him. By early May Hilsey had again changed his mind. He wrote to Chancellor Bagard that his previous advice and the consequent silencing of Latimer had not been effective in calming the town. Nor had his own preaching and that of four others against Latimer served to set the matter at rest as he had hoped. He also felt that his position had been distorted by the way his previous letter had been presented to Bagard, but he did not want to elaborate. His primary point was that he not only had misjudged the situation and the participants, but also had misunderstood Latimer's position: Latimer was more against the abuse of things than the things themselves. Most important, he advised Bagard to license Latimer to preach so that he could 'open his mind in these matters that the people would be content, and this would please the council of the town well, for before this they be agreed, and hopeth upon your good help in it'.[34]

Hilsey had moderated his criticism of Latimer and gone over to the Corporation's side. The timing of the letter, after Powell's preaching, was significant, for Powell was an outspoken enemy of the King's divorce of Queen Catherine.[35] Latimer wrote to a colleague that Powell had preached in Bristol with little regard for the King and that the Mayor had 'twitted him' for it.[36] The position of Latimer at court, on the other hand, was strong, because of his position on the royal divorce.[37] Thus, Hilsey's change of heart related to Latimer's political strength, the political vulnerability of his opponents, and the mutual interest of the Crown and Corporation in supporting him.[38] The Corporation's plea to the Chancellor through Hilsey was successful and Latimer preached again in Bristol during Rogation Week, 12–18 May.[39]

The battle between the Corporation and the determined local clergy escalated when Hubberdine followed Latimer again, preaching on Ascension Day and the following Sunday, 22 and 25 May.[40] Not to be outdone, the Mayor sent a representative to Wells seeking a license for Hilsey to preach in that diocese.[41] No doubt he was to preach before the municipal body in St Mary Redcliffe during Whitsun Week.[42] He had already been preaching, probably at his own friary in Worcester diocese where no license was required, and now was to answer Hubberdine's latest sermons which were delivered in one of the parish churches in Bath and Wells diocese, perhaps St Mary Redcliffe.[43]

The governing elite did indeed hear three sermons at St Mary Redcliffe during Whitsun Week, but Hilsey was not the preacher. They had run into real trouble with the hierarchy of Bath and Wells over licensing him to preach. The Bishop of the diocese was John Clerke, a conservative who had served the King well as a diplomat but who had been the only bishop to refuse outright the submission of the clergy in 1532 and refused to support the divorce.[44] One of Clerke's chaplains, George Dogeon, probably already was the vicar of Bristol's Temple church in Bath and Wells, where Hubberdine had preached on Ascension Day.[45] Clerke or his deputy may also have licensed Edward Powell to preach in Bristol.[46] In the case of Hilsey, however, the diocesan authorities balked, and therefore the Corporation was not able to acquire a licence for its chosen preacher at one of the year's most important civic occasions. In mid-July Hilsey was still trying to get a licence from Archbishop Cranmer, who was seeking the Council's approval for the issuance.[47] During the first week of June, therefore, the Corporation had to sit through three sermons knowing that they were powerless to control even official preaching before them, much less other pulpits in their town.

The response of the Corporation to this humiliation was indirect. On 5 June a number of the corporate elite joined Hilsey and three other clerics in asking the King's Council to certify the 'synstrall' preaching of Powell and Hubberdine to the Corporation, no doubt so that they, Aldermen acting as Justices of the Peace, could act against the preachers. They included a book of articles against the two.[48] Since this petition was not an official one from the Corporation and since at least four of the laity involved were sympathetic to religious reform, it could have been a factional request and the signers may have been among those burgesses who earlier had petitioned the Mayor and Council to act against Hubberdine.[49] Among the reformists signing were David Hutton (Sheriff in 1527), William Shipman (Sheriff in 1520 and Mayor in 1533–4), William Cary (Sheriff in 1531 and Mayor in 1546), and William Kelke (Sheriff in 1529). Hutton, as already shown, may have been connected to Lollardy and to the distribution of proscribed books. He also was a friend of Thomas Cranmer and had a connection with Anne Boleyn. Shipman, whose own will indicated strong protestant leanings, and Cary, were overseers of Hutton's will. Shipman, Cary, and Kelke also had relatives who were Protestants of the hotter sort.[50]

The presence of reformists, however, did not preclude broader political support for the petition to Cromwell. It was probably unofficial so that it could include clergy as well as laity and portray the trouble as being the community against outsiders. That the Corporation did in fact back the request is indicated by the Mayor's letter of 10 July to Cromwell, wherein he thanked him 'for tendering & preferring of our petition concerning the lewd demeanour of Hubberdine, & for your friendship shown to your poor bedeman Dr. Hilsey of the Black Friars'.[51]

Cromwell's response to the Corporation-backed petition was two-pronged. First, he either ordered Hubberdine to the Tower or certified his misbehaviour to the Corporation, allowing them to jail him. He was in jail by 4 July.[52] This saved the Corporation's face and demonstrated Cromwell's sympathies. At the same time, however, he commissioned an investigation of the affair, putting it in the charge of John Bartholomew, the Customer of Bristol, rather than the Mayor and Aldermen, which was the ordinary procedure.

On 5 July Bartholomew received the commission with directions to appoint a group of four or five men to investigate the preaching of Latimer and Hubberdine. His selection suggests that Cromwell, who had been Chancellor of the Exchequer since 12 April 1533, did not yet know the Mayor and Council and had opted for using an Exchequer official.[53] Possibly he had dealt with Bartholomew and trusted him to create an impartial committee which would report the facts. Bartholomew actually selected a conservative group including the Abbot of St Augustine, William Burton, three former mayors, and Thomas Abowen, gentleman.[54] The commission went to work immediately, calling for depositions from both clergy and laity.

The Corporation countered with a campaign to influence the results of the investigation by intimidating the clergy and stacking the witnesses against Hubberdine. The warden of the Grey Friars reported that Councilman Gilbert Cogan, soon to be Chamberlain of the city, visited him and warned him concerning what he might communicate to the commission, saying that four hundred men were prepared to contradict him.[55] An attorney, John Drews, worked for the Corporation, securing witnesses against Hubberdine, but he was not as successful as Cogan's threat to the warden implied. Drews appeared before the commission with a book containing the three articles against Hubberdine signed by those willing to bear witness to them. When the commission began calling on the men, however, it became clear that some who had signed all three articles were willing to depose concerning only one. At that point Drews asked the commission to allow each man to write up his own testimony since the oral proceeding was becoming too lengthy, and the commission agreed. Drews's book of articles contained only twenty-five different signatures and a list of twenty-nine names which Drews said represented men who were willing to depose.[56]

The testimony against Hubberdine included three articles: one accusing him of saying in the pulpit of St Thomas that there were twenty or thirty heretics among the inhabitants of the town; a second claiming that in several places and churches he had said that whoever spoke against the Pope or his acts or ordinances was a heretic; and finally, an accusation that he had made a negative reference to the King's new power over the choice of bishops. Unfortunately, there are no extant clerical depositions and this probably explains the absence of complaints concerning Latimer. Only one deponent, sheriff John Smyth, testified concerning Latimer's preaching, and he addressed Latimer's views of purgatory.[57]

The report of the commission itself, however, criticized Latimer and supported Hubberdine. The commission concluded that Latimer preached 'diverse schismatic and erroneous opinions: as in hell to be no fire sensible; the souls that be in purgatory to have no need of our prayers, but rather to pray for us; no saints to be honoured; no pilgrimages to be used; our blessed lady to be a sinner, as it has been reported and taken by the hearers.' The report said of Hubberdine that he 'preached sharply against Latimer's articles, proving them by authorities as well by the Old as the New Testaments schismatic and erroneous'.[58] The commission appended the articles against Hubberdine to the report and noted the circumstances surrounding the collection of those depositions, circumstances which showed that the Corporation attempted to influence the hearings to the discredit of Hubberdine.[59]

Mayor Clement Base, however, fired off his own letter to Cromwell on 10 July, one day before the commission dated its report. The bearer of the letter was none other than John Drews and he was to inform

Cromwell of the truth regarding the commission's findings.[60] Drews's endeavour on the Corporation's behalf was successful. Hubberdine remained in the Tower for at least two years and on 8 August the Corporation offered Cromwell the position of town Recorder, with a fee of £19. 6s. 8d., telling him that the labour was not much.[61]

Cromwell had not found it necessary to investigate the preaching of Powell in Bristol, for his views on the king's divorce were well known at court. He was an advocate of Queen Catherine. In January 1534 his proctorship of the Salisbury clergy was threatened, and a few months later, refusing the oath of succession, he was condemned for treason by the same act of parliament as Fisher and others. His influence disappeared in Bristol when he was deprived of all his preferments, including the prebend of Bedminster and Redcliffe, and was imprisoned in the Tower. On 30 July 1540, he was one of the three Catholics who, along with Barnes, Garret, and one other Protestant, were executed at Smithfield after being dragged two and two on hurdles from the Tower.[62]

The fates of the local clergy involved in the anti-Latimer campaign were not so dramatic, nor so unfortunate.[63] Hilsey, of course, had become an ally of the Corporation and a favourite at court. There is little information about the prior of St James, who preached against Latimer, or about John Fleming, curate of St Nicholas in Bristol, where Hubberdine had preached at Easter.[64] St Nicholas is the only known parish in Worcester diocese where Hubberdine preached, and he did so without licence.[65] On 17 September 1533, Archbishop Cranmer summoned Fleming to appear before him, but there is no evidence of further consequences.[66]

Two other clerics were involved in action against Latimer: John Goodriche, who preached, and John Floke, who as dean of Bristol must have consented to Hubberdine's preaching and whose advice on omitting prayer for the King and Queen was called into question.[67] Both were men of standing in the clerical community and were well established in the town. They, like most of the other refractory clergy, had graduate degrees. Hilsey, Powell, and Floke were Doctors of Divinity, the prior of St James at least a Bachelor of Divinity, Goodriche a Master of Arts.[68] Floke had become vicar of All Saints in 1517 and Goodrich rector of Christ Church in 1525.[69] Both were pluralists but were resident in their Bristol livings.[70] Goodriche, as an executor of Robert Thorne's will in 1532, was instrumental in the foundation of the free grammar school.[71]

Their break with the Corporation surely surprised its members, but there is no evidence that the break was irrevocable. Goodriche continued as rector of Christ Church until 1538, although he probably had become non-resident at least by 1536.[72] He was licensed to preach in Worcester diocese in July 1534, but there is no evidence that he was involved in any further conflict.[73] He died, the vicar of Clevedon in Bath and Wells diocese, by 1544.[74]

The career of Floke following the controversy included some immediate trouble followed by reconciliation with the corporate elite. He resigned the living of All Saints by 9 December and on 5 September 1533, was instituted vicar of Bedminster, with the 'chapels' of St Mary Redcliffe and St Thomas attached.[75] His patron, of course, was none other than Edward Powell. On 22 December 1534, Floke became a subdeacon and vicar of Westbury College in Gloucestershire near Bristol, a move that followed Powell's deprivation.[76] That position he held only for a few months, however, moving back to Bristol as prior of the Kalendars' Guild at All Saints on 24 March 1535, a post he kept until his death in the autumn of 1540.[77] This position was in the patronage of the mayor, who traditionally presented the candidate offered by the guild's priests. Given the Mayor's approval of the appointment and the absence of further conflict, undoubtedly Floke had agreed to curtail his activities and follow the Corporation's line.

Both Floke and Goodriche buckled under enormous pressure, not only from the Corporation but also from the Crown and the new Bishop of Worcester. Goodriche, however, did leave a parting shot in the person of his curate, John Rawlyns, whose conservative preaching earned him a jail sentence in 1537.[78]

The Corporation's success in managing the Latimer affair was no guarantee of stability. Although the clergy who opposed Latimer are not known to have caused any further trouble, the incident continued to rankle clerics and populace alike, particularly after Latimer became Bishop of Worcester late in the summer of 1535. That Latimer never visited Bristol in his four years as diocesan indicates the delicacy of the peace which had been achieved.[79] More important, the Corporation's success clearly owed more to their good fortune in supporting Cromwell's own favourite, Latimer, against enemies of the King's divorce, than to their manipulation of the investigation. Their efforts were, in fact, rather clumsy, and they must have felt very deeply their dependence upon Cromwell in the face of both a clerical challenge supported by the ecclesiastical hierarchy and the popular religious controversy it engendered. Having bestowed the recordership upon him, they were yet to learn that Cromwell's aid was an unreliable crutch during further conflict over local pulpits.

We can see that the Latimer episode was a critical juncture for the clerical and civic communities, although this view was not so apparent to the participants. For the resisting clergy it was another episode in the national story of the Crown's assault on clerical independence. It also represented a failure of unity among the city's clerical community, although monks, friars, and parish clergy did challenge Latimer and the Corporation. While it demonstrated the potential power of clerical consciousness operating in a cohesive manner, it also indicated the clergy's divided loyalties since many local clergy did not participate. For the lay elite, the clerical opposition came as a surprise which had to be dealt with firmly in order to maintain their own authority and lessen the threat of disorder, not to mention maintain good relations with the Crown.

To some of the secular elite the incident must have been merely 'one of those things' in the life of the city; to others it must have served as a warning to be vigilant. Both were right. This affair did reflect the latent tension in any urban centre caused by the clergy's mixed loyalties to Church and city. In other times this tension might have found expression, been dealt with, and receded. These times, however, were extraordinary. The Crown's extended attack on the church would gut the city's ecclesiastical institutions and redefine the urban church. The clergy would be weakened beyond imagination. Popular religious conflict, encompassing clergy and laity alike, would require the Corporation's continuous effort to maintain their authority and thus keep order. The Latimer affair was the beginning of the end of the medieval church and clerical community and thus the medieval civic community itself. The balance between local church and local state, the integration of the two into the civic microcosm, would never be regained.

CONTINUED RELIGIOUS CONFLICT

Religious conflict temporarily disappeared from view after the Latimer episode, and in the spring of 1534 Archbishop Cranmer visited Bristol and placed a ban throughout the province on sermons dealing with a number of controversial subjects.[80] By the summer of 1535, however, things began to heat up again, and the corporate elite initiated several investigations.

The Mayor and Aldermen first conducted an investigation of a hermit named Hugh Lathbury, who on 2 June 1535, appeared before them and admitted favouring Queen Catherine and speaking openly about supporting her. The Mayor himself wrote Cromwell on 22 August sending a second copy of depositions concerning Lathbury, in case by chance Cromwell had not received them. He indicated that Lathbury would remain in custody until the King's pleasure was known.[81] In another letter of the same date the Mayor gently but firmly answered Cromwell that the office of town clerk was not vacant or likely to be, and begged that future appointments be left to local authorities according to the ancient rule.[82] Cromwell obviously hoped to increase the value of his recordership with a bit of patronage, but the Corporation firmly drew the line against incursions into their own domain, even though they were left holding Lathbury.

Another commission, some of whose members were among the officials involved in the Lathbury affair, were investigating 'seditious preaching' in the city during the same period, and also were being ignored by Cromwell. Two of the three men known to have been on this commission were sympathetic to reform and they may have sought the commission to harass conservative preachers. On 26 August just three days after the Mayor's request for instructions concerning Lathbury, they sent Cromwell a message by Latimer, the bishop elect of Worcester.[83]

We have heard nothing from you touching the correction of offenders which counseleth the preachers to continue full in their indiscrete preaching encouraging all them that be adversaries to God's Word and putteth us somewhat to rebuke which were commissioners because they be not punished for their deserts, not yet commanded to surcease their preaching to such time they knew your mastership's pleasure . . . surely it will stay our town marvelously if they might be corrected according to those demerits whereas else farther inconveniences may ensue.[84]

If this commission represented a reform faction in the Corporation, they nevertheless received the same treatment as the Mayor and other Corporation officials. Although the executions of Fisher and More in June and July demanded Cromwell's attention, this does not explain his dealings with Bristol. He appears to have been more interested in local patronage than in the local government's problems, in reform, or even 'seditious preaching' in the city. He may, however, already have indirectly answered the complaint against preachers who were the adversaries of God's word with the election of Latimer to the bishopric of Worcester on 12 August. His refusal to act on the recommendations of local officials and of his own local commission nevertheless left the corporate elite in an extremely embarrassing situation and weakened their authority. In the future the Corporation would be less likely to act against offenders in religious matters. They could not afford to go out on a limb to control preaching unless the situation was critical because their role in investigating and condemning could potentially be more damaging to their authority than the preaching itself. There is no indication of the final outcome of the investigations of 1535, but the incidents throw into relief the local elite's dependence on the Crown and Cromwell, if they were effectively to enforce royal policies and still maintain order and their own authority. And if there were reformist activists among them, they too were undermined by Cromwell's behaviour.

During 1536 there were no commissions or investigations in Bristol. The only sign of inquiry into religious matters was a report by Bishop Latimer and a Worcester Justice of the Peace, John Russell, on 18 October. They had examined John Scurfield, 'the prisoner of Bristow,' according to Cromwell's orders. Although Scurfield had written very suspicious letters, he seemed innocent of malice and subtlety: 'His delight was to have them punished, which bruited to deny the Sacrament'. His lack of discretion was also attributed to his being less than 19 years old. Latimer concluded, 'He has been hampered therefore meetly well already, and is now carried again to Bristol to put in sureties, lacking sureties here for his forthcoming'.[85] This incident and its handling suggest that the Corporation was keeping a low profile in religious controversy following the embarrassing events of 1535.

Cromwell may have largely ignored Bristol because he had a trustworthy assistant in Latimer, but this was not an effective strategy. Worcester was far from Bristol and as a matter of fact, seditious preaching did continue in the city in 1536. It was ignored until February 1537, when an investigation developed, undoubtedly prompted by Cromwell's own concern with the Pilgrimage of Grace and the fear that things might be going out of control in Bristol. The commission's oath for inquiry, dated 25 February, emphasized the government's concern over seditious preaching, seditious and slanderous bills, and attacks on Bishop Latimer.[86] The government may have feared that local authorities were ignoring the expression of conservative, even traitorous, sentiment in the city. The commissioners, who reported on 7 May, were the Mayor, Richard Abingdon, seven former or future mayors, and William Appowell, a merchant.[87] They heard 100 to 110 witnesses and took over two months to complete the investigation, a far cry from those of 1533 who did their work in six days.[88] Perhaps this was because the commission was better balanced between reformists and non-reformists and because of the greater number of people and issues under investigation, but it also suggests a more cautious approach. They had not sought the investigation and did not rush to complete it.

The government's fear that the local authorities had backed away from a strict enforcement of official religious policy was realistic. The local Dominican prior, William Oliver, one of the reformist preachers to be investigated, had from his pulpit reproved the appearance in town of seditious bills of the 'infest and corrupted' *Pater noster, Ave,* and *Creed* and hoped the local authorities would not 'wink at it'. He also prayed God there were no 'privy Northern hearts nor close festered stomachs among them'.[89] He thus censured the authorities for ignoring the actions of those who posted seditious bills and for possibly harbouring among them conservative sympathizers. The injunctions of August 1536 had been brought to Bristol by 'the King's visitor' and included instructions to the clergy for teaching the paternoster and creed to their parishioners in English. The omission of the *Ave* or 'Hail Mary' was particularly provocative in Bristol where controversy over the place of the Virgin in religion had arisen when Latimer preached in 1533. It is not certain that the seditious bills represented the conservatives' response to the new policy omitting the *Ave,* but it is likely particularly given that the complaining preacher was a reformer.[90] The preacher's concern indicates that the authorities had been looking the other way even when religious activism conflicted with or ridiculed official policy.

The investigation revealed a fearlessness in the conservative John Kene which showed that he too had assumed the authorities would overlook the controversy. Perhaps he was among those preachers the commission had complained of in the summer of 1535 and whom Cromwell had ignored. Kene had jumped into the popular fray when he defended the sanctity of the Virgin, asserting from his pulpit that

some women do say they be as good as Our Lady; for we have borne four or five children and know the father of them and she bare but one and knew not the father. They do despise our blessed Lady which is most worthy of all honour; but if it had pleased God he might have made me his mother or have been born of a calf or a sheep.[91]

Latimer himself had distinguished between esteeming the Virgin and worshipping her when he clarified his criticism as of the 'abuse' of things rather than things in themselves.[92] But the dispute in Bristol had gone further.

The conservatives didn't attack Latimer by name from their pulpits, but Kene did attack the new preachers. He accused them of preaching new learning with their new books; and though they claimed 'to have as much learning as a student [studiar] that hath been at university forty or fifty years . . . they are as far wide as is Jerusalem and Jericho, which is three score miles and odd'.[93] Presumably these new preachers had been at work in the city.

Witnesses said that Kene despised good and faithful people, saying their learning was

old heresy new risen like unto old rusty harness new furbished. And whereas they say they have brought in the light into the world, no, no, they have brought in damnable darkness and endless damnation. Choose you go to hell and ye will, for I will not be your lodesman.[94]

Railing, he called them 'heretics, heretics and newfangled fellows', trusting that 'some honest men and women will take my part. I think I have made them somewhat better than they were wont to be, for they have used in times to grin and laugh at me, but they have well left it, wherefore I will pray for these heretics'.[95]

His parishioners were offended further because he had not prayed for the King during the northern rebellion or preached against the Pope as commanded by the King's visitor.[96] They also thought it 'not the King's will that he should call them heretics and newfangled fellows'.[97]

Both Kene and John Rawlyns, parson of St Ewen, also spoke privately against Bishop Latimer. Kene referred to Latimer as a 'false harlot', while Rawlyns said he was a 'harlot heretic'. Rawlyns also said, 'I trust to bring a fagot and to see the bishop of Worcester burned [brande]. And it is pity that ever he was born.' Witnesses attributed similar statements to two laymen. One of them, William Glaskeryon, had also been heard to say, at the time of the rising of the northern men, 'We may bless the time that we were born; they rise to strengthen our faith.' Piers Bak echoed Glaskeryon's sentiments saying, 'I hope they will rise again, and that a little stronger than before, and I will be one of them myself.' Only one of the laymen, Glaskeryon, was jailed, for four days. For their offences Kene spent twenty, Rawlyns three days in jail.[98]

The conservative reaction to Latimer in 1533 had obviously not been eradicated, and yet the local authorities were reluctant to take action. Given their past experiences with Cromwell, the municipal governors would act to curb religious division only when there was a direct challenge to them. In this case, neither their religious policy nor their own authority was at stake.

In February, shortly before the investigation began, the priors of the Dominicans and Franciscans had debated the worth of the religious life from their pulpits, and they, too, came under the commission's scrutiny. The Franciscan defended the religious while his opponent, William Oliver, made the most direct presentation of a Lutheran doctrine of which we have evidence. He connected Luther's solefideism to the worthlessness of the religious, preaching that 'a whole ship laden with friar's girdles, nor a dung cart full of monks' cowls and boots [botes] would not help to justification'; none of it could avail without faith. He also delineated the doctrine of Christian liberty, saying that one could not fruitfully work before justification by faith in Christ, while one so justified would naturally do charitable work for his neighbour.[99]

Although the commission examined the friars, there is no evidence that they were disciplined. The focus of the investigation was on the maintenance of royal and episcopal authority rather than on religious doctrine or even the dissolution of religious houses, most of which lay in the future. However, that three of the accused spent some time in jail doubtless also bolstered respect for the Corporation's authority, which had been called into question by the handling of earlier investigations. This time their caution, combined with Cromwell's concern, was rewarded with penalties for those guilty of resisting royal religious policy.

THE WISHART EPISODE

When George Wishart, the Scottish Protestant radical, preached in Bristol in 1539, the Corporation again reacted cautiously, this time finding itself in John Kene's camp and again caught between popular religious conflict and external authorities. A contemporary chronicler wrote that Wishart preached in St Nicholas church May 15 'the most blasphemous heresy that ever was heard, openly declaring that Christ neither had nor could merit for him nor yet for us'. The heresy, he added, 'brought many of the commons of this town into a great error and diverse of them were persuaded by that heretical lecture to heresy'.[100]

After John Kene, the Rural Dean of Bristol for the year, and others complained about Wishart's preaching, the Mayor wrote Cromwell on 9 June seeking his approval for action against the preacher, who 'was lately before your Lordship'.[101] The preaching in May and the Mayor's letter in June were not, however, the initial round of the controversy. Three letters written by a religious radical indicate that Wishart had preached in the city before 10 January, possibly in the parish church of Christ Church, had been jailed by local authorities, and then freed when popular disorder loomed.[102] When Wishart preached again at St Nicholas in May, the danger of popular protest thus provided a prophylactic against his detention in spite of the complaints of Kene and others.

The threats in the religious radical's letters were not generalized; they were aimed directly and personally at the city's established authorities, both clerical and lay. The first letter said

O you enemies to God's word, why have you accused the same faithful young man that did read the lecture, the very word of God? . . . I trust you shall all repent it shortly when my lord Privy Seal hears of it. And you foolish mayor, and that knave Thomas White, with the liar Abynton, the prater Pacy, the flattering Hutton, and drunken Tonell, foolish Coke, dreamy Smith, and the niggard Hart, and grinning Pryn, proud Addamys, and poor Woddus, the sturdy parson of St. Stevens, the proud vicar of St. Leonard's, the lying parson of St. John's, the drunken parson of St. Ewen's, the brawling master of the Calendars, the prating vicar of All Hallows, with divers other knave priests shall all repent this doing.[103]

The second letter, dated 10 January, was even more menacing and contemptuous of the city's established leadership and hinted that Bishop Latimer, as well as Cromwell, was on Wishart's side.

Yet once again to the enemies of God's word . . . you may see what cruelty you did use in putting this faithful young reader in prison and now be glad to put him out again. If you had not you should have been burned out of your housing. You shall repent this doing if some of us do live.[104]

He turned first to the 'knave priests':

the vicar of St Leonard's, rowling his nightcap of velvet every day and not able to change a man a grote, and the drunken parson of St. James, and that perpetual knave, the parson of St. Stephen's, and brazen-face knave of All Hallows, baburlyppe knave the priest of St. Leonard's, with long Sir Harry and little Sir Thomas, with the vicar of St Austin's, the old fool. All these of this diocese that have cure shall go like knaves to sing *Ave Regina* when the bishop come; for they have warning the last visitation and take this my warning you knaves all.[105]

Turning to the temporality, the writer claimed 'that same knave Thomas White now begins to shrink in his horns but that shall not help him. And the foolish mayor must follow a many of knaves counsel'. He also attacked the sheriffs, the town clerks, and others before concluding,

Therefore I do advise you beware and discharge the sureties of the reader by time; or else you will repent it for he shall make as many as 20 of you if need do require. Fare you well all you knaves all that do hold against the same honest man the reader for he doth regard the king of heaven before the king of England. And thus fare you well. You shall know more of my mind when our bishop comes from London.[106]

The third letter continued in the same vein although it was even more abusive and was addressed to a cleric, the vicar of St Leonard, Thomas Sylke, rather than to a layman. 'Thou shitting and stinking knave', it began; the writer was particularly angry because Sylke had not followed instructions for delivery of a previous letter cast into his chamber. 'Be sure', he wrote, 'thou shall lose one day one of thy ears and that ere it be middle Lent Sunday'. Sylke was the same cleric referred to in the previous letter as 'rowling his nightcap of velvet every day and not able to change a man a grote'. At the end of the letter the writer told Sylke, 'Commend me to all the knave priests that be the enemies of God's word . . . for the knaves have no learning, nor none will learn'. The critic referred, of course, to the lack of correct doctrine rather than lack of education among the clergy.[107]

The writer went on to link the threat of violence with the pointmakers, a group of leatherworkers. A reference to William Chester, a pointmaker and a member of the corporate elite, suggests that those involved in the threat were journeymen or apprentices.

Say not but you have warning for if the pointmakers do rise some of you will lose their ears and that shortly . . . that double knave William Chester, for sometimes he is with us and sometimes he is with the knaves; but he shall be a long knave for it, and his wife a foolish drab; for she is the enemy of God's word.[108]

The writer concluded with a last assertion of the bishop's sympathy: 'Fare you well for this time . . . Commend me to all the knave priests that be enemies of God's word; for if we live and the bishop together, they shall not trouble this town except the King do fail us'[109]

These letters reflect a deep disaffection with local lay and ecclesiastical authorities and show that a core of parish clerics supported the corporation against Wishart. The familiarity, hatred, and contempt expressed added credibility to the threat of violence.[110]

Once again the local officials had to exercise great caution, seeking to determine the least of several evils before deciding on a course of action. They could ignore heretical sermons. It would not be the first time the authorities had failed to act. Moreover, Wishart was not a local man and there was a good chance he would move on and not return. On the other hand, an ecclesiastical official, albeit a lowly rural dean, had pressed a complaint; this could not be ignored even though the anonymous radical's letters emphasized the danger of popular disorder if the complaint were acted upon. And there was Cromwell's unreliability to consider. After Wishart's earlier appearance before him, presumably following the first sermon in Bristol, Cromwell had not jailed him. And Wishart's enthusiast was certain that both Cromwell and Latimer would support the preacher (although there was a suggestion of doubt concerning the outcome in the phrase, 'except the King do fail us').[111] Did the local officials dare take further action against Wishart or his sureties after he repeated his offense in May? Did they dare not? By 9 June, when the Mayor wrote to Cromwell asking for direction, the Six Articles had been introduced into Parliament some three weeks before with the King's support.[112] It was becoming ever more difficult to judge the consequences from the centre for any local action or inaction. Best to hold still but guard against accusations of inaction by seeking direction from Cromwell.

Fortunately for the Corporation and unfortunately for the Wishart faction, the king did indeed fail Wishart and his supporters. The passage of the Six Articles Act set in motion the King's religious reaction. Latimer, who was among the bishops opposing the Six Articles, resigned on 1 July and thus was unable to provide the expected support.[113] There is no record of Cromwell's response, but events proved that he, too, failed the Wishart party. Wishart came before Archbishop Cranmer, who with several other bishops and doctors 'examined, convicted and condemned' him for heresy. Following their injunction, the preacher did penance by bearing a faggot in the local parish and church of St Nicholas on 13 July and in Christ Church and parish on 20 July.[114] There is no evidence of any action by Wishart's supporters; faced with resistance from royal, ecclesiastical, and local authorities, they retreated.

The Wishart affair again demonstrated the extreme vulnerability of the local authorities to external elements. Had the King continued on the path directed by Cromwell and Cranmer, Latimer no doubt would have remained as Bishop of Worcester and Wishart might have gone unpunished. The radicals would have been strengthened. Conservatives, led by Kene, would have been outraged, and serious popular disturbance might have ensued. Fortunately for the Corporation the confluence of national events precluded any interference from Latimer. At this critical juncture, the interests of the Crown and the Corporation coincided, albeit by chance, to support the Corporation's authority and ability to maintain order.

The Wishart episode also showed that a core of parish clergy were perceived by religious radicals as part of the establishment which was effecting and ensuring royal policy in the city. For the most part they were those who had been absent from the clerical movement against Latimer in 1533. Except for John Floke, who was rehabilitated after the Latimer affair, these clerics had remained loyal to the city rather than to the larger Church. The very prominent Thomas Sylke exemplified the clerics who by following the lead of the Corporation and the Crown, made successful careers through over four decades of changing royal religious policy. Throughout the Reformation, however, clergy at all points on the religious spectrum were subject to denigration by those who did not share their views, whether of left, right, or middle. While religious conflict continued, the clergy, divided and vulnerable, were forced to ally with like-minded laity in order to survive, and this had important ramifications for the relationship between clergy and laity.

In February 1540 Bristol's Mayor and Aldermen requested that Cromwell's representative in Gloucester come to Bristol to 'reform certain points'.[115] The request came only about three months before the visitation of the new bishop of Worcester John Bell, and they must have wondered what course was necessary to steer between this appointee of a conservative King and the King's other servant, Thomas Cromwell.[116] The Corporation was exercising the caution it had learned during the previous decade. Religious conflict was a difficult problem, particularly when the responses of the Crown, the diocesan authorities, and local laity and clergy were unpredictable. This experience and the continuation of local religious conflict help to explain the lay elite's lack of response to the debilitation of the clergy over the decades of the Reformation, even though it meant reduced service to the laity.

The death of Cromwell in 1540 and the creation of the diocese of Bristol in 1542 simplified the local government's tasks of maintaining order and its own authority. Yet the religious conflict continued. This we know because in the 1530s and 1540s the conservative preacher Roger Edgeworth was periodically in Bristol preaching at Redcliffe Cross.[117] Through his sermons we are able to relate the immediate stresses of religious conflict and the spread of Protestantism and to examine their impact on the clergy and their relationship to the laity.

4

Religious Conflict: Resistance and Change

THE religious divisions which so concerned the Corporation were played out among the clergy and laity in the city's streets and churches. The furore itself contributed to the diminution of traditional clerical authority, particularly since it required the divided clergy to make lay allies. Moreover the spread of Protestant ideas propelled a new lay assertiveness and discouraged traditional distinctions between clergy and laity. The balance of power in the relationship between the two collapsed in favour of the laity. Out of these developments emerged competitiveness among the clergy, an important element in their atomization. And here lay the culmination of the medieval clerical community's destruction.

The sermons of Roger Edgeworth give a great deal of insight into the lived reality of religious strife in Bristol and its impact on the clergy.[1] Preaching late in Henry VIII's reign or early in Edward VI's reign, Edgeworth said there were those in Bristol who would 'not use prayers in the church nor in other places, but rather with their babbling in the church, and mocking of divine service letteth and hindreth other men from their prayers, and from attending and hearing God's service'.[2] Reformers challenged mass-goers openly, calling, 'Will you see this Pope holy horeson? . . . We shall have a prophet, or a preacher of him', and other 'blaspheming and railing words'.[3]

Edgeworth encouraged his conservative listeners to ignore the epithets which reformers were casting at them, particularly for fasting or abstaining during Lent. 'These days', he lamented, 'folk think it no fault but a merry jest to rail and slander their neighbor, and to bring a man into infamy which many times turneth to his destruction and undoing'.[4] Edgeworth compared the plight of those who observed the traditional fast in Lent with that of Christ, who, 'When he was railed against, and called a heretic, and traitor, a benchwhistler, a blowboll, a fellow with ribalds, knaves, whores, drabbes, all this wind shook no corn.'[5]

The clergy were in the middle of these boisterous disturbances. Those priests who observed prescribed divine services daily were mocked and jested at

and not only of light brains of the laity, but also of men of our own coat and profession, lewd and foolish priests, that neither serve God devoutly, nor the world justly nor diligently, but give themselves to walking the streets, and beating the bulks with their heels, clattering light and lewd matters full unseeming for their profession.[6]

These heckling clergy and their lay counterparts made it impossible for the conservative or conforming clergy to proceed with dignity. Clerical divisions were rife.

Moreover, the clergy, Edgeworth claimed, were the focus of the hostilities:

for well is he that can do any hurt or displeasure to a priest, to take their lands and livings, is thought gotten good, and no good so safely gotten, to jest rail and mock at them, and to do them despites, is thought best pasttime, not regarding the prohibition of God.[7]

However, if Edgeworth was concerned about attacks on the conforming clergy, he also was capable of attacking their reformist counterparts, encouraging his listeners to avoid these 'pseudapostles, and lewd preachers' who had seduced them into 'sinister opinions, in which you walked darkly and blindly'.[8] Edgeworth's sermons show very clearly the divisions among the clergy, their weakened condition, and the necessity of alliance with the laity.

PROTESTANT DOCTRINES

Although not as important as religious conflict itself, Protestant ideas, which demanded a totally new view of the clergy's role, were extremely important in the assault on clerical authority during the Reformation. Probably the most important of these ideas was the redefinition of the sacrament of the altar.[9] The Catholic belief in transubstantiation placed the priest in a critical position since he performed the consecration rite. Furthermore the repeated sacrifice of Christ in the mass celebrated by the priest was seen as a necessary aid to the sinner's salvation. The Catholic view had been challenged since the late fourteenth century by Lollard heretics, whose underground activity kept their dissenting views alive in spite of intermittent persecutions.[10] Their denial of transubstantiation was based largely upon a simple critical empiricism—the bread and wine clearly did not change their appearance after consecration. Martin Luther's critique of transubstantiation had little in common with the Lollards', for he maintained the real presence of Christ's body and blood in the sacrament and held that the faithful received sacramental grace. The reformist critique of the Eucharist, however, irrespective of the precise content of each reformer's view, was also a critique of the clergy's central function.

Continuing debate about transubstantiation and change in official doctrine in England up until the statutory endorsement of the Thirty-nine Articles in 1571 possibly was as damaging to the clergy's status as the denial of transubstantiation itself.[11] During the reign of Henry VIII, transubstantiation was not questioned officially either during the 1530s or during the religious reaction which characterized the last six and one half years of the reign. The Edwardian Prayer Book of 1549 allowed a definition of the sacrament which admitted of transubstantiation, but the 1552 Prayer Book explicitly denied transubstantiation and was Zwinglian in tone. After the Catholic reign of Mary, transubstantiation again was denied, but Elizabeth's influence placed words in the 1559 Prayer Book which admitted the real presence as in 1549. In 1563 she would not agree to the twenty-ninth article of the Thirty-nine Articles of Religion, which by asserting the presence of Christ in heaven, greatly qualified the nature of the real presence, making it spiritual only. Not until 1571, when the Articles received parliamentary approval did she give the article her assent.

The reduction of the number of sacraments from seven to three and then two also had the effect of reducing the significance and power of the clergy. Debate over the sacramental nature of penance included discussion of auricular confession, a critical element in the relationship of clergy and the laity.[12]

Questions concerning the sacraments stemmed, of course, from Luther's central doctrine of justification by faith, which changed the focus of salvation from the Church to the individual.[13] Luther's new emphasis on the Scripture as the authority in matters of faith, in conjunction with the advent of printing and a rise in lay education, took power from the clergy and placed it in lay hands.[14] Both the doctrine of justification by faith and an emphasis on Scripture in the vernacular were in evidence in Bristol in the 1530s.[15] The changing balance of power inherent in reformed doctrine was made explicit in Luther's doctrine of the priesthood of the believer. The layperson no longer had to depend on a priest as an intercessor with God. Luther's doctrine of Christian liberty from the precepts of the law, furthermore, suggested the Christian's freedom from good works related to the medieval church's practices such as almsdeeds and pilgrimages. While Luther was convinced that inward and outward works of charity were certain manifestations of faith, good works were neither necessary to salvation nor tied to the church. These ideas too were manifest in Bristol as early as the 1530s. While Calvin and others modified Luther's view of the Christian's obligation to the law of God, they did not re-establish clerical oversight of good works nor emphasize their accomplishment in an ecclesiastical setting as the medieval Church did with pilgrimages, processions, candles, fasts, prayers for the dead, and numerous other activities regulated by the Church and controlled by the clergy.[16]

During the reign of Henry VIII the Crown recognized the distinction between things necessary to salvation and 'ceremonies' not necessary, which were within the Crown's competence.[17] These generally were traditional practices which could be continued for the sake of order or ended if they encouraged superstitious abuses. This distinction, as well as the Crown's plans for the dissolution of religious houses, made reformers' criticism of purgatory, pilgrimages, prayers to saints, and other 'ceremonies' acceptable, and these critics played an important role in Bristol's reform movement. Practices which contributed to clerical power and which had been considered good works became suspect, and the suspicion included doubt about the motivations of the clergy in encouraging the practices.

THE CLERGY

The spread of Protestant theology and ideas critical of traditional religious practices (in tandem with the dissolution of religious houses) contributed to the redefinition of the clergy's role during the Reformation. In Bristol as changes in the clerical role unfolded and contributed to other developments among the clergy, Roger Edgeworth defended the traditional priestly character and function. Edgeworth argued, apparently late in the reign of Edward VI, that the order of the priesthood was different from the laity, and he appealed for recognition of priestly authority and power.[18] Priests were like aldermen and had a leadership role which should be respected.[19] They were specialists who had been appointed by God to be 'lanterns of light' who would lead and guide people toward the salvation of their souls. Just as in trade and merchandise, merchants would listen to a merchant of grave and long experience, and a carpenter or mason would listen and learn from the King's craftsmen, 'Evenso it is in matters of higher learning pertaining to our souls health'.[20]

In Bristol, however, by the end of Edward VI's reign the traditional route to a clerical career, which ordinarily began in youth, was being abandoned as craftsmen became clerics. St Peter, Edgeworth claimed, was not a priest who was

at all adventurous, as these lewd ministers be made now a days of shoemakers, smiths, cobblers, and clouters, as well married as single, but one taught and brought up under the prince of priests our Savior Jesus Christ. Therefore they should assure themselves that he would teach them nothing but that should beseem a priest.[21]

The knowledge which these men had acquired in their crafts clearly was not, in Edgeworth's opinion, seemly to a priest.

He also agreed with Paul's thinking that new converts (or the newly called) should not be promoted to priest or bishop lest they soon forget themselves and their calling.

As who should say, yesterday at the cart, or in the barn among his corn and his threshers, or in the common market, and today at the open sises, sessions, law days or the courts, and today to minister in the church, yesterday at dice and cards, and all unthrifty games, and today to turn and read the holy books of Scriptures, or the holy mass book, yesterday to dancing and dallying, and today to consecrate priests, widows and virgins.[22]

Edgeworth was concerned that the dignity of the priesthood was damaged by those who left other trades or professions to become clerics.

Even more damaging, however, was the tradesman who became a priest but did not give up merchandising. That which is seeming and honest to one man, Edgeworth said, is not so to another. It was all right for a draper, a mercer, a shoemaker, or a hardwareman to stand in the open market and sell his wares to the most advantage in order to sustain himself, his family, and his household. For a knight, a squire, or a well-landed man, such activity would be a 'filthy shame and dishonesty' and equally so for a priest. A priest should be ashamed to give himself to merchandising, 'chopping and changing, buying good cheap, selling dear'. That which is 'tolerable and somewhat honest' in others should be regarded as shameful gains in a priest.[23] Edgeworth's criticism showed that concrete changes in the composition and practices of the clergy contributed to clerical divisions. They reinforced the ideological loss of authority by creating clergy little different from the laity.[24]

Other changes among the clergy also contributed to a loss of authority by further lessening the distinction between clergy and laity. A very radical change was clerical marriage, for clerical celibacy represented an important societal ideal. Edgeworth accused the married clergy of 'shameful and incestuous bawdry, which they would cover with the name of matrimony, so by them slandering that holy sacrament'.[25] In addition, priests had cast off clerical dress in favour of clothing worn by the laity. There were 'a great many' priests who went about in lay garments as if they were ashamed of the order of the priesthood and would be glad to 'pull their heads out of that yoke' if possible.[26]

Added to these changes among the secular clergy was the dissolution of all the city's religious houses by the end of 1539. This not only removed the religious, the clergy most distinct from the laity, from the scene, but also pushed many of them into jobs in local parishes. Although this was not a totally new phenomenon, the loss of the friar's ideal of poverty and the monastic ideal of the life of prayer, brought the clergy closer to lay activity.

THE LAITY

In Edgeworth's view the clergy's movement towards living like the laity was complemented by a new lay assertiveness in religion, a movement towards clerical authority if not always towards clerical activity. Edgeworth attacked the laity's assumption of authority in religious matters which had been made possible by increased literacy and better access to the Bible, and which owed much to both Lollard tradition and Lutheran invention. In 1538 Royal Injunctions ordered the placement of the Bible in English into every parish church for the use of the parishioners, and in Bristol many of the laity doubtless possessed their own copies. Edgeworth protested around 1539 that of all the faculties of learning, Scripture was in the worst condition, for it was the only knowledge 'that all men and women challengeth and claimeth to themself and for their own, here and there, the chattering old wife, the doting old man, the babbling sophister, and all other presumeth upon this faculty, and teareth it and teacheth it afore they learn it'.[27]

Furthermore, he questioned the laity's motives, asserting that as these 'green divines' taught and distributed books, they encouraged others to labour so they could oppose the best priest in the parish and tell him he lied.[28] He thought the reformists' study of Scripture, and by implication their assumption of clerical authority, was clearly discredited by their mockery of conservative clergy and laity. There were many, he said, who boasted and gloried in their learning from study of the English Bible, and seditious English books 'sent over from our English runagates now abiding with Luther in Saxony'. But the effects of the study demonstrated faulty motivation. When men and women thought themselves learned, others perceived little else but envy, disdain, and mockery towards traditions and ceremonies of the Church and those who would practice them.[29] Moreover, he warned, the study of the Scripture without the presence of the Holy Ghost would result in heresy.[30]

In the early 1540s it also incensed Edgeworth that people refused to come to sermons, preferring the sweet words of some to the bitter sayings of others.[31] Some even eschewed services and sermons for 'bawdy songs, unhonest and filthy plays, or pageants, interludes of schisms, dissension and heresies'. These carnal men and women would rather pay money to poison their souls than to come to hear a free sermon for their souls' health.[32] These were not only those who studied Scripture or English books but those who exercised simple rational criticism of the sacrament of the altar and the fire of hell. Edgeworth argued that the merit and reward of the faithful would be small if the things hoped and believed were not so removed from the carnal senses. But there were many 'so addicted and wedded to their bodily senses that they will not believe much more than experience showeth them, or than that they may attain to by their own gross reasons'. From this stance came 'diffidence and wavering' about the Eucharist and about the state of souls in the afterlife and many other matters of faith.[33]

Among the targets of Edgeworth's preaching were those such as Robert Jordeyn alias Bowyer of Bristol, who was accused in 1541 of asking one Roger Waxmaker 'when he did see God', a classic Lollard reference to the sacrament of the altar.[34] Jordeyn denied the accusation. He did, however, admit to having met with two other men 'in a cellar of one Patrickes in Bristol' and saying that 'no man did see God at any time (as far as he could hear) with his bodily eye'. Jordeyn also admitted discussing whether one could see the devil, arguing that no man could because 'it was a spirit and had neither flesh nor bone'.

Jordeyn's testimony had the ring of medieval Lollardy by virtue of its simple rationalism and suggests the possibility that investigation of Scripture was not necessarily the only means to reformist discussion and activity. If literacy was an important component in the spread of the movement, those with common sense could also participate.

Edgeworth reserved some of his criticism of the laity's new role in religion specifically for women, who in Bristol were not only studying the scriptures but also teaching and disputing it.[35] There were a variety of reasons why women should 'not play the reader . . . not keep the schools, but rather . . . learn in silence without many words and without clattering, with all obedience and subjection'.[36] Some of his reasoning related to common notions of women's inferiority. A woman, he said, should consider her subordinate place as the second created and the first to sin. Since once her teaching had marred all, she should be subject to and not reform and teach men.[37] Responding no doubt to reform activity in which local women were engaged, he emphasized women's incapacity for study. They were frail, very obedient to their fancies, and too earnestly and eagerly followed their own lusts. They were 'very unmeet scholars of moral philosophy'.[38]

In addition to the natural and moral inferiority of women, which was the basis of Edgeworth's argument, there was also the fear that bad things might happen if women stepped out of a traditional role, out of control. He warned that if women were allowed to be teachers, they might 'wax proud and malapert'.[39] And if they were allowed to reason or ask questions of learned men, 'by overmuch familiarity some further inconvenience might mischance to both parties'.[40] Edgeworth's view of women and their place in the world was common to his time. Court records show, however, that this view did not prevent women from speaking their minds in public.[41] To some extent the involvement of women in reform was simply an extension of normal life. Nevertheless Edgeworth wanted to emphasize the prescribed role of women and portray all aberrations as exceptional. If women were to teach, then they were to do it modestly and secretly and certainly were not to openly dispute and teach men.[42] If there must be exceptions, they should at least keep a low profile. Referring to women to whom St Jerome wrote, Edgeworth said they were 'well exercised in Holy Scriptures' but they were not 'readers, preachers, or disputers of Scriptures'.[43]

The conservative preacher recognized that the activities of women reformists threatened more than lay usurpation of clerical authority. In order to demonstrate the societal dangers inherent in the assumption of clerical roles by women, Edgeworth turned to the 'Lutherians' (presumably in Germany), who misused Scripture to

> confound and deface all good order of divine and human things, allowing the women to serve the altar, and to say mass while the men tarry at home and keep the children and wash their rags and clothes: and as well they might allow the women to be captains of their wars and to lead and give an army of men in battle, while their husbands tarry at home to milk the cow and to serve the sow, and to spin and card.[44]

The picture which Edgeworth presented was a world turned upside down by the usurpation of clerical roles by the laity. Pushed to its limits, the concept of a lay priesthood allowed women to become priests, an outrage comparable to the admittance of women to combat. The implication was not simply that women's new role harmed the clergy, but that it threatened the superior position of all men. By exploring the profound challenge to the accepted relationship between men and women inherent in Luther's 'priesthood of the believer', Edgeworth also defended the traditional role of the clergy against all reformist attacks.

As the traditional role of the clergy broke down in the face of religious divisions and Protestant doctrine, the clergy on both sides of the conflict became more and more vulnerable. Edgeworth's defensive posture is clear and his situation ironic. Forced to attack the new Protestant and nontraditional clergy, he contributed to the loss of clerical dignity even as he defended it. His most serious criticism of his fellow clerics rings true. Some of the local clergy, he claimed, were following the people rather than leading.[45] For fear of losing promotion, favour, or friendship both clergy and laity were preaching and teaching pernicious heresies. Many others spoke against reason and talked 'with their mouth that they have not thought with their hearts'.[46] Edgeworth also chastised the reader, schoolmaster, or preacher who taught falsely out of ignorance. These could not have a good conscience any more than those who changed their opinions to please the world or for promotion, profit, or advantage, 'as the wind bloweth & as the world changeth'.[47] Of course, Edgeworth was not an unbiased observer. Among those he criticized undoubtedly were men motivated by their own beliefs and commitments. Nevertheless in a situation where religious divisions threatened the clergy, new ideology supported lay leadership, and royal policies brought instability, clerical compromise was the order of the day. Edgeworth himself managed to hold on to preferments until his death in 1560, even though he was imprisoned for a time.[48]

By the end of the 1530s the clergy were in a growing crisis not of their own making. The emergence of conflicting religious views in that decade destroyed the medieval consensus on the local clergy's role in religion and society, making it impossible for a cleric to receive general societal approval regardless of what he did. Throughout the Reformation, the clergy came under fire as a result of competing doctrinal views rather than clerical inadequacies. The destruction of the traditional consensus and the long period of indecisiveness which followed contributed heavily to a decline in clerical status and the disintegration of the clerical community.[49] What had been an easily recognizable and definable body, albeit with many sub-groups, was becoming a loosely defined group of individuals, many of whom claimed no collegial relationship. The individual cleric was left to find support where he could among both fellow clerics and the laity.

The Protestant ideal of a preaching clergy, furthermore, did little to restore the lost status of the clergy or to recreate the coherence of the medieval clergy. Ordination no longer admitted one to the true clergy. This office could be achieved primarily by the individual's development of preaching skills and the approval of his congregated listeners. Of course the city's well-educated parish clergy and friars of the pre-Reformation period had undoubtedly also sought to preach well, but this skill was not the essence of their authority, and their positions were more secure. The development of free-lance preaching during the Reformation brought a different kind of competition and separated preaching from the pastoral function. The eventual establishment of corporation lecturers (even when they were incumbents) emphasized the separation of preachers from the clergy and even the laity of the parishes and dramatized their dependence on the élite laity of the Corporation.

While religious conflict and Protestant ideology promoted the decline of the clergy's status and the fragmentation of the community, the dissolution of religious houses under Henry VIII and of chantries under Edward VI cemented the losses by removing substantially independent institutions and leadership in the case of religious houses, and in the chantries elements of worship which drew the most lay support for the church. This destruction had far-reaching effects for the clerical community, diminishing its resources and creating a competitive climate for those clergy seeking employment.

5

Religious Houses and Chantries: Dissolutions and Surrenders

THE dissolution of religious houses, which occurred in Bristol between 1536 and 1539, and the suppression of chantries in 1548 involved two very different kinds of ecclesiastical institutions. The religious lived communally and were far more independent of lay influence than the chantry priests, many of whom were stipendiaries paid by lay trustees. Nevertheless the eradication of the religious houses and the chantries both mirrored and brought about dramatic changes in the urban community and caused lasting harm to the local church and clerical community. The dissolutions also reflected and effected changes in the status of the city's clergy. Given the drama and significance of the changes, it is notable that there was no lay resistance to the dissolutions and among the clergy, only friars defied the authorities.[1] It is understandable that by 1538 most of the beleagured clergy would see resistance as futile and would be ducking for cover. Much had occurred since 1533 when clergy of various groups had co-operated to oppose Latimer. It is, in fact, remarkable that three houses of friars refused to surrender for a brief time. The response of the city's laity, however, requires further investigation.

THE CORPORATION'S RESPONSE

The position of religious houses in and about a city necessarily created tension, for though the religious and friars were inhabitants of the city and members of the community their loyalties were divided. Their extra-urban connections, of course, also gave them independence which parish clergy were less likely to have. As we have said, civic ceremony was one way to emphasize local loyalty and overcome the tension. Nevertheless there were times when conflict erupted. In several instances the authorities in late medieval Bristol faced jurisdictional disputes with two local ecclesiastical institutions.

In 1491 a protracted conflict broke out when the abbot of the monastery of St Augustine claimed manorial jurisdiction over St Augustine's Green and the Hospital of St Mark and their precincts.[2] The disputed jurisdiction included the view of frankpledge and the abbey's right to hold its own courts and collect all dues and fines, including those for breaking the assize of bread and ale. The Mayor and commonalty argued that these areas had always been within the city and county of Bristol, that local officials had always exercised jurisdiction there, and that the inhabitants of the area had always been assessed with those of Bristol.

Before the case was settled other issues also intruded. The Corporation accused the Abbot of doubling his mills from two to four and drawing business away from the town's mills. Moreover, they said, the Abbot was forestalling grain coming into Bristol, using some for making malt and illegally exporting most to Ireland. The Abbot claimed that the convent was unable to purchase victuals in the town and that the town's inhabitants had been ordered not to use the monastery's mills. Rents due the convent from the town were being withheld while suits of those connected to the monastery had been delayed in local courts. Further, said the Abbot, local authorities had stirred a private suit against the abbot and others in the court of King's Bench in order to cause conflict and insert themselves into the abbot's jurisdiction. Also at issue were the Corporation's actions in removing great stones from the Avon river, which had served to protect the monastery's lands. The Corporation claimed the removal necessary for shipping and denied all other charges. The issue of sanctuary also arose when the Mayor and Sheriffs entered the disputed area in search of vagabonds. The abbot's servants attacked them and conflict ensued. It appears that the Corporation was using all the means at hand to overcome the abbey's assertion of jurisdiction.

The end of the dispute over a law day came through the mediation of Archbishop Morton, Chancellor of England, and John Fyneux, Chief Justice of the King's Bench in 1496. It was determined that town officials should hold a law day in the disputed area, keeping the records and meeting the costs, but profits should be divided between the town and the abbey. This presumably kept the Corporation's franchise of the assize of bread and ale intact, as well as the appearance of control, but gave the abbey added income, which was probably the original goal. In the 1530s the Corporation was paying 3s. 4d. to the town clerk each year for keeping court at St Augustine.

Conflict broke out again in 1515. When some choristers of the abbey refused to pay 'the King's silver', local officers entered the jurisdiction of the abbey and confiscated some of their possessions. The Abbot thereupon arrested the municipal officers, and the Mayor and commonalty retaliated by imprisoning retainers of the convent. The Abbot, 'with a riotous company', attempted unsuccessfully to release his men. This dispute, too, finally was referred to arbitrators who decided that the choristers should pay their taxes and all prisoners should be released. In addition the Mayor and Council were to attend divine service in the monastery as usual, while the Abbot and his successors, in token of submission for their contempt, were to wait for them at the door of the grammar school at Frome gate every Easter Day in the afternoon and Easter Monday in the forenoon. The Corporation had won at least a symbolic victory and, it would appear, was making significant headway in pulling the monastery into the dominion of the city.[3]

If the abbey's claims were not an immediate problem in the 1530s, a dispute between the Corporation and the Hospitallers, who had manorial rights in the city's Temple Fee area across the Avon, concerned similar claims.[4] In 1533 Edmund Hussey, the commander of Temple Cloud (a larger administrative area encompassing Temple Fee), and William Weston, prior of the Hospitallers in Bristol, claimed right of sanctuary, legal jurisdiction, and assize of bread and ale in Temple Street, a major artery of the city. The Corporation responded by taking the case to the Star Chamber in 1534 with a strong attack against Hussey. They accused him not only of assuming Corporation franchises by holding a law day for those given sanctuary (from Corporation or county justice) and by giving the assize of bread and ale, but also of baser actions: he had stolen a servant girl from another man and was holding her in Temple Street against her will. He was also accused of operating an unlawful ale house to the ill example of the town. When confronted by the constable, they further charged, Hussey refused to pay sureties and supported his refusal with some forty or so armed men. The extended charges probably reflected the Corporation's determination to receive a hearing on the regulatory issues. The issue of sanctuary was decided in favour of the Corporation and the Mayor's officers were given the right to serve processes in Temple Fee without resistance from the prior. Decision in the other matters was postponed, and there is no evidence that it was ever given.

The similar claims of the abbey of St Augustine and the Hospitallers sought to limit the rights of the Corporation which had been won through royal charters. In normal times these challenges to municipal authority would have been seen as a nuisance, the price to be paid for the benefits these institutions provided. In the context of religious conflict, the nuisance may have seemed slightly more hazardous. In any case, the negative aspects of these institutions for corporate power and civic unity could have provided a strong rationale for accepting Crown actions when resistance was virtually unthinkable anyway. Moreover, during the 1530s the religious houses supported clerical opposition to the Corporation on occasion and contributed to religious conflict among clergy and laity alike. The Abbot of St Augustine was a member of the commission which found fault with Latimer rather than Hubberdine in 1533, and the priors of the Franciscan friars and the monks of St James also were involved in opposing Latimer.[5] In 1537 religious conflict between the priors of the Franciscans and the Dominicans figured in another commission investigation.[6] Obviously the religious and the friars were not preponderant in the conflict, but their contributions made the Corporation's job of maintaining order and their own authority more difficult. The dissolutions of religious houses thus may have seemed a partial solution to the problems of order and control. At least members of the corporate elite may have justified their failure to defend this part of the local community in this way.

Although there is little evidence that the religious houses were using their patronage rights in Bristol in opposition to Corporation or local lay interests, the events of 1533 also demonstrated the corporate elite's vulnerability in that regard, thus providing another reason or rationalization for the Corporation's acceptance of the Crown's attack. The abbey of St Augustine had the patronage of the appropriated vicarages of All Saints, St Nicholas, St Leonard, and St Augustine-the-Less.[7] Tewkesbury, the mother house of the local Benedictine priory of St James, was patron of the vicarage of Sts Philip and Jacob and the rectories of Christ Church, St Ewen, St John, St Michael, and St Peter, and provided a perpetual curate for the parish church of St James.[8] The rectories of St Mary-le-Porte and St Werberg had as their patron the priory of Keynsham, and the rectory of St Stephen was in the patronage of Glastonbury Abbey.[9] The Hospitallers were patrons of the parish church of Temple, and the prebendary of Bedminster and Redcliffe in Salisbury Cathedral was patron of St Mary Redcliffe and St Thomas, which were officially chapels of the church of Bedminster.[10] Only St Lawrence had a secular patron, Lord Lisle.[11]

Ostensibly patronage was a weapon which the church could have wielded against Bristol's lay elite, who went along with the Crown's religious policy. Pulpits manned by opponents to the royal divorce, to reform, to the dissolution of religious houses would have made the Corporation's efforts to follow Crown policy much more difficult. The stasis of the parochial system of tenure, however, left little opportunity for the monasteries to fight the King's attack on the Church in the 1530s. The conservative preacher and Salisbury prebendary Edward Powell used his patronage of Bedminster to allow John Floke to move from All Saints to Bedminster and St Mary Redcliffe in 1533, while Tewkesbury replaced John Goodriche with the equally rebellious John Kene at Christ Church, but neither case represented a numerical increase in conservative parish clergy. Tewkesbury also replaced Edward Waterhouse, whose views are not known, with John Rawlyns, an opponent of Latimer, as parson of St Ewen.[12] These changes at least suggested the possible implications of ecclesiastical patronage in the city. Local livings could be used to protect conservative clergy who countered King and Corporation, encouraging religious conflict. Monastic patronage gave yet another reason for the Corporation to welcome the dissolution of the religious houses.

Unlike the more independent religious, the chantry priests remained under fairly tight lay control.[13] At the dissolution in 1548, ten priests occupied nine chantries called 'services', an indication that the endowments and tenures were controlled by lay trustees who hired stipendiary priests to meet the requirements of the chantries' founders. Another thirteen priests also were stipendiaries, although some of them were protected by episcopal institution, which mitigated lay control over the clerics. Nevertheless none of these twenty-three controlled the endowments of their chantries in the way that incumbents controlled parish livings. In addition to this economic control, some fourteen chantry priests of eleven chantries were required to give an annual oath to the Mayor, acknowledging his authority to oversee the fulfilment of their duties. Eight of these were not among the twenty-three known stipendiary chantry priests. Seven of the chantries paid the Mayor and town officials to attend anniversaries of the founders and to oversee the chantries; two of these were not among those identified as having priests who were stipendiaries or owed an oath to the Mayor. Beyond these forms of lay influence, lay patronage affected another six chaplaincies.[14] Thus, at least thirty-nine of forty-four chaplaincies fell under some degree of lay control or influence.

The extent to which lay influence permeated the city's chantries demonstrates the character of those foundations as exemplars of medieval mercantile religiosity and the integration of religious expression, economic success, civic pride, and communal responsibility. These institutions, however, were not outside ecclesiastical control. In some cases where ecclesiastical institution was necessary, the Bishop rather than the lay trustees had authority over tenure. In the 1530s, when religious divisions threatened the exercise of power by local secular authorities, ecclesiastical power intruded into the city through this mechanism. On 5 December 1533, William Benet, who signed the certificate of the preaching of Powell and Hubberdine in June 1533 and who was chaplain to Bishop Latimer in 1536, became chaplain of Spicer's Chantry in the parish church of St Nicholas. That he was elected by the Council with the Mayor's consent as provided by the foundation, rather than nominated by the Mayor as was customary, suggests that there was some controversy over his selection.[15] Benet held the position in St Nicholas until 1539 when a parishioner complained to the new Bishop, the conservative John Bell, that he had long been absent from his post, and the Bishop removed him.[16] The complaint, of course, corresponded to the Crown's swing towards religious conservatism and Latimer's resignation from the episcopacy of Worcester. Most important, the action showed that the authority of the lay elite could be challenged by other local laity through an appeal to the Bishop. The chantries were subject to greater control by laity in a number of parishes than any other pre-Reformation ecclesiastical institution. Thus they could provide a means by which lesser laity used outside ecclesiastical authority to affect local affairs, potentially in defiance of the majority of the corporate elite. Although episodes such as this threatened local control, it is highly unlikely that the Crown would have received the Corporation's support for dissolving chantries in the 1530s, given their integration into the community.[17]

THE POPULAR RESPONSE

Several elements undoubtedly contributed to the lack of popular resistance to the dissolutions of 1536–9 and 1548. Religious reform certainly had raised doctrinal questions concerning the validity of the functions of the religious, the friars, and the chantry priests. Latimer's criticism of pilgrimages, relics, and prayers to saints in 1533 was aimed at the religious, and his questions about purgatory challenged the purpose of chantry priests as well. The priors of the Franciscans and Dominicans debated the worth of the religious from their pulpits in February 1537 and in the same year Latimer, then Bishop of Worcester, ruled that no friar or religious person was to be allowed to participate in parish church services.[18] The combination of Lutheran and Lollard activity in spreading reformist ideas undoubtedly also undermined the position of the institutions and priests targeted by the Crown for dissolution. This is not to say that the city's populace was united in its support of religious change; popular conflict belies that. But the conflict itself undermined the *status quo*; clerical squabbling undoubtedly created apathy or even anticlericalism among many lacking strong doctrinal convictions.

It is equally likely, however, that the conflict also created fear, especially among those who might have defended the religious against the dissolutions. Edgeworth's descriptions of the harassment of conservatives strongly suggests this possibility, and who would have wanted to risk jail, the fate of outspoken conservatives just the year before? Moreover the co-operation of local authorities with the Crown's representatives certainly would have made resistance a difficult proposition. It is also likely that the attention of those who might have protested was fastened on their own parish churches where images and relics were being removed in accordance with the royal injunctions of 1538.[19]

While the immediate religious and political climate contributed to fear, apathy, or lack of esteem for the threatened ecclesiastical institutions, wider social change may also have contributed to the lack of resistance. These clergy fulfilled several social responsibilities. All prayed for the community and the friars preached. Perhaps more important, by living communally the religious represented the civic ideal of communal, or social, co-operation. The ideal, of course, was never realized in the urban community, which was comprised of clergy and laity from many groups, but it represented the operative myth which maintained the *status quo*, gave meaning to it, reduced tensions, and helped to keep people in their assigned places in the communal hierarchy. The friar's idealization of poverty fulfilled a similar purpose by discouraging overt competitiveness. In Bristol the early sixteenth century was characterized by developments which contradicted these ideals. There was conflict among the lay elite over shrieval duties and expenses, and long-distance merchants attempted to exclude retailers from overseas trade. Conflict also occurred between journeymen and masters. Locally a depression in the mercantile economy combined with inflation to produce a situation which may have further encouraged competitiveness, given the example set by some of the city's leaders.[20] Changing attitudes towards the poor, which were reflected in the development of punitive poor laws, also were occasionally reflected in wills of Bristolians who refused benefactions to any able-bodied poor.[21] The onset of religious conflict in 1533 represented a further breakdown of the communal ideal. The myths of communal co-operation and the holiness of poverty which the religious represented were increasingly contradictory to developments in the city, not to mention the country.

For some the religious houses may have represented cherished values in an increasingly troubled world. For others they may have been a bothersome reminder that these new developments denied traditional values. These may have viewed religious houses as obstacles to personally profitable changes, as prickers of conscience, or as simply increasingly irrelevant institutions. The Crown's depredation resolved the troublesome contradiction, giving permission as well as opportunity for pursuing self interest in the most direct and previously unacceptable manner. If a Latimer could portray religious houses as a waste of resources in relation to both personal salvation and rejuvenation of the commonwealth, others undoubtedly were less unselfishly motivated. So the lack of popular resistance to the dissolutions may indicate degrees of support for the action. However, the evidence of religious conflict suggests very strongly that there were many supporters of traditional religion who had good reason to fear the consequences should they have opposed the Crown, the Corporation, the Bishop, and obstreperous local reformists by resisting the attack on the religious houses.

By the time the scheme for the eradication of chantries was initiated in 1545 and the process begun in 1548, the decline of community had been exacerbated much more by religious conflict, religious change, and royal religious policy (including the first series of dissolutions) than when the earlier dissolutions had occurred. Had the chantries been attacked a decade before, they might not have fallen so easily, for laity and clergy alike shared in the extraordinary communal quality of these foundations. While K. L. Wood-Legh emphasizes the self-interest of chantry founders, she acknowledges the communal quality of chantries, saying, 'all the foundation deeds bear witness to the belief that spiritual benefits should be shared' by including 'all the faithful departed' as well as relatives, friends, and benefactors.[22] Alan Kreider implies the communal nature of chantories, noting the many roles played by chantry priests in the parish. They interceded for departed souls, heard confession, officiated at parish masses, participated in the cure of souls, taught parishioners' children, participated in church services and provided music.[23]

The work of Clive Burgess on chantries in Bristol, however, makes the communal quality of chantry foundations explicit. Not only did the founders of chantries intend that their chantry priests serve their parishes in a variety of ways, they also intended the lavish vestments, vessels, and books with which they were equipped to enhance or 'increase' divine service in perpetuity. That founders of temporary chantries were among those who gave most generously of equipment when they could have extended the duration of intercessory prayers suggests their concern for their parish communities as well as for themselves and the wider community of souls departed.[24] Ameliorating the liturgical standards of their churches and augmenting the parish clergy, founders of chantries 'equated the benefit of their parish with that of their soul', for these were services 'on which both the living and the dead depended.' Thus the founding of chantries was not a self-centred activity, and chantry priests were certainly not the 'isolated servants of the dead'.[25]

The evidence for giving great emphasis to the communal quality of chantries is convincing. But the nature of this community was, of course, hierarchical. The chantries founded by the well-to-do before death not only bore witness to the bonds they shared with all the faithful dead and their fellow parishioners but also ensured that their economic and social position in the parish community would not be forgotten.[26] This undoubtedly also helps to explain the choice of lavish equipment over an extended duration of intercessory prayers. Not only did vestments and vessels make a more vivid impression than longer-lived prayers by more simply equipped clergy but also both benefactor and benefaction were remembered in perpetuity with the annual reading of who had given what to the parish. It was the parish's way of saying thank you and encouraging the continuance of the benefactions which did so much to elevate the beauty of the liturgy, to increase divine service for the benefit of all.

The lack of resistance to the dissolution of chantry foundations thus suggests the dissolution of the hierarchical but closely bonded parish community, and it reflects the breakdown of the wider urban community shown in the local conflicts and in the earlier dissolutions. The dissolution of the chantries, of course, did not simply reflect the breakdown of communal life; it contributed to it by eradicating a very important symbol of the traditional community. And it is wise to consider that their eradication came some twelve years after the dissolutions of religious houses had begun. Had the Crown initially proposed all the measures eventually taken against ecclesiastical symbols of community, it is doubtful that the laity would have bowed to them so easily.[27]

If the Crown had not suppressed the religious houses and chantries, they probably would have continued indefinitely, but some adjustment in their institutional purposes might have been necessary. Such an adjustment may, in fact, already have been occurring in some city chantries. The appointment of Benet and another reformer to chantry positions in the two decades before their suppression suggests that some chantries were being transformed to support the cause of reform rather than the designated purpose of intercessory masses and prayers. In the case of Benet it appears that a majority of the Common Council elected him to the position following the satisfactory resolution of the Latimer conflict in the spring of 1533. One sees the hand of pragmatic patronage rather than the spirit of reform influencing the local Council, but the chantry's endowment nevertheless was supporting an absentee reformer. This provoked a presumably conservative parishioner to take action as soon as Latimer was replaced as Bishop of Worcester by the more conservative John Bell.

In the 1540s another reformer, William or Walter Bower, apparently became priest of Foster's Service in St Werberg and Eborard le Frenche's chantry in St Mary Redcliffe while he was a fellow of Magdalen College, Oxford.[28] The parishioners of St Werberg included reformists among the secular elite in the 1540s, in Elizabeth's reign, and in the first four decades of the seventeenth century while the parish of St Mary Redcliffe supported an outspoken Puritan curate in the 1560s and 1570s.[29] Bower, who may have been a native of Bristol, was expelled from Oxford with other reformers, including the Bristolian and future prebendary Arthur Saule, at the visitation of Bishop Gardiner in 1553.[30] Both he and Saule were supporters of the Puritanical party in the Lower House of Convocation in 1563, and by that time Bower had become the assistant teacher in the cathedral grammar school.[31] Given that some chantries initially were endowed to aid a particular priest, as well as serve the needs of the parish, the appointments of Benet and Bower continued in that tradition of patronage (and if they preached in the parish, possibly the tradition of parish community) while transforming the ideological basis of chantries.[32]

The utilization of chantry endowments to support reformist clerics suggests a resilience in ecclesiastical institutions which might have allowed them to adapt to religious and ideological change had it continued. Chantry resources might later have been used to support a parochial preaching clergy had they not been confiscated by the Crown.[33] In Bristol the parochial livings became impoverished during the sixteenth century, and lay support for a preaching clergy developed outside the parochial system.[34] Although chantry endowments in local rentals probably were not keeping up with inflation, those endowments in the hands of parish incumbents, or even parish lecturers or preachers paid by the parishioners, might have saved the parish clergy from the extreme decline experienced in the mid-sixteenth century, a decline from which they had not recovered by the century's close.[35] Thus, although the loss of the chantries did not represent the loss of clerical independence such as resulted from the dissolution of religious houses, it may have denied the church resources which, even though largely lay controlled, were important to the future of the Church and clergy.

Even more significant for the Church and its place in the larger community was the realization that the Crown's dissolution of local ecclesiastical institutions was also an intrusion upon the city. It represented an attack not only on the Church but also on the civic community. Through the Church the city became vulnerable not just to outside ecclesiastical authority but also to royal authority in both its secular and ecclesiastical guises. While this was clear with the dissolution of religious houses and friaries, it was probably felt even more keenly with the destruction of chantries. Whereas the religious houses had been founded either by the aristocracy or their own mother houses, the chantries were established by the city's mercantile elite and their resources were largely lay rather than ecclesiastically controlled. The Crown's attack on the chantries destroyed the medieval integration of mercantile wealth and religiosity in the Church.

The intrusion of the Crown upon the community represented by the dissolutions of religious houses, and even more so of chantries, was connected to the tremendous secularization of philanthropy in the city which W. K. Jordan has described.[36] Between 1480 and 1540 almost one half (47.59 per cent) of all benefactions in Bristol went to religious uses. During the Reformation decades, from 1541 to 1560, the percentage dropped to 5.30 per cent, while between 1561 and 1600 the figure fell to 1.13 per cent. Jordan is basically correct in his emphasis upon rising secularism, but he fails to acknowledge that this represented the rejection of a Church which could no longer be trusted to represent the interests of the civic community. Thus his picture of a farsighted laity vigorously pursuing well-conceived secular goals lacks depth and perspective. It ignores the implications of the Crown's attack on local wealth through the church as well as the disappearance of institutions which had significant responsibility for some community needs which the new secular philanthropy addressed. The Crown's attack on the local church was an impetus to the secularization of society primarily because it signalled the lay elite that the Church was not a safe repository for local wealth, nor a satisfactory focus for local aspirations, because it was vulnerable to the Crown. The line between medieval philanthropy, which focused on the Church, and post-Reformation philanthropy, which turned away from ecclesiastical institutions, marked a response to institutional change, not an abandonment of religious values. It is true, however, in regard to the clergy, that this line was an important one, for lay religiosity no longer depended on the Church and clergy in the way that it had, either for the benefit of the single soul or for the community.[37]

The consciousness that the attack on the Church was an attack on the community appeared in the loan of church plate to the Corporation by city parishes for the purchase of property from the dissolved religious houses.[38] By pooling parish wealth, the lay community not only kept some of the wealth of religious houses in Bristol but also enabled the Corporation to consolidate its jurisdiction and gain some patronage of local livings. The possibility that the Crown would confiscate parish wealth as well, a possibility not realized until 1553, also motivated the parishes.[39] By lending parish plate to the Corporation, they mitigated the Crown's confiscation of local wealth as much as possible.[40]

THE SALE OF THE LANDS OF THE DISSOLVED HOUSES

Although the Corporation had made suit for the house of the Grey Friars when it surrendered 10 September 1538, it appears that the chance to acquire the house and lands of St Mark after its dissolution 9 December 1539, prompted a surge of action.[41] Over a year was to pass nevertheless between the time the church plate was sent to London (February 1540) and the Corporation's reception of their first grant of property from the dissolved religious houses. In May 1541 they acquired the hospital of St Mark and its lands, the manor of Hampe, Somerset, formerly belonging to the monastery of Athelney, a close and pasture on St Michael's Hill which had belonged to the priory of St Mary Magdalen, the houses and sites of the Franciscans and the Carmelites, and the prise of fish in the city which had been shared by the Franciscans and Dominicans.[42] In 1544 they bought the manor of Temple Fee and the Templecombe preceptory with rents and appurtenances as well as a piece of void ground on Bristol Bridge which formerly had been owned by Wyttham priory. With the acquisitions of property of St Mark and Temple they were addressing claims of exclusion from municipal authority made previously in relation to the properties.[43] Their purchase also included numerous lands in and around the city which the Crown had acquired from Lord Lisle and which included the advowson of the parish church of St Lawrence.[44] Following the dissolutions of chantries the Corporation purchased only the Chapel of the Assumption on Bristol Bridge, retaining its lead, but lacking any of its endowments.[45]

Along with the community's purchase of lands, of course, individuals also profited from the dissolutions of religious houses. The most dramatic transfer of property from ecclesiastical to lay hands in Bristol at the time of the dissolutions of religious houses was that of the priory of St James. The abbot and convent of Tewkesbury, seeing the approach of the inevitable and perhaps fearing an early attack on St James, which had been visited briefly by Crown visitors in 1536, leased the priory and its appurtenances to Anthony Kingston, esq., on 26 January 1539, a year before the dissolution of Tewkesbury. The indenture was extremely detailed, suggesting that the monks wanted to cover anything the Crown might have eyed in regard to this priory or cell.[46] The lease may have prevented the early confiscation of the priory by the Crown, and it also may explain why the priory did not surrender although its monks were present for the dissolution of the mother house. Not until 25 April 1543 did Kingston surrender the demise and indenture of St James to the King, who regranted the property to him.[47] Less than two months later Kingston transferred his interests in the property to Henry Brayne, citizen and merchant of London.[48] Two years later, on 8 July 1545, the Crown granted a great deal more Bristol property to Brayne, including some 100 tenements, messuages, gardens, closes, and pastures formerly belonging to various religious houses.[49]

Some pieces of city property purchased by Brayne filtered to other of the city's laity while some of the lay elite purchased monastic property from others like Brayne or from the Crown. John Smythe, one of the city's wealthiest merchants, made a number of purchases both within and without the city between 1543 and 1554.[50] William Chester, John Sprynge, and Thomas White, sometime Mayors of Bristol, also purchased monastic properties as did John Wylle, the city's Chamberlain.[51] The *Great Red Book* recorded a number of local property sales following the dissolutions, but reveals few of the possible connections to the Crown's confiscations.[52] The primary purchaser of the city's chantry lands was Miles Partridge of Gloucestershire.[53] Further study is necessary to determine the extent to which local property moved from ecclesiastical to lay ownership and who among the local laity profited most.

THE FATE OF THE HOUSES AND THEIR SITES

Although the sale of confiscated property meant a significant replacement of ecclesiastical by lay landlords, the changed ownership of the religious houses themselves was even more devastating to the status of the Church and clergy. The slow ruin and use of some as quarries was the most conspicuous evidence of the church's vulnerability to the laity. It appears that the priory of St Mary Magdalen became a private dwelling, and this apparently prevented its early ruin.[54] At St James the parish church remained in use, but Leland said that the ruins of the priory stood 'hard butting to the east end of the parish church'.[55] A print of 1630 shows the priory ruins, roofless and crumbling.[56] There is no record, however, of its use as a quarry, which was the fate of portions of at least three of the city's friaries.[57]

All of the city's friaries ended up in the hands of the local lay elite, two being purchased first by the Corporation. Precisely what became of the Austin friary is not known, but according to one of the suitors for it, it was shielded from thieves and defacers on one side only by a ditch. William Popley, gentleman of Bristol, who was one of the receivers of the friary on 10 September 1538, petitioned Cromwell the following day for possession of the site. He apparently did not get the house until 1544, after it had passed through the hands of at least two other owners, neither of whom were Bristolians. Popley sold it in 1550, and after another transfer of ownership it came into the hands of Walter Pykes, a member of the local elite, in 1565.[58] That this house was smaller than the others may explain why it did not fall immediately into the hands of the Corporation or a member of the corporate elite for use either as a quarry or dwelling. The use which the lay owner did make of it is unknown.

The Corporation bought the Carmelite site in 1541, and in 1543–4 the parish of St Thomas was using free stone and tile stone from the house for repairs of the church.[59] The prominent merchant John Smythe was also paying the same man for stones from the 'friars' in 1546, and for two years rent of a garden there.[60] During Mary's reign the site provided the parish of All Saints with stones to rebuild the altars which had been demolished during the reign of Edward VI.[61] Leland deemed the house itself very fair and the King's visitor called it 'meet for a great man'. When Queen Elizabeth visited Bristol in 1574, she stayed there in what had become the house of John Younge.[62] It appears that the buildings and walls of the Carmelites became a quarry, while the best building was reserved as a dwelling.

When the Corporation asked the Crown for the house of the Franciscans, they specifically mentioned the need for stone with which to repair the town walls and the quay and to build a wharf; it is likely that this friary, too, became a source of building stone.[63] Many of its buildings were demolished immediately, some of the timber going to the local gaol for repair of a privy and a well.[64] In 1558 William Tyndall's will noted ground in Lewen's Meade 'late the church of the grey friars', which was suitable for building, and the cessation of rents to the Corporation for buildings on the property in that year suggests that the site was cleared. Probably only the church remained; it was leased in the same year to a Mrs Davis, but its subsequent uses are unknown.[65]

The Dominican friary also was a substantial site with a large house and buildings. In March of 1540 former Mayor William Chester was seeking the house and in June he bought it for £37. 10s., a sum which also bought a vacant place outside the wall.[66] In 1553–6 the parishioners of St Werberg rebuilt their altars and Easter sepulchre using stone from this site.[67] Part of the friary remained a dwelling house for the Chester family, however, and in 1560 Dominick, the son of William, was living there.[68] In 1579 there was a stable 'within the Blackfriars', and two of the buildings later became a meeting house of the Quakers and the Bakers' Hall.[69] The use of the remains of the friaries to rebuild altars and repair churches was ironic, suggesting a church feeding off itself and a community unwilling to invest further in vulnerable ecclesiastical institutions. The eventual use of Blackfriars by the Quakers is a particularly apt expression of the transformation of the medieval civic church into the non-conformist church of the late sixteenth and seventeenth centuries.

THE FATE OF THE CLERGY

For the local church and community the most immediate problem presented by the dissolutions of both the 1530s and of 1548 were the jobless clergy, who would have to be absorbed by the parish churches or, after 1542, the cathedral chapter. It is difficult to determine the impact of the dissolutions on clerical employment because clerical availability involved not only the number of ex-religious and ex-chantry priests remaining or coming into the city, but also the number of clerical deaths and new ordinands. If the pre-dissolution clerical population remained stable, the influx of ex-religious into the parochial job market would have created a serious unemployment problem. Since there are no extant ordination lists for Bristol diocese during this period, however, no judgement can be made on the stability of new ordinations. Even if such lists did exist, they would present serious interpretive problems, given Bristol's peculiar diocesan history.[70]

It is possible that, as Margaret Bowker has shown was the case in the diocese of Lincoln, ordinations declined as a result of the religious clergy's entering the job market. The apparent result, a clerical shortage, seems also to have occurred in a number of other dioceses as well. Bowker allows that if clerical availability did not decline in areas such as Lancashire, as Christopher Haigh has suggested, financial inducements offered to the clergy must have prevented a decline in numbers.[71] Apparently no such inducements were available in Bristol. Michael Zell contends, based on his work in Kent, that the influx of religious clergy probably kept the clerical population stable until the deprivations and epidemic mortality of the Marian period brought the clerical population more in line with the number of available benefices.[72] It is important in the case of Bristol to consider the city's position as a provincial capital, capable of drawing clergy from the countryside of more than one diocese. It seems likely that regardless of fluctuations in ordinations, the city would have attracted more than its share of clerical proletariat and ex-religious to compete for stipendiary parish positions. That a significant number of ex-religious remained to work in the city's parishes could suggest either that competition was not too intense or that they were able to compete successfully. The latter possibility seems the more likely.

The elimination of religious houses eradicated some fifty-five or more clerical positions, but not all of them were filled at the time various houses surrendered.[73] Each house must be considered to determine the numbers of clergy who stayed to the end and who remained in the city. The small numbers of friars present at the surrender of their houses suggest that dispersal had begun before the houses were confiscated. The friars were alone in having offered resistance to royal pressure for their surrender, and this probably related to the fact that, unlike the monks, they were pensionless. Priors were absent at the Carmelite house, where only four men remained, and at the Franciscan friary, where six were present. The prior and four friars signed the surrender of the Dominicans, while the prior and eight men signed for the Augustinians.[74] As early as 8 May 1537, a friar of one of Bristol's orders gained dispensation to change his habit for that of a secular priest, and a Carmelite friar received dispensation to wear the habit of his order beneath that of a secular priest six months later on 20 November. Another White Friar was granted dispensation to change his habit on 27 May 1538, almost exactly two months before his house surrendered.[75]

The early departures could have been produced by fear of the dissolution or a turn to Protestant ideas critical of the religious. Friars had been involved in both sides of religious controversy in the years before their surrender in 1538. John Hilsey, prior of Bristol's Dominicans, first preached against Latimer in 1533 and then became his defender. Latimer, of course, introduced serious questions concerning the legitimacy of the religious clergy and their role. John Cardmaker, a Bristol Franciscan in 1533, was also a Latimer sympathizer. Both Hilsey and Cardmaker left their orders before 1538.[76] In 1536 the prior of the Franciscans in Bristol defended the validity of the religious life from his pulpit and was answered by the

Dominican prior, who denigrated the role of the religious clergy in the sinner's quest for salvation. Their exchange became part of a local royal commission's investigation.[77] Thus during the 1530s friars were exposed to criticism from within their own ranks as well as attacks from the outside. Undoubtedly ideological questions as well as apprehension of the coming dissolution figured in their dwindling numbers.

The four friars who surrendered the Carmelite house on 28 July 1538 received dispensations to change to secular garb on 10 September, the day the other three houses surrendered. None of these are known to have remained in Bristol. Four of the Black Friars received dispensations on 1 December, almost three months after their surrender, but they too seem to have left the city. Of the six Grey Friars who signed the surrender of their house, only one, John Duke, is known to have received a dispensation. Oddly enough, it is dated 31 July, almost two weeks before the house's surrender.[78] We do not know Duke's fate, but three of the six took parish positions in the city, another in the deanery.[79] There are no extant dispensations for the Augustinian friars either, but of these nine, four remained as secular priests in the city and one in the deanery.[80] In 1540 seven of twenty-three friars who had signed the surrenders of their houses were serving in parish churches in the city and one in the deanery. This does not account, of course, for those who remained in the city unemployed or engaged in part-time work.

Like the friars, the monks also began leaving their houses before the institutions were dissolved. The four or so monks of St James probably left town when the mother house of Tewkesbury leased the priory and all its appurtenances in January 1539, a year before the dissolution of the monastery. When the monks of St Augustine surrendered in December 1539, they numbered eleven, down seven from 1534 when eighteen had signed the supremacy oath.[81] Four of the five men who signed the supremacy oath at the hospital of St Mark were still there at its surrender in 1539.[82] Taking parish positions in Bristol following the surrender were five ex-monks of St Augustine (one of whom had left before the surrender); five of Tewkesbury, at least one of whom had been at St James; and three of the four clergy of St Mark.[83] Thus, some nine to twelve of the nineteen or so monks and brothers (plus one who was not present at the surrender of St Augustine's) stayed in the city. Among those who did not, two remained as curates of deanery churches, one became a chantry priest of Berkeley, Gloucestershire, one apparently accompanied St Augustine's abbot, Morgan Guilliam, to the Isle of Wight, and another spent some time in Norfolk before returning to Bristol as a prebendary in 1554. The fate of only one is unknown.[84]

Out of a total of some twenty-three friars and nineteen religious, some sixteen to nineteen (plus one) or around 40 per cent remained to work in city parishes. In addition the city drew some ex-religious from outside. At least three were holding positions in the city in 1540, five or six more by 1548, and two others by the mid-1550s. The first bishop and dean of the new cathedral also were ex-religious.[85] Two lists of clergy, one made 26 April 1540, the other early January 1541, show that ex-religious made up about one-third of all parish stipendiaries. In 1540 seven of sixteen parishes employed at least one ex-religious and in 1541 ten of these same parishes did so. The 1541 list also included the parishes on the Bath-and-Wells side of the Avon, showing that a total of thirteen of the city's nineteen parishes had ex-religious as stipendiaries.[86]

Although the community apparently accepted the ex-religious, and it is possible that structural unemployment did not occur, the ex-monks and friars could hardly have felt at ease in situations which called for individual enterprise. They also were set loose from their orders to find and keep jobs at a time when Bristol was suffering religious controversy which hurt the status of the clergy. Those who became chantry priests faced another dissolution in a few years and the flow of the ex-chantry priests into the employee pool presented another potential employment crisis, the dimensions of which are unknown.

The suppression of chantries in 1548 undoubtedly put some pressure on the city's ecclesiastical structures to absorb the loss of some forty-four positions and the thirty-two clergy left jobless, but it is doubtful that it was any greater than that following the dissolution of religious houses. By 1552, seventeen of the ex-chantry priests appear to have been living in or near Bristol. These men appeared personally before the pension commissioners in Gloucestershire to collect their pensions. Pensions were paid to another six who were unable to be present. Two of these had gone to London; one to Warwick. One was in Hennocke, Devon, one in Roode, Somerset, and another lived in the parish of Westbury, Gloucestershire. One of Bristol's ex-chantry priests had died in 1551. Eight men were not mentioned in the commission's report, and this suggests that they had completely lost contact with those who remained in Bristol.[87]

Of the seventeen whose appearance placed them in Bristol or the vicinity, one had been a prebendary in Bristol's cathedral since 1546, two were in minor cathedral offices, and three took positions as vicar, curate, and stipendiary in their respective parishes. Four working in the vicinity included a rector, a vicar, and two curates. Of the other seven nothing is known.[88] One of those who did not appear before the commissioners in 1552, however, did reappear in Bristol within a decade.[89] Unfortunately we know nothing of the immigration of unemployed ex-chantry priests from outside the city. It seems, however, that in the years immediately following the suppression of the chantries no more than seventeen, perhaps as few as six of the thirty-two ex-chantry priests stayed in or near the city.

Aside from the unknown quantitative competition for clerical positions, the unemployed religious and chantry priests were entering a climate which was becoming increasingly competitive by virtue of changes in religious practices. The reformist emphasis on Scripture study and preaching, on clerical merit rather than clerical office, may have put many of the ex-religious and chantry priests at a disadvantage, even though official policy took a reactionary turn in 1539.

Education, if not a necessity, certainly was a help to the newly unemployed clergy of the religious houses and chantries who now had to compete for positions within the parishes. Among the friars at their surrender four of twenty-three possibly had university degrees. A few who certainly were graduates had left before 1538. At the hospital of St Mark the prior was almost certainly a graduate, and one of the three brothers present at the house's dissolution may have had a degree. At the monastery of St Augustine Abbot Morgan Guilliam, styled magister, probably was a graduate and John Rastell, 'student', undoubtedly was studying somewhere.[90]

Among fifty-eight chantry priests identified from 1524 to 1548 only three are known with certainty to have been graduates. It is probable that one other and possible that eight others were graduates. Thus twelve of fifty-eight or some 20 per cent of identified chantry priests may have been graduates in the two and a half decades before the chantries' dissolution. Five of the possible graduates and one of the certain graduates made up the 19 per cent of possible graduates among the thirty-two cantarists at the dissolution in 1548.[91]

If Clive Burgess is right about the growing importance of musical training to the success of chantry priests, it is not surprising that few of them were university graduates. Musical training was not inaccessible and developing liturgy required singers competent in polyphony in the parishes.[92] The trend among Protestants, however, was away from music, especially polyphony, although we might imagine a brief respite during Mary's reign. Under Edward VI the organs of St Paul's Cathedral and York Minster were silenced, and plans were made to end their use in all the country's churches. In the Convocation of 1563 an unsuccessful movement to remove the organs from all churches arose.[93] In 1577 the Puritan John Northbrooke of Bristol stated the limitations necessary for the use of music in the church. Of utmost importance were the words; only words from Scripture were to be sung and they were to be sung in unison. Music 'broken and quavering' was not to be used. And, of course, singing was not to take time away from preaching. Nor were stipends for musicians to be so great as to leave little or nothing for the preachers.[94] Clearly the musical training of chantry priests was not an asset in the new environment. After 1548 the loss of vocation for some and the necessity of finding employment once again for the ex-religious among them must have been discouraging. One must remember that in regard to perpetual chantries, secure tenures with incomes almost comparable to parish livings were being destroyed in many cases.

Although Alan Kreider has accepted Margaret Bowker's assertion that the goal of ordained clerics was a parish living, he asserts that chantry positions were valued. 'Though hardly a luscious ecclesiastical plum', the chantry 'must have seemed deliciously welcome . . . after years of hand to mouth existence'.[95] Burgess, however, asserts that chantry priests 'need not have been merely disappointed benefice hunters'. Financially their salaries in fifteenth-century Bristol were comparable to those of the beneficed clergy in the West Country. In the early decades of the fifteenth century, chantry founders set £5 or £5. 6s. 8d. as an intercessory priest's income. In the latter half of the century this went up to £6. This rate of pay consistently exceeded the statutory maximum income of £4. 13s. 4d. for stipendiaries. In Bath and Wells diocese in 1414 the average annual income for beneficed clergy was between £5. 6s. 8d and £6. 13s. 4d. The average in Exeter in 1426 was similar.[96] Within the city of Bristol chantry priests' incomes also were comparable to, though somewhat lower than, the beneficed clergy's in the first half of the sixteenth century. In 1535 the mean worth of benefices was £8. 19s. 5d. If the exceptionally high income of the parish of St Nicholas is excluded, the mean drops to £7. 4s. 7d.[97] The incomes of perpetual chantry priests in 1548 averaged £5. 18s.

4*d*.; the median income was £6.[98] It is likely that the incomes of temporary chantry priests (Kreider calls them stipendiary priests) was about the same average and median, but they did not have as much security. Neither incurred many of the costs of parish incumbents, such as hospitality or maintenance of the sanctuary and in many cases the parsonage. For both the multifarious duties explain the relatively high pay.[99] But more than finances was at stake. Many chantry priests may have been drawn to their work by the choral, liturgical, and perhaps educational duties. For some these duties may have been paramount, their chantry duties important but largely a source of income which enabled them to pursue a musical or educational vocation.[100] Once the chantries were eradicated these men would have been hard pressed in a society where clerical merit was becoming associated with preaching skills.

And there is evidence that even those skilled in preaching were becoming quite competitive just as these men entered the job market. The conservative Bristol preacher Roger Edgeworth claimed late in the reign of Edward VI that there were some clerics who 'maketh a merchandise of the word of God, using their preaching and teaching all for lucre and advantage.' They were grieved, he said, 'that any men should open their mouths in a pulpit but themselves, that so they might gather in their sermon nobles'. If money were given to have sermons preached, these clerics 'make shift, then they make friends, that they may be the doers of it, more for the lucre's sake, than for the zeal to the soul's health of their audience'.[101] The competition which Edgeworth criticized reflected a move away from the traditional funerals and observances of month's and year's minds which employed numbers of clergy to celebrate mass and pray for the dead. The endowment of the sermons and their use at funerals represented both a further contraction of clerical jobs and the requirement of a new skill to compete successfully for those which were available.[102] After the security of the religious life and the steady income from a chantry position, the clergy left jobless by the dissolutions undoubtedly were at a disadvantage in the new climate of clerical competition. Furthermore, more than one-half of the priests of the suppressed chantries were over 50 years old, certainly an added disadvantage.[103] In general, the spectacle of newly unemployed ex-religious and ex-chantry priests reduced to hustling for work surely undermined respect for the clergy even if it inspired some sympathy as well.

Given the random and limited nature of much of the evidence

concerning the ex-religious and ex-chantry priests, it is impossible to generalize concerning their fates. A number of elements influenced the futures of these men, including income, contacts, religion, and education. First, an important distinction has to be made between the financial circumstance of the friars and the other religious because the friars were not pensioned.[104] The monks of St Augustine received pensions ranging from £6 to £8, and the abbot received £80.[105] The monks of Tewkesbury who probably were of St James received pensions ranging from the prior's £13. 6s. 8d. to £6.[106] Pensions for the clergy of the hospital of St Mark were as high as £40 for Master John Colman and from £6 to £8 for the other three brothers.[107] A monk who became a stipendiary could combine his pension with a wage which in the 1530s usually ranged between £5 and £6.[108] The friar would have been left with his wage alone. The wage was, however, comparable to the pay of most chantry priests and to the livings of some parish incumbents.[109] Nine of the city's parish livings were worth less than £8 in 1535 and at least two were stipendiary curacies probably not worth more. Six of the livings were worth £6 or less. The ex-religious who added pensions to stipendiary wages were in a better financial situation than many others. It should be kept in mind, however, that Bristol's parish livings were notoriously poor and that stipendiary curates were replacing tenured incumbents from the mid-1550s. By that time the inflation that was undermining the city's cash-based parish livings was also eating into pensions.[110] If the pensioned ex-religious were better off relative to other clergy in the city, they nevertheless were not holding their own as stipendiaries.

Two ex-monks, who were fortunate not only in having pensions but also in receiving livings formerly in the patronage of their house, the monastery of St Augustine, nevertheless also faced different financial circumstances.[111] Humphrey Hyman, who had been prior of the convent, and John Rastell, who had been a student at the dissolution, each received a pension of £8.[112] The living received by Hyman in 1542, however, was that of All Saints worth only £4. 3s. 4d., while in 1546 Rastell received that of St Nicholas, the city's wealthiest living at £21. 13s.[113] Both men were pensioned and received livings which probably were insured by arrangements made before the dissolution, but Rastell clearly was better off than Hyman, probably because he was better educated.

Other pre-surrender contacts also probably enabled some of the jobless clergy to enhance their situations. Richard Wale of the

Kalendars' Guild no doubt had the help of Thomas Sylke, who was both master of the guild and a prebendary and canon in the cathedral chapter, in getting a position as deacon in the cathedral by 1550. With a yearly stipend of £6. 13s. 4d. and a £6 pension, his income was quite a bit more than the £8 he had received as a priest of the guild.[114] While Nicholas Corbett left the monastery of St Augustine before its dissolution and thus received no pension, he did benefit from arrangements made when the abbot conveyed the vicarage of Powlett in Bath and Wells diocese to three laymen. They presented Corbett to the living and he was instituted on 22 August 1542. His predecessor in the living, Thomas Sprint, also was a Bristol cleric.[115] The constellation of Augustinian friars which appeared in the parishes of St Thomas and St Mary Redcliffe also probably related to pre-dissolution contacts which they had as the only group of friars on that side of the river.[116]

Age also made a difference in the quality of life achieved by the ex-religious or ex-chantry priests. Any elderly friar who could not work was completely dependent on the goodwill of others and an elderly priest with a pension would have been hard pressed to live on a fixed income during a period of inflation. John Shereman, priest of Fraunce's Chantry in Temple church, was 76 when the chantries were suppressed, and he was given a pension of only £2. 16s. 8d., based upon his exceptionally low income, which he still received in 1555. In 1557, however, Shereman, by then aged 85 returned to work as the curate of St Ewen, receiving a stipend of £7.[117] In contrast to Shereman, Thomas Pinchin was only 27 when he was expelled from the hospital of St Mark with a pension of £6, and his subsequent career demonstrated the vitality of a man young enough to scramble. In 1540 he was a stipendiary in the church of St John, but in 1544 he became priest of Ball's Chantry in Christ Church. His combined income was £14. When he lost his chantry position in 1548, however, he appears to have become a minor canon in the cathedral at £10 per year for a total income of £15 or £16. He took a cut in income when (by 1555) he left the cathedral to become the curate of Christ Church at a wage of £7. The timing of the move suggests he left the cathedral when conservatives took over the diocesan apparatus at the accession of Mary. By 1560, at age 48, he had moved to the rural and presumably more lucrative parish of Eastchurch in Bristol deanery, and in 1563 he had become the curate of St Mark, Bristol, which curacy probably paid around £8.[118] Pinchin's moves suggest he searched aggressively for better situations. Certainly he was in a much better position to do so than the aged John Shereman.

Also among elements affecting the clergy's fates were religion and the related issue of marriage. We know very little about the religious beliefs of these groups of clergy, but in the case of William Bower his religious commitment was almost certainly the key to his employment in 1561 as assistant teacher in the cathedral grammar school and in 1570 as the master.[119] It is unlikely, however, that any of these clergy could have taken strong religious stances without a base of support within the laity.

There is very little to indicate that many of Bristol's clergy married during the Reformation, and evidence exists of no married ex-religious and only one married ex-chantry priest. Marriage could make a difference in the level of survival, not only in regard to the economic demands of a family, but also because during Mary's reign, married clerics were deprived of their livings, and those who refused to give up their wives were forced to give up their careers.[120] Roger Lewys, the former incumbent of Stoke's Chantry in St Thomas, was deprived of the living of Bedminster in 1554 because of his marriage to Catherine Weaver, a widow.[121]

Pensions and wages, pre-dissolution contacts, age, religion, and marriage combined to create different futures for individual ex-religious and ex-chantry priests. All were thrown into a competitive situation wherein changing standards were being applied to the clergy, religious conflict divided clergy and laity alike, and for a number of reasons disrespect for the clergy was growing. The meaning of the situation for different individuals, however, was not identical.

The dissolutions of the religious houses and the chantries were dramatic events in the life of the city and the church, and they irrevocably changed the balance of power between the city's laity and clergy. The independent monastic clergy had been instrumental in the conservative clergy's challenge to Latimer, the Crown, and the Corporation in 1533. The dissolution eradicated the economic and political base of that independence. Moreover the ruthless show of secular power over ecclesiastical demonstrated to all that the Church was no longer the partner of the state on either the national or the local level. The ideal of the city community in which the clergy had a prominent and powerful place became a thin fiction. The status of the clergy was damaged further by the movement of ex-religious and ex-chantry priests into stipendiary jobs. Regardless of the extent of competition or unemployment, these clerics were less secure and more dependent on the laity than before their institutions were dissolved. The creation of Bristol's cathedral did little to ameliorate the clergy's loss of status and resources, and the remaining parochial system suffered from structural weaknesses which contributed to a dramatic decline in the quality and status of the parochial clergy. If the institutional framework of parishes remained untouched, the story of the parish clergy nevertheless represents an equally dramatic pattern of events with great significance for the deterioration of the clergy's position in the city.

6

The Decline of the Parish Clergy

IN 1530 the parochial system of Bristol seemed part of the natural order of things, as unchanging as the tidal flow of the Avon which was the city's lifeline to distant lands. A new parson could look forward to twenty years or so in his parish and his parishioners depended on this kind of continuity as a stabilizing force.[1] Many of the incumbents were university graduates, a number of whom even held post-graduate degrees. They were an educated elite who could offer their parishioners personal guidance as well as instruction from their pulpits.[2] Most had the assistance of stipendiaries and presided over churches whose chantry priests offered a continual and colourful liturgy. Forty years later, however, parishioners were accustoming themselves to intermittent service by uneducated curates, whose status was also diminished by their lack of tenure and dependence on wages. The parson who had the cure of souls, conducted divine service, said mass, preached, collected tithes, and managed a number of parish responsibilities largely had been replaced by a stipendiary curate or even a salaried incumbent.[3] The seemingly timeless parochial system which in 1530 offered a certain amount of security to parson and parishioners alike had been distorted by 1570: the power which had rested with the tenured incumbent was in the hands of the laity who collected and paid the cleric's wage. If the Corporation had asserted its dominance over the city's clergy in the 1530s and the Crown augmented that power by dissolving the religious houses, the decline of the parish clergy over the next thirty years represented an intimate dimension of lay control, heretofore limited to parishioners' relationships with some stipendiary chantry priests.

When Henry VIII began collecting a grant from the clergy in 1531, not a single Bristol living of the fourteen in Worcester diocese lacked a parson, although the incumbents of St Nicholas and Sts Philip and Jacob may have been non-resident and the vicars of All Saints and Christ Church were pluralists.[4] In 1565, however, an episcopal survey reported that eleven of the city's fifteen rectories and vicarages were vacant by reason of the poverty (*exilitatem*) of the fruits.[5] Four livings had been vacant for at least eight years: St Mary-le-Porte, St Augustine-the-less, St Ewen, and St Lawrence. Five had been vacant seven years: St Werberg, St Leonard, St Peter, Sts Philip and Jacob, and Christ Church. The parish of St Stephen had been without an incumbent for four years; that of St John the Baptist, three. Nine of the eleven livings apparently were still vacant in 1570. The parishes of St John and Sts Philip and Jacob suffered the shortest vacancies, the former being filled in 1568 after a six-year vacancy and the latter in mid-1564 after six years. Sts Philip and Jacob, however, apparently lost its vicar in 1568 and did not gain another until 1576.[6] Although the parish of St Ewen gained a pluralist parson in 1568 after an eleven-year vacancy, it appears that the parishioners were not even aware of his existence, and he did not reside until 1579.[7] The vacancy at St Mary-le-Porte lasted twenty-six and possibly thirty-six or more years (although the untenured curates were stable) and at St Stephen, nineteen years. Five others were vacant for some period over twelve years. The living of St Lawrence was never filled and the parish was combined with that of St John in 1580.[8] Thus, beginning in the late 1550s most of Bristol's parish livings fell vacant for periods spanning six to twenty-six or more years.[9]

During these vacancies parishes were served by stipendiary curates whose status was greatly diminished in comparison to the clergy who earlier had occupied the livings. They were, of course, untenured and they received a stipend from the parish which sequestered the tithes rather than collecting tithes themselves. They were poorer than the incumbents unless they had second incomes. In addition the educational quality represented by the curates was markedly inferior to that of the parochial clergy at the beginning of the period, a decline made even more dramatic by the rise in lay education.[10]

CLERICAL EDUCATION

The decline in educational attainments of the parochial clergy had been under way throughout the period. It is impossible to know with certainty the number of educated men among Bristol's parish clergy during the Reformation, but within limits patterns of education can be established. Sometimes, but not always, degrees were indicated with names during this period and this is the best indication of educational status. In some instances the printed biographical registers give enough information to identify a student as a Bristol cleric with certainty or with a high degree of probability.[11] For others, one must attribute the possibility that a Bristol cleric attended a university when a like name appears and the dates and biographical data do not conflict with other information known about the man. Thus it is likely that some who have been identified as possibly having taken degrees, in fact did not. On the other hand, given the poor quality of the period's records and their preservation, it is also likely that some who appear not to have been at a university will in fact have studied or taken degrees.[12] Thus we must trust that the one balances the other, and since the patterns revealed concerning the education of Bristol's parish clergy coincide with what is known about other aspects of their development, it appears that that trust is well-founded. In a situation where the Crown was destroying the medieval civic church and clerical community, where livings were poor and growing poorer because of inflation, where merchant philanthropy began to target secular programmes rather than parish churches, and where some of the laity were extending control over the clergy, it is to be expected that the number of educated parish clergy would decline.

The decline was steady throughout the period 1530–70 as Table 1 shows. At the beginning of the Reformation and for some time prior only about one fifth of Bristol's parish clergy were almost certainly

Table 1. *Education of Bristol Incumbents*

Years	Degree	Poss. degree	No degree
1515–34	13 (41%)	12 (37%)	7 (22%)
1534	8 (44%)[a]	7 (39%)	3 (17%)
1540	5 (31%)[b]	5 (31%)	6 (38%)
*c.*1550	8 (40%)[c]	2 (10%)	10 (50%)
*c.*1560	2 (20%)	1 (10%)	7 (70%)
*c.*1564–70	—	1 (12%)	7 (88%)

Notes: The perpetual curate of St James and the curates of St Thomas and St Mary Redcliffe are included as incumbents since these parishes were always served by curates.

Total number of individuals identified was 95, of which 63 were incumbents.

[a] All eight possessed of postgraduate degrees.

[b] Four of all those with postgraduate degrees in 1534 were still incumbents. Some individuals appear more than once.

[c] Five of these held postgraduate degrees; one incumbent remained from the 1534 group; two had Bristol ties from the 1530s; two were apparently Bristol natives and were instituted in the 1540s.

non-graduates. Their number grew throughout the period, until during the last six years only one of the eight incumbents even possibly was a graduate. The decline appears from Table 1 to have been fairly gradual, but in fact it began early in the period and was slowed by the longevity of many incumbents. Between 1535 and 1545 eighteen identified clergy came into possession of livings in Bristol. Of those eighteen only five are certain to have taken degrees and the remaining thirteen apparently did not. Thus, though only 17 per cent of parochial incumbents in 1534 were certainly not educated, 72 per cent of the clergy entering livings in the following decade were non-graduates.

By the end of the Reformation, the picture in Bristol included the non-tenured curates who had largely replaced the parochial incumbents as primary parochial clergy. Table 2 shows the rise in numbers of primary parish curates by the last decade of the period and the continuing paucity of educated men among them, as well as the appearance in the first decade of Elizabeth's reign of readers, who also lacked education.[13]

While graduate clergy were not necessarily preachers, it seems reasonable to postulate that in Bristol the decline in numbers of graduates among the parish clergy also represented a decline in able preachers. That the graduate clergy preached is also suggested by the standards set in the city by the four orders of friars and the traditional

Table 2. *Education of Bristol Curates and Readers*

| Years | Curates | | |
	Degree	Poss. degree	No degree
1530	—	2 (33%)	4 (67%)
1540s	—	—	6 (100%)
1550s	—	2 (40%)	3 (60%)
1560s	—	1 (11%)	8 (89%)
	Readers		
1560–6	—	1 (17%)	5 (83%)

Notes: The assistant curates of St Nicholas, St Thomas, and All Saints in the 1560s are not included. John Lee (or Lyll, Lynche), who was first reader and then curate of St John is included as curate.

Total number of individuals identified was 95, of which 26 were curates and 6 readers.

need for preaching as an antidote to Lollardy. In addition, almost all of them were resident.[14]

The issue of clerical quality was related to that of quantity. At the beginning of Elizabeth's reign the bishops were concerned with a widespread clerical shortage which could only be remedied by lowering standards required for ordinands. Margaret Bowker has traced a clerical shortage in Lincoln diocese to the impact of the dissolutions beginning in 1536. Fears of the influx of ex-religious into the parochial job market brought a dramatic decline in ordinations. D. M. Barratt has suggested that the Elizabethan shortage could be traced to higher standards set for ordination during the reign of Edward VI. Michael Zell contends that the influx of ex-religious into the clerical job market propped up the clerical population until the 1550s when the Marian deprivations and epidemic mortality brought a decline which made benefices more readily available than before. Rosemary O'Day reasons that the 'unstable state of affairs' and 'the contempt in which the ministry seems generally to have been held' were responsible for the pre-Elizabethan decline in the numbers of ordinands. She also notes the declining opportunities for advancement within the Church, regulations concerning pluralities, and the Marian deprivations of married clergy as factors influencing declining ordinations. The large numbers of vacancies at Elizabeth's accession, she admits, may have stemmed from the high death rate between about 1556 and 1560 as well as from deprivations and resignations.[15] We might add to this litany of suggestions that in cities like Bristol where the medieval civic church had been changed dramatically, if not totally destroyed by the Crown, there was less in the way of status and of clerical community to draw men to ordination. The same reality existed within many towns and cities or indeed any parish church which lost chantries and thus lost extended and beautiful liturgies and communities of priests.

At the accession of Elizabeth 10 to 15 per cent of the nation's livings were vacant and as many as one-third in populous areas such as the archdeaconries of London and Canterbury.[16] Over two-thirds of Bristol's livings were vacant.[17] We must be cautious, however, about equating vacancies, even extended ones, with a simple shortage of clergy. Populous areas were most likely to have poor livings, which were more profitably served by curates than by incumbents or which necessitated pluralism. Even the lay readers in Bristol may have represented men who avoided ordination in order to combine secular jobs with their clerical work. It is likely that the clerical population of Bristol had declined, but there also is evidence that those who were available were not pursuing benefices.[18]

CLERICAL INCOME

The Bristol survey of 1565 attributed the large number of parish vacancies to the poverty of the livings, and it is clear that the declining values of the livings were both a part of the clergy's decline and a cause of further slippage. Even early in the Reformation when educated incumbents still were present in livings, shrinking incomes undoubtedly lowered clerical social status at a time when the lay attack on the church was doing likewise. Declining income and social status, in turn, contributed to the educational decline and the failure to fill the livings.

The incomes of urban livings were, with some exceptions, notoriously poor in the sixteenth century, and at the beginning of the Reformation those of Bristol were no different.[19] The primary source for establishing the official (taxable) value of clerical livings during the Reformation is the *Valor ecclesiasticus* made in 1535 when Henry VIII ordered a survey of church property and income.[20] Unfortunately, the extant *Valor* does not include the city of Bristol although it does include the rest of the deanery.[21] To establish the incomes as they were valued in this survey it has been necessary to consult compositions for first fruits as well as a 1534 subsidy list from the *Visitation Act Book* of Bishop Bell in Worcester diocese.[22] In some cases it has been possible to compare these sources: the results show them to be reliable indicators of the official (taxable) values of livings. These figures are shown in Table 3.

Various scholars have questioned the reliability of the figures given by the *Valor*. Some believe the rectories to have been underassessed because parsonages were not included, while vicarages were over-valued by counting the value of all tithes great and small rather than just the small (which was as much as most vicars received) or none at all (as could sometimes also be the case).[23] Other scholars see no reason for assuming these reservations about the valuations to be true.[24] In Bristol's valuation there was a good chance of accuracy since three of the five vicarages probably did not have great tithes to collect anyway. Map 1 in Chapter 1 shows that the vicarage of St Philip and Jacob was an outlying parish, and an eighteenth-century glebe terrier indicates that the vicar received great tithes from part of the parish.[25]

Table 3. *Bristol Parish Livings*

Parish	Value
St Nicholas (v)	£21. 1s. 1d. ob.[a]
Sts Philip and Jacob (v)	£15[b]
St Stephen	£14. 15s. 2d.[c]
St Mary Redcliffe	£12. 6s. 3d.[d]
St Leonard (v)	£12[e]
Christ Church	£11[f]
St Werberg	£10[g]
St John	£7. 4s. 6d.[h]
St Mary-le-Porte	£7 (£5. 5s. 9d., 1544)[i]
St Peter	£6. 7s. 6d.[j]
St Michael	£6[k]
St Augustine (v)	£6[l]
St Lawrence	£4. 3s. 4d.[m]
All Saints (v)	£4. 3s. 4d.[n]
St Ewen	£3. 6s.[o]
Temple	£3. 4s.[p]

Notes: While the church of St Mary Redcliffe was officially a chapel of the vicarage of Bedminster outside Bristol rather than a living in itself (and was served by either the said vicar or a curate also sometimes referred to as the vicar), the subsidy returns of 1558 valued its living as shown. St Thomas, also a chapel of Bedminster, was served by a curate as was the perpetual curacy of St James. Curates were salaried while the incumbents (rectors and vicars) held livings.

(v) vicarage. Other livings are rectories.

Compositions for first fruits from PRO E 334 are listed below by volume and folio. Subsidy payments, which were 2s. in the pound or one-tenth of the living's value, were recorded in 1540 (H&WRO, 802 BA 2764, fos. 269–72) unless otherwise noted and are shown below with 'Sub'.

[a] Vol. 3, fo. 104 (1546); vol. 8, fo. 21 (1564). Sub.

[b] Vol. 3, fo. 13 (1544). Sub.

[c] Vol. 6, fo. 35 (1556).

[d] Sub. (PRO E 179/6/2, 1558).

[e] Sub.

[f] Sub.

[g] Vol. 3, fo. 28 (1544).

[h] Vol. 8, fo. 149 (1568).

[i] Vol. 2, fo. 108 (1542); vol. 2, fo. 167 (1543); vol. 3, fo. 36 (1544); vol. 4, fo. 5 (1548).

[j] Vol. 2, fo. 91 (1542).

[k] Sub.

[l] Sub.

[m] Vol. 2, fo. 141 (1543). Sub.

[n] Vol. 2, fo. 58 (1541). Sub.

[o] Sub.

[p] Vol. 6, fo. 7 (1555).

This explains why it was one of the city's wealthier livings. The parish of Temple also lay on the city's fringes, but the low valuation of the living suggests that the vicarage was not endowed with the great tithes. The appropriator was the rector in livings with vicars, of course, and collected the great tithes.[26]

Absolute accuracy aside, the figures for Bristol are comparable to the rest of the valuation; and they tell something about the relationships among Bristol's own parishes. These figures are limited, however, in what they reveal about the clergy's economic status, for the source of a cleric's income determined his ability to keep up with rising prices. Incumbents with glebe and tithes in kind survived the great inflation better than those who collected either personal tithes or tithes commuted to money payments. There were, moreover, a myriad of benefits and expenses which varied from parish to parish. Still, the valuations of the *Valor ecclesiasticus* and the counterpart established here for Bristol are the best figures available on clerical income in the 1530s.

The value of Bristol's livings does not compare favourably with those of the nation at large. Peter Heath suggests that three quarters of all parochial livings in the late fifteenth century were worth less than £15, that a half of all were not worth £10, and many less than £7.[27] Christopher Hill estimates that about half of all livings in the country were worth less than £10 in the *Valor*.[28] In Bristol fourteen of sixteen benefices (87 per cent) were valued at less than £15; ten of sixteen (62 per cent) were below £10; and seven parishes (44 per cent) were valued at less than £7. Table 4 compares the values of livings in Bristol with those of other English cities of similar parish structure, the nation, and the rural parishes of Bristol deanery.[29]

The figures suggest that the rural livings of Bristol deanery were better than those of city livings. Although the average of the rural livings was comparable to that of Gloucester, the smallest city registered here, the spread from top to bottom was greater among the rural parishes. Bristol's values were similar to those of Exeter though a bit poorer, and the values of both far surpassed those of York. The poverty of York's livings appears to have resulted from the larger number of parishes in the city at the beginning of the Reformation.[30] Appropriated livings are among the wealthiest as well as the poorest of these urban livings (which include inner-city and outer-city parishes) and this suggests that in cities appropriation was not a primary cause of poor livings.

Table 4. *Comparison of Livings*

	Bristol	Exeter	Gloucester	York[c]	Bristol Deanery
Population	10,000	8,000	4,000	8,000	8,000
Number of Parishes	16 of 18[a]	17 or 19[b]	8	26 of 40	10
Livings:					
below £15[d]	14 (87%)	15 (88%) or 17 (90%)	6 (75%)	26 (100%)	6 (60%)
below £10[e]	10 (62%)	11 (65%) or (58%)	3 (37%)	25 (96%)	5 (50%)
below £8	9 (56%)	7 (41%) or (37%)	3 (37%)	23 (88%)	5 (50%)
Income:					
Median	£7. 2s. 3d.	£8. 14s. 6d.	£9. 10s.	£4. 2s. 8½d.	£8. 17s.
Average	£8. 19s. 4d.	£9. 3s. 4½d.	£12. 15s. ob.	£4. 4s. 6d. or £4. 5s. 9d.	£12. 14s. 4½d.
Highest	£21. 1s. 1½d.	£34. 2s. 2d or £15. 4s. 8d.	£25. 5s. 9d.	£10	£30
Lowest	£3. 4s.	£4. 13s. 4d.	£3. 17s. 3d.	£1. 3s. 1½d.	£2. 14s. 4d.
Impropriated livings	6 (37%)	1 (6%)	3 (37%)	9 (35%)	3 (33%)
Average income of impropriated livings	£12. 4s. 10½d.	£15. 4s. 8d.	£8. 3s. 2d.	£4. 13s. 6d.	£22

[a] The curacies of St Thomas and St James are not included.

[b] Exeter had one living with two chapels annexed valued at £34. 3s. 2d. In the 'Livings below' categories the figures have been computed using this sum as a single parish living and as three parish livings at £11. 7s. 3d. each. The latter is somewhat askew because in fact the stipends of the two chaplains were lower than the living of the incumbent. The first is diminished by the fact that probably the incumbent was paying stipends to the two chaplains. The median and average livings have been computed on the basis of three equal livings, bringing the mean up slightly (from £8. 6s. 8d.) and the average down (from £10. 4s. 11d.). It is possible that after deductions for stipends, the highest income would be in the neighbourhood of those of Bristol and Gloucester.

[c] York had forty parish churches at the beginning of the Reformation, but the *Valor* registers only 26 (Palliser, *The Reformation*, 3).

[d] 75% nationally.

[e] 50% nationally.

But what do the figures mean in regard to the standard of living of the clergymen themselves? Peter Heath, using clerical accounts of the late fifteenth century, says of clerical incomes,

After payment of a chaplain, of occasional stipendiaries, and of occasional pensions, to meet the small and regular expenses, to support the incumbent and his household, and to pay for the costly repairs, frequently needed, medieval building being what it was, an income of £15 would seem desirable and reasonable, or where there was no chaplain £10.[31]

Alan Kreider calls £8 the 'ecclesiastical poverty line' because in cases where income was lower than this the Faculty Office allowed pluralism. His assessment is that in the 1530s and 1540s an incumbent needed a net income of nearly £10 from his benefice with supplementary income from baptism and mortuary fees to carry out his duties. Felicity Heal has suggested that £8 was sufficient, if the living included five or more acres of glebe and some tithes in kind.[32]

THE ABSENCE OF GLEBE OR TITHES IN KIND

At least nine of Bristol's parish livings fell below minimums of either £8 or £10, and it is doubtful that many of Bristol's livings had much glebe or many tithes in kind.[33] C. S. Taylor, in discussing the appearance of Bristol's churches in the *Domesday Book*, said that 'the parish churches held little or no land in later days'.[34] William Smith's perspective map of 1568 depicts the contrast between the concentration of dwellings within the medieval walls and the open land outside the walls.[35] The only churches set near open lands were the suburban churches of Sts Philip and Jacob, St Michael, St James, St Mary Redcliffe, St Thomas, and Temple. Since St James, St Mary Redcliffe, and St Thomas were perpetual curacies, lawfully their curates would never have enjoyed any tithes or glebe.[36] It is likely, however, that the other three did collect tithes in kind and had glebe to farm. Significantly St Michael and Temple never suffered long vacancies, even though in 1535 they ranked only eleventh and fifteenth respectively in livings' values.

The vicarage of Sts Philip and Jacob apparently was endowed with great tithes of corn and hay and mixed tithes of lamb, wool, and pig in one portion of the parish. The impropriator claimed them in the other part. All the other small tithes in the whole parish belonged to the vicar. It appears that there was little if any glebe for farming; the vicar had only the vicarage with a garden and stable behind it.[37] Millerd's map of 1675 depicts quite a lot of open space in the parish of St Leonard, and it is possible that the vicar of this parish, which was ranked fifth in livings' values in 1535, enjoyed tithes in kind and glebe although this probably did not include crops of grain or hay.[38] There are two other parishes which may have had valuable glebe although not for farming. The vicarages of All Saints and St Nicholas were inner-city livings which were among the four livings not to suffer vacancies, and this may have been because they had glebe which could be rented as shops and because of the port for large ships in the latter.[39] St Nicholas was the most valuable living in Bristol in 1535; All Saints, however, ranked a low thirteenth. It is probably significant in regard to tithe values that during the period of extant records, beginning in 1556, though not continuous, the only clergy suing for tithes were the incumbents of St Nicholas, St Michael, Temple, and Sts Philip and Jacob.[40] A cleric did not risk alienating parishioners and important townspeople unless the income at stake was both substantial and needed.

Although there was little for the clergy to gain from great tithes in most of Bristol's parishes, they probably collected mixed tithes, such as butter, cheese, and small animals, and small tithes from orchards and gardens. Most of these were mentioned in tithe suits in Bristol during the 1550s and 1560s although primarily in the parish of St James where a perpetual curate served and the impropriator brought the suits.[41] In general, however, there was a tendency to commute small tithes to money payments, a practice which further diminished their value in an inflationary period.[42] In the parish of St Philip a number of commutations were recorded.[43] It was customary to pay 1s. yearly for every cow and heifer that had a calf in lieu of the calf and milk and 2s. per year for the tithe of 'carretts' in the part of the vicarage that was not endowed. Eight shillings was owed yearly for every drift of horses, and 4d. for every other horse kept by a parishioner for his own use, excepting one for a market horse.[44] It was also usual to compound yearly for the tithes of apples and other fruits of orchards. Innkeepers and others who used their grounds to feed unprofitable cattle were to pay 2s. for their feeding grounds. In the sixteenth century tithes for newly mined sea coals in the parish were at issue in the consistory court of Bristol.[45] By the eighteenth century the vicar customarily collected 8s. yearly for every 'colework' in any part of the parish.[46] Apparently a *modus* had been reached, leaving the vicar with a fixed sum.

The trend towards cash payments also appeared in other parishes. When Henry Brayne, the impropriator of a number of local livings, sued John Northall for tithes in the parish of St James in 1556, Northall testified that for the last two years he had paid the curate 4*d.* for tithes of the orchard and 4*d.* for the tithes of the gardens each year.[47] Twelve years later, in 1568, the parish of St Mary-le-Porte sequestered, in addition to personal tithes, 3*d.* for pigs. The extant accounts of 1557–8 and 1564–5 do not mention pigs or any other small tithes in kind (mixed tithes) making it appear that they also were very scarce.[48] Even if earlier rectors had collected small tithes in kind, it is doubtful that they amounted to much. The trend toward commutation was probably encouraged during vacancies in livings when parishioners sequestrated the tithes, basing the incomes even more firmly on a cash basis.

To what extent cash income from *modi* was augmented by fees for marriage and burials is unknown, but these may have been substantial in a parish like St Nicholas or St Mary Redcliffe, which had 800 and 600 parishioners respectively in 1548.[49] Up until 1548 some extra money also came in from attendance at funerals, obits, and other memorial services and masses for the dead.[50] By the early 1540s clerics were receiving bequests for sermons, a sign that the role of the clergy was being redefined by reformist thought. Those clerics who could not preach lost income as a result of this transition.[51] Many wills also recorded 'tithes forgotten', which went to the parson and could range from a few shillings to several pounds, the former being more common. These may have been more important in cities, where personal tithe obligations may often have been underassessed or gone unpaid.[52]

THE TRANSITION FROM PERSONAL TITHES TO RATES

The most important source of income for urban clergy was personal tithes, originally assessed on profits of trade and income from wages. As small tithes they were due to both rectors and endowed vicars. By the time of the Reformation personal tithes in Bristol apparently had been transformed into rates based upon rents. This transformation has been traced for London and it is probable that the pattern was similar in Bristol.[53] In the thirteenth century London attempted to stabilize customary parish offerings (oblations) by initiating a rate based upon rents. Debate over whether this included personal tithes continued until it was finally settled in the affirmative in 1536 by the Act for tithes in London, which also reduced the rate. While this act was limited to the capital, in 1549 the Act for the true payment of tithes applied to the nation.[54] Among other things, this act abolished the oath (which virtually ended true assessment of personal tithe), exempted those who had not been paying personal tithes the previous forty years from paying them, and freed day labourers from tithes on wages. It exempted London and Canterbury and their suburbs, however, together with 'any town or place that hath used to pay their tithes by their houses'. Bristol almost certainly was one of these.

Several pieces of evidence indicate that Bristol's parishioners did indeed pay personal tithes at a rate based upon rents. At issue in a 1556 tithe suit was the tithe of those who lived in one parish but had shops or cellars in another.[55] When the consistory court in Bristol tried the suit, brought by John Rastell, vicar of St Nicholas, against Richard Muckley and John Langeley, testimony of one witness revolved around the shop which Muckley occupied in High Street within St Nicholas parish. Articles apparently concerned Muckley's use of the shop, the rent he paid, the resident of the shop's house, and its ownership.[56] The request for this information suggests that personal tithes were based upon rent as in London where rules concerning responsibilities of owners, tenants, and sub-tenants were carefully laid down. It also suggests the tremendous problems inherent in assessing and collecting tithes based upon rents. It appears that in Bristol, as in London, it was one thing to lay down rules, another to collect tithes.[57]

Evidence bears this out for other city parishes as well. In the parish of St Ewen a list of receipts was labelled 'a rate upon every house-holder towards the priest's wages' in 1567–8 and 'Rental towards the ministers yearly' in 1574–5.[58] A tithe suit which the churchwardens of St Ewen brought in 1563 against parishioner Joan Adams for 6s. tithe proves that the rates recorded in the accounts were legally personal tithes.[59] She appeared in the account of that year paying exactly that sum, and the account also included the 3s. expense 'For having goodwife Adams into Mr. Chancellers court'.[60] Another annual list of receipts at Easter from the children, maids, servants, men, and apprentices of householders was labelled 'oblations' in 1567–8 and usually ranged from 3d. to 6d.[61] This probably represented the ½d. traditionally paid at the four principal feasts and a commuted personal tithe for servants on annual wages.

The parishioners of St James were listed in 1572 according to street of residence, with one group (apparently householders) paying various sums (apparently rates) as well as 2*d*., and another group (apparently non-householders) paying 2*d*. each.[62] Evidently everyone paid 2*d*. oblations in that parish. Receipts at Easter in the parish of St Mary-le-Porte were not labelled rates, tithes, oblations, or offerings. Nevertheless they are similar to the collections in St Ewen, with householders paying various sums (rates) ranging from 2*s*. to 20*s*. and children, 'servants', 'maidservants', journeymen, apprentices, and others paying smaller sums ranging from 2*d*. to 12*d*.[63] All the city's parishioners apparently paid personal tithes which had been transformed into rates; only the assessment of oblations appears to have differed, being specifically required of all parishioners in the parish of St James and only of non-householders in others.

In London after 1546 householders paying more than 10*s*. rent per year were exempted from Easter offerings, while other family members were required to pay 2*d*. for their four offering days.[64] The appearance of some distinctions among the Bristol parishes in this regard suggests that unlike London the development was never legitimized or regularized by a central authority, either national, municipal, or diocesan. It appears that within the context of the substitution of rates for personal tithes and oblations each parish worked out its own system to deal with householders and non-householders, personal tithes and oblations.[65]

DIMINISHING INCOMES

The most important feature of clerical income in Bristol was its dependence on tithes in money and the relative insignificance of tithes in kind. During the inflationary sixteenth century tithe rates based upon slowly rising rents lost in real value, even if correctly assessed and promptly collected, while tithes in kind, particularly foodstuffs, gained.[66] It seems, moreover, that rents did not rise significantly, if at all, in sixteenth-century Bristol. The figures from John Smythe's ledger in the 1540s suggest static or declining population in the city and probably a strong resistance to rising prices in rents.[67] In at least one parish rates were lower for some parishioners in 1581 than they had been before.[68]

Clearly inflation was a significant factor in the poverty of fruits which contributed to extended vacancies in eleven Bristol livings early in Elizabeth's reign. The work of E. Phelps Brown and Sheila Hopkins shows the rising price of a composite unit of consumables in southern England during the early–mid-sixteenth century. While there were numerous fluctuations up and down during our period, the median price index level rose each decade from 1500 to 1580.[69] The average index levels of each decade reveal a similar rise although they suggest a drop during the 1560s and a greater increase in the next decade. The medians and averages are shown in Table 5.

Table 5. *Price Indexes 1500–1580*

Decade	Median	Mean
1500s	105	104
1510s	111	111
1520s	142	148
1530s	154	150
1540s	184	162
1550s	273	289
1560s	281	279
1570s	309	315

These two sets of figures indicate that the cost of living rose about 175 per cent in the first half of the sixteenth century in southern England. Between the first decade and the end of the 1560s the rise was about 268 per cent. The urban parson who relied largely on a cash income based upon rents would have seen his real income reduced during this period.[70] Even if rates or tithes had risen with rents, this process would have been slower than the rise of prices and would have demanded an exaggerated efficiency in the parson's assessment and collection of tithes. In addition to the problem of inflation, D. H. Sacks contends that Bristol suffered a depression in the sixteenth century as trade turned from English woollens and Gascon wine to Spanish and Portuguese imports.[71] If the large number of vacancies suggest clerical reluctance to accept a living with a diminishing income, it may also point to lay desire to keep control of tithe rates at a time when they, too, were feeling the effects of a faltering economy.

Tax increases were another cause of clerical poverty. The legislation for first fruits and tenths under Henry VIII broadened taxation from 1535 to include all clergy with livings of eight marks or more and added these taxes to the usual subsidy of one-tenth of the living per year. Only four of Bristol's livings escaped payment of first fruits and tenths. Furthermore, the payments were based upon a new valuation which increased the papal appraisal.[72] The increase in taxation created a substantial inequality between lay and clerical taxation of which ecclesiastical writers complained vociferously.[73] As the real value of the livings declined, the taxes became progressively more burdensome.[74] From 1559 on, however, first fruits and tenths were paid only on vicarages worth £10 and up and on rectories £6. 13s. 4d. and up, freeing three more Bristol livings from these taxes.[75] During Mary's reign clerical taxation diminished and under both Mary and Elizabeth the rates of the subsidy tax were graded so that benefices worth under £5 paid nothing at all and those under £8 only 6s. 8d.[76] Thus the four poorest Bristol livings ostensibly were freed from taxation altogether. Stipendiary curates, however, still were required to pay the subsidy. In 1557 John Sherman, curate of St Ewen, owed 6s. 8d., based on his stipend of £7.[77] He and his successors may have continued in debt because in 1562 the parish began to make the yearly payment, calling it a 'subsidy' or the 'queen's tenth'.[78] Actually the parish living was exempt, but they continued paying to the subsidy on the basis of a £7 stipend for a curate. The parish retained a number of curates at different times, many part time, with varying stipends, and the payment must have reflected some agreement between the parish and diocesan authorities.[79] The parish's payment of the curate's subsidy reflected the mobility of curates in and out of the parish, which made payment of the subsidy by the parish really the only effective means of collection.

The tax reductions for poor livings had little effect on the impoverished livings and clergy of Bristol; most of the livings already were vacant by the end of Mary's reign. During vacancies, when parishioners were sequestering the tithes, as was the case for eleven or more of the eighteen livings in 1565, they were responsible for the living's taxes, although their stipendiary curates paid subsidies according to their stipends.[80] This may in essence have resulted in double subsidy bills since the curate's stipend actually represented the tithes or rates of the living. This may have been a moot question, however, in light of the non-payment of taxes by both parishes and curates. Between 1558 and 1561, eight livings were in decay or without fruits and unable to meet at least one subsidy payment.[81] Stipendiaries, too, were unable to meet their tax responsibilities: between 1556 and 1567, the curates of at least eleven parishes missed one or more of their subsidy payments.[82] By 1581 the diocesan authorities who were responsible for collecting taxes owed the Crown £970. In that year they and the authorities of four other dioceses were facing orders for seizure of goods to cover tax debts; the debts of others, however, ranged only from £84 (Chichester) to £296 (Coventry and Lichfield), well below the enormous sum owed in the diocese of Bristol.[83] While taxation became an increasing burden, which no doubt contributed to the impoverishment of the city's parsons and its vacant livings, by the early part of Elizabeth's reign income from the livings was so poor that parish sequestrators and stipendiary curates alike sometimes paid no taxes at all.

While their economic situation obviously worsened during the Reformation, we have few details concerning the parish clergy's standard of living. There are indications, however, that income from their livings was simply inadequate. In 1539, for example, Thomas Yereth, the vicar of All Saints, owed the parish £3 that he had borrowed from the church stock, and apparently had taken £4 for an obit which he had yet to serve.[84] In 1560 another vicar of that parish borrowed 13s. 4d., 10s. of which he still owed in 1563.[85] The parson of St Stephen, Thomas Hanson, owed his parish £5 in 1550, a sum which he too had borrowed.[86] We can only imagine that informal clerical borrowing from individual parishioners also occurred.[87] The parishioners of St Ewen apparently were aware of the economic hardship faced by their incumbent and were supplementing the tithe income of parson John Rawlins from parish receipts at least by the early 1550s. In 1550–1 payments were made 'towardes his living'.[88] Inadequate livings were already blurring the line between incumbents and stipendiary curates.

STIPENDIARY CURATES

With a declining real income and a growing tax burden, it is not surprising that nine of Bristol's livings were vacant by 1558, eleven by 1563.[89] As these vacancies occurred, the incumbents were replaced by stipendiary curates whose stipends were almost always less than the 1535 values of the livings they served. It was perhaps only a small step from the parish incumbent, who collected tithes but whose economic survival depended to a greater or lesser extent on the generosity of his parishioners, to the parish curate, whose whole income came from a parish-paid stipend, but a measure of independence was lost, particularly with the loss of tenure.

The growing number of vacancies, furthermore, signalled the disappearance of an important factor conditioning lay–clerical relationships. It is likely that a man who served a parish for many years would have developed personal relationships with many parishioners and that these relationships would soften the clergy's loss of status individually even as the group lost respect. Between 1555 and 1563 ten livings lost long-serving parsons: four who had served over twenty years, two over fifteen, and four who had served over ten either died or resigned.[90] Among the four livings which did not suffer extended vacancies upon loss of their long-time parsons, only two appear to have gained parsons who in turn became long-serving.[91] Curates, on the other hand, were notably mobile. In the nine years from 1562 through 1570 the parish of St Peter had three curates; in the twenty-two years from 1553 through 1574 St Mary Redcliffe had six.[92] The parish of St James had three curates in the eleven years from 1556 until 1566, and Sts Philip and Jacob had four in the six years from 1562 to 1567.[93] The parish of St Ewen had six curates and the services of six occasional ministers or curates in the twenty-three years from 1557 until 1579.[94] The average stays of curates in these parishes ranged from one and a half years to almost four years.

There were exceptions, however. Two parishes did gain the services of the same cleric for long periods. The parish of St Mary-le-Porte, which seems to have had trouble keeping a parson early in the period, acquired parson John Pylle, who served from 1548 until 1557, and curate John Gregory, who served from at least 1564 until his death in 1579.[95] By 1583 Richard Arthur was curate and was still there in 1593. The parish church of St Thomas, which as a chapel always was served by a curate, had the services of John Tewe from at least 1557 until at least 1583, although a reader served the parish in his absence from May 1561 until at least the end of 1564.[96] In addition some curates who served only briefly may have been known to their parishioners through earlier service in other capacities, perhaps in other parishes.[97] In spite of these exceptions, however, the trend was away from the long-serving parson and towards the mobile curate, who was less likely to have gained the loyalty of his parishioners.

In addition to all the other disadvantages under which curates worked, they, unlike the incumbents at the beginning of the period, seldom had assistants, and thus, were spread thinner, so to speak, over the parish. Table 6 shows the ratio of clergy to parishioners near the beginning of the Reformation.[98] While in some instances the ratio

Table 6. *Ratio of Priests to Parishioners*

Parish	Clergy in 1534	Communicants in 1548	Priests : Parishioners
All Saints (includes Kalendars' Guild)	6	180	1 : 30
Christ Church	5	326	1 : 65
St Augustine	3	unknown	unknown
St Ewen	2	56	1 : 28
St James	3	520	1 : 173
St John	4	227	1 : 57
St Lawrence	3	100	1 : 33
St Leonard	3	120	1 : 40
St Mark (not parochial in 1534)			
St Mary-le-Porte	1	180	1 : 180
St Mary Redcliffe	7 or more	600	1 : 86
St Michael	1	252	1 : 252
St Nicholas	9	800	1 : 89
St Peter	2	400	1 : 200
Sts Philip & Jacob	5	514	1 : 103
St Stephen	5	461	1 : 92
St Thomas	6 or more	600	1 : 100
St Werberg	2	160	1 : 80
Temple	6	480	1 : 80

seems high even then, it compares favourably to the ratio of 400 to one, most often favoured by chantry commissioners in 1548.[99] In all the parishes except St Michael and St Mary-le-Porte it undoubtedly was considerably worse at the end of the period, when chantries had been abolished and the livings did not afford assistants.

If the curates were faced with serving large numbers of parishioners without assistance, most were also expected to do it for less money than their incumbent predecessors. Between 1556 and 1570 the salaries of primary and perpetual curates of at least nine parishes ranged from £6. 13s. 4d. to £11, with most hovering around £7. Only the stipends of St Mary-le-Porte and St Ewen were more than the 1535 valuations of their livings, the former paying £3 or £4 over the £7 valuation, the latter more than doubling its valuation of £3. 6s.[100] The stipends did not compare favourably to the stipends of curates in

London, which varied from as little as £8 per year in one parish from 1565 through 1605 to £20 per year in another in 1564. H. G. Owen suggested that the market price in London in the 1570s was the £16 received by at least two curates, while Bishop Sandys's allowance of £5 for a half-year's wages in 1573 was perhaps the officially approved price.[101] Thus the stipends of curates in Bristol at the end of the Reformation did not compare favourably to the incomes of either the city's pre-Reformation incumbents or London's post-Reformation curates.

The low stipends make it difficult to believe that many of the incumbents or primary curates were surviving on single incomes by the latter part of the period, and indeed, many were not. Both pluralism and pensions helped to cushion the economic decline.

PLURALISM

Pluralism, which is difficult to measure because it included livings outside the local sphere, played a larger role in the 1560s than before. Bristol's pluralists ranged from formal ones, who had been instituted to two livings, to informal ones who held one living and another position or served two cures though instituted to only one. Formal pluralism was regulated by statute, providing that no incumbent whose benefice was worth £10 per annum could add a second benefice.[102] Exceptions were made for royal and noble chaplains, for those to whom the Crown gave dispensation, and for clergy of noble or gentle birth or those who were Bachelors or Doctors of Divinity or Bachelors of Canon Law. In the early years of the Reformation Bristol's pluralists reflected this statute's picture of elite clergy. In the 1530s perhaps as many as five incumbents were pluralists, four formal and one informal. Three were from the city's wealthier livings, two from among the four poorest, and only two were resident in Bristol. Four held graduate degrees.[103] During the next decade four other parsons held more than one ecclesiastical position, not all pluralists in the strict sense of holding two parish livings. Three of the Bristol livings involved in pluralism in the 1540s came from above the median value of livings and three from below. The combination of local livings by two of these clerics, however, signalled the appearance of clerics who worked at two jobs.[104] Pluralism was becoming less a privilege and more a necessity for Bristol's clergy.[105]

Only two other pluralists are recorded during the 1550s, one the rector of eighth-ranked St John, who was rector of Wearcon in 1551, and the other the vicar of Temple, the lowest-valued benefice in the city, who became vicar of Hungerford, Berkshire, in 1550. Apparently, both were resident in Bristol and must have acquired rural livings to augment their incomes. The rector of St John also became curate of St Lawrence in 1557 when a vacancy occurred in the living.[106] At least five Bristol clerics were pluralists of sorts during the 1560s, when most of the livings were vacant. Three incumbents and two curates held more than one living or briefly served more than one cure at a time, and these informal pluralists were more likely to be serving two cures within the city than the more elite clergy at the beginning of the Reformation. Four of the five combined local cures in some fashion.[107]

By the end of the Reformation, most of Bristol's livings were vacant as a result of their poverty and of taxation. The question of formal pluralism became virtually a dead issue in the city, while informal pluralism persisted as a means by which some local clergy augmented their incomes. By 1563, however, this practice may have been limited by a policy of local diocesan authorities which apparently prohibited a cleric's serving two cures unless he was incumbent of one of them. The policy distinguished between incumbents who could hold a second cure and stipendiary curates who could serve only one cure without admission to a living.[108] Allowing incumbents to serve second cures and collect second incomes may have been designed to encourage men to accept institution to livings and thus, to benefit collection of first fruits for which the diocesan authorities were responsible. Fewer vacancies no doubt also would have improved the authorities' image with the Crown, which was threatening the diocese with extinction by 1562.[109] In addition the ecclesiastical authorities may have recognized the growth of lay control inherent in the payment of stipendiary curates and tried to shore up incumbents by allowing them alone to serve second cures. It is doubtful that the policy resulted from clerical unemployment, given that some livings were served by unordained readers. Perhaps it was a limited exercise in pastoral concern.

PENSIONS

For those incumbents and curates who were ex-religious or ex-chantry priests, pensions were another source of income which cushioned the declining wealth of Bristol's livings during the Reformation. Two of the four livings which never became vacant were served for long periods by former monks of St Augustine's monastery in Bristol, their presentations no doubt insured by grants made before the dissolution. Humfry Hyman, vicar of All Saints from 1541 until around 1555, combined a pension of £8 with the living valued at £4. 3s. 4d.[110] John Rastell, the vicar of St Nicholas from 1543 until his death in 1563, added an £8 pension to his top-ranked living of £21. 1s. 1. ob.[111] Of course, they had to wait some years after the dissolution of the abbey before the livings became vacant. As we have seen, Rastell may also have become a pluralist in 1560 when he was non-resident. In addition these two vicarages, which were appropriated by the monastery of St Augustine and later the dean and chapter of the cathedral, were informally augmented during the tenures of Hyman and Rastell when the dean and chapter allowed them perennial arrears on the tithe portions they owed to the chapter.[112]

MARRIAGE

We have noted in regard to ex-chantry priests in Chapter 5 that age was a factor which affected a cleric's chance of bettering his economic position. Marriage was another element which may have intensified economic problems for some clergy, requiring them to scramble in various ways to effect a viable income. Christopher Hill and others have speculated that families of rural clergy contributed to the family's income while those of urban clergy were likely to be dependants.[113] It seems reasonable to suggest that the urban parson's family did not contribute through farm work, but it is hard to believe that women who married into the economically strained circumstances of the urban clergy would have failed to contribute economically or that their children would have remained idle. There is little evidence, however, of clergy's being deprived of their Bristol livings for marriage upon the accession of Mary. This indicates the slowness with which poor city clergy reacted to a new but potentially burdensome possibility.[114] Or perhaps it indicates the lack of potential partners. Traditionally pious women would have been horrified at the idea of marrying a priest while many reformists were at least temporarily anticlerical. Those in the middle would have hesitated to attract opprobrium from both sides by marrying a priest amid the raucous contention evidenced by Edgeworth's sermons.[115] Moreover, declining incomes generally also made the clergy less desirable for marriage.

In any case, marriage also undoubtedly contributed to the demise of clerical community and perhaps in Bristol it was also something of a replacement. To some extent families took time and emotion which before went to professional friends with common interests. To the extent that the clerical community was breaking down and being replaced with more competitive arrangements, however, family life must have been a comfort, an emotional buffer—at least in those marriages which were based on affection. Any economic burden was certainly matched by the emotional support of a positive relationship, which contributed not only to personal fulfillment but also to the ability to compete.[116]

There is no way of knowing how many parish clergy married in the 1560s (or took back former wives), but there is little doubt that marriage was one of the factors which contributed to the search for greater income among them.[117] At the birth of his son in 1565, John Gregory held three positions, a greater number than most. He was rector of St Michael, curate of St Mary-le-Porte, and subdeacon in the cathedral, for a combined income of around £22.[118] Problems with his living, however, caused him to abandon the rectory in 1568. The costs of tithe collection—both court costs and the social cost of suing the town's elite—were potentially substantial and the suits not certain of success.[119] Furthermore, the upkeep of the rectory, which was in decay in 1556, and of the chancel reduced the living's value to Gregory.[120] The value of his curacy at St Mary-le-Porte was enhanced by the curate's house, located next to the church, and by absence of responsibility for the chancel since he was not incumbent.[121] By 1570 his stipend in the cathedral had grown from £5 to £6. 8s. 4d. which, added to his £10 or £11 stipend as curate, gave him a total income of around £17.[122] Gregory remained at St Mary-le-Porte until his death in 1579.[123]

The career of Roger Rise also suggests the difficulties of married clergy. Rise first appears in the accounts of St Mary Redcliffe where he received a stipend of 18s. and 6s. 8d. for a chamber in 1554. In 1556 he was the highest paid stipendiary, receiving £5. 6s. 8d., but the following year he was paid for only one half year's service. He turns up next in the records at All Saints where he received £5 per year as a stipendiary from 1558 until 1560. Although his housing may have been provided in the quarters of the dissolved Kalendars' Guild, it appears that this step did not signal any increase in income. He probably then moved to St Ewen where he was curate at least from 1564 until the end of 1567.[124] This move brought a greater income, but it is doubtful that housing was provided since he did not live in the parsonage.[125] The parish paid stipends of £6. 13s. 4d. in 1561, £7 in 1562, £7. 10s. in 1563, and £7. 14s. in 1567–8.[126] The increase to £7. 10s. paralleled Rise's marriage to a local woman from the parish of St Leonard late in 1563.[127] About a year later Rise was assigned to serve the cure of nearby Clifton for a short period, adding £2 or so to his income.[128] Rise left the cure of St Ewen at the end of 1567 to become the incumbent of the parish of St John, a living valued at £7. 4s. 6d. in 1535. In that capacity he also became curate of the parish of St Lawrence, whose church stood across the gate from the church of St John, and whose living had been valued at £4. 3s. 4d. in 1535.[129] Even if both livings had remained the same since Henry VIII's valuation, the combined income of over £11 would have surpassed Rise's wage at St Ewen. Between 1558 and 1568, in fact, his income had more than doubled, and at St John's he probably had use of a parsonage. Even so, his nominal income was less than that of five local livings in 1535, was lessened by inflation, and possibly burdened by family.[130] His responsibilities for taxes and upkeep of rectory and chancel, moreover, were greater than those of curates, whose single incomes remained around £7. For Rise personally, some gratification may have come from his increased income and from his tenured position in a church where many of the city's lay elite worshipped. Nevertheless he must have felt the effects of inflation and the burden of supporting a family even if he did not fully recognize his position among a clergy in reduced circumstances.

At least one Bristol curate appears to have opted for a rural living to finance marriage. Stephen Popyngaye received a stipend of £8 in 1556 and 1557 as curate of Clifton, apparently leaving that cure to become rector of St Werberg, valued at £10 in 1535.[131] He succeeded the reformist Christopher Pacy in this parish, where a number of reformists among the secular elite lived, and possibly was ousted at the accession of Elizabeth and the return of Pacy to the city.[132] In 1560 and 1561 he was perpetual curate of St James at a stipend of about £7.[133] He also did part-time work to supplement his income, receiving 1s. 4d. for his services in the parish of St Ewen.[134] By the time of his marriage to Margaret Pope of the parish of St Werberg in 1562, he was the rector of a living in the county of Dorset, presumably a rural living with a better income.[135]

In spite of the difficulties faced by many curates, some of them may not have been terribly dissatisfied with their roles.[136] There were some advantages to serving the vacant livings. The most obvious was tax benefits. For an untenured curate there were no first fruits due to the Crown, and the tenth and subsidy due on the living were paid by the parish. The curate owed only a subsidy based upon his stipend.[137] A second advantage which the curate gained was escape from the burden and uncertainty of tithe collection. Parish sequestrators paid regular stipends, sometimes augmenting their 'tithe' collections from other parish receipts. Loss of some independence may have seemed a small price to pay for these advantages. For those who had been stipendiary assistants, positions as primary parish curates actually may have exceeded their expectations. Moreover, there was one new group of semi-clergy which fell below the curates. Between 1560 and 1567 at least seven laymen were designated as readers in Bristol, five of them where the parish livings were not vacant. They read divine service but were prohibited from ministering the sacraments or preaching, and they were very poorly paid. The reader of All Saints received a stipend of only £2 in 1560–1 and £2. 13s. 4d. in 1562–3, so the step from reader to curate meant a raise in pay as well as responsibility.[138] In addition, pensioners may have been grateful for their jobs while lamenting the economic conditions which made them necessary. We simply do not know the extent to which personal circumstance stood outside the decline which the clergy as a group were suffering.

THE LACK OF LAY RESPONSE TO THE CLERGY'S DECLINE

A most remarkable element in the clergy's deterioration was the lack of lay response to the decay of parish livings and the concomitant decline in clerical education. There are no indications of lay discontent with clerical quality even at the clergy's nadir in the early years of Elizabeth's reign. At a time when education among the laity was increasing and Protestant theology was emphasizing the preaching and teaching role of the clergy, however, the poor educational quality of Bristol's clergy can hardly have gone unnoticed.

The nature of the parochial system played a significant role in the lack of lay response to the clergy's decline in education. The inner-city tithe system's reliance on cash contributed to the impoverishment of most city livings, and the patronage system discouraged additional endowments by the lay elite. Patronage of nine of the city's livings

came into the hands of the Brayne family shortly after the dissolution
of religious houses; that of four went to the dean and chapter of the
cathedral.[139] One went to the corporation and one remained in the
hands of the Crown.[140] By 1565, however, the corporation had
purchased advowsons of two livings from the Braynes.[141] It is
significant that the living of Temple, of which the Corporation became
patron in 1544, never suffered an extended vacancy, and the living of
St John, the patronage of which was later acquired by the Corporation,
suffered a relatively short vacancy of only five years between 1563 and
1568. The Corporation's other advowson of the living of St Lawrence
was never exercised. The living was served by the rector of St John,
and in 1580 the two parishes were combined and the church of St
Lawrence destroyed. It is very likely that the Corporation was
augmenting the livings of Temple and St John in some informal way.
We have already noted the informal augmentation of the livings of All
Saints and St Nicholas when the dean and chapter of the cathedral
allowed a permanent state of arrears. The Brayne family, however,
apparently had no interest in augmenting the livings of which they
were patron, and there is no indication that they were troubled by
parish sequestration of the tithes, although they did do battle over tithe
control in the parish of St James where parishioners challenged the
right of the impropriator to collect tithes and provide a perpetual
curate.[142]

Neither the Braynes nor the lay elite had an interest in augmenting
the livings because none of the factors were present which could have
motivated such a step. If the Braynes had had strong religious
convictions, they might have upgraded the livings in order to attract
clergy who could preach those convictions from local pulpits. The
Corporation, on the other hand, regardless of religious beliefs, would
not have profited by augmenting a living when they had no control over
the choice of clergy. The city's governors may in fact have chosen not
to purchase more advowsons because they were not unanimous in their
religious views. In addition the Crown's attacks on the city's church
had made it clear that the Church was an unsafe repository for local
wealth. Certainly the local laity at the parish level (including those in
municipal government) had more control over the tithe or rate
payment and choice of clergy, if one ignores the issue of quality, when
the livings were vacant and served by parish-chosen, parish-paid
curates. Apart from the issue of pulpit control lay the reality that
advowsons were private property which could be bought and sold.

There was certainly no motivation for the lay élite to contribute to Brayne's private property, and this point was sharpened by the tithe suits which Henry Brayne and his son Robert brought against many of the lay elite in parishes where the lay impropriator was rector.[143]

Nor were there any attacks on the patronage system. The fact that advowsons were private property was an obstacle to national reform throughout the Elizabethan period as both clergy and laity sought better qualified clergy, but refused to attack a system which hindered this goal because it was based upon the principle of private property.[144] Larger stipends might have attracted educated clergy to Bristol from Oxford or London, but that would have meant raising rates for unguaranteed results. In addition, these clergy would have sought institution to the livings, institutionalizing the higher rates as tithes. The laity would have transferred choice of cleric to the patron and control of the pulpit to the cleric himself, both at the price of higher rates. At the same time the patron could have profited from the sale of the advowson. There may also have been fears that additional endowments might have increased the valuation of the living and thus its taxes. The presence of uneducated, untenured, stipendiary clergy as primary parish curates was almost unavoidable without an overhaul of the patronage system which would have threatened assumptions about private property and opened up questions concerning control of the pulpit.

Given the problems which independent clergy and popular religious divisions caused, the clergy's impoverished and uneducated condition may not have been entirely unwelcome to those whose authority had been threatened.[145] While the parish leadership was not limited to members of the Corporation, it did fall to the prominent men of each parish whose concerns were similar to the corporate elite in regard to the advantages of order and obedience to authority. There is no denying that the payment of a stipend to an untenured parish curate constituted a new level of lay control even though it is questionable whether tithe collection could have benefited the city's clergy economically at the time. Parish incumbents had relied on their parishioners' good will for loans and augmentations, but theirs had been tenured positions and their tithes had been protected by legal remedies. The curate's situation was different. When the livings became vacant, diocesan authorities ordered sequestration of tithes by parishioners, who then paid their curate.[146] The collapse of the balance of power between parish incumbents and their elite parishioners left these laity in control and the clergy concerned with meeting the parish laity's approval. Relationships among the clergy could only be secondary at best.[147] The parish laity's control of pulpits, of course, could be as threatening to the Corporation's desire to maintain its authority as were independent clergy and popular religious conflict. But it seems that the continued poverty of the livings and the establishment of the Corporation's preachers (supported by parish rates) in the mid-1580s lessened this threat at least until the end of the century.[148]

Those laity for whom religion was a paramount concern also were unlikely to have addressed the clerical decline because they were engaged in the process of changing the very definition of clerical education. It is important to acknowledge the rise of demands nationally during Elizabeth's reign for a better educated, preaching clergy, although we have not found evidence of that in Bristol during the first decade of the reign. Our focus on the Reformation period in Bristol has found that clerical education was probably not a concern of early reformists because so many of Bristol's best educated clerics were among the defenders of traditional religion and many of the educated parish clergy were Corporation-oriented moderates. Concern for clerical quality was related to doctrinal positions rather than to the clergy's formal education. When Wishart's radical supporter attacked local parish clergy in 1539, he was critical of a parson who had an MA from Oxford because he could not 'change a man a grote'.[149] On the other hand, John Kene, the conservative parson of St Ewen, condemned preachers of the 'new learning', a term alluding to humanistic education but emphasizing its relationship to reform ideas.[150] Another conservative, Roger Edgeworth, was concerned that nonspecialists were interpreting Scripture and that craftsmen and tradesmen were entering the priesthood. His was not so much a plea for a better educated clergy, however, as for a traditional clergy whose authority was respected and whose role as religious guide was not threatened by the entry of reformers into the clergy or by the laity's assumption of authority. He said that the clergy who read English books were not true expositors of the Scripture.[151]

Throughout the Reformation the doctrinal debate meant that there also was no consensus on the proper education of a clergyman. No unequivocal call for an educated clergy could be made by those with passionate religious commitments because the call could have been used by the enemy. Only when the battle was essentially won could reformers call for a better educated clergy and by then the clergy had declined to an abysmal state. Thus if the moderates and pragmatists among the corporate and parish elites had good reason to remain passive in the face of the parochial clergy's decline, the religious zealots on both sides also had little motivation to call for higher incomes or better educated clergy. Not until the very end of the sixteenth century did graduate incumbents begin to reappear in Bristol. While they slowly became the rule rather than the exception, whether they were resident is unknown. Further investigation undoubtedly would reveal the extent to which in the decades up to 1640 they reconstituted a clerical community, the character of this community or grouping, and its relationship to the laity.[152]

If the pre-Reformation parish parson had played the role of peacemaker among hostile parishioners envisioned by John Bossy, this role no doubt was shaken by the trend away from the long-serving parson with assistants and by other changes during the Reformation. Early in the period some of the parish clergy abandoned such a role by taking strong stands during the religious conflict over Latimer's preaching. It is unlikely that the vulnerable curates at the end of the period could have either taken a strong stand on an issue or played peacemaker. Their influence in parish affairs was probably negligible. If there is no evidence of anticlericalism (other than Lollard) before the Reformation, there is little evidence after the early 1540s of the anticlericalism shown by George Wishart's supporter and others against the parish clergy. The clergy were no longer independent or educated enough to excite the attention of the corporate elite nor rich or respectable enough to attract attacks from the likes of the Wishart supporters. Poorly educated, lacking tenure, receiving poor stipends, combining jobs and pensions to create viable incomes, the parish clergy at the end of the Reformation were vulnerable to and dependent on the parish laity to an extent unknown by their predecessors three decades before. The only bright spot during the Reformation for Bristol's sorely weakened Church was the creation of the diocese of Bristol by Henry VIII in 1542. As the next chapter will show, however, the new ecclesiastical hierarchy had their own problems and their presence did not signal a major exception to the clergy's decline.

7
The New Diocese and its Clerical Elite

THE establishment of the diocese of Bristol in 1542 signalled the creation of a new clerical elite in the city. Unlike their medieval counterparts, however, the cathedral clergy were not an integral part of a diverse clerical community nor did they enjoy independence from the lay elite. Their roles as clerical tax collectors and ecclesiastical judges separated them from the parochial clergy whose lives they regulated, while their superior educational qualifications and multiple preferments gave them more in common with the lay elite than with the lesser clergy, whose qualifications were declining. They were nevertheless subordinate to the lay elite, largely because of institutional realities. The new diocese, which could not have been erected without local lay support, was poorly endowed and its existence continuously threatened. Its clergy were extremely vulnerable to local lay influence except during the reign of Mary when new personnel relied on the Crown. Although canons were required by the cathedral statutes to preach and to maintain a grammar school, lay-controlled institutions lessened the cathedral clergy's influence in these areas. The Consistory Court was an important instrument of social as well as religious control, but institutional changes during the period guaranteed that the secular authorities would also influence the ecclesiastical court, even in religious matters. In addition the presence of men with local connections among the cathedral canons suggests that the local lay elite were influencing royal presentations to cathedral posts. It is ironic that the creation of a new diocese and a new clerical elite also promoted the lay elite's power over the clergy.

THE CREATION OF THE NEW DIOCESE

The creation of the new diocese of Bristol was part of a larger plan which Henry VIII effected from 1540 through 1542. The circumstances of its creation and its odd composition, however, suggest the influence of the local lay elite on the final inclusion of Bristol in the scheme. The idea of establishing a number of new bishoprics had originated with Wolsey in the 1520s and later was expressed in written form by the King himself.[1] When a parallel plan for the creation of suffragan bishops was enacted in 1534, Bristol was among the titles created. This did not alter the existing diocesan structure, however, and Bristol's inclusion as a suffragan see indicates that at that time the King was not considering it as a potential diocese.[2]

Although Bristol was considered as a site of a new see in 1539, neither the King nor the local laity seems to have been set on the idea until a few months before the new diocese was founded over two years later. When the local monastery was dissolved in December of 1539, the abbot and monks of St Augustine were dismissed. At Gloucester, on the other hand, services were continued at St Peter's monastery, also dissolved in December, and when the new diocese of Gloucester was erected in September 1541, the rural deanery of Bristol was included in it.[3] Sometime soon after the creation of Gloucester, however, the King had a change of mind, and on 4 June 1542 he established the diocese of Bristol.

The geographical dimensions of the diocese themselves suggest the last-minute nature of the decision and the patchwork character of the creation. This diocese, unique in English ecclesiastical history, consisted of the deanery of Bristol except for nine or ten Gloucestershire parishes left in the new diocese of Gloucester, the three trans-Avon city parishes originally from Bath and Wells diocese, the manor of Leigh, Somerset, and the county of Dorset out of the diocese of Salisbury. Bristol and Dorset were separated by the dioceses of Salisbury and Bath and Wells, a separation of some forty miles.[4] The creation of such a diocese clearly had little relationship to the desire for efficient diocesan administration or pastoral care. It was an afterthought on the part of the Crown which suggests some outside influence.[5]

The circumstances of the new bishopric's establishment point to the influence of Bristol's secular elite. Certainly there were motivations for pursuing a see, and the timing paralleled those motivations. The Corporation first encountered problems with the city's two diocesan authorities in 1533 during the Latimer affair. Although Cromwell was in control of ecclesiastical policy, Bishop Clerke of Bath and Wells and the Vicar General of Worcester did not always follow his lead, and complications had arisen for the local secular authorities.[6] They do not seem to have seriously pursued a new bishopric in the 1530s, however, probably because the institution of Latimer to the see of Worcester in 1535 and the newly obsequious behaviour of Clerke towards Cromwell made matters somewhat less complicated in regard to ecclesiastical policy.[7] In addition rumours concerning the confiscation of bishops' property in the late 1530s made a new bishopric less desirable.[8]

The King's religious reaction in the spring of 1539 and Latimer's resignation in the summer clouded the situation again, giving the corporate elite reason to be concerned. The religious reaction and the harsh punishments dictated by the Six Articles Act inspired 500 indictments for heresy and many arrests in London.[9] In Gloucester there were protests against the dissolution of monasteries and sermons against the King's Articles. Cromwell's representative in the area, Thomas Avance, was in Gloucester in February 1540, giving out light punishments to those detected during the last visitation, when Bristol's mayor and aldermen requested that he come to Bristol to 'reform' certain points.[10] Apparently the corporation wanted his help before the city was visited by the new bishop of Worcester, John Bell, in April.[11] There is no extant evidence that the visitation caused any problems, but the death of Cromwell in the following summer signalled the victory of conservative forces in the battle for the monarch's ear and the end of an era for local authorities. They were left to wonder if the King would return to more direct reliance on diocesan authorities and if harsh punishments of Bristol's religious dissidents would follow. The six men executed at Smithfield only two days after Cromwell's death included both Catholics and Protestants, and three of them had been active in Bristol.[12]

In addition to these worries another factor was added. In September 1541 the King created the diocese of Gloucester; this may have been the trigger which set in motion some effort by Bristol's elite to gain their own diocese. The inclusion of Bristol in the diocese of Gloucester, a rival city, was threatening. The cities had recently feuded over scarce food supplies, and the prospect of Bristol's having an episcopal authority influenced by this rival urban oligarchy was a serious matter.[13] In addition civic pride suffered when Gloucester gained the title of city. To make matters worse, the newly named bishop was John Wakeman, who had been abbot of Tewkesbury, and probably a foe of the corporation during the Latimer affair.[14] Clearly at this point the Crown had no plan to create Bristol diocese, and the only other force interested and strong enough to change the royal direction was Bristol's secular elite. Their concern with diocesan authority and their rivalry with Gloucester were strong motivations for seeking a diocese of their own. The new diocese was founded less than a year after the establishment of the diocese of Gloucester and more than two and one-half years after the dissolution of the monastery of St Augustine and the dispersal of the monks.

THE VULNERABILITY OF THE NEW DIOCESE

The weakness of the new see from its beginning suggested strongly that it would not threaten Bristol's secular authorities in any way. It was poor, lacking in effective episcopal leadership, and under threat of destruction. These three factors fed and sustained each other. Impoverished bishops could not stand up to the Crown, and threats of further impoverishment or even dissolution made the bishop and the dean and chapter dependent on local lay support.

The Poor Endowment

The endowment of the new diocese was £679. 3s. 11d. with the bishopric itself worth £383. 8s. 4d. of that.[15] Like the other new sees founded by Henry VIII, Bristol was poor in comparison to most of the older bishoprics. In 1535 the average net pre-tax income of the seventeen English bishoprics was £1,568. 7s. 6d. per year; Rochester at £411. 1s. 9d. was the lowest valued. Of the new sees, the Bishop of Chester had an income valued at £420. 1s. 8d., Peterborough at £368. 11s. 6d. ob., Oxford at £381, and Gloucester at £315.[16] The bishop of Bristol held about 57 per cent of his wealth in lands, the other 43 per cent in appropriations, or 'spiritualities'.[17] His wealth compared favourably with that of the Bishop of Chester, who had little land and who also administered a much larger diocese, but less favourably with that of Peterborough, whose income was primarily landed and whose diocese was, if larger than Bristol, nevertheless more compact. The dean and chapter of Bristol were endowed with the remaining £295. 15s. 7d. of the diocese's endowment, out of which each of six canon-prebendaries was allowed £20 per year, plus added sums for assuming certain offices.[18] Paul Bush, the first bishop, was allowed to retain the canonry and prebend of Bishopstone in Salisbury Cathedral, while the prebendaries of Bristol generally held a number of other preferments, including parish cures, though none in Bristol.[19] It is impossible to determine the incomes of bishop and chapter members with precision because little diocesan evidence is extant and because preferments were scattered. Nevertheless it is clear that the endowment of the diocese itself was so small by traditional standards that it certainly did not provide a strong position for the new clergy.

Weak Diocesan Leadership

The diocese was further weakened by the lack of strong leadership. Not a great deal is known about the tenures of the first two bishops, Paul Bush (1542–54) and John Holyman (1554–8).[20] Bush, who is buried in the cathedral, probably was more active in diocesan affairs than Holyman, who was buried in his long-held rectory of Handborough, Oxfordshire. Bush's Chancellor John Cotterell made his career in Bristol and probably ran the diocese for Bush, but there is little evidence of early diocesan administration.[21] Although Holyman was present for the heresy trials of Latimer and Ridley in Oxford, his Chancellor William Dalby sat at the trials of Bristol's heretics.

Bush's position was weakened by his loss of the manor of Leigh, his only manor, to the Crown in 1551.[22] His weak position was also indicated by an incident which occurred in the following year. In 1552 Dean John Whitheare and three members of the chapter, including the Bishop's Chancellor John Cotterell made a deal with a local layman behind the Bishop's back. They sold stone from a projected cathedral extension, for which Cotterell received £20 and the dean and other two members Thomas Sylke and Roger Edgeworth an equal amount, presumably for their personal use. The deal became public only during the reign of Mary when a suit for delivery of the stone was brought in the Court of Requests.[23] The incident did not speak well of diocesan leadership. While the bishop was unaware of the sale of the cathedral stone, the chapter members who made the shady arrangement were long-tenured leaders of the cathedral community and the Consistory Court.[24]

John Cotterell was perhaps the most important man in the cathedral hierarchy during the first thirty years of its existence although his authority was not that of a bishop. He was the leading figure in the ecclesiastical court, serving as Chancellor to Bishop Bush from at least 1543 until 1554, and resuming a similar role in December 1559 as vicar general (delegate) of the Archbishop of Canterbury during vacancy of the see of Bristol. He continued this role as deputy to Bishop Cheyney of Gloucester, who was given the see *in commendam* in 1562, finally replacing Cheney as spiritual guardian of the see by commission from the Archbishop on 23 May 1563.[25] He became a canon and prebendary of Bristol in 1545 and Archdeacon of Dorset in 1551, retaining both offices until his death in 1572. In probably March or April 1554 he was commissioned (under title of Archdeacon of Dorset) with two others to deal with married clergy in the diocese of Bath and Wells. On 8 April 1554, he became vicar general of the bishop of Bath and Wells and on 18 May he was admitted canon and prebendary of the same diocese. In the same year he became Archdeacon of Wells, a post he held until his death.[26] Cotterell's career indicates strong ties to Bristol. He received his doctorate in civil law from New College, Oxford, in July 1542 at the age of 34 and within a year of receiving the degree he had begun his legal career in Bristol as Bush's Chancellor. His move to Bath and Wells during the reign of Mary suggests that he was avoiding the troubles which were to come in Bristol. If he had remained as Chancellor, he, rather than William Dalby, would have sat at the heresy trials which resulted in the condemnation and burning of some four to eight Bristolians.[27] His move preserved his career, which was resumed in Bristol at the accession of Elizabeth. While his career gave some continuity to diocesan leadership, his authority was limited initially by the existence of bishops, then by the break in his local career, and, of course, by his want of the episcopal title.[28]

After the death of Bishop Holyman in 1558, the see was vacant until 1562 when it was given *in commendam* to the Bishop of Gloucester, Richard Cheyney, who held it until his death in 1579.[29] Cheyney, however, did not exercise the ordinary's powers in Bristol diocese, which were left to Cotterell. In 1568 Cheyney became involved in a dispute over his preaching in Bristol Cathedral, provoking a complaint to the Crown by local citizens.[30] The bishop was excommunicated in 1571 when he failed to appear at Convocation for the required subscription to the Thirty-nine Articles.[31] He was absolved in the same year, but he exercised very little authority over corrupt diocesan officials, whose bribe-taking left ecclesiastical authority in Gloucester in a shambles. His failure to collect the Queen's tenths promptly from the clergy, furthermore, almost resulted in confiscation of his land and goods.[32] While Cotterell's oversight of Bristol diocese appears to have been more effective, the lack of episocopal leadership throughout the period contributed to the institutional vulnerability of the diocese.

The Threat of Disintegration

The weakness of the diocese, suggested by its poverty, its confusing array of leaders, and its odd geographical configuration, made it a ripe target for disintegration, if not dissolution. The first manifestation of this trend was the Crown's confiscation of the manor of Leigh from Bishop Bush in 1551, but the Crown was not the only predator.[33] In his report to the Queen's council on the diocese of Gloucester in 1563, Bishop Cheyney explained that when the diocese of Gloucester was created, it extended into the towns and counties of both Gloucester and Bristol. At present, he wrote, the diocese of Bristol contained ten Gloucestershire parishes although there was 'no mention made in the erection of Bristol to have any part or parcel of the County of Gloucester'. He promised more on the subject, but the portion of the report concerning the diocese of Bristol is not extant, and we hear no more.[34] Apparently Cheyney was touching on diocesan history with an eye to recouping territory lost from Gloucester diocese or even to restoring the whole of Bristol deanery. He was not able to retrieve any of Bristol's territory, but the possibility that Bristol would lose a Gloucestershire portion or even be subsumed in the diocese of Gloucester remained a threat to the integrity and even the existence of the diocese, particularly as long as the bishop of Gloucester held Bristol *in commendam*.

By early 1572 threats to the diocese of Bristol came from another direction. Cheyney's excommunication in 1571, combined with the death of John Cotterell in 1572, apparently brought disjunctures to diocesan administration which threatened to end the obviously odd union of Dorset with Bristol and reunite it with contiguous Salisbury diocese. It seems that on his excommunication Cheyney lost all jurisdiction in the Archdeaconry of Dorset, and John Cotterell received a commission to visit the diocese. Cotterell may have become incapacitated, however, for in November 1571 a similar commission went to the Bishop of Bath and Wells. Cotterell's will was dated 21 February 1572, and in the same month the Bishop of Bath and Wells received another commission to visit the diocese of Bristol.[35] In May care of the diocese was transferred to the bishop of Salisbury Edmund Guest who had replaced John Jewell only six months before.[36] Within a year and a half the Bishop was participating in the suit of James Procter against the Archdeacon of Dorset, Henry Tichenor, for jurisdiction within the archdeaconry. Tichenor argued that the archdeaconry of Dorset had been, by act of Parliament and the grant of Henry VIII erecting the Bishopric of Bristol, 'clearly and absolutely separated from the cathedral church of Sarum'. It had been united to the cathedral church of Bristol and was in the gift of the Bishop of that see (presumably Cheyney, who still held Bristol *in commendam*).[37] The question raised concerned who would exercise the patronage power of the Bishop of Bristol in regard to the office of Archdeacon of Dorset. Initially Procter (and Bishop Guest) won in practice if not in principle. In 1575 he was acting as substitute for the Archdeacon of Dorset under the Bishop of Salisbury and was removed from that position for taking bribes and failing to punish criminals.[38]

In the following year competition for jurisdiction in Dorset continued between diocesan authorities in Gloucester and Salisbury. In January 1576 a messenger or apparitor of the ecclesiastical commission in Gloucester, which was working in tandem with the Consistory Court, had his papers taken from him by force when he went into Dorset.[39] In 1577 even the Privy Council seemed confused about jurisdiction in the county, writing the Bishop of Bath and Wells for a list of recusants in the archdeaconry. The Bishop passed the request on to the deputy-Lieutenants of Dorset, who replied that Dorset was sometimes *in commendam* to the see of Gloucester and sometimes to the see of Sarum, and that they had no means of collecting particulars about recusants in a short time.[40] Apparently the archdeaconry of Dorset was a fairly stable part of the diocese of Bristol during the lifetime of John Cotterell, who by virtue of his several offices had a firm grip on jurisdiction in the county. Without his personal control, however, Dorset's link to Bristol became tenuous.

The threat of disintegration, combined with impoverishment and lack of strong episcopal leadership, left the diocese weak and vulnerable to the Crown and other ecclesiastical authorities, and dependent upon the support of Bristol's secular elite. The diocese as an entity probably was at its strongest early in Elizabeth's reign when Cotterell was at the helm. In 1562 the corporation informed the Crown that they desired the maintenance of an independent Bishopric. Otherwise they preferred union with Bath and Wells. This preference undoubtedly related to Cotterell's position in Bath and Wells diocese and their satisfaction with his career in Bristol as well as to their antipathy towards Gloucester.[41]

RELATIONSHIP OF THE LAY ELITE TO THE CHAPTER PERSONNEL

The ties which some of the deans and prebendaries had to Bristol suggest that the secular elite were not relying upon the vulnerability of the diocese as the only means of influencing the cathedral clergy and the diocesan authorities. These local connections suggest that Bristol's laity were influencing some Crown appointments to the cathedral hierarchy or developing ties with new canons. Of the twenty-six deans and canons in office by 1580, nine had previous local ties. Four or five were natives of Bristol, and eight formerly held local ecclesiastical positions.[42]

The Foundation and Early Years

The corporation's influence was not immediately apparent, however, at the foundation of the diocese in 1542. Of the first six canons none can be identified with certainty as having positive ties to the corporation although Roger Hughes certainly did by the time he died in 1545.[43] Of John Gough's origins we know nothing, and it appears that Henry Morgan's position in Bristol was only one of many preferments resulting from his favour with the Crown. The appointment of three conservatives with local ties, however, suggests the impact of the royal religious reaction as well as ties to local conservatives. Roger Edgeworth had been prior of the Kalendars' Guild in Bristol for several years in the late 1520s, but his conservative preaching in the city after he went to Wells in 1535 may have caused discord.[44] The two other new canons had been in opposition to the Corporation during the brouhaha of 1533. George Dogeon was chaplain to Bishop Clerke of Bath and Wells as well as incumbent of a local living, and Richard Browne had been Commissary in Bristol for the Bishop of Worcester and had preached against Latimer.[45] The impression given by the initial contingent of canons is of ecclesiastical professionals rather than local loyalists.

The corporation's influence showed itself, however, when John Barlowe, with strong local ties, replaced Gough in February 1544, and Bristol native John Williams replaced Richard Browne the following month.[46] Undoubtedly, John Cotterell Chancellor of the diocese also proved an ally of the corporation when he took Roger Hughes's stall in 1545. Thomas Sylke, almost certainly a native of the city, took Williams's place upon his death in 1546.[47] Thus, within a few years Barlow, Sylke and Cotterell provided the corporation with a grip on the chapter; Roger Edgeworth appears to have become allied with Sylke and Cotterell for governance of the diocese even though his primary residence was at Wells. That Barlowe also knew how to play ball with the establishment was evidenced in letters to Cromwell in 1536, and his connection to the Thorne family of Bristol in 1546. He seems to have been resident during the early years of his tenure at Bristol.[48]

Thomas Sylke was among the canon-prebendaries most closely related to the secular elite. He not only was almost certainly a native of Bristol but also probably was related to members of the corporate elite.[49] Having received his MA degree from Oxford in 1526, Sylke began his career in Bristol by 1529 as vicar of St Leonard.[50] His relationship to the corporation was reflected in his absence from the conflict of 1533, his association with the secular elite in the Wishart affair of 1539, and his appointment as prior of the Kalendars' Guild in 1540, a post he held until its dissolution in 1548.[51] This appointment as well as his position as canon suggests that he had no problems preaching during the reigns of either Henry VIII or Edward VI, and his survival of religious changes under all four Tudor monarchs indicates great flexibility. Sylke was very active in chapter affairs, signing accounts, serving as receiver of the rents, and speaking for the group in cases brought against them in chancery.[52] He also seems to have had an ongoing relationship with the corporate elite. John Smythe, a prominent merchant, recorded in 1539 that he had received £20 from John Rokesby, sent from Wells by Master Sylke of Bristowe. In 1545 Smythe received 4 marks from Master Sylke and on 4 January 1547, received £9. 6s. 8d., which he paid to Smythe's wife.[53] His continuing relationship to the elite was shown by his appointment as a governor of the free writing and grammar school of Queen Elizabeth in Redcliffe in 1571.[54] Sylke died sometime before 14 September 1575, when he was replaced as a cathedral canon and prebendary.[55]

John Williams (1544–6) also was a native of Bristol and probably related to an elite family.[56] He was vicar of St Nicholas from at least 1534, having become non-resident by 1540.[57] Whether he returned to the city upon becoming a canon is unknown, but he kept his preferment as well as his living at St Nicholas until his death in the first half of 1546.[58] Thomas Sylke, defending the chapter against a suit by Williams's predecessor, asserted that Williams had paid the previous prebendary and canon, Richard Browne, £80 for the position. Browne, who had been a foe of the corporation in 1533 when he was an episcopal commissary, was suing the chapter for his last stipend and asserting that he had been forced to resign.[59] The arguments suggest that money as well as influence was used to replace Browne with Williams.

The appointment of John Barlowe (1544–54) also pointed to local influence. Although Barlowe held a number of preferments before becoming canon and prebendary at Bristol, he had been known in the area as the dean of the college at Westbury-on-Trym in Gloucester-shire, near Bristol, a position he held from 1530 until its dissolution in 1544.[60] In 1546 the will of Nicholas Thorne, a prominent merchant of Bristol, described him as 'late dean' of this college, and made him, along with two local merchants, an overseer of the free grammar school at St Bartholomew. In 1547 he received a royal grant of non-residence from his position as dean of Worcester.[61] It seems safe to assume that he was resident in Bristol at least during part of his tenure. There is not any other evidence, however, that he was active in Bristol's affairs. Undoubtedly he spent some time in Worcester where he was dean of the chapter from 1544 until 1554 and vicar delegate of the chapter of Canterbury during the vacancy of the see of Worcester, and in Wales where he was Archdeacon of Carmarthen in 1547.[62]

Roger Hughes (1542–5), who previously was a proctor in the Worcester Consistory Court, may not have been known to the corporate elite before he became a member of the chapter.[63] His will testifies, however, that he came under their influence. When he died in December 1545, he left the advowson of St Leonard in Bristol to John Sebright, chamberlain of the Corporation.[64] This was an important bequest because the parson, who was none other than Thomas Sylke, left the living within a year to become a prebendary and canon in the cathedral. The living ranked fifth in income among Bristol's parishes and a bequest of £300 in 1527 for general uses probably had made it a plum for Sylke.[65] Hughes's legacy made certain that the corporate elite would name Sylke's successor at St Leonard. Hughes also left money to Sebright and his wife and put Sebright in charge of a bequest to the church of Wolverly. Among the seven clerical beneficiaries was Sir Philip, the 'vicar' of St George's in the Guildhall.

During the Marian period personnel changes supported the Crown's conservative religious policy rather than the Corporation's influence by bringing such men as Henry Joliffe and William Dalby into the chapter. Joliffe, who was installed as dean 22 August 1554 after the deprivation of George Carewe, had been imprisoned during the reign of Edward. As a prebendary of Worcester, he had publicly challenged the views of Bishop Hooper.[66] Dalby, the Chancellor who presided over the heresy trials, also became a prebendary and canon.[67] During their tenures the mayor and aldermen showed their disapproval of the administration of ecclesiastical policy by refusing to worship at the cathedral, forcing the dean and chapter to 'fetch them out of the city'. This earned the officials a reprimand from the Privy Council and an order to attend the services.[68] The reprimand came on 26 August 1557, the eve of the death of Thomas Banion, the last of some four to eight Bristol inhabitants to be burned as heretics during Mary's reign.[69] The conjunction of events suggests that the mayor and aldermen had attempted to dissociate themselves from the burnings.

In any case, the mayor and aldermen clearly had some disagreement with the diocesan authorities, who represented the Crown and its intrusion into the local community. The Crown's re-institution of Catholicism may very well have exacerbated religious differences within the corporate elite, particularly if conservatives in religion had been named to a local commission which superseded the justices of the peace, that is the mayor and aldermen. Banion, the last to be burned, was brought before the ecclesiastical court for condemnation on the commandment of the 'commissioners'. Whether this was the commission of the peace (virtually identical to the mayor and aldermen) or a special commission of clergy and laity for ecclesiastical affairs is unknown but it was probably the latter.[70] Without more evidence it is impossible to determine the extent to which the mayor and aldermen's disagreement with the ecclesiastical authorities focused on religion, local autonomy, or possibly potential popular disorder at the time of another burning. It can hardly be doubted that all three of these closely related issues were of great concern to the municipal authorities and were exacerbated by the Crown's changing religious policies. We do not know whether the mayor and aldermen obeyed the council's command to attend services at the cathedral, but no more burnings were reported. Matters became somewhat easier for municipal officials to manage when, at the accession of Elizabeth, Dalby and Joliffe were replaced once more by Cotterell and Carewe, whose professional flexibility had been proven.[71]

The Elizabethan Period

The appearance of two new prebendaries in 1560 showed the influence of the local elite again and this time, the influence of reformist sentiment among them.[72] Christopher Pacy (1560–90), a reformer, was made a canon on 8 February 1560. In 1544 Pacy had been instituted vicar of St Werberg, a parish in which a number of Bristol's elite reformers lived, and in 1552 he was the beneficiary of a reformist's will.[73] His sureties for the composition for first fruits were

London residents, one of whom lived in the parish of Aldermanbury, where Lollard distributors of Lutheran books also had lived.[74] At the accession of Mary, Pacy went into hiding, probably leaving Bristol. The free-lance preacher John Huntingdon claimed he and Pacy had been stalked by the authorities, who would have burned Pacy 'stump and all' had they caught him.[75] Where he spent the Marian years is unknown, but he returned to his living in Bristol soon after the accession of Elizabeth. The parishioners of St Werberg augmented the living of £10 by £2 per year.[76] By 24 July 1562, he was also rector of Olveston, a rural living in the deanery of Bristol. He may have faced some financial difficulties in 1562, for in that year he owed the parish of St Werberg £6. 5s. and sued a parishioner of Olveston for tithes.[77]

Arthur Saule (1560–*c*.1585), one of the new chapter members, also was a reformer and a native of the diocese of Bristol. A fellow and one of the extreme reformers of Oxford's Magdalen College, he probably was among those expelled in 1553. He spent the Marian period at Strasbourg and the University of Heidelberg, returning to Bristol early in Elizabeth's reign. On 2 November 1559, the Crown presented him to the prebend of Bedminster and Redcliffe in Salisbury cathedral, a post of great significance to Bristol, since it made him patron of nearby Bedminster and the local 'chapels' or parish churches of St Mary Redcliffe and St Thomas. He was instituted to a canonry in Bristol cathedral 25 January 1560. In 1563 Saule, also a prebendary of Gloucester, was proctor for the cathedral chapter and for the dean of that diocese in Convocation and was a member of the proto-Puritan 'precisian' party, which pushed for reforms. John Cotterell, who held proxies for the clergy of Bristol and of Wells, argued against the precisians' program during a fierce debate. Nevertheless he and George Carewe, dean of Bristol, were among those chosen by the lower house to present the reformist program they adopted to the upper house, probably in order to give the impression of wider support for their proposals.[78]

The reform activity of Saule and Pacy is reflected in their connection to the local puritan preacher John Northbrooke. By the late 1560s, Northbrooke was curate of St Mary Redcliffe, a 'chapel' of Bedminster, of which Saule was patron. In 1568 Northbrooke was involved in the protest against Bishop Cheyney of Gloucester, who also held the see of Bristol *in commendam*. John Calfhill, a visiting puritan preacher who also was involved in the protest, had been a precisian, along with Saule, in the Convocation of 1563.[79] Saule's support of

Northbrooke's position at St Mary Redcliffe and their mutual connection to Calfhill suggest that they shared similar reformist views and goals.

The protest against Bishop Cheyney also indicated important divisions among the secular elite, some of whom supported Northbrooke and Calfhill in their condemnation of Cheyney's preaching. The dispute centred on the issue of free will, against which Calfhill preached during Cheyney's visitation and preaching in Bristol.[80] While in Bristol, Cheyney wrote the Council, he had dealt gently with both Calfhill and with Northbrooke, who had been 'grieved against him'. Calfhill had refused his invitation to supper and to conference, and Northbrooke had repeated to Calfhill those things which Cheyney had told him privately. Calfhill had repudiated Cheyney in his own hearing, using a term new to the Bishop, 'freewilliomes'. In his initial letter, Cheyney thought their 'great causes' were free will and the eucharist. A week later, however, as his adversaries in Bristol were preparing articles to send to the Council and the High Commission, the Bishop wrote the Council that unless he was deceived, 'their chief mark that they shoot at is not freewill or such like', but rather his own defeat. The changed emphasis implied that the issue was one of authority rather than doctrine. Cheyney was convinced that 'If young and hotheads [whoteheads] shall be suffered to say and preach what they lust in matters of great weight (as no doubt certain of they do very rashly to . . . great hindrance of the gospel) there must needs issue a Babylonical confusion'. Northbrooke had continued to preach against Cheyney and was among those threatening their adversaries with action before the High Commission.

On 2 October, only five days after Cheyney's second letter to the Council, 'certain citizens of Bristol' sent a list of articles concerning Cheyney's sermons to the Council and the commissioners for matters ecclesiastical. They used the same strategy as Cheyney had used with the Council, emphasizing not only the 'strange, perilous and corrupt doctrines' which he preached but also 'the no small hazarding of the common tranquility' which his preaching threatened. The articles also accused him of supporting free will, preaching against Calvin, and advising extreme caution in interpreting and emphasizing Scripture. Obviously they thought the authorities would share their condemnation of these views.

Another article dealt with his position on the question of *adiaphora* or things indifferent. Cheyney had claimed the Protestant theologian

Peter Martyr as authority for the view that though the body is at an 'idol service', the heart can be with God and no offence or sin incurred. The latter statement undoubtedly was in response to objections to the Elizabethan Prayer Book adopted in 1559. Based on the second Edwardian Prayer Book, it represented a compromise on the communion service and retained use of clerical vestments, pictures, crucifixes, and church music. Cheyney was arguing for acceptance of the Queen's religious policy, which in the previous four years had imposed the surplice on resistant clergy in London. Those remnants of papistry which the moderates would argue were matters of indifference were to the more fervent reformists occasions of offence and sin.

Among the twenty-five Bristol men signing the letter were at least fourteen who probably were members of the Corporation: two aldermen, the two current sheriffs, four who had already served as sheriff, and seven who would take up the office over the next decade. Of these fourteen, the two aldermen had been mayor and seven others would gain the office. The list also included the Chamberlain and a schoolmaster. While these were clearly men of high standing in the city, their number in the Corporation was not sufficient to bring official censure of Cheyney, which would have required a majority vote.[81] Among the Corporation members involved were representatives of both merchant and retail interests, although the former appear to have outnumbered the latter eight to four. Among the other signers were four merchants and two retailers. Thus of twenty-five men signing the letter complaining about Cheyney's preaching at least twelve were merchants and six retailers. This is important because there was longstanding economic rivalry between these groups as merchants tried to exclude retailers from long-distance trade.[82] Attached to the letter were the articles which were signed by twelve other men. Only two of these would hold positions in local government, but others had connections to the corporate elite. They included at least three whose interests were probably with the retailers and at least two whose sympathies lay with a merchant monopoly of long-distance trade.[83] The complaint against Cheyney suggests that religion cut across lines of economic interest among the corporate elite.

Members of the corporate elite who sent their complaint about Cheyney to royal authorities represented a fervent Protestant faction in the corporation.[84] These men opposed a bishop because of religious doctrines he preached in their city. They clearly thought his doctrines would be condemned by the highest ecclesiastical authority, and thus believed themselves in the Protestant mainstream. Their views on doctrine and their opposition to Cheyney probably were shared by many others, but they were the more zealous ones, the ones compelled to act when they perceived a threat to right religion. Patrick Collinson has convincingly argued that in Elizabethan and Jacobean England puritans were integrated into the established Church, struggling to bring a reformation of religion, and that the Church was Calvinist. By this reckoning the anti-Cheyney faction in Bristol was both mainstream Protestant and puritan.[85]

The Corporation itself, always cautious and preferring to avoid interference from the Crown, took no official role. Cheyney did not represent a threat to local control, and his position was weak *vis-à-vis* Bristol, where he was not commissioned to hold spiritual power and thus had no power to discipline the laity. Although he did ordain some men to the priesthood, his visitation and preaching were apparently largely symbolic. His administration of Gloucester diocese was lax and it was not likely that he sought controversy in Bristol.[86]

Since the puritans were a minority of the corporation in 1568, they were forced to gather support from other members of the community for their complaint to the council and commission. In the next few years, the puritan minority appears to have gathered strength, for Northbrooke became the local clergy's representative to Convocation in 1571. In June of that year he and Thomas Sylke were the only clerics among the twelve governors of the newly licensed free grammar and writing school of Queen Elizabeth in St Mary Redcliffe parish. He was still curate of St Mary Redcliffe in 1574 and may have remained there even beyond 1577 when he became vicar of the nearby and wealthier rural living of Henbury.[87] Since the puritans were more aggressive than the moderate corporation members, it seems likely that they were at least trying to dominate local religious policy and the presence of Saule and Pacy in the cathedral hierarchy undoubtedly supported this attempt.

Shaping local policy, of course, was not confined to local issues. The complexity of the situation was revealed again when Pacy and Northbrooke became involved in the controversy over the descent of Christ into hell. In August 1563 testimony in the Consistory Court accused Christopher Pacy of preaching in the cathedral church that Christ's soul descended no farther than the monument where the body lay. The doctrinal description was scored through and replaced with the words 'a certain doctrine'. Pacy presumably was addressing the doctrine of Christ's descent to hell, which was being disputed in the Convocation of 1563; in the end it remained in the Thirty-nine Articles.[88] It may be that Pacy was among those attempting to change it, and later, not wanting his position known officially, had it crossed out of the court record.

In 1571, the year the Articles were finally ratified, Northbrooke defended himself in a published work against charges that he too had denied this article of the creed in a sermon at St Mary Redcliffe. Apparently having opposed the doctrine's inclusion in the creed and lost, he was careful now to make his belief in the creed explicit while still implying that it should not have been included.[89] As a representative to Convocation in 1571, Northbrooke undoubtedly subscribed to the Articles of religion, for he later became vicar of Henbury near Bristol.[90] This doctrinal conflict indicated the clergy's tendency to conform, a tendency which reflected conformity among the corporate elite; even the reformist elite would not have supported disobedience to the law.[91] Arthur Saule also had a record of support for conformity. He had encouraged it in the English congregation at Strasburg, and the long tenures of both Saule and Pacy in Bristol bear out their conformity during Elizabeth's reign.[92]

The presence of reformers Saule and Pacy and the conservative-to-moderate old professional hands Carewe, Cotterell, and Sylke in the early Elizabethan cathedral hierarchy is striking in its reflection of a secular elite who long had practised policies of pragmatic moderation while being pushed towards the religious left by reformers within their midst. (The model would hold for the nation as well.) By 1576 Cotterell and Sylke were dead and Carewe made Saule and Pacy (and Thomas Bayley) his proctors for the rule of the cathedral church.[93] In 1580 Carewe was replaced by John Sprint, the son of a Bristol apothecary of the same name who was prominent in the parish of St Ewen.[94] Saule and Pacy were dead by the end of 1590.[95]

THE LIMITED POWER AND SCOPE OF THE CLERICAL ELITE'S FUNCTIONS

While the lay elite's influence on the selection of chapter personnel helped to determine how ecclesiastical power would be exercised, there also were institutional realities which limited the power and scope of the chapter's and the ordinary's functions. Services at the cathedral did remain a focus for civic worship on certain days and on special occasions like the thanksgiving service for the defeat of the Armada.[96] By statute the dean of the chapter or his proxy was to preach at Easter, Corpus Christi Day, and Christmas, and each of the canons was responsible for four sermons per year.[97] The preaching of the dean and chapter, however, became less important when the corporation began to sponsor its own preachers in the latter part of Elizabeth's reign.[98] The lay elite also had their own grammar school at St Bartholomew, founded by 1532, which prevented the cathedral grammar school from achieving the prominence which similar ones did in other cities.[99]

The most important function of the diocesan clergy was rendered in the Consistory Court, which functioned as an agent of social control. While the cathedral chapter and diocesan authorities were technically separate, there were overlapping appointments which blurred the distinction, and a weak episcopacy furthered this process. For most of the period the Chancellor of the diocese, who was head judge of the Consistory Court, was also a canon and prebendary (Cotterell and Dalby). Early in Elizabeth's reign, Thomas Sylke and Christopher Pacy actually joined John Cotterell to hear the case of accused heretic Hugh Guillam.[100]

The Consistory Court records do not offer a complete picture of its work or its effectiveness. Except for the year 1556 the deposition records for our period are lost. There are many cases where no cause is shown, while other cases show no action or cannot be traced to completion. The court regulated some ecclesiastical activity, hearing tithe cases and cases concerning church rates, ordering the sequestration of fruits during vacancies, licensing readers and regulating curates, and (rarely) ordering repairs on church buildings and churchyards.[101] It also dealt with refusals to follow proscribed religious practices and with heresy. Will probation also figured as an important part of court business, and marriage licences were sought there.[102] Most of the cases before the court, however, dealt with defamation, marriage, and sexual behaviour, important facets of social control.

It is possible to get a sense of the effectiveness of the court as an agent of social control by examining one year's records in regard to excommunications, penances, and commutations. A total of some 112 cases can be isolated from the rest of the court's business in 1562; forty-three were from city parishes, thirteen from unnamed parishes, and fifty-five from deanery parishes outside the city.[103] Given the number of excommunications for matters such as non-appearance when cited, non-certification of having done the prescribed penance, and failure to render account, it appears that those living within the city were slightly more likely to disregard the court than the rural parishioners. Of the fifty-five defendants from within the city, eighteen or almost one-third were excommunicated, while only ten of sixty-two defendants (16 per cent) from deanery parishes outside the city were so penalized. Three defendants of the nineteen from unnamed parishes were found contumacious, but there is no record that they were excommunicated. From within the city only ten appear to have remained excommunicated, while only four from outside the city remained so. These fourteen represent about 10 per cent of the total 136 defendants. These figures suggest that the city dwellers were somewhat less intimidated by the court and its penalties, but that overall, few were willing to ignore it completely.

It is significant that of the forty-three cases involving city parishioners only sixteen were office cases, cases initiated by the court; one was an office case promoted by laity; and twenty-six were instance cases, cases of lay plaintiff against lay defendant. These numbers were similar in the non-city cases as well: four office and nine instance cases among those of unnamed parishes; thirteen office, eight promoted, and twenty-eight instance cases, five of which were tithe cases brought by clergy in the rural parishes. The predominance of instance cases suggests that the court was a vital part of the community rather than an imposed judicial force, a place where justice was being sought by some and resisted by others, but where most, in the end, obeyed.

Consistory Court documents record very few cases concerning religious belief and behaviour. In 1561 there were a few cases of nonattendance at church in the parish of All Saints and one in the parish of St Michael, which could have represented those from either the left or the right.[104] The same could be true of those few who were brought into court for refusing the eucharist.[105] In 1561 and 1564 there were single cases of women using rosaries (*preculis*). These were handled by the court in routine fashion.[106]

In 1564 an unusual case of religious nonconformity or heresy came before the court, an office suit brought against Hugh Guillam which demonstrated a more concerted effort by the ecclesiastical authorities.[107] It is impossible to pinpoint Guillam's heresy but part of it has the ring of Christian mortalism, a heresy concerning the nature of the soul and its fate after death.[108] Questions about the soul's fate after death had first emerged publicly in Bristol when Hugh Latimer had addressed the question of purgatory. Given that the strength of England's mortalists was among the semi-literate and illiterate poor, it is not surprising that Guillam lived in a hospice and signed his abjuration with a cross.[109]

Guillam's brand of mortalism was not only heretical but also a threat to the social order in that it eradicated the traditional sanctions supporting the Christian moral system. His comparison of the soul to the light of the candle paralleled the thetnopsychist branch of mortalism which believed in the reliance of the 'soul', an insubstantial 'breath of life', on the body. Those among them who believed in the resurrection of the body could also be called 'soul sleepers', but Guillam's response that the rising of the body was a 'strange matter' suggests he did not share this belief. He seems rather to have belonged to the most radical element among the mortalists, the 'annihilationists'. The soul, or at least the personal soul, dissolved with the body. Thus there was no personal judgment in the afterlife. Heaven was to be enjoyed in this world, if at all.

This threat to the social order was intensified by Guillam's apparent denial of the Old Testament, that is, the Mosaic law, which was the foundation of Christian morality. The antinomian connotations in these views had long been associated with religious radicalism and thus were anathema to both moderate and puritan Protestants.[110] That additional officials appeared during Guillam's hearing in the ecclesiastical court indicates the seriousness with which they regarded the case, which represented a challenge to the established order. There is, however, nothing to link him to other religious radicals in Bristol. The only other evidence of religious radicalism in the city during the 1560s is a local calendarist's account of trouble stirred up by apprentices over the christening of a child. The gathering of armed inhabitants in the marsh was pacified by Mr Chester, a pointmaker, and his company and thus echoed the Wishart episode of 1539. While this uproar and Guillam's case seem superficially unrelated, both underlined the difficulty of enforcing uniformity in a city with a strong reformist tradition which sometimes intertwined with economic disjuncture.[111]

While the Consistory Court played a consistent, important, and largely independent role, in a few instances its authority was superseded by that of local secular officials.[112] In both 1560 and 1562 cases of defamation were moved from the ecclesiastical court to the mayor or the 'mayor and justices' for determination. The earlier case involved defendants who were excommunicated for non-appearance and then absolved. The defendant's proctor then informed the court that the case was closed, having been determined by the mayor and justices by consent. After consideration and after the plaintiff's refusal to appear again, the judge dismissed the suit. This case suggests that on occasion the jurisdiction of the mayor and justices supplanted that of the Consistory Court in cases not related to religion, and it indicates a reluctance on the part of the ecclesiastical judges to challenge secular jurisdiction. Still the Corporation needed the co-operation of a loyal and effective ecclesiastical authority, and it is unlikely to have provoked unnecessary conflict with these ecclesiastical officials who represented the Crown. A balance of power existed that was better left untested.

THE RELATIONSHIP OF THE CLERICAL ELITE TO THE PARISH CLERGY

Another important function of the diocesan elite was the regulation of the lower clergy. Their power over the parochial clergy not only promoted religious consonance in the city's pulpits but also separated the clerical elite from the rest of the clergy. The diocesan authorities collected clerical taxes, regulated pluralism and heard tithe cases in the Consistory Court. As we indicated in Chapter 6, these were matters of importance to the parish clergy, whose incomes were declining throughout the period. The authorities were not very successful as tax collectors, but did regulate the pluralism of parish curates. Tithe cases, of course, became largely matters of laity against laity and in the few cases where the clergy sued, the court's decisions are not extant. This function did, in any case, place the diocesan clergy in a position of power over the parish clergy.

It was also to the ecclesiastical court that suits concerning clerical behaviour were brought. In 1562 an office case was brought against the curate of Sts Philip and Jacob, John Edwardes. Twelve persons swore that he was a drunkard, 'a comon al[ehouse] h[a]unter, a gamester, and a swerer'. He denied the charge but failed in his purgation, which required the favourable testimony of four clerics and four parishioners. He was forbidden to serve in the diocese.[113] In 1564 Edward Butt, a cleric apparently of the parish of All Saints, was more fortunate in his purgation, and he was freed from jail and bonds.[114] In that same year the authorities brought Bartholomew Phillips, the curate of St James, into court, requiring that he prove his marriage.[115] Two clerics who appeared in court were schoolmasters in the parish of St Mary Redcliffe. John Austen had to prove in 1560 that he had received absolution and been released from the excommunication which had been given him by the Bishop of Salisbury.[116] In 1564 James Hylman was suspended from the administration of sacred rites and from the education of boys in the city because he had spoken defamatory and libellous words against preachers of the word.[117]

The diocesan authorities also came into conflict with parochial clergy on the issue of preaching, for which a licence was required during most of the period. In 1560 an office case was brought against the vicar of St Nicholas, John Rastell, and Thomas Tewe, the curate of St Thomas, for allowing John Figge, the vicar of Calne, to publicly preach in their churches without inspecting or requiring his license. They were admonished not to repeat this infraction.[118] On 5 December 1561, the court ordered Robert Fortune or Warten, the curate of Redcliffe, not to preach outside his cure and to bring in his letters of orders 'by Sunday week'. On the following 28 February the judge inhibited Fortune from further preaching within the diocese and within the province of Canterbury. It appears that Fortune had been given a licence by the Bishop of Norwich, and the Bristol authorities refused to recognize it or to give him another one.[119] Almost three years later, on 2 December 1564, the court ordered the church-wardens of Redcliffe not to allow unlicensed preaching in the church.[120] Earlier in that same year David Marten the curate of St Nicholas was the subject of an office case. Marten denied having preached in his parish church without a licence, and he was ordered to bring in the written sermons which he had delivered. He returned with a book of comments (*postillae*) by one Richard Taverner and alleged that he had preached nothing beyond what was contained in the book. The judge ordered him henceforth not to engage in the exposition of the gospels.[121]

The regulatory function of the Consistory Court and the close connection of the cathedral chapter with it created a division between the city's clerical elite and its parish clergy. This division was heightened by the wide differences in the educational qualifications and the preferments of the two groups. We have shown in Chapter 6 how the qualifications of the parish clergy declined during the Reformation decades and how pluralism by the end of the period was largely a matter of making ends meet. This contrasted with the qualifications of the cathedral prebendaries, which remained uniformly high, and with their many preferments. All of the twenty-four prebendaries in office between 1542 and 1584 were university graduates. Indeed only three were limited to a single degree. Five had studied law; four, theology; and the rest held degrees in the arts only. Roger Edgeworth held a doctorate in theology, while John Cotterell was a doctor of canon law. Most of the men (thirteen) received their degrees from Oxford, but there were four Cambridge students. Two others received degrees from both universities. The universities of five men are unknown. As was very common in the clerical hierarchy, all the men for which information is available were pluralists, twelve holding prebends in other cathedrals as well as various parochial livings. Eleven held offices such as dean, precentor, chancellor, or treasurer in other cathedral chapters; four were archdeacons and one a vicar general in other dioceses.[122]

It seems certain that Bristol's five deans were graduates, although there is no extant evidence of the attendance of John Whitheare (1550–2) at either university. William Snow (B.Th., 1542–50), George Carewe (BA; 1552–4 and 1559–80), and John Sprint (BA, MA, B.Th., D.Th., 1580–90) were graduates of Oxford, while Henry Jolyffe (BA, MA, B.Th., 1554–9) was a Cambridge graduate. Carewe probably received his MA and D.Th. degrees abroad. At least three of the deans held preferments in other cathedrals as well. Carewe held many, including prebends and chapter offices at Wells, Salisbury, and Exeter. Jolyffe remained a prebendary of Worcester, while Sprint was a prebendary of Salisbury and treasurer of the chapter there in 1584. Snow held several parish livings in Salisbury diocese but was not a member of any other cathedral chapter. Of Whitheare's preferments nothing is known.[123] The educational attainments of the cathedral clerical elite were unremarkable in a national context. But in our urban context, it is clear that their education separated them from the parish clergy. This was quite different from the situation in pre-Reformation Bristol.

There are no precise measurements by which to compare the new clerical elite with the old, but some differences are clear. The power and independence of the pre-Reformation clerical elite were based upon the existence of institutions which did not depend upon lay approval. Even some parish clergy among the old elite had benefices elsewhere on which they could depend, as well as tenure and the legal right to tithes. As we have shown, the institutional weakness of the new diocese was a severe limitation on the new clerical elite's independence from the secular elite. Both old and new clerical groups were characterized by superior education and economic resources. However, communal institutions existing before 1540 and the educational qualifications and tenure of the beneficed parish clergy before the Reformation prevented a great gulf between the clerical elite and the rest of the city's clergy. Moreover the diversity of the city's late medieval ecclesiastical institutions meant that ecclesiastical power was not centralized. Ironically the concentration of ecclesiastical power in the cathedral chapter and the ecclesiastical authorities simply made its limitation by the lay elite easier. The establishment of the new diocese created and institutionalized a division between the clerical elite and the rest of the clergy and promoted the power of the elite laity, which was itself becoming a more narrowly defined group.

THE IMPACT OF CORPORATION LECTURERS

The process of centralization was carried further when the corporation established a stipend for a lecturer or preacher around 1585.[124] Although regulatory functions were left with the cathedral clergy, the responsibility for preaching given them by the cathedral charter was subverted and the dean and chapter's resistance may have been evidenced in the refusal of the parish church most closely associated with them, St Augustine-the-Less, to contribute to the rate for the preacher's stipend.[125] However, that two of the first three preachers identified were canons suggests continuing co-operation until the early Stuart years. Not until November 1605 do we have evidence of the Corporation's desire to seek a learned preacher from outside the city, Edward Chetwynd, recent DD of Oxford.[126] This may have signalled trouble between the secular and clerical elites, for only a few months later the dean and chapter were resisting the Corporation's plan to build raised seats for themselves and their wives in the cathedral. While the secular elite won both their seats and a preacher from Oxford, they lost the seats two years later when the Bishop, with the support of the dean and chapter, pulled them down. Following this, the Mayor and Council refused to continue worshipping at the cathedral (still referred to in the seventeenth century as 'the college of St Augustine') as they had traditionally done.[127]

In 1617 events took an interesting turn, although the direction is not clear. Edward Chetwynd, the preacher who came from Oxford in 1606 and who subsequently became chaplain to the Queen, became dean of the chapter in Bristol Cathedral. He remained until his death in 1639, after which he was buried in the cathedral choir.[128] Was this a coup by the Corporation? The Corporation's seats went up again in the cathedral during his term, but were a point of complaint by the chapter at Archbishop Laud's visitation of 1634. The cathedral clergy also complained of Sunday afternoon lectures at the nearby parish church of St Augustine-the-Less, attendance at which, especially with contribution, was said to distinguish the holy from the profane, 'as they term them'. We do not know if these were Corporation-sponsored, but there does seem to be a point in their occurring next door to the cathedral.[129] Regardless of the meaning of Chetwynd's later career for relations between the Corporation and the cathedral clergy, his initial employment as town preacher represented further centralization of the secular elite's power. Already the diversion of preaching into a non-ecclesiastical institution had demonstrated further the abandonment of the local church shown in the decline of bequests and stemming from the recognition that the local church was not safe from the Crown.

Between 1616 and 1631, possibly longer, the Corporation's preacher or lecturer was another local cleric, Mr William Yeamans, the vicar of Sts Philip and Jacob since 1603.[130] At first glance, this suggests something other than abandonment of the Church, but the suggestion is hardly warranted. This was an economical measure, which though it might have lent financial support to a parish incumbent, was not an investment in the local church. Yeamans was a bargain; his stipend of £25 was lower than that of any predecessor.[131] When Robert Temple, canon in the cathedral chapter, was hired as lecturer in 1586, he received £34. 13s. 4d. to deliver lectures every Tuesday and Thursday, fifty-two weeks of the year. If he were to 'make default' without good cause, 6s. 8d. would be subtracted.[132] One suspects him more likely to have defaulted on sermons due in the cathedral where his £20 stipend was based upon residence. In 1601, when the Corporation decided against the dismissal of a Mr Baxter and hired Canon John Gulliford as a second preacher, both preachers were to receive stipends of £40.[133] Chetwynde, brought down from Oxford, had received £50 annually.[134] Yemans, like the cathedral clergy earlier, was available and a known quantity. He was not totally dependent on his lectureship, and his parish living, while not great, was one of Bristol's most lucrative.[135] The Corporation did not use the lectureship to bring a preacher to a local parish; they took advantage of one already there. Moreover, they, the secular elite, henceforth undoubtedly had more influence over him than did his parishioners.

We do not know the motivation for the Corporation's creation of lectureships, but one likely reason was a desire to keep control of preaching in the city. We have seen the problems throughout the Reformation which preaching presented for the local government. In the first decade of Elizabeth's reign, the presence of unlicensed preachers in some parishes suggests that parishes were finding the resources to afford preaching even though most of the livings were vacant; these sermons, of course, did not always accord with the authorities' views of appropriate preaching.[136] If this continued, the Corporation may have been more interested in control than in edification. By taxing inhabitants to pay the city's lecturers, the local government took resources from individual parishes which could have been used to afford the preaching of the vestry's choice. Thus the creation of Corporation lectureships not only ultimately removed power from the elite clergy of the diocese but also from the elite laity of the parishes.

Nor were the sermons an attempt to provide preaching for all the city's inhabitants. The earliest known lecturer, Arthur Temple, was to preach in the parish church of St Nicholas; by 1616 the sermons were occurring in the parish church of St Werberg.[137] The Mayor, Aldermen and Councillors with their wives would have left some room for others in these parish churches, but not much; these sermons were intended for the city's secular elite, not the general populace, nor even all the parish elites. And how did the parishioners and parish clergy respond to the creation of a Corporation preacher who drew on their resources but provided nothing for the parish? Resistance was evidenced in the refusal of some to contribute or pay the rate towards the preacher's stipend. Lists of parish payments extant for the years 1585, 1586, 1598 and 1599 show that initial resistance came from six of the city's 18 parishes. In 1586, two of these contributed, but three others did not.[138] Most of these parishes had incumbents or long-term curates. Roger Rise must have been in his prime at St John; Richard Arthur, embroiled in conflict over the living of St Ewen in 1579, was installed at St Mary-le-Porte, probably as curate. Thomas Colman was vicar of Sts Philip and Jacob, where he would remain until his death in 1603 or 1604. Richard Martin was vicar of Temple, where he, too, would remain for some years. In the parish of St Thomas, John Tewe, curate since 1558 and still in 1583, may have led opposition.[139] That these beleaguered parish clergy would have resisted the withdrawal of parish resources for the support of the Corporation's preacher can hardly be doubted. Their resistance would have meant little, of course, without their parishioners' agreement. Other parishes that failed to contribute in 1585 were St Michael and St James, both outlying parishes, and St Augustine-the-Less, closely associated with the cathedral chapter. Only three however, St Michael, St Augustine, and Sts Philip and Jacob, are absent from all four extant lists, while St Mary Redcliffe, after appearing on the initial list of contributors, made no further contribution either. Undoubtedly this reflected the tradition of preaching there in Bristol's largest and finest parish church and quite possibly in the other three as well. Resistance, however, went beyond refusal to pay. Complaints reached London, and in 1593 the Privy Council ordered the municipal government to make an assessment on all 'inhabitants of ability' to support the parish clergy, especially the preachers, because the livings were so poor. There is no evidence, however, that the Corporation co-operated.[140]

There are many questions about the precise shape of the Corporation's domination of preaching and of ecclesiastical institutions in Bristol by the end of Elizabeth's reign, but there is no doubt that it existed. Even canons who became city lecturers were kept on a tight leash, with stipend closely connected to performance. Through this new institution the Corporation attempted to take preaching out of the hands of the cathedral clerical elite and parish vestries and clergy, sparking resistance with institutional and possibly religious roots. Thus the growth of a new clerical elite in the cathedral following the destruction of the pre-Reformation clerical elite did not signal an ecclesiastical renaissance. Rather, they and the new city lecturers were elements in the centralization of power by the secular elite. The cathedral chapter and the Corporation's preachers (sometimes in tandem, sometimes at odds) were conduits for maintaining order and the Corporation's authority, tools by which the city's lay elite could attempt to bring the city, both lay and clerical, more tightly under its control.

8

Conclusion

THE clergy of Bristol suffered a crisis during the first forty years of the Reformation. Between 1530 and 1570 the complex medieval community was transformed into a simple configuration comprising the cathedral elite and the clergy of the parishes. Economic, institutional, and religious change contributed to the development of clerical competition and fragmentation, the decline of clerical independence, and the growth of lay control. It should be emphasized that while the Reformation certainly contributed to the crisis, structural factors would have weakened the clergy in any case. Given the city's poor, cash-dependent livings and the period's inflation, as well as the dependence of religious houses and chantries on declining rents, a crisis of lesser dimensions would have occurred even without the institutional changes promulgated by the Crown, the tumult of popular religious conflict, or the Protestant redefinition of the clerical role. Without the institutional and ideological changes wrought by the Reformation, however, the clerical decline would have been less dramatic, less significant, and perhaps more open to remedy.

The 1530s were critical years for the clergy in Bristol. They made a powerful and organized response to Latimer and the Corporation, whose actions they rightly considered a local manifestation of the Crown's attack on the national Church. An alliance between leaders of religious houses, parish clergy, and diocesan authorities fought their attackers and created a wave of religious conflict in the city. If this was their last hurrah, it was nevertheless extremely significant because it demonstrated an organized clerical movement which possibly could have made itself felt on a broader scale. The failure of the movement to include all the city's clergy and stand firm in the face of tremendous political pressure from national and local authorities does not dilute the significance of the attempt.

The city's clerical community was represented in this alliance, which included clergy from various ecclesiastical institutions, and the Corporation's response showed that they took this community very seriously. Not all the city's clergy joined the clerical alliance, however, and this suggests, apart from religious considerations, that clerical loyalty was divided between Church and city. It was the latter loyalty, whether motivated by love or by fear, that made the Corporation's victory possible. Had the clergy revolted *en masse* they doubtless would have carried more of the populace with them, and the Corporation might have been forced to back away from their support of Latimer, in spite of his being a favourite at court. Thus, while the Latimer affair demonstrated the existence of a far from impotent clerical community, the episode also showed that the community had difficulty maintaining its unity under pressure and therefore could not achieve a collective clerical victory. Thereafter clerical protests were rendered individually rather than collectively, except when clerics joined like-minded laity to harass each other. What power they might have had as a group, what support they might have offered each other, was dissolved in the Latimer episode.

By the end of the decade this dissolution of power was ensured for the long term by the destruction of the city's religious houses, institutions which largely had provided the economic and political base for the clerical action of 1533. The foundation of the diocese of Bristol in 1542 created what could conceivably have been a new power base for a new clerical elite. As we have shown, however, the see was so weak economically and politically that the well-educated and relatively well-to-do diocesan clergy were forced to rely on the support of the local lay elite, except during Mary's reign. A split between the 'professional' and 'puritan' prebendaries during the first decade of Elizabeth's reign may also have diminished their ability to exercise collective power in their own behalf, much less in behalf of the rest of the city's clergy. Indeed, their vulnerability to the lay elite made them instruments for controlling the non-elite clergy and laity.

Except for the dissolution of the chantries and the confiscation of church goods, the parish church structure did not experience institutional alteration at the hands of the Crown. These, however, brought no small changes. The appearance of ex-chantry priests in the clerical job market and their absence from the parish churches contributed to the clerical crisis. Parish incumbents were left to deal with a lack of assistance and to preside over churches whose leaner liturgies must have reduced clerical status among the city's inhabitants.

The condition of the remaining parish clergy also changed dramatically in other ways. Parish livings, which were not wealthy to begin with, were largely dependent upon personal tithes and thus did not keep up with inflation. This circumstance probably contributed to the declining educational quality among parish incumbents and finally, to the many extended vacancies which had begun by the accession of Elizabeth. That most of the parishes had stipendiary curates or regular readers suggests that financial considerations, rather than poor clerical recruitment *per se*, may have been responsible for the vacancies. In addition the fact that parish sequestration of tithes placed the untenured parish curates under the control of parochial laity cannot be ignored. In just a few decades the well-to-to, well-educated parish incumbents, whose parishioners had legal obligations in regard to tithes, were reduced to untenured, stipendiary clergy wholly dependent for their wages on the laity they served. The possibility, moreover, that diocesan authorities might protect the local clergy from the power of the local laity, as had happened to some extent in 1533, no longer existed. Clerical loyalty of necessity now lay with the laity rather than with each other. Institutional change, some of which emanated from the magisterial Reformation and some of which was structural, gutted the church of Bristol and left the clergy firmly under the domination of local laity at both the city and the parish levels.

Institutional change also contributed to clerical rivalry. The eradication of religious houses and chantries helped to create a competitive environment as individuals struggled for a livelihood. Funeral practices, which reflected religious belief and official policies, also contributed to shrinking clerical employment and income, as the single preacher replaced the clerical contingents which traditionally attended to pray for the deceased. In the early 1540s Edgeworth, admittedly not an unbiased observer, was already commenting on the development of competitiveness among the clergy over opportunities to preach at funerals or to preach endowed sermons. Despite Edgeworth's interest in demeaning reformist clergy, it is likely that there was truth in what he said. If some ex-religious were unable to preach, pensionless friars and parish incumbents, whose resources were shrinking under the impact of inflation, were doubtless eager to supplement their incomes with sermons. The opportunities for preaching in a large city like Bristol, moreover, attracted able preachers, probably motivated by economic as well as religious concerns, to compete with the resident clergy.

Clerical rivalry and the concomitant growth of lay domination also gained force from religious conflict. With declining institutional support for clerical power, the clergy, regardless of their religious views, were forced to ally with lay groups in order to survive the religious tumult. Given the views of the left, the right, and the middle, the clergy could not avoid criticism from one group or the other. It was important, therefore, to be allied with some laity, even if that meant fighting with others. Roger Edgeworth essentially was asking for lay support for conservative clerics even as he attacked the reformist clergy who joined lay reformers in their harassment of conservatives. And although Edgeworth portrayed the harassment as going one way, we know that the conservative John Kene was capable of haranguing his reform-minded parishioners and that he, like Edgeworth, unleashed his tongue against reformist clergy as well. Religious conflict had the twofold effect of setting the clergy against each other and of making them dependent on the laity. The clergy became fragmented along ideological lines.

Apart from the religious conflict, Protestant theology itself reduced the power of the clergy by its redefinition of transubstantiation, and its emphasis on the role of the individual layperson in salvation. No longer were the laity totally dependent upon their priests. The minister, who was expected to preach and to teach his congregation, was more dependent on the laity. Whereas traditionally every priest, by virtue of his office, could be equally effective in mediating between God and sinners through the sacraments, the reformist view would rank clergy on how well they presented the Word to their hearers. The Protestant redefinition of the clerical role implied clerical competition for lay approval.

Thus institutional and religious change combined with intense religious conflict during the Reformation to isolate Bristol's clergy from each other, even to set them working against each other, while placing them firmly under lay control. This atomization of the clergy occurred, paradoxically, in the context of lay-dominated ecclesiastical centralization. The new diocese established a clerical elite in the cathedral, who were dominated by the governing laity. Later in the century this centralization went further with the creation of Corporation preachers. If the problems which the pulpit first raised for the Corporation in the 1530s were solved only partially by the dissolution of the religious houses, the creation of a local diocese, and the gutting of parish livings, the Corporation went even further in the late sixteenth century by taking the financing and selection of preachers into their own hands. If the hire of some canons as town preachers suggested co-operation between Corporation and cathedral, it was nevertheless a relationship between employer and employee. And even that balance was lost, it seems, when the Corporation asserted even further control over preaching and over the cathedral clergy in the early seventeenth century.

Bristol's clerical crisis had culminated in the transformation of a complex, competent, and independent clerical community into a simple construction containing an elite clerical nucleus and an impoverished, uneducated, and fragmented clerical periphery, both lay dominated. Nor was the crisis resolved. The church was left bereft; resources and religious impulses were largely channelled in other directions. Still the Church remained, a weak but living reminder of what had been and what could be, a reminder of a time when community meant diversity, when the Church had been crucial to that sense of community, and when this diversity and the Church itself had threatened local autonomy and the authority of the local governing elite. The remaining configuration of cathedral and parish churches weakly contradicted the new reality of a city dominated by a narrowed lay elite. Should the church be revived through the growth of an educated parish clergy, a more independent clerical elite, and the support of the Crown, the contradiction would intensify. But this is a story for another book. Ours is the story of a changing concept of community, of ecclesiastical disintegration and decline, of crisis left unresolved.

Appendix 1

Parish Clergy and the Religious

ALCOCKE, EDWARD. Curate, St James, 26 Apr. 1540; Dean of Gloucester, ordered to inquire into pollution of church and cemetery of Erlington, Worc. diocese, 15 Jan. 1535 (H&WRO, 802 BA 2764, fo. 270; 716–093 BA 2648, Reg. Ghinucci, fo. 34ᵛ).

ALLRED, JOHN. Priest, apparently of St Mary-le-Porte, 1556; involved in probate dispute over goods of Thomas Hanson, rector of St Stephen (BAO, EP/J/1/1, p. 137).

APPLEBEE, JOHN. Priest, curate, St Mary-le-Porte, 1558 (Churchwardens' accts. transcribed in *Hockaday Abstracts*, vol. 442; PRO, PCC, Noodes, 32 (Robert Correy; proved 5 July 1558)).

ARONDTE, ROBERT. Chantry priest, St Stephen, 1534 (H&WRO, 802 BA 2764, fo. 99).

ARTHUR, RICHARD. Minister, St Ewen, 1577–8; rector, St Ewen, Instituted 4 Apr. 1579, removed 1 Oct. 1579 (Masters and Ralph (eds.), *Church Book of St Ewen's*, 234, 237, 258–9; Lambeth, Reg. Grindal, fo. 309, transcribed in *Hockaday Collection*, 9 (4), from Bristol Cathedral Library, fo. 133, exhibition of institution to the visiting ordinary; see Chapter 6 n. 7). Curate St Mary-le-Porte, 1583, 1593; witnessed will of St Peter parish, 1596 (Nicholls and Taylor, *Bristol, Past and Present*, ii. 227; McGrath and Williams, *Bristol Wills*, i. 76, ii. 81).

ATENS, WALTER. Died by 1531 when replaced as rector of St John the Baptist by Thomas Tasker (H&WRO, 716–093 BA 2648, Reg. Ghinucci, fo. 14ᵛ).

ATWELL (ATWALL), THOMAS. Priest, probably of St Mary Redcliffe; paid trustees of Canynges Chantry in St Mary Redcliffe 6s. 8d. for a chamber, 1528; paid for a 'Tucking girdle' for the priest, 1d., 1534 (E. Williams, *Chantries of William Canynges*, 241, 244). Priest, apparently of St Mary Redcliffe, 1535 (Weaver (ed.), *Wells Wills*, 21, 28).

AUSTEN, JOHN. Status unclear. Paid year's wages of £6 by trustees of Canynges's Chantry in St Mary Redcliffe; undated account prior to 1548 (E. Williams, *Chantries of William Canynges*, 252) (not titled 'sir' as was customary for priests). Also appears in Churchwardens' Accounts of St Mary Redcliffe 1557; teacher of children, 1559, 1560. In trouble in Bristol Consistory Court, 1560, where appears to be both minister and teacher (see Chapter 7, p. 143). Probably Oxford scholar in Oct. 1534; fellow, admitted 1538; vacated 1545–6;

BA, admitted 18 Feb. 1538; MA Mar. 1542 (*BRUO 1501–1540*, 17–18).

BACHELLER, —— Curate, All Saints, 1556, 1557 (PRO, E 179/6/12 and 6/ 10). Possibly attended or took a degree from Oxford (*BRUO 1501–1540*, 19; Foster, i. 52).

BALE, WALTER. Priest, Frampton's Chantry, St John the Baptist, 1534; vacated by 4 July 1545 (H&WRO, 802 BA 2764, fo. 100; PRO, E 334/3, fo. 60).

BARNE, OLIVER. Stipendiary, St Mary-le-Porte, 26 Apr. 1540 (H&WRO, 802 BA 2764, fo. 272). Clerk, St Mary-le-Porte, 27 July 1545 (PRO, PCC, Alen, 5 (Richard Abyndon; 17 July 1545; 23 Feb. 1546)). (See also OLIVER BROWNE.)

BARRET, THOMAS. Stipendiary, All Saints., Jan. 1541 (H&WRO, 802 BA 2764, fo. 193). Possibly Oxford BA (Foster, i. 78).

BARVEY (BARREY), PHILIP. Priest, Blankettes Chantry, St Stephen, at dissolution 1548 (age 52) (Maclean, 'Chantry Certificates', 243); not on pension list 1552 (Baskerville, 'Dispossessed Religious of Gloucestershire', 106); on pension list, 1555 (Taylor, 'Religious Houses of Bristol', 121).

BARWICKE, RICHARD. Vicar, Temple, 8 Apr. 1571 (McGrath and Williams, *Bristol Wills*, i. 7). Possibly attended Cambridge (Venn, i. 102).

BECHE, JOHN. Clerk of St Thomas, 1527, and of Canynges' Chantry, St Mary Redcliffe, 1534; paid by All Saints for pricking mass and song books, etc., 1525, 1527, 1528; witnessed will, St Mary Redcliffe, 1530; overseer will of Edmonde Dauncer, priest (which see herein), 1535 (BAO, AS/ChW/under dates; E. Williams, *Chantries of William Canynges*, 248; Weaver (ed.), *Wells Wills*, 18, 21).

BEDE (BOODE, READE), THOMAS. Ordained subdeacon 21 Sept. 1521; deacon 14 June 1522, both at Chapel of Virgin Mary, Wells, to title of canon of monastery of Keynsham, order of St Augustine (SRO, D/D/B Reg. 11/ Wolsey, B&W, fos. 28 and 29). Stipendiary, Sts Philip and Jacob, 26 Apr. 1540 (when ordered to exhibit letters of ordination on morrow of St Michael), 6 Oct. 1540, Jan. 1541 (H&WRO, 802 BA 2764, fos. 270 and 193; PRO, PCC, Allenger, 21 (John White; 6 Oct. 1540; 21 Jan. 1541)). Priest, Kemys Chantry, Sts Philip and Jacob, at dissolution 1548 (as Thomas Boode, age 40) where reported he was already receiving a pension of £5. 6s. 8d. (Maclean, 'Chantry Certificates', 236). Curate, Sts Philip and Jacob, 1552 (Thomas Beede) (Wadley, *Notes*, 188). Pension lists 1552 (Thomas Boode, appeared before the commission); 1555 (Thomas Reade, Kemys Chantry) (Baskerville, 'Dispossessed Religious of Gloucestershire', 105; Taylor, 'Religious Houses of Bristol', 122). (See also THOMAS GREADE and THOMAS READE.)

BELEY (BULLE), ALEXANDER. Stipendiary, St Nicholas (Bulle), Jan. 1541; stipendiary, St Leonard (Beley), also Jan. 1541 (H&WRO, 802 BA 2764, fos. 193, 269, 270). Monk, Tewkesbury (Beley), at dissolution 9 Jan. 1540; could have been at St James, Bristol, earlier (Baskerville, 'Dispossessed Religious of Gloucestershire', 85).

BELLYNGER, THOMAS. Stipendiary, St Ewen, 26 Apr. 1540, Jan. 1541 (H&WRO, 802 BA 2764, fos. 193, 272). Probably attended Eton and Cambridge; of Bristol; age 18 on 16 Apr. 1509 (Venn, i. 130).

BENET, ROBERT. Brother, Hospital of St Mark, 11 Sept. 1534 (*LP* vii. 1216). Possible Oxford B.Th. (sup. 8 July 1523); D.Th. (sup. 22 Nov. 1527) (Foster i. 107).

BENET, WILLIAM. Clerk, signed certificate of preaching of Powell and Hubberdyne, 5 June 1533; priest, Spicer's Chantry, St Nicholas, instituted 5 Dec. 1533, deprived 14 Oct. 1539 (*LP* v. 596; H&WRO, 716–093 BA 2648, Reg. Ghinucci, fo. 62; Reg. Bell, fo. 3). Possibly 'Mstr Benett, priest' who witnessed will of David Hutton (PRO, PCC, Hogen, 30 (27 Oct. 1535; 13 Mar. 1536). Chaplain to Bishop Latimer of Worcester (*LP* x. 1099). *Same name*, doctor of laws, Salisbury diocese, an auditor of the Cardinal Archbishop of York; advisor in the election of heads of several religious houses in B&W diocese, 1523, 1524 (*Regs. B&W*, nos. 473, 474, 479). BCL, Oxford, admitted 18 Feb. 1528 (*BRUO 1501–1540*, 43); possibly DCL (see above). *Same name* instituted Axbridge, B&W diocese, 25 Sept. 1560; incumbent, Warminster, Salisbury dioc., 27 Oct. 1539 to 1554, restored at accession of Elizabeth (Field, *Province of Canterbury*, 14 and 265).

BERRY, WILLIAM. Stipendiary, St Mary Redcliffe, 1557 (St Mary Redcliffe Parish Archive, ChW Accts, 1557).

BEST, THOMAS. Priest, Bristol, 1531 (Weaver (ed.), *Somerset Medieval Wills*, 10–11). Stipendiary, St Mary Redcliffe, 1559 (St Mary Redcliffe Parish Archive, ChW Accts, 1559). *Same name*, Rector of Coates, deanery of Cirencester by 1540; d. 1557 (Geoffrey Baskerville, 'Elections to Convocation in the Diocese of Gloucester under Bishop Hooper', *EHR* 44 (1928), 24); also BA, Oxford, admitted 26 June 1515; determined 1516; sup. for MA 9 Apr. 1519; in priest's orders by 1519; MA by 1526; vicar of Sandford St Martin, Oxon.; vacated by Dec. 1526 (*BRUO 1501–1540*, 47).

BETTY, RICHARD. Overseer of will, St Thomas, 1535 (*Wells Wills*, 28); minor canon, Bristol Cathedral, 1550, 1554, 1561 (BAO, DC/A/9/1/1, fos. 4, 5, 42; instituted Ilmyster, B&W diocese, 1554 (*Regs. B&W*, no. 697). Clerk delegate of John Cotterell, vicar general, Bristol diocese, 8 Jan. 1560 (BAO, EP/J/1/5, p.7).

BLAKE, JOHN. Reader, St Thomas, 29 May 1561; 2 Dec. 1564 (BAO, EP/J/1/5, p. 212, EP/J/1/6, p. 93.

BOWER (BONER, BOUER, BOWRE, BOURNE), WALTER (WILLIAM). Priest, Eborard le French's Chantry, St Mary Redcliffe; composition for first fruits 18 Sept. 1543; at dissolution 1548 (age 33) (PRO, E 334/2, fo. 80; Maclean, 'Chantry Certificates', 238). The composition shows his sureties as Robert Boner, innholder of Bristol, and John More parish of St John in Walbroke, London, shoemaker. Priest, Foster's Service, St Werberg, at dissolution 1548 (age 33) (Maclean, 'Chantry Certificates', 232). Still receiving pensions, 1552

(Bonor) (did not appear before pension commission; curate of Hennocke, Devon); 1555 (Baskerville, 'Dispossessed Religious of Gloucestershire', 117; Taylor, 'Religious Houses of Bristol', 122, 126). Son of Edmund Bower of Wiltshire. Oxford, Magdalen College, fellow, admitted 26 July 1542; BA (admitted 8 Nov. 1542); MA by 1547. Ordained acolyte 4 June 1547; subdeacon, 17 Dec. 1547; deacon 31 Mar. 1548 (in Oxford dioc.); priest, 26 May 1548 (in Salisbury dioc.); expelled from Magdalen College 1553 at Bp. Gardiner's visitation. Rector, Farmborough, Som., 1559, until death; rector Long Bredy, Dorset, presented 23 Dec. 1561; vacated by 1578; canon of Wells and prebendary of Henstridge, by 1562, until death; rector, Nympsfield, Gloucs., presented 9 Feb. 1566 (*BRUO 1501–1540*, 63). Bristol Cathedral Grammar School, assistant teacher (*hipodidascqulus*) 1561; teacher (*preceptoris*), 1570 (BAO, DC/A/9/1/2 Computa, under date). Supporter of puritanical party in Lower House of Convocation, Feb. 1563 (Strype, *Annals*, i. 502, 204, 512). Died 1580 (PRO, PCC, Arundell, 32 (18 July 1530; 23 Aug. 1580)). Walter Bower instituted Baghurst, Winchester diocese, 14 Oct. 1558, resigned by 18 Jan. 1559, to take up Long Bredy, Dorset, 30 Jan. 1561; composition for first fruits and instituted Nympsfield, Glos. diocese, 9 Feb. 1566; d. 1580 (Field, *Province of Canterbury*, 126, 284).

BOYCE, RICHARD. Rector, St Mary-le-Porte, 1534, 1535 (H&WRO, 802 BA 2764, fos. 99–100; 716–093 BA 2648, Reg. Ghinucci, fo. 36ʳ). Possibly Oxford, attended or BA (Foster, i. 160, 163).

BRADLEY, JOHN. Priest (*socius*) of Westbury College, 1534, 1535 (H&WRO, 802 BA 2764, fo. 101; *Valor ecclesiasticus*, ii. 435). Priest, Canynges Chantry, St Mary Redcliffe, 1538, at dissolution 1548 (age 58); received £5 for three quarters' wages and 25s. for another quarter and received 15d. for bread and wine at his altar (undated) (*Hockaday Abstracts*, vol. 443, transcript of lease from Calendar of muniments of Berkeley Castle, p. 210; Maclean, 'Chantry Certificates', 245; E. Williams, *Canynges Chantries*, 252). Priest, free chapel of Knoll in Bedminster parish, instituted 18 Apr. 1547; 1548 (*Reg. B&W*, no. 650; Emanuel Green (ed.), *The Survey and Rental of the Chantries, Colleges and Free Chapels . . . of Somerset* (Somerset Record Society, 2, 1988), 91). Collecting pension, 1552; of parish of Westbury, Gloucestershire (Baskerville, 'Dispossessed Religious of Gloucestershire', 117); pension list, 1555 (Taylor, 'Religious Houses of Bristol', 121). Given an octavo volume in Latin, written in the fifteenth century in England: 'An exhortation to virtuous living', and 'Albertus Magnus de virtutibus animae', by John Colman 'Magister domus le Gauntes juxta Bristolliam' (T. W. Williams, 'Gloucestershire Medieval Libraries', 85.)

BRISTOW, THOMAS. Monk, Tewkesbury, at dissolution Jan. 1540; priest, Fraternity of St John the Baptist, the Company of the Tailors, St Ewen, at surrender 1548, (age 58); perhaps Lady Priest of Cheltenham, at dissolution 1548 (age 58) (Maclean, 'Chantry Certificates', 248; Baskerville, 'Dispossessed

Religious of Gloucestershire', 116). Perhaps *alias* Ball, rector, Great Witcombe, 1550–62 (Baskerville, ibid. 85).

BROMFIELD (BROMFELDE), RICHARD. Vicar, All Saints, admitted 3 July 1503; re-admitted Nov. 1513; vacated 1517 (H&WRO, 716–093 BA 2648, Reg. S. Gigli, fos. 26, 105ᵛ,124ᵛ). Master, Hospital of St John, admitted 22 July 1513 (Henry Maxwell-Lyte (ed.), *The Register of Oliver King, Bishop of Bath and Wells, 1496–1503, and Hadrian de Castello, Bishop of Bath and Wells, 1503–1518* (London: SRS, 54, 1939), no. 163); still 1522, 1528, 1530, 1535, and at surrender, 1544 (PRO, PCC, Porche, 23 (Henry Kemys; 1 Oct. 1522; 7 Feb. 1529); PCC Porche, 39 (Elyn Kemys, dated 12 Sept. 1528); Weaver, *Wells Wills*, 18; *LP* ix. 1025 and xix. pt. 1, 157). *Communa* paid on proceeding MA or to other higher degree 1485–6; to be distinguished from another of same name (*BRUC*, 96). Nicholas Thorne, merchant of Bristol, asked Cromwell to direct RB to deliver timber for rebuilding ship, 28 Dec. 1535 (*LP* ix. 1025).

BROMLEY, RICHARD. Curate, St James, 1534; witnessed will of Morgan Gwilliams (PRO, PCC, Pynning, 8 (20 Mar. 1544; 30 May 1544)), who was former abbot of St Augustine's, Bristol, and then parson of Yaverland, Isle of Wight (H&WRO, 802 BA 2764, fo. 100; Baskerville, 'Some Ecclesiastical Wills', *Trans. B&GAS* 52 (1930), 284). *Same name*, instituted Brede, Chichester diocese, 20 Jan. 1562; according to Field he had been ordained 16 Mar. 1526, by Thomas Parker, suffragan Bishop of Worcester; he was married and was buried at Brede in 1588 (Field, *Province of Canterbury*, 67). (See also RICHARD CARSY.)

BROWNE, OLIVER. Rector, St Lawrence, resigned by 14 Nov. 1525 (H&WRO, 716–093 BA 2648, Reg. Ghinucci, fo. 24ᵛ). (See also OLIVER BARNE.)

BROWNE, THOMAS. Stipendiary, St Werberg, 1534 (H&WRO, 802 2764, fo. 100). Possibly Oxford or Cambridge degree (*BRUO 1501–1540*, 78; Foster, i. 297; Venn, i. 237). *Same name*, Dominican friar, Worcester convent, ordained subdeacon 18 Dec. 1473; deacon 5 Mar. 1474; priest 17 Dec. 1474 (A. B. Emden, *A Survey of Dominicans in England, 1268–1538* (Rome: Istituto Storico Domenicano, Santa Sabina, Dissertationes Historicae, 1967), 211, 293).

BRYAN, MATHEW. Stipendiary, St Augustine-the-Less, 1534 (H&WRO 802 2764, fo. 100). Vicar, Portbury, B&W diocese, instituted 12 Sept. 1556 (*Regs. B&W 1518–1559*, no. 837).

BRYLERDE, THOMAS. Priest, probably stipendiary, St Augustine-the-Less, 26 Apr. 1540 (H&WRO, 802 2764, fo. 272).

BURNELL (BINNELL?), PETRIUS. Rector, St Peter, instituted 7 Dec. 1525; titled doctor in decrees (H&WRO, 716–093 BA 2648, Reg. Ghinucci, fo. 24ᵛ; *BRUC* 109). (See also successors WILLIAM MOULDER and JOHN WHITE.)

BURTON, JOHN. Vicar, St Nicholas, 1498 (Lambeth Reg. Archbp. Morton, fo. 177ᵛ, transc. in *Hockaday Accounts*, vols. 445–6, under date); instituted prior, Kalendars' Guild, 10 Apr. 1480; d. by Feb. 1499. Of London; fellow of Balliol College, Oxford, B.Th.; received only £2 of prior's salary until 1486; to

Bologna for doctor's degree, 1483; buried London; bequests of books and other goods to Kalendars' and two parish churches of which he was incumbent (Reg. John Alcock, fo. 65; Lambeth Reg. John Morton, I, fo. 185; *BRUO* 319; PRO, PCC, 37, Horne, all cited in Orme, Guild of 'Kalendars', 44, 46). *Same name*, Priest, Spycer's Chantry, St Nicholas, instituted Dec. 1526, vacated by 14 May 1528 (H&WRO, 716–093 BA 2648, Reg. Ghinucci, fos. 5^r, 28^r, 36^r).

BURTON, WILLIAM. Abbot, Abbey of St Augustine, 1533–9 (not 1537 as in *VCH Gloucester*, ii. 79; *LP* xiv. pt. 1, 333 and 1354 (39); see also *LP* vii. 4, 103 and 215). Possibly Oxford BA, admitted June 1527; determined 1528 (*BRUO 1501–1540*, 88).

BUTT, EDWARD. Convicted clerk subjected to purgation in Bristol Consistory Court, 23 Oct. 1564 (BAO, EP/J/1/6, p. 65).

BYRCHE, ELLIS. Stipendiary, St Leonard, 1534 (H&WRO, 802 2764, fo. 99).

CAPYS (CAPES), ROGER. Priest, Pollardes Chantry, St Lawrence, 1534, at dissolution 1548 (age 56) (H&WRO, 802 BA 2764, fo. 100; Maclean, 'Chantry Certificates', 232). Appeared before pension commission of 1552; still receiving pension, 1555 (Taylor, 'Religious Houses of Bristol', 125; Baskerville, 'Dispossessed Religious of Bristol', 107).

CARDMAKER, JOHN (alias TAYLER). Franciscan friar, of Exeter, entered under age. Bridgewater Convent, 1512; Cambridge Convent before 1532; Oxford Convent, 1532; Bristol Convent, 1533 (licensed to preach in Worcester diocese 11 Sept. 1533); Exeter Convent, warden, 1534, still Dec. 1534. Dispensed to hold a benefice and change of habit 1 Dec. 1537. After sixteen years study at Cambridge and Oxford, supplicated at Oxford for B.Th., Dec. 1532; B.Th. by 1533. Rector, Tatenhill, Staffs., instituted July 1537; until death; dispensed to hold an additional benefice 17 Nov. 1543; vicar, St Bride's, London, instituted 21 Nov. 1543; vacated by July 1551; Chancellor of Wells, admitted 1547; deprived by Apr. 1554; canon of Wells and prebendary of Combe, 1547; deprived by Apr. 1554. Under Edward VI appointed lecturer at St Paul's Cathedral, London, where his preaching three times a week at Paul's Cross evoked violent disapproval. At Mary's accession tried with his bishop, William Barlow of B&W, to escape under disguise to the continent (through Bristol). Discovered and committed to the Fleet. Burned in Smithfield, London, 30 May 1555 (*BRUO 1501–1540*, 101). Married Catherine Testwood, widow, who bore him three children (*Regs. B&W*, no. 669 n. 1). Possibly schoolmaster to son of Marquis of Exeter before 1538; at Louvain 29 Aug. 1538 (*LP* xiii. pt. 2, 217).

CARLEON (CARYLN, CARLYNE), JOHN. Probably stipendiary, St Leonard, 1516 (*GRB*, pt. III, pp. 181–3, witnessed will of that parish); 1521 (BAO, P/AS/ ChW 3, paid for father's grave in parish of All Saints). Curate, St Leonard, 1534 (H&WRO, 802 BA 2764, fo. 100). Witnessed will, parish St Mary Redcliffe, 4 Aug. 1535 (Weaver (ed.), *Wells Wills*, 21). Rector, St Mary-le-Porte, composition for first fruits 19 Nov. 1544; vacated by 20 Feb. 1548

(PRO, E 334/3, fo. 36; E 334/4, fo. 5). Rector, St Michael, Cornwall, composition for first fruits 16 May 1557 (PRO, E 334/6, fo. 44ᵛ). Oxford, BA, admitted 19 Nov. 1527; in priest's orders by 1527 (*BRUO 1501–1540*, 103). *Same name*, instituted St Michael Penkivel, Exeter diocese, 31 July 1554; ejected at accession of Elizabeth (Field, *Province of Canterbury*, 109). (See also THOMAS CARLETON.)

CARLETON, THOMAS. May be same as John Carleon. Curate, St James, 1556, 1557 (PRO, E 179/6/12; E 179/6/10).

CARPENTER, HENRY. Bristol Franciscan friar at surrender, 1538 (*LP* xiii, pt. 2, 321).

CARRE, WILLIAM. Stipendiary, St Werberg, 26 Apr. 1540; ex-religious (H&WRO, 802 BA 2764, fo. 270).

CARSY (KERSEY), RICHARD. Monk, St Augustine, Bristol, at dissolution, 1539; still received pension 1552 (did not appear before pension commission; dwelling with the Lord Chamberlain of the King's household), 1555 (Baskerville, 'Dispossessed Religious of Gloucestershire', 95, 112; Taylor, 'Religious Houses of Bristol', 119). Witnessed will of former Abbot of St Augustine, Morgan Gwilliams, who probably was the rector of Yaverland in the Isle of Wight from Feb. 1544 until death (PRO, PCC, Pynning, 8 (20 Mar. 1544; proved 30 May 1544)). Presumably identical with the brotherhood priest of St Peter's Cornhill, London, 1548, and with the curate of Beddington, Surrey, who was restored to office in 1556 after giving up his wife (Baskerville, 'Dispossessed Religious of Gloucestershire', 281, 283, 285). (See also RICHARD BROMLEY.)

CARTER, THOMAS. Stipendiary, possibly curate, St Thomas, 1535, 1543 (Weaver (ed.), *Wells Wills*, 28, 29; BAO, P/StT/ChW/1/1543–4).

CARYE, JOHN. Monk, St Augustine, Bristol, at dissolution, 1539 (Baskerville, 'Dispossessed Religious of Gloucestershire', 95). Stipendiary, Olveston, Deanery of Bristol, 26 Apr. 1540, Jan. 1541 (H&WRO, 802 BA 2764, fos. 273, 195).

CAVERLY, THOMAS. 'Clerk', probably minister, St Stephen, 1577; living filled in 1580 by Thomas Tyson (*Hockaday Abstracts*, vols. 449–50, under St Stephen, 1577; PRO, E 334/9, fo. 99).

CHALONER, ROGER. Curate, Sts Philip and Jacob, 1567, 1569 (PRO, E 179/6/23; Wadley, *Notes*, 204).

CHAMPNEIS, THOMAS. Exhibited letters of priests' orders dated 4 Apr. 1556, by Gilbert, Bishop of B&W; admonished henceforth not to hold two cures together; in Bristol Consistory Court, 24 May 1563 (BAO, EP/J/1/5, p. 529).

CHELTENHAM, ROBERT (RICHARD) (alias RICHARD NETHEWAY?). Robert and Richard both appear on the pension list at the dissolution of Tewkesbury, the former with a pension of £10 and the latter, £6. 13s. 4d. (*LP* xv. 49). Other records suggest, however, that the two names were used for one person. Robert was used for the prior of St James, 1523; the prior of Deerhurst, 1535;

and possibly the curate of St James, 15 Feb. 1542 (*VCH Gloucester*, ii. 75; *Valor ecclesiasticus*, ii. 484; PRO, PCC, Spert, 7 (Henry Kemys; 15 Feb. 1542; 28 June 1542)). Emden takes the name Robert from these sources and lists him as B.Th. (*BRUO 1501–1540*, 688). Foster lists him as B.Th.; sup. 1 Mar. 1506; and D.Th.; sup. 13 June 1513 (Foster, i. 261). That Robert Cheltenham did not collect his pension in 1552 and 1555, while Richard did, suggests the possibility that they were the same person (Baskerville, 'Dispossessed Religious of Gloucestershire', 63–121; Taylor, 'Religious Houses of Bristol', 31–126). This is supported by the fact that Richard Cheltnam was curate of St James in Jan. 1541 (H&WRO, 802 BA 2764, fo. 194) (while Robert was curate in Feb. 1542; see above). Baskerville records Richard Cheltenham alias Netheway, curate of St James; i.e. Richard Cheltenham in 1542 and Richard Netheway in 1545 ('Dispossessed Religious', 86). Richard was vicar of Wraxall, Somerset, 1546, 1552; deprived for marriage, 1554 (Baskerville, 86). CIRENCESTER (CIRCETER, etc.), ROBERT. Monk, Benedictine; Tewkesbury Abbey, by 1512. Ordained deacon 18 Sept. 1512; priest 17 Mar. 1514. Prior, St James, Bristol, 1535 and at dissolution(?); pensioned £13. 6s. 8d per year, 12 Jan. 1540. Oxford, Gloucester College, scholar in 1532 [*sic*] and 1524. After nine years study in logic, philosophy, and theology, supplicated for B.Th. 20 Mar. 1523; B.Th., admitted 30 Oct. 1524. A book probably of Kalendars library, inscribed 'Rob. Cyscetur, "studens"': 'Catholicaon fratris joh. Januensis ord. predicat. Lugduni Nich. Sulf. 1503.' (*BRUO 1501–1540*, 117; *VCH Gloucestershire*, ii. 75; *LP* xv. 49; Baskerville, 'Dispossessed Religious of Gloucestershire', 122; Taylor, 'Religious Houses of Bristol', 117; Williams, 'Gloucestershire Medieval Libraries', 90). Possibly still a priest in the parish, 'Mr. Kachar, Priest', witness to will of Henry Kemys, 15 Feb. 1542, 28 Jun 1542 (PRO, PCC, Spert, 7).

CLERKE (CLARKE), JOHN. Stipendiary, St Nicholas, 1534 (H&WRO, 802 BA 2764, fo. 99). *Same name, cantatoru* or singing man in Bristol Cathedral, 1570; Oct. 1588, Gryffyth Hughes of Bristol, schoolmaster, accused JC, singing man in the cathedral, of taking money, which he told GH was necessary to pay to the dean in consideration of his desire for the job as schoolmaster at the cathedral grammar school; in fact, JC kept the money (BAO, DC/A/9/1, Computa 1570; PRO, Req. 230, Oct. 1588, cited in *Hockaday Abstracts*, vol. 433, under 1588).

CLOGGE, NYCHOLAS. Cleric, received 5s. for his wages, All Saints, 1558 (BAO, P/AS/ChW, 1558).

CLYFTON, THOMAS. Sub-prior, Carmelite friars, Bristol, at surrender, 18 July 1538 (*LP* xiii, pt. 1, 1485). Dispensed to leave his order and to hold a benefice, 10 Sept. 1538 (Chambers (ed.), *Faculty Office Registers*, 162).

COKE, JOHN. Chantry priest, All Saints, 1534 (H&WRO, 802 BA 2764, fo. 99). Stipendiary, St James, 26 Apr. 1540 (ibid., fo. 270). Possibly John Cooke, instituted Whetehill, 26 Jan. 1525; John Coche, instituted vicar, Stokelande,

14 Nov. 1526; John Coke, d. by 27 Jan. 1542, vicar Estchynnoke (*Regs. B&W*, *1518–1559*, nos. 212, 274, 509). Possibly took an Oxford or Cambridge degree (*BRUO 1501–1540*, 144 (Cox); Foster, i. 340; Venn, i. 384, 408 (Cook, Cokke, Cocks, Cox)).

COKE (COOKE), THOMAS. Vicar, St Nicholas, instituted Nov. 29, 1508; until death by Oct. 1515 (H&WRO, 716-093 BA 2648, Reg. de Gigli, fos. 57, 143). BA; Paris MA; supplicated for incorporation 30 Jan 1509, Oxford, B.Th. (admitted 31 Jan. 1513); D.Th. by 1515 (*BRUO 1501–1540*, 126).

COLES, RICHARD. Clerk, Christ Church, 1547 (paid 12*d*. for looking out the deeds of Martin Polardes cellar and 4*d*. for writing of the King's business) (BAO, P/ChC/ChW, 1547).

COLLYNS, HENRY. Vicar, St. Augustine-the-Less, 1534, 1540 (H&WRO, 802 BA 2764, fos. 100, 272). Possibly Oxford BA, MA (*BRUO 1501–1540*, 670; Foster, i. 308); their assertion of death by 1530 may have been made by a possibly incorrect identification of the Oxford graduate with the vicar of Fowey, Cornwall (*Hockaday Abstracts*, vol. 355, St Augustine, 1541, refer to our cleric as 'Mr.').

COLLYNSON, EDWARD. Priest, Ball's Chantry, Christ Church (Holy Trinity), instituted 3 May 1530; 1534, 1540 (H&WRO, 716–093 BA 1648, Reg. Ghinucci, fo. 43ʳ; 802 BA 2764, fos. 99, 269).

COLLYS (COLES, COLE, COLYNS, COLYS), JOHN. Vicar, Sts Philip and Jacob, instituted 5 Aug. 1526; witnessed will 12 Sept. 1528; 1534; 1540 was pluralist and non-resident; vacated by 9 May 1544 (H&WRO, 716–093 BA 2648, Reg. Ghinucci, fo. 26ᵛ; 802 BA 2764, fos. 100, 270; PRO, PCC, Porche, 39 (Elyn Kemys; 1528); PRO, E 334/3, fo. 13). Probably *same name*, rector, Preston, B&W diocese, by 1533–4, 1535; deprived by 1554; styled *magister* (*Valor ecclesiasticus*, i. 184; *Regs. B&W*,133, 162; *BRUO 1501–1540*, 670); restored at accession of Elizabeth (Field, *Province of Canterbury*, 11). *Same name*, rector, Churchill, Halfshire, Worcs., instituted 19 Mar. 1527 (H&WRO, 716–093 BA 1648, Reg. Ghinucci, fo. 40ᵛ). *Same name*, vicar, Shoreham, Kent, instituted 31 Oct 1554; vacated May 1555; rector, St Clement's Eastcheap, London, instituted 26 Apr. 1555; until death, 1565 (*BRUO 1501–1540*, 131). Colyns, curate, Mangotsfield, Glos., 1534 (H&WRO, 802 BA 2764, fo. 101). Probably Oxford graduate (*BRUO 1501–1540*, 310, 131, 669, 670, 718).

COLLYS (COLYNS?), WILLIAM. Carmelite friar, Bristol; dispensed to wear habit of his order beneath that of a secular priest, 20 Nov. 1537 (Chambers, *Faculty Office Registers*, 115). Perhaps William Colyns, parson, Street, B&W diocese, instituted July 1546 (*Regs. B&W*, no. 947). Possibly Oxford or Cambridge graduate (Foster, i. 311; Venn, i. 375).

COLMAN, JOHN. Master, Hospital of St Mark (Gauntes), 11 Sept. 1534; at surrender, 9 Dec. 1539 (*LP* vii. 1216; xv. 139; PRO, E 315/245, fo. 7). Probably of Salisbury diocese. Probably Oxford BA by 1515; ordained acolyte 22 Dec. 1515; subdeacon 15 Feb. 1516; deacon 22 Mar. 1516; priest 17 May

1516. Owned books; gave one to John Bradley, which see (*BRUO 1501–1540*, 131; T. W. Williams, 'Gloucestershire Medieval Libraries', 85).

COLMAN, THOMAS. Clerk, probably minister; commission to sequester tithes of Sts Philip and Jacob, 1576, on death of last incumbent (Lambeth Reg. Grindall, fo. 293, transcribed in *Hockaday Abstracts*, vol. 448, under date). Vicar, Sts Philip and Jacob, by 1584, until death, 1603–4 (Wadley, *Notes*, 234; Seyer, *Memoirs*, 259).

COLYER, JOHN. Priest (*socios*), Westbury College, near Bristol, 1535 (*Valor ecclesiasticus*, ii. 435). Priest, Spycers Chantry, St James, at dissolution 1548 (age 53) (Maclean, 'Chantry Certificates', 233). Still receiving pension of £4, 1555 (Taylor, 'Religious Houses of Bristol', 120). Perhaps John Collea, priest, who took inventory of Blankets Chantry, St Stephen, 1527 (BAO, ChW/StS/ Inventories 1494–1550, fo. 34ᵛ).

COME, RICHARD. Priest, Crowde Chantry, St Nicholas, 1531 (St Nicholas MS cited in Nicholls and Taylor, *Bristol Past and Present*, ii. 163). Possibly same as Robert Came, assistant cook of the dean and chapter of Bristol, 1561 (BAO, DC/A/9/1 Computa, 1561).

COMPTON, ROGER. Monk, Tewkesbury; almoner, pensioned at dissolution 9 Jan. 1540; appeared before pension commission, 1552 (Baskerville, 'Dispossessed Religious of Gloucestershire', 85, 103). No longer receiving pension, 1555 (Taylor, 'Religious Houses of Bristol', 120–6). Priest, Ponam's Chantry, St James, at dissolution 1548 (age 66) (Maclean, 'Chantry Certificates', 233).

COMPTON, WILLIAM. Stipendiary, St Mary Redcliffe, 1551 (St Mary Redcliffe Parish Archive, ChW Accts., 1552).

CONDON, DAVID. Vicar, Sts Philip and Jacob, 1547 (PRO, E 334 (Index, set 3, vol. 1—the page of vol. 4, which should contain the details, is missing)).

CORBETT, NICHOLAS. Monk, St Augustine, before dissolution (Geoffrey Baskerville, 'The Dispossed Religious', in Baskerville (ed.), *Essays in History Presented to R. Lane Poole* (Oxford: Clarendon Press, 1927), 454). Curate, St Peter, 1540 (H&WRO, 802 BA 2764, fos. 193, 271). Vicar, Pawlett, instituted 27 Aug. 1542; resigned by 28 Mar. 1545 (*Regs. B&W*, nos. 526, 596). Vicar, Sts Philip and Jacob, composition for first fruits 9 May 1544 (PRO, E 334/3, fo. 13); vacated by 1547 (see DAVID CONDON).

CORNEGE, JOHN. Clerk?, Hospital of St Mark, 1525; received 6*s*. 8*d*. from parish of All Saints for pricking five books of songs (BAO, P/AS/ChW, 1525).

COVENTREE, ROGER. Chantry priest, St Lawrence, 1534 (H&WRO, 802 BA 2764, fo. 100).

COWD (COWDE), BARTHOLOMEW. Rector, St Mary-le-Porte, instituted 26 June 1542; vacated by 27 Oct. 1543 (PRO, E 334/2, pt. 2, fos. 25, 84). Incumbent, Coleridge, Devonshire, Exeter diocese, 25 Oct. 1544 to 1554, restored at accession of Elizabeth. Incumbent Eggesford, Devon., Exeter diocese, 10 Feb. 1549 to 1554; restored at accession of Elizabeth; instituted incumbent, Basildon, Archdeaconry Berkshire, Salisbury diocese, 26 Apr. 1555, resigned by 20 Feb. 1567; incumbent Stow St Jacob, Widworthy and Uplyme, *c*.1566, Exeter diocese; d. in possession of Widworthy, 1571 (Field, *Province of Canterbury* 111, 265).

COWPER, THOMAS. Reader, St Leonard and Hospital of the Three Kings of Cologne, 1560 and probably 1564 (BAO, EP/J/1/5, p. 36; EP/J/1/6, p. 108). Possibly parson, Lamiat, B&W diocese, instituted 1555 (*Regs. B&W 1518–1559*, no. 791). Possibly graduate of Oxford or Cambridge (Foster, i. 339; Venn, i. 392; *BRUO 1501–1540*, 145). Cf. a case in the local Consistory Court: *Cibartha Gilbarne of Redcliffe* v. *Thomas Cowper of All Saints*; matrimony; 4 and 18 Mar. 1559; Thomas Cowper, sen., asserted that his son could not attend because he was dead; judge ordered testimonial letters to be produced under the seal of the Mayor to that effect (BAO, EP/J/1/4, pp. 8–10). *Same name*, instituted 27 Mar. 1561, to living of Wyfordby, Lincs. diocese (Field, *Province of Canterbury*, 168).

COWPER, WILLIAM. Priest, Eborard le French's Chantry, St Nicholas, 1534, 1540; vacated by 30 Apr. 1542 (H&WRO, 802 BA 2764, fos. 99, 269; PRO, E 334/2, fo. 16). Beneficiary of will of Edmonde Dauncer, chantry priest of St Mary Redcliffe, 10 Feb. 1535 (Weaver (ed.), *Wells Wills*, 21). Witnessed will of Robert Fychett, clerk, priest, Eborard le Frensch's chantry, St Mary Redcliffe, 16 Aug. 1510 (PRO, PCC, 36, Bennett, cited in Williams, *Canynges Chantries*, 26.)

CROFT (CRAFT, CROFTE, -S), GEORGE. Master, Hospital of St Bartholomew, instituted 31 July 1525; still 1532. Son of Sir Edward Croft of Hereford and Joyce, d. of Sir Walter Skull. Oriel College, Oxford, BA, admitted 13 Dec. 1512; determined 1513; MA by 1518. Ordained acolyte 17 Feb. 1518; deacon 3 Apr. 1518, to title of fellowship. Rector, Mappowder, Dorset, instituted 15 Dec. 1519; deprived 1539; Rector, Upper Sapey, Herefs., instituted 28 Aug. 1523; vacated Aug. 1524; rector, Winsford, Som., instituted 19 Sept. 1524; Rector, Deane, Hants, instituted 13 Mar. 1525; vacated Oct. 1527; Canon of Chichester and prebendary of Hova Ecclesia, collated 4 May 1526; vacated by Aug. 1529; Rector, Broughton, Oxon., instituted 19 Sept. 1527; until death; bursal prebendary in Chichester, collated 13 Aug. 1529; vacated Aug. 1531; rector, Shepton Mallet, Som., instituted 20 Sept. 1529; until death; rector, Newton Ferrers, Devon., instituted 8 Mar. 1534; until death. Chaplain of the King by 1531; preached before the King, Passion Sunday 1531. Arrested for utterances concerning the royal supremacy associated with the proceedings taken against Lord Montague, the Marquess of Exeter, and Sir Edward Neville; subjected to three examinations. Indicted for high treason 4 Dec. 1538, and executed shortly afterwards (*BRUO 1501–1540*, 150).

DAUNCER (DAWNSER), EDMONDE. Curate?, priest, St Mary Redcliffe, 1533; chantry priest, 1535; d. 1535 (Weaver (ed.), *Wells Wills*, 19, 21).

DAVIS (DAVYS), JOHN. Priest, Chapel of Holy Trinity Hospital, parish of Sts

Philip and Jacob, 1534; stipendiary, St Stephen, 1534 (H&WRO, 802 BA 2764, fos. 99 and 100). Stipendiary, St Mary Redcliffe, 1552 (half a year), 1554 (1 mo.) (St Mary Redcliffe Parish Archive, ChW Accts., under date).

DEAN, WILLIAM. Priest, Kalendars' Guild, All Saints; instituted 8 May 1527, 1534, 1539, 1540, at dissolution 1548 (age not given) (H&WRO, 716–093 BA 2648, Reg. Ghinucci, fo. 30ᵛ and Reg. Bell, fo. 1ᵛ; 802 BA 2764, fos. 99 and 271; Maclean, 'Chantry Certificates', 246). Still collecting pension 1552, when curate of St Margaret's in New Fish St, London, and in 1555 (Baskerville, 'Dispossessed Religious of Gloucestershire', 118; Taylor, 'Religious Houses of Bristol', 126).

DEANE, RICHARD. Vicar, Temple, 23 Oct. 1564 (BAO, EP/J/1/6, p. 65).

DEVEROUX, CHRISTOPHER. Curate, St Peter, 8 Apr. 1570 (McGrath and Williams, *Bristol Wills*, i. 5).

DOBINS, THOMAS. Curate, Sts Philip and Jacob, Aug., Sept., Oct. 1563 (BAO, EP/J/1/5, pp. 560, 571, 582). *Same name*, curate, Stroud, 1541; curate, Forthampton, 1551; vicar, Trynley, Wynche Deanery, 1552; vicar, Tirley, 1551, deprived for marriage, 1554; perhaps vicar of Leigh, Worcs., 1556, d. 1579 (all in Gloucester dioc.) (Baskerville, 'Elections to Convocation', 27).

DOGEON (DEGYON, DOGEN, DOGESON, DOGGESON, DOGION, DOGYON, DOOGEN, DUDGEON), GEORGE. Vicar, Temple, by 28 Dec. 1533, 1534, 1536, resigned 1538 (Weaver (ed.), *Wells Wills*, 23, 24; PRO, PCC, Hogen, 37 (Thomas Broke; 10 Feb. 1536; 24 June 1536); see Edward Togood, below). Deputy of visitory general of the King in the dioceses of Sarum, Bath and Wells, and Exeter (PRO, PCC, Crumwell, 20 (Edward Cowrtelove; 10 Mar. 1538; 10 Apr. 1538)). Chaplain to Bishop John Clerk of Bath and Wells, 1540 (Hembry, *Bishops of Bath and Wells*, 69; Weaver, *Somerset Wills*, 61–2). Precentor of Wells by May 1541, until death; canon and 6th prebendary of Bristol, 1542, until death. Vicar, Chew Magna, Som., by 1543, until death; rector, Langton Matravers, Dorset, composition for first fruits 13 May 1545, until death; dispensed to hold an additional benefice 12 May 1546; canon of Wells and prebendary of Holcombe, 1547; rector, Welford, Berks., composition for first fruits 19 Nov. 1548 (*BRUO 1501–1540*, 171). Licence of non-residence, 15 Apr. 1547 (*Hockaday Collection*, 9(4), 159). D. 14 Dec. 1552; will dated 1 Oct. 1552; proved 19 Feb. 1553; requested burial in Wells Cathedral. MA, Paris, incorporated Oxford as MA and B.Th., 8 Nov. 1542; granted licence to study abroad for 5 years, 15 Apr. 1547; D.Th. conferred in Italy, 1551, by Transagardus, a young gentleman of Padua, by a special privilege conferred by Emperor Sigismund (*BRUO 1501–1540*, 171).

DOLLE (DARLE, DOOLE, DALL), RALPH. Dominican friar, Bristol, at surrender, 10 Sept. 1538 (*LP* xiii, pt. 2, 320). Dispensed to hold a benefice with complete change of habit (Chambers (ed.), *Faculty Office Registers*, 166). Probably Ralph Dall, vicar, North Curry, Somerset, 1569; d. 1587 (Baskerville, 'Dispossessed Religious of Gloucestershire', 96). A Ralph Dowell was admitted to the living of Westhampnett, Chichester diocese, 5 June 1560 (Field, *Province of Canterbury* 70). Possibly related to Ralph Dole, who signed the complaint of citizens against Bishop Cheyney, 1568, and was sheriff of Bristol, 1578–9 (see Chapter 7, n. 81).

DONDAS (DYE), ROWLANDUS (ROWLANDE). Vicar, Temple, 1535 (*Valor ecclesiasticus*, i. 184). Subdeacon (and then apparently *cantatore*), Bristol Cathedral, 1550, 1554, 1561 (BAO, DC/9/1/1, under dates; EP/J/1/5, p. 483).

DOWELL, DAVID. Monk of Cleeve, Som. before dissolution (Baskerville, 'Dispossessed Religious of Gloucestershire', p. 104). Priest, Holwaye's Chantry, All Saints, composition for first fruits 18 Jan. 1544; at dissolution 1548, (age 53) (PRO, E 334/3, fo. 1; Maclean, 'Chantry Certificates', 246). Curate, Stepleton, 1557 (PRO, E 179/6/10). Still collecting pension 1552, 1555 (Baskerville, 'Dispossessed Religious of Gloucestershire', 104; Taylor, 'Religious Houses of Bristol', 121).

DOWGLAS, JOHN. Preacher, 1550. To preach ten sermons 'where he shall think expedient by the advice of my brother.' (PRO, PCC, Coode, 19 (Roger Wigmoure, gent.; 31 July 1550; 16 Dec. 1550). (See THOMAS GUILLIAM.)

DUKE, JOHN. Franciscan friar, Bristol, at surrender, 10 Sept. 1538 (*LP* xiii, pt. 2, 321). *Same name*, Oxford Convent at surrender, 1538, and dispensed to hold benefice and change habit, 31 July 1538 (*BRUO, 1501–1540*, 178). (See also THOMAS GRIFFITH.)

DURANTE (DURRANT, DURHAM), MORICE. Curate, St Ewen, 1574 (Mr Durham) and a fortnight's service there, 1579–80 (Masters and Ralph (eds.), *Church Book of St. Ewen's*, 238, 179). Of St Werberg, 1597 (McGrath and Williams, ii. 35). Probably graduate (Mr); if of Cambridge, possibly former Dominican friar (Venn, ii. 77).

DYER, JOHN. Possibly clergy. Bequest of a 'book of chronicles' to Sir John Dyer from William Rycart (PRO, PCC, Jankyn, 18, 13 Sept. 1528; 18 June 1530). A bequest to the master of Gauntes (St Mark's) of a parchment book containing physic and surgery suggests the possibility that John Dyer was also of Gauntes.

EATON (HAYTON, HEYTON), JOHN. Curate, preacher, Holy Trinity (Christ Church), 1564, 1565, 1567 (PRO, E 179/6/18, 6/23; BAO, EP/J/1/6, p. 196). Possibly 'Mr. Eiton, preacher', to whom former mayor, Nicholas Williams gave 10s. for a funeral sermon, 1565 (Wadley, *Notes*, p. 225; cf. William Eydon). Present in Bristol Consistory Court for the abjuration of heretic Hugh Gwilliam, 1564 (BAO, EP/J/1/5, p. 706; see Chapter 7, pp. 140–1).

EDGEWORTH (EDGWORTHE, EDGEWOURTHE, EDGWURTHE, EGEWORTH, EGGEWORTH, EGWORTH), ROGER. Born at Holt Castle, Denbighshire. Ordained subdeacon 5 June 1512; deacon 8 Sept. 1512; priest 18 Dec. 1512. Fellow, Eton College, admitted 22 Sept. 1518; vacated 1521; precentor,

1520–1; vicar, Christchurch, Monmouthshire, presented by Eton College 13 June 1521; vacated 1544; vicar, Chalfont St Peter's, Bucks., admitted 1523; vacated by Dec. 1528; Prior Kalendars' Guild, Bristol, 1525; vacated by Apr. 1528 (BAO, Deeds, 12966 (37), cited in Orme, 'Guild of Kalendars', 47; H&WRO, 716–093 BA 2648, Reg. Ghinucci, fo. 36); canon, Salisbury and prebendary of Slape, by 1535, until death; canon of Wells and prebendary of Warminster, by 1535; probably vacated 1554; canon and 2nd prebendary of Bristol, admitted 1542, until death; vicar, St Cuthbert's Wells, admitted 10 Oct. 1543; vacated Mar. 1559; Chancellor of Wells, collated 30 Apr. 1554, until death?; rector Brandesburton, Yorks., vacated by Dec. 1556; rector, Bledon, B&W diocese, vacated at death (*CPR* (Elizabeth), 339). Banbury School, Oxon., exhibitioner of William Smith, Bishop of Lincoln; Oriel College, probationary Bishop Smith fellow, elected 8 Nov. 1508; fellow 11 June 1510, vacated 15 Mar. 1519; treasurer, 1513; granted leave to lecture on Canon Law for 2 years 18 Dec. 1511; chaplain 1512–18; St Martin Hall, battelar in Dec. 1524; still in 1530; Oxford, BA, admitted 27 Feb. 1508; determined Lent 1508; MA, incorporated 9 Feb. 1512; Scholar of Theology 19 Dec. 1515; B.Th. admitted Oct. 1519; D.Th. incorporated 1 July 1526. D. by Jan. 1560; will dated 24 Dec. 1559; proved 1 June 1560. Requested burial in Wells Cathedral. Bequeathed works to Oriel College. Author of *Sermons very fruitfull, godly and learned* (London, 1557) (*BRUO, 1501–1540*, 184–5).

EDWARDES, JOHN. Curate, Sts Philip and Jacob, July–Dec. 1562. Failed in purgation and forbidden to serve in any way within the diocese after the feast of nativity (BAO, EP/J/1/5, pp. 417, 429, 460, 476, 477). See Chapter 7, p. 142.

EDYNGTON (EGGINGTON, EGINTON), THOMAS. Stipendiary, St Nicholas, 26 Apr. 1540; Jan. 1541 (H&WRO, 802 BA 2764, fos. 269, 193). Priest, Eborard le Frenches Chantry, St Nicholas, composition for first fruits, 1543 (PRO, E 334/2, fo. 16).

ELIS (HELYS), JOHN. Brother, Hospital of St Mark, at dissolution, 9 Dec. 1539; pension of £8 if curate of St Mark's, but £6 if refuses; curate, St Mark, 16 Apr. 1540; still 1546 (H&WRO, 802 BA 2764, fo. 275; McGrath and Williams, *Bristol Wills*, i. 1; PRO, E 315/245, fo. 7; *LP* xv. 139).

ETON, HUMFRIDI. Priest, Ball's Chantry, Christ Church (Holy Trinity); d. by 3 May 1530 (H&WRO, 716–093 BA 2648, Reg. Ghinucci, fo. 43ʳ).

EVANCE, ROGER. Stipendiary, St Stephen, 26 Apr. 1540 (H&WRO, 802 BA 2764, fo. 269).

EYDON (EDON, IDEN), WILLIAM. Instructor (preceptor), teacher (*didastuli*) in cathedral grammar school 1550, 1554, 1559, 1561 (Eydon); proctor, Bristol Consistory Court, 4 Dec. 1561 (BAO, DC/A/9/1/1, Computa, under dates; EP/J/1/5, pp. 78, 323 and 332; *Hockaday Abstracts*, vol. 441, under 1559, will of Cicily Lady Berkley, transcribed from Berkley Castle MSS. Box 18). Possibly 'Mr. Eiton, preacher', to whom former mayor, Nicholas Williams gave 10s. for a funeral sermon, 1565 (Wadley, *Notes*, 225; cf. John Eaton). Oxford, BA, 1525; MA, 1529 (Eden, Edon, Eydon); imbued with Lutheran sympathies, concerned with activities of Thomas Garrett in the university, 1517, and possibly was obliged to vacate his fellowship on that account (*BRUO, 1501–1540*, 288).

FATHIR, WILLIAM. Rector, St Peter, d. by 7 Dec. 1525 (H&WRO, 716–093 BA 2648/Reg. Ghinucci, fo. 24ᵛ). Oxford, BA, 1506–7 (Foster, ii. 486).

FLEMYNG, JOHN. Curate, St Nicholas, 17 Sept. 1533, 1534 (*LP* vi. 1133; H&WRO, 802 BA 2764, fo. 99).

FLETCHER (FETCHETT, FYCHETT), RICHARD. Ordained deacon, 24 Mar. 1520; priest 22 Sept. 1520 (B&W diocese) to title of Hospital of St Mark (SRO, D/D/B, Reg. 11, fo. 26). Brother, St Mark, 11 Sept. 1534; at dissolution, 9 Dec. 1539 (*LP* vii. 1216; xv. 139). Possibly Oxford, B.Gram. 10 July 1531 (Foster, ii. 508). D. *c*.1546; will dated 11 Aug. 1546; burial in St Mark's; owned five books, including the whole works of Vyncentt, *Sermones discipuli*, and a dirige book of vellum with a clasp of silver and gilt (McGrath and Williams, *Bristol Wills*, i. 1).

FLOKE (FLOOKE, FLOOK, FLUKE, FLOK), JOHN. Of Llandaff diocese. Ordained subdeacon 23 Dec 1508, Worcester diocese; rector, Sulham, Berks., admitted 23 Mar. 1514, exchanged Jan. 1526; vicar, All Saints, Bristol, instituted 8 May 1517, vacated by Dec. 1533. Rural Dean of Bristol, 1533, possibly 1528 (*LP* vi. 72; J. Foxe, *Acts and Monuments*, v. app. vi). Rector, Chalfield Magna, Wilts., admitted 23 Jan. 1526, vacated Nov. 1526; vicar, Weare, Som., admitted 8 Nov. 1526, vacated by Oct. 1528; vicar, Portbury, Somerset, admitted 12 July 1529, until death. Vicar, Bedminster, Som., instituted 25 Sept. 1533, vacated by 1535 (*Valor ecclesiasticus*, i. 183). Curate and 'vicar', St Mary Redcliffe, 30 Dec. 1533; curate, St Thomas, 6 May 1534 (Weaver (ed.), *Wells Wills*, 20, 28). Subdean and vicar, Westbury College, admitted 22 Dec. 1534, vacated by 21 Apr. 1535. Prior, Kalendars' Guild, instituted 24 Mar. 1535, until death (H&WRO, 716–093 BA 2648, Reg. Ghinucci, fo. 73ᵛ and Reg. Bell, fo. 12). Dispensed to hold an additional benefice, 18 Apr. 1535. Oxford, BA, admitted 1508; determined 1509; MA, incorporated 30 June 1511. Will dated 11 Sept. 1540 (H&WRO, BA 3585/4b, 1540, no. 61); d. by 8 Oct 1540 (*BRUO, 1501–1540*, 207–8, under Fluke, for references not shown here).

FONTAYNE (FONNTEY), JOHN. Rector, St Lawrence, instituted 14 Nov. 1525, 1534, 1535; non-resident 1540 (H&WRO, 706–093 BA 2648, Reg. Ghinucci, fo. 24ᵛ; 802 BA 2764, fos. 100, 272; PRO, PCC, Hogen, 26 (Philip Bokke; 18 Jan. 1535; 10 July 1535). Oxford, supplicated BA, Jan. 1532 (*BRUO, 1501–1540*, 212).

FORTUNE, ROBERT (J.). See ROBERT WHARTEN.

FOSTER, ROBERT. Stipendiary (perhaps chantry priest), Christ Church (Holy Trinity), 26 Apr. 1540; Jan. 1541 (H&WRO, 802 BA 2764, fos. 193, 269);

priest, Erells Chantry, Christ Church, at dissolution 1548 (age 76) (Maclean, 'Chantry Certificates', 242). No longer receiving pension, 1552 (Baskerville, 'Dispossessed Religious of Gloucestershire', 104–18, 116–8, 120). 'Ghostly father' (confessor) and beneficiary, 1543, to William Glaskeryon (PRO, PCC, Spert 16 (4 Feb. 1543; 22 Feb. 1543) See Chapter 3, pp. 50–1.

FOXE, THOMAS. Stipendiary, St Mary Redcliffe, 1552, 1553, 1554 (St Mary Redcliffe Parish Archive, ChW Accts., under date).

FRANKYS, LAURENCE. Augustinian friar, Bristol, at surrender, 10 Sept. 1538 (*LP* xiii, pt. 2, 319).

FYLYON (FYGEON?, PHYGEON?), ROGER. Augustinian friar, Bristol, at surrender, 10 Sept. 1538 (*LP* xiii, pt. 2, 319). Probably Roger Fygeon or Phygeon, vicar, Winterborne Stoke, 1542; deprived 1554; vicar, St Edmund, Salisbury, 1556–60; vicar, Berwick St James, 1556 (Baskerville, 'Dispossessed Religious of Gloucestershire', 97).

FYSSHE (FISHE, FYSCHE), JOHN. Rector, St Michael, instituted 4 Sept. 1523; 1534, 1540; vacated by 1556; farmed the parsonage to Thomas Richardes for four years before he left (H&WRO, 716–093 BA 1648, Reg. Ghinucci, fo. 33^v; 802 BA 2764, fos. 100, 270; BAO, EP/J/1/1, p. 149 and EP/J/1/2, p. 40). Oxford, BA, 1507; MA, 1511; of West Dean, Wilts.; Winchester College, scholar, admitted 1495, aged 13; New College, scholar, admitted 2 May 1502; fellow, 9 May 1504; vacated by May 1511; ordained subdeacon 20 Dec. 1510; deacon 5 Apr. 1511; chaplain, Holy Trinity chantry, All Saints, Oxford, admitted 17 Apr. 1511; vacated Nov. 1529 (Foster, ii. 499; *BRUO, 1501–1540*, 224). (See also THOMAS MOLENCE.)

GARDINER, JOHN. Vicar, Sts Philip and Jacob, instituted 19 Aug. 1513, until d. by 5 Aug. 1526; ordained subdeacon 16 Mar. 1512; from Coventry and Lichfield diocese (H&WRO, 716–093 BA 2648, Reg. Ghinucci, fos. 26^v, 182). Oxford, B.Gram.; BA, admitted 18 June 1511; MA, incorporated 30 June 1511 (*BRUO, 1501–1540*, 227).

GARDYNER (GARNAR), WILLIAM. Dominican friar, Bristol, at surrender, 10 Sept. 1538 (*LP* xiii, pt. 2, 320). Dispensed to hold a benefice with complete change of habit, 1 Dec. 1538 (Chambers, p. 166).

GATEWEY, RICHARD. Stipendiary, Temple, Jan. 1541 (H&WRO, 802 BA 2764, fo. 195).

GAYNER, EDWARD. Rector, St Werberg, 1534; 26 Apr. 1540 (H&WRO, 802 BA 2764, fos. 100, 270).

GEFFREY (GEFFEREY, GEFFRAY, GEFFERES, GEPHEREY, PERFREY, PERFEY), ROBERT. Austin friar, Bristol, at surrender 10 Sept. 1538 (Perfrey) (Gerfrey?) (*LP* xiii, pt. 2, 319). 7 May 1537, testified to King's commission on preaching in Bristol; called late clerk of Christ Church (Holy Trinity) (Gefferes) (*LP* xii. 1147). Originally parish St Mary Magdalene, Mill St, London, and later St Peter's parish, Cheapside, London. Son of Winchester tenant. Winchester College, Oxford, scholar, admitted 1514, aged 13, vacated by May 1531 on entering Order of Austin Friars; BCL, admitted 25 Feb. 1527; B. Canon Law, admitted 3 Mar. 1530 (*BRUO, 1501–1540*, 230).

GENNYNS, JOHN. Priest, Whites Chantry, St Stephen; d. by 20 May 1527 (H&WRO, 716–093 BA 2648, Reg. Ghinucci, fo. 31ʳ).

GERMAN (JERMON, ZARMAN), JAMES (JACOBUS). Dominican friar, Bristol, ordained subdeacon 23 Dec. 1508, in Lady chapel by the cloister, Wells cathedral (Emden, *Survey of Dominicans*, 49); at surrender, 20 Sept. 1538 (*LP* xiii, pt. 2,320). Dispensed to hold a benefice with complete change of habit, 1 Dec. 1538 (Chambers (ed.) *Faculty Office Registers*, 166).

GOODCHILD, THOMAS. Priest, Chepe's Chantry, St Nicholas, instituted 3 Sept. 1524, (vacant by resignation of John Masday), on presentation of Richard Sowthall master of the fraternity of the Assumption of Our Lady on the Bridge, and William Shypman and Robert Aventre, of the same fraternity (*Reg.B&W*, no. 192).

GOODRICHE (GOODRICH, GOODRYCHE, GOODRIDGE, GUDRYGE), JOHN. Rector, Holy Trinity (Christ Church), called 'parson', 1522 (PRO, PCC, Porche, 28 (Henry Kemys; 1 Oct. 1522; 7 Feb. 1529); instituted 17 Mar. 1525 (H&WRO, 716–093 BA 2648, Reg. Ghinucci, fo. 20ᵛ); 1530, 1534; licensed to preach in Worcs. diocese, 24 July 1534 (H&WRO, 716–093 BA 2648, Reg. Ghinucci, fos. 43, 68; 802 BA 2764, fo. 99); vacated by May 1538 (H&WRO, 716–093 BA 2648, Reg. Latimer, fo. 6ᵛ); of Bristol, 1531, 1532, 1533 (*LP* iv. 6; v. 909, grant 20; vi. 433, iii). Vicar, Clevedon, B&W diocese, by 1535, until d. by 27 June 1544 (*Valor ecclesiasticus*, i. 186; *Regs. B&W*, no. 581); farmed four rectories from Deerhurst Priory (Tewkesbury), 1535 (*Valor ecclesiasticus*, ii. 484). Oxford, MA, B.Th. (supplicated 8 June 1509); D.Th. (supplicated 18 July 1519) (Foster, ii. 583).

GORYNS, WILLIAM. Priest, apparently of St Leonard, 1529 (PRO, PCC, Jankyer, 22 (Johan Vaughan; 23 Dec. 1529; 31 Oct. 1530)).

GREADE, THOMAS. Rector, St Mary-le-Porte, composition for first fruits 27 Oct 1543; vacated by 19 Nov. 1544 (PRO, E 334/2, pt. ii, fo. 84). (See also JOHN CARLEON; THOMAS BEDE and THOMAS READE.)

GREGORYE, JOHN. Rector, St Michael, presented 1564; 1565; resident by 15 Apr. 1568 (BAO, Presentation Deed Bundle; EP/J/1/6, pp. 52, 75, 147; *Registrum Matthei Parker*, 35(i), 269 and 36 (ii), 510). Curate (minister), St Mary-le-Porte, 1564, 1565, 1576, until d. 10 Apr. 1579 (PRO, E 179/6/18, 6/20, 6/23; Wadley, *Notes*, 211). Subdeacon, Bristol Cathedral, 1553, 1561, 1570 (BAO, DC/A/9/1/2, Computa, under dates). Son of same name matriculated at Oxford, 29 Nov. 1588, aged 23 (Foster, ii. 603; *BRUO, 1501–1540*, 244). *Same name*, instituted to Benagre 14 Apr. 1545 (*Regs. B&W*, no. 599). *Same name*, incumbent East Dean, Chichester diocese (near Chichester), 1549–54, restored on accession of Elizabeth (Field, *Province of Canterbury*, p. 62).

GRENE, JOHN. Stipendiary, Holy Trinity (Christ Church), 1534 (H&WRO, 802 BA 1764, fo. 99). Possibly Oxford graduate (Foster, ii. 598; *BRUO, 1501–*

1540, 245). Same name instituted to Barwyke, Merston Deanery, B&W diocese between 1518 and 1559 (*Regs. B&W*, no. 937).

GRIFFITH, THOMAS (RICHARD). Priest, Burtons Chantry, St Thomas, composition for first fruits 18 July 1541 (Thomas); at dissolution 1548 (Richard, age 62); chantry commissioners noted he had a pension of £8 in addition to his salary of £6—this suggests he was an ex-religious (PRO, E 334/2, fo. 61; Maclean, 'Chantry Certificates', 235). Still receiving pension (Richard), 1552 (when appeared before pension commission), 1555 (Baskerville, 'Dispossessed Religious of Gloucestershire', 105; Taylor, 'Religious Houses of Bristol', 121). Possibly d. 1571, when vestry of St Thomas reported the death of a former chantry priest to the authorities (Taylor, 'Religious Houses', 110). *Same name* (Thomas), Augustinian friar of Oxford Convent at dissolution, 1538; dispensed to hold a benefice and change habit, 31 July 1538 (*BRUO 1501–1540*, 148–9). (See also JOHN DUKE.)

GWYNNE (GWYN), THOMAS. Curate, St Nicholas, 14 Oct. 1539; 26 Apr. 1540; Jan. 1541 (H&WRO, 716–093 BA 2648, Reg. Bell, fo. 3; 802 BA 2764, fos. 193, 269). Of St Nicholas parish, 1547 (PRO, PCC, Alen, 45 (Walter Lodbroke; 26 June 1547; 8 Aug. 1547). Priest, Lady Service, St Nicholas, at dissolution 1548 (age 50) (Maclean, 'Chantry Certificates', 238). Curate, St Mary Redcliffe, 10 Sept. 1542 (PRO, PCC, Spert, 18 (19 Apr. 1543)). Rector, Sudeley, 1549–51; d. *c.*May 1551 (Baskerville, 'Dispossessed Religious of Gloucestershire', 120).

GUILLIAM (GWILLIAM, GWILLIAMS, GWILLIEMS, GWILLEAMS), MORGAN. Abbot of St Augustine, Bristol; ordained priest to title of that monastery after 1523 (SRO, D/D/B Reg. 11, fo. 28). Became abbot after 5 July 1533 and by 9 Sept. 1534, when signed acknowledgement of royal supremacy (BL, Cotton MS, Cleop. iv., fo. 73; *LP* vii. 1216); at surrender, 9 Dec. 1539, pensioned £80 with mansion of Abbots' Leigh (Baskerville, 'Dispossessed Religious of Gloucestershire', 94); probably rector, Yaverland, Isle of Wight, instituted 7 Feb. 1544; until death (*BRUO 1501–1540*, 680); will, dated 20 Mar. 1544, proved 30 May 1544 (Baskerville, 'Some Ecclesiastical Wills', 281, 284). Styled magister (*BRUO 1501–1540*, 680).

GUILLIAM (GILLAM), THOMAS. Preacher, witness, and beneficiary of will requesting ten sermons in parish church of St Mary-le-Porte, 1550 (PRO, PCC, Coode, 29 (Roger Wygmoure, gent.; 31 July 1550; 16 Dec. 1550). Also beneficiary of £4 to preach twelve sermons in parish church of St Werberg, 1552 (PRO, PCC, Powell 4 (William Shipman; 16 July 1551; 5 Feb. 1551)). (See also JOHN DOWGLAS.)

HALL, HENRY. Stipendiary, St Augustine-the-Less, 1534 (H&WRO, 802 BA 2764, fo. 100).

HALL, THOME. Rector, St Michael, admitted, giving pension to resigning rector, Johannes Morys, 3 Apr. 1523; resigned by 4 Sept. 1528 (H&WRO, 716–093 BA 2648, fos. 116, 33).

HANSON, THOMAS. Rector, St Stephen, probably instituted before 1516; 1534, 1539, 1540, 1549, 1550, probably until d. by 1555 (H&WRO, 802 BA 2764, fo. 99; BAO, St Stephen's Inventory, fos. 51ᵛ, 54ᵛ; EP/J/1/1, p. 137; PRO, E 334/6, fo. 35ᵛ). Possibly Cambridge BA, 1524–5 (Venn, ii. 300).

HARRIS, BARNARD. Priest, Mede Chantry, St Mary Redcliffe, at dissolution 1548 (age 40) (Maclean (ed.), 'Chantry Certificates', 244). Appeared before pension committee, 1552; still receiving pension, 1555 (Baskerville, 'Dispossessed Religious of Gloucestershire', 105; Taylor, 'Religious Houses of Bristol', 122).

HARRIS, GEORGE. Vicar, St Nicholas, instituted 8 June 1564; 1593 (*Registrum Matthei Parker*, 39(iii), 963; PRO, E 334/8, fo. 21; McGrath and Williams, *Bristol Wills*, i. 55).

HARRY. 'Sir Harry' received two weeks' wages of 7s. 6d., St Mary Redcliffe, 1557 (St Mary Redcliffe Parish Archive, ChW Accts., 1557).

HARRYS, NICHOLAS. Chantry priest, St Stephen, 1534, 1540 (H&WRO, 802 BA 2764, fos. 99, 269). Priest, Kalendars' Guild, All Saints, at dissolution 1548 (age 46) (Maclean, 'Chantry Certificates', 246). Still on pension list, 1555 (Taylor, 'Religious Houses of Bristol', 121). Possibly Oxford, BA, admitted 13 July 1528 (Foster, ii. 657; *BRUO, 1501–1540*, 270).

HARVYST, THOMAS. Stipendiary, All Saints, 1526, 1528 (for keeping of our lady mass) (BAO, P/AS/ChW, 1526, 1528).

HASTLYN (HASTLEY, HASTLYE), WILLIAM. Exhibited letters of orders in Bristol Consistory Court, 2 Mar. 1560, given by Bishop of Lincoln in parish church of Hychyn in Lincoln diocese, dated 2 Oct. 1552 (BAO, EP/J/1/5, p. 26).

HAULTON (HALTON), WILLIAM. Curate, minister, St Ewen, 1577, 1577–8 (Masters and Ralph (eds.), *Church Book of St Ewen's*, 231, 234).

HAWARDYNGE, ROBERT. Ex-religious; stipendiary, Sts Philip and Jacob, 26 Apr. 1540 (H&WRO, 802 BA 2764).

HEWYS (HEWES, HUYS, GUY), RICHARD. Monk, St Augustine, at dissolution, 9 Dec. 1539; still receiving pension, 1552 (as parson of Brandeston, Norfolk; did not appear before commission) (Baskerville, 'Dispossessed Religious of Gloucestershire', 96); still on list, 1555 (Taylor, 'Religious Houses of Bristol', 119). Magdalen Coll. Oxford, BA, admitted 24 July 1541; determined 1542; MA, incept 5 Feb. 1548; taxor of Halls, 1548; Junior Proctor of the University 1549–50. Rector, Brandiston, Norfolk presented by Magdalen College, instituted 26 July 1551; vacated by Aug. 1556; canon and third prebendary, Bristol, presented 10 Sept. 1554, until death; rector, Pwllcrochan, Pembrokeshire, instituted 19 Jan. 1556; canon of Wells and prebendary of Henstridge, instituted 1558; canon and cursal prebendary of St Davids, collated 7 Oct. 1560, until death; d. by July 1563 (*BRUO, 1501–1540*, 286–7). Vicar, Berkeley, Glos., presented 10 Nov. 1557, instituted 1559, until death (*Hockaday Collection*, 9(4), 179). Proctor of clergy of city and deanery of Bristol to Convocation, 1563; elected with John Cotterell, 7 Jan. 1563 (BAO, EP/J/1/ 5, p. 483). Haugaard identified Richard 'Guy' as proctor for the clergy of Bristol, but distinguished him from Richard Hughes, whose position he was unable to identify (*Elizabeth and the English Reformation*, 357, 358, 381, 383). Undoubtedly the two were identical.

HILL, RICHARD. Monk, St Augustine, at dissolution, 9 Dec. 1539 (Baskerville, 'Dispossessed Religious of Gloucestershire', 95). Listed next to Richard Oriell, and the similarity of names suggests they might have represented the same man. Oriell later appeared on pension lists; Hill does not appear on any other documents. But cf. *same name*, rector of Edgeworth, Glos. diocese, 1539, d. 1556; and another of *same name*, rector of Eastleach Martin or Burthorp by 1532; of Burthorp, 1552–3; dep. for marriage, 1554; probably rector of Cold Aston, 1554–9 (Baskerville, 'Elections to Convocation', 27, 22). *Same name*, incumbent Leintwardine, Hereford diocese, 3 Mar. 1552 to 1554 and restored at accession of Elizabeth; also restored to Ruckland, Hereford diocese; instituted Sidmouth, 29 Apr. 1560; *same name*, presented by Crown to Aston Blank, Glos. diocese, 7 May 1554; composition for first fruits 8 May 1554; ejected at accession of Elizabeth (Field, *Province of Canterbury*, 112, 140, 163). (See also RICHARD ORIELL.)

HILSEY (HILDESLEIGH, HYLSEY), JOHN. Of Berkshire, Dominican friar; Oxford Convent, 1527; B.Th., 1527; after 14 years study supplicated for D.Th. Nov. 1532; D.Th. by 1533. Ord. subdeacon 10 Mar. 1514; deacon 17 May 1516. Bristol convent prior, 1533; Prior Provincial of England, appointed by Thomas Cromwell, Apr. 1534. Commissioned with Prior Provincial of Austin friars to visit friaries of English province and secure their adherence to royal supremacy. Became Bishop of Rochester, 1535, until death, 1538. Exposed relics of Hales, Boxley, 1538. Prepared a service book and extracts from it for children, both of which appeared 1539, and other works (*BRUO, 1501–1540*, 289–90; *DNB*, under name). For his role in the religious unrest in Bristol, 1533, see *LP* vi. 433 (iii), 596 and 796, and see Chapter 3 herein.

HOCHEKYN, EDWARD. Stipendiary, Holy Trinity (Christ Church), 1534 (H&WRO, 802 BA 2764, fo. 99).

HONYBRIGGE, JOHN. Priest, renting chamber from trustees of Canynge's Chantries, St Mary Redcliffe, 1509, 1528, 1534 (E. Williams, *Canynges Chantries*, 111, 231). Fed at abbey of St Augustine for eleven weeks in 1506–7 (Sabin, 'Compotus Rolls of St. Augustine's Abbey', 199).

HOPER (HOUPER), JOHN. Ordained priest to title Carmelite friars, Bristol, 14 June 1522 (SRO, D/D/B, Reg. 11, fo. 29). Carmelite at surrender, 10 Sept. 1538 (PRO, E 36/115, p. 19). Dispensed to leave his order and hold a benefice, 10 Sept. 1538 (Chambers, *Faculty Office Registers*, 162).

HOUSEMAN (HOUSMAN), RICHARD. Stipendiary, Christ Church, 1559 (BAO, P/XCh/ChW/1(3), 1559). Reader, All Saints, licensed 3 Sept. 1561; ordered to procure letters of ordination to continue, 2 Dec. 1564; literate (BAO, EP/J/

1/5, p. 266; EP/J/1/6, p. 93). Curate, Christ Church, 1575 (Wadley, *Notes*, 213–14, 216, 217).

HOWGREVE, FRAUNCIS. Possibly rector or curate, St Michael, 1574, when witnessed two wills (McGrath and Williams (ed.), *Bristol Wills*, i. 12–13).

HOWKE, RICHARD. Stipendiary, St Mary Redcliffe, 1553 (one quarter year) (St Mary Redcliffe Parish Archive, ChW Accts., 1553).

HUNT, WILLIAM. Ordained subdeacon and deacon 17 Dec. 1524; B&W diocese (SRO, D/D/B/Reg. 12, fos. 9, 11). Priest, Chantry of St Katherine, Byrport, Archdeaconry of Dorset, 1535 (*Valor ecclesiasticus*, i. 234). Stipendiary (chantry priest?), St Nicholas, 1534 (H&WRO, 802 BA 2764, fo. 99). Witnessed will, St Mary Redcliffe, 10 Sept. 1542 (PRO, PCC, Spert, 18 (Lewis Yevans; 19 Apr. 1543)). Priest, Spicers Chantry, St Nicholas, 1540, at dissolution 1548 (age 40) (H&WRO, 802 BA 2764, fo. 269; Maclean, 'Chantry Certificates', 239). Bristol Cathedral Chapter precentor, sacrist, minor canon, 1554, 1561, 1570 (BAO, DC/A/9/1/1, fos. 40ᵛ, 41ᵛ; DC/A/9/1/2, under 1561, and fos. 196ʳ, 196ᵛ, 197ᵛ). Deputy of vicar general delegate John Cotterell, Bristol diocese, 8 Jan. 1560 (BAO, EP/J/1/5, p. 7). Possibly Oxford, BA, admitted 19 Nov. 1527, determined 1528 (*BRUO, 1501–1540*, 306). D., burial, 4 Dec. 1582 (Sabin, *Registers of the Church of St. Augustine-the-Less*, 6). *Same name*, instituted Beaworthy, Exeter diocese, 31 July 1554, ejected at accession of Elizabeth (Field, *Province of Canterbury*, 110).

HUNTINGDON, JOHN. Preacher in Bristol and elsewhere, who went to Strasbourg during Mary's reign, returning to England by 30 Aug. 1559 and to Bristol soon after, and 1570, 1572; Canon of Exeter and pluralist during Elizabeth's reign; attended Oxford (Seyer, *Memoirs of Bristol*, i. 234–5; Garrett, *Marian Exiles*, 194; Powell, *Marian Martyrs*, 17; Foster, ii. 773; Wadley, *Notes*, 205, 210). Chaplain to Francis Russell, the second Earl of Bedford and a strong Protestant, who recommended him to the Mayor of Exeter in 1560, trusting that he would be accepted as a 'good workman in God's harvests' and assisted 'in all things within your liberties and change for the better setting forthe of God's truethe and the Queene's Majesties godly proceedings'. *Same name*, instituted Sampford Brett, B&W diocese 21 Aug. 1560 (Field, p. 12). *Same name*, instituted Sowton, Devon., Exeter diocese, 15 Aug. 1560 (Field, *Province of Canterbury*, 112).

HYLL, JOHN. Stipendiary, St Nicholas, 1534 (H&WRO, 802 BA 2764, fo. 99). Possibly vicar, Mydsomer Norton, B&W diocese, instituted 1554 (*Regs. B&W*, no. 745). Stipendiary, St John, 1557 (Nicholls and Taylor, *Bristol, Past and Present*, ii. 152). Possibly Oxford, BA (Foster, ii. 710; *BRUO, 1501–1540*, 309).

HYLMAN, JAMES. Deacon and priest, orders from Matthew, Archbishop of Canterbury, dated 7 Jan. 1560, exhibited in Bristol Consistory Court 8 Mar. 1560; clerk, St Werberg, 4 Oct. 1560; curate, St Mary Redcliffe, 7 Dec. 1560; 1 Jan. 1561. Suspended from the administration of sacred rites and from the education of boys within city of Bristol 'by reason of diverse vicious and contumelious libels and other words of a defamatory kind, declared, set forth, and spoken by him against preachers of the word', 10 Jan. 1564 (BAO, EP/J/ 1/5, pp. 39, 102, 129, 144, 619).

HYMAN (HYMA), Humfry (John). Monk, prior of St Augustine at dissolution, 9 Dec. 1539; appeared before pension committee, 1552; not on pension list, 1555 (Baskerville, 'Dispossessed Religious of Gloucestershire', 94, 99; Taylor, 'Religious Houses of Bristol', 119). Vicar, All Saints, instituted 27 July 1541 (H&WRO, 716–093 BA 2648, Reg. Bell, fo. 22ᵛ); composition for first fruits 9 Oct. 1541 (PRO, E 334/2, fo. 72); 1544, 1551, 1553 (PRO, PCC, Alen, 16 (William Davye Lewes; 23 Aug 1546); BAO, DC/A/9/1/1 Computa, under 1551, 1553); vacated by 1556. (See also ROBERT ROWE.)

INGE, WALTER. Vicar, St Augustine-the-Less, 1544 (Sabin, *Registers of Church of St Augustine-the-Less*, p. xiii).

INGMAN, JOHN. Augustinian friar, Bristol, at surrender, 1538 (*LP* xiii. 319). Curate, St Mary Redcliffe, 1540; 1543 (Baskerville, 'Dispossessed Religious of Gloucestershire', 97). Curate, St Thomas, Jan. 1541 (H&WRO, 802 BA 2764, fo. 194).

JAMES, JOHN. Stipendiary, St Nicholas, imprisoned (*incarcetus*), 1540 (H&WRO, 802 BA 2764, fo. 269).

JAY, WALTER. Vicar, Temple, composition for first fruits 16 Feb. 1555 (PRO, E 334/6, fo. 7); vacated by 1559. (See also JOHN PYLLE.)

JEFFREIS (JEFFREYS, GEFFREYS, JEFFERS, JERVIS), JOHN. Stipendiary, All Saints, 1528 (BAO, P/AS/ChW/1528). Chantry priest, St John the Baptist, 1534, 1540, 1543 (H&WRO, 802 BA 2764, fos. 100, 194, 271; BAO, St John's Church Book, fos. 47ʳ 52ʳ). Proxy for John Flooke's admission as subdeacon, Westbury College, 22 Dec. 1534 (H&WRO, 716–093 BA 2748, Reg. Ghinucci, fo. 35). Overseer and beneficiary, will of John Flooke (H&WRO, BA 3585/4b, 1540, no. 61). *Same name*, instituted vicar Bathford, B&W diocese, on presentation of Walter Gleson, notary public (and registrar, diocese of Bristol), 31 Mar. 1556; deprived or removed by 4 June 1558, when another presented by Henry Joliffe, dean of cathedral, Bristol. *Same name*, executor, will of Alice Krykelande, Temple parish, 29 Jan. 1563 (BAO, EP/J/ 1/5, p. 496).

JENKENSON (JENYSON, HEYNKYNGSON), HUGH. Priest, one of Canynge's chantries, St Mary Redcliffe, 1538; vacated by 24 Mar. 1546 (*Hockaday Abstracts*, vol. 443, under parish and year; PRO, E 334/3, fo. 84). Beneficiary of will of Edmonde Dauncer, chantry priest of St Mary Redcliffe, 10 Feb. 1535 (Weaver (ed.), *Wells Wills*, 21).

JENNYNGES (JENYNGES), WALTER. Priest, Katheryne Jones Chantry (Service), Christ Church, at dissolution 1548 (age 55)(Maclean, 'Chantry Certificates', 242). Still receiving pension of £4 in 1555 (Taylor, 'Religious Houses of Bristol', 122).

JENYNS, ROWLANDE. Priest, witness to will with chantry priest of St Mary Redcliffe, 1547 (Weaver (ed.), *Wells Wills*, 97).

JERMON (ZARMAN), JACOBUS (JAMES). See GERMAN.

JOHNSON, JOHANNES. Of Bristol dioc. Ordained deacon and pst. at Lambeth by Scory, Bishop of Hereford, 22 Dec. 1559 (*Registrum Matthei Parker*, 35 (i), 338).

JONES, HUGH. Rector, St Stephen, Bristol, composition for first fruits 12 May 1555 (PRO, E 334/6, fo. 35ᵛ); 1557 (*Hockaday Abstracts*, vols. 445–6, under St Nicholas and date). Clerk, St Mary-le-Porte, 1558 (*Hockaday Abstracts*, vol. 442, transcription of churchwardens' accts., under parish and date). Deputy of John Cotterell, Vicar General in Spirituals of Archbishop of Canterbury in Bristol diocese during vacancy of the see, 13 Jan. 1560 (BAO, EP/J/1/5, p. 11); made deputy (with Cotterell) of Bishop Richard Cheyney, holding Bristol *in commendam*, 20 Nov. 1562 (BAO, EP/J/1/5, p. 462). *Same name*, probably same man, rector, Tredunnoc, Monmouthshire, 1535, still 1563; dispensed to hold an additional benefice, 29 Jan. 1544; vicar, Almondsbury, Glos., composition for first fruits 29 Jan. 1544; vicar, Llanvihangel Crucorney, Monmouthshire, presented 5 May 1554; vicar, Llanrothell, Herefordshire, admitted 29 May 1556; vicar, Banwell, Som., admitted 4 Jan. 1558 (vacated by resignation of Thomas Silke, on presentation of dean and chapter of Bristol), vacated on promotion to bishop; canon and prebendary of Llandaff, vacated on promotion to bishop; bishop of Llandaff, elevated 17 Apr. 1567; consecrated 5 May 1567; temporalities restored 6 May 1567; until death; vicar, Cornwood, Devon, collated 31 Dec. 1571; d. Nov. 1574; buried in Matherne church, Monmouthshire. Oxford, BCL (*BRUO 1501–1540*, 321; *Regs. B&W*, no. 875).

JONES, LUDOVICO. Apparently rector, St Mary-le-Porte, vacated about one year before Jan. 1535 when successor Richard Boyce agreed to pay a pension for one year (H&WRO, 716–093 BA 2648, Reg. Ghinucci, fo. 35ʳ; 802 BA 2764, fo. 100); subdeacon and vicar church and college of Westbury, instituted 21 Apr. 1535 (H&WRO, 716–093 BA 2648, Reg. Ghinucci, fo. 74ʳ; *Valor ecclesiasticus*, ii. 435).

JONES, NICHOLAS. Cleric, witnessed will of St John the Baptist parish, 23 Aug. 1545 (PRO, PCC, Pynning, 36 (Robert Ellyett; 7 Oct. 1545)). Confessor of Alice Smythe, of St Leonard, probably curate, 16 Apr. 1546 (Vanes (ed.), *Ledger of John Smythe*, 274).

JONYS, WATYR. Sexton or second clerk, All Saints, received 26s. 8d. for one year's wage and borrowed £4, 1528; repaid 20s. and received 26s. 8d., 1529; repaid 26s. 8d. but apparently did not receive wage, 1530 (BAO, P/AS/ChW, under year).

KENE (KERELL, KERLE, KERNE), JOHN. Ordained subdeacon, Wells Cathedral, 21 Dec. 1521 to title of Hospital of St John, Bridgewater (SRO D/D/B Reg. 11, fo. 28). Instituted Tellysford, B&W diocese, 1520 [*sic*], vacated by 1530;

rector, Yatton, Som., admitted 1522 (*Regs. B&W*, no. 52, pp. 62, 20). Curate, Holy Trinity (Christ Church), 1537 (*LP* xii. 447 (iii)). Rector, Holy Trinity (Christ Church), instituted May 1538; 1540 (H&WRO, 716–093 BA 2648, Reg. Latimer, fo. 6ᵛ; 802 BA 2764, fo. 269); vacated *c.*1555–by 1558 (*CSPD* (Elizabeth), xii. 108). Rural dean of Bristol, deputy of the Bishop of Worcester, 1539 (*LP* xiv, pt. 1, 1095; *Mayor's Kalendar*, 55). Witness to will of Thomas White, 10 Sept. 1542 (*GRB* pt. 3, pp. 130–3). Rector St Lawrence, composition for first fruits 9 Apr. 1543 (PRO, E 334/2, fo. 58); vacated by 1553 (see also THOMAS STAUNTON). Beneficiary and witness, Robert Ellyett, 1545 (Wadley, *Notes*, 182); Christian Whyte, 1546 (PRO, PCC, Alen, 20 (24 May 1546; 24 Nov. 1546)). Instituted, Preston, 8 May 1559; deprived 10 Feb. 1560; instituted High Ham in succession to Anthony Salvin (*Regs. B&W*, no. 922; *Registrum Matthei Parker*, 35(i), 176–7; Field, *Province of Canterbury*, 9, 11). Styled MA; probably Oxford, BA, MA (*BRUO 1501–1540*, 329, 685).

KNIGHTE, JOHN. Minor Canon, Bristol Cathedral, 1570 (BAO, DC/A/1/2 Computa, 1570, fo. 196ᵛ). Curate, St Stephen, 1574 (McGrath and Williams (eds.), *Bristol Wills*, i. 11, 13; Wadley, *Notes*, 218). Vicar, All Saints, at death, between 31 May and 23 July 1597 (McGrath and Williams (eds.), *Bristol Wills*, ii. 34–5). Possibly attended Cambridge or Oxford (Venn, iii. 299; Foster, ii. 861).

KYNGE, THOMAS. Priest, Assumption of our Lady Chapel on Bristol Bridge, at dissolution 1548 (age 44) (Maclean, 'Chantry Certificates', 240; PRO, PCC, Populwell, 22 (Agnes Compton; 1 Aug. 1548; 24 Jan. 1549). Canterbury diocese; Queens' College, fellow, admitted 1496; vacated 1501; quaestionist, admitted 7 Mar. 1494; MA, incepted 1497. Ordained subdeacon 26 Feb. 1496, to title of fellowship; priest, 2 Apr. 1496, to same title. Rector of Elkstone, Glos., admitted 16 Apr. 1500 (*BRUC*, 344).

LANE (LAWNNE, LAWE, LANG), HUGH (HUGO, HENRY). Franciscan friar, Bristol, at surrender, 1538 (*LP* xv. 321; Baskerville, 'Dispossessed Religious of Gloucestershire', 16). Curate, Sts Philip and Jacob, 1534; stipendiary, St Peter, Jan. 1540 (H&WRO, 802 BA 2764, fos. 100, 271). Stipendiary, Bristol Cathedral, 1554 (BAO, DC/A/9/1/1, Computa, 1554, fo. 41ᵛ).

LANGBURNE, ANTHONY. Letters of orders by John Bishop of Hereford, dated 22 Mar. 1562, in parish of Whitburne, exhibited in Bristol Consistory Court, 12 Sept. 1562 (BAO, EP/J/1/5, p. 430).

LAURENCE, JOHN. Priest, witness to will of Christian Whyte, St John the Baptist, 24 May 1546 (PRO, PCC, Alen, 20 (24 Nov. 1546)). 'Maister Laurence' to preach at funeral of John Whyte, merchant, 1569–70 (Wadley, *Notes*, 202). Possibly Oxford BA, or attended Cambridge (Foster, iii. 887; *BRUO, 1501–1540*, 344; Venn, iii. 53).

LAURENCE, THOMAS. Curate, St Mary Redcliffe, 1531 (Weaver (ed.), *Wells Wills*, 19). Stipendiary, St Peter, 1534 (H&WRO, 802 BA 2764, fo. 100).

LEE (LYE, LYLL, LILL, LINCHE, LYNCH, LYLE?, LILE?), JOHN (THOMAS).

Franciscan friar (Thomas Lee), Bristol, at dissolution 1538 (*LP* xv. 321). Franciscan friar (John Lye), Bristol, 1534 (*LP* viii. 1607). Stipendiary (Thomas Lye), St Lawrence, Jan. 1541 (H&WRO, 802 BA 2764, fo. 194). Stipendiary (John Lill), St Thomas, 1543 (¾) (BAO, P/StT/ChW/1 (1543–4). Perhaps curate, Estbrynte, B&W diocese; will witness between 7 Dec. 1543 and 4 Apr. 1546 (John Lyle, Lile) (Shilton and Holworth (eds.), *Medieval Wills from Wells*, 2–193, *passim*). Possibly (unlikely) vicar Kelston, Som. by 1545; died 1558 (Baskerville, 'Dispossessed Religious of Gloucestershire', 96). 'John Linche' surety for James Linche and Thomas Wether, who became sequestrators of tithes of rectory, Littleton-on-Severn, Bristol diocese, 14 June 1561 (BAO, EP/J/1/5, p. 503). Reader (John Lyll), St John the Baptist, 2 Dec. 1564; pronounced contumacious for not appearing in the Consistory Court after citation and suspended from his office (BAO, EP/J/1/6, p. 93). On this date other readers were ordered to procure letters of ordination, something a former friar may not have possessed. Apparently, however, Lyll obtained the letters. Curate (Johes Lynche), St John the Baptist, Sept. 1567 (PRO, E 179/6/23). (In determining that all these entries probably refer to the same person, it is useful to know that Bristolians then and now often add an 'l' to words which end in vowel sounds. For example, the city itself was called Bristow before the natives added the final 'l' sound. Thus the transition from 'Lee' or 'Lye' to 'Lyll' or 'Lill' is understandable. While there is no similar reason for the transition to 'Linche' or 'Lynche', this nevertheless seems probable given that 'Lyll' and 'Lynche' were reader and curate, respectively, of St John the Baptist within a period of three years.) Possible Cambridge, BA, MA (Venn, iii. 65).

LEWIS, RICHARD. Stipendiary?, All Saints, 1558, paid 10*s*. for each of four quarters (BAO, P/AS/ChW/1558). Possibly vicar, Shepton Montis, B&W diocese, 1519 (*Regs. B&W*, nos. 42, 44). Possibly Oxford BA (Foster, iii. 909).

LEWYS, N. 26 Mar. 1562, exhibited dimissory letters at Bristol, granted at Wells 'on this date', that he may obtain all sacred orders from some Bishop; literate (BAO, EP/J/1/5, p. 361).

LEWYS (LEWES), ROGER. Stipendiary St Stephen, Jan. 1541 (H&WRO, 802 BA 2764). Priest, Stokes Chantry, St Thomas (mistaken as St Mary Redcliffe), composition for first fruits 15 July 1545; at dissolution 1548 (age *c*.30) (PRO, E 334/3, fo. 60; Maclean, 'Chantry Certificates', 235). Sureties included John Pyke of Bristol, mercer, and Robert Esington of All Saints, Horrylane (Honeylane?), London. Thomas Garrett, the Lutheran activist with Bristol and Bedminster connections, was parson of All Saints, Honeylane, London, in 1527 and was inducted to the living 14 June 1537 (see Chapter 3, p. 37). Vicar, Bedminster (and thus curate, St Mary Redcliffe, St Thomas?), deprived by 5 Nov. 1554 (age 40, having married Catherine Wever, a widow) (*Regs. B&W*, no. 777 and p. 136 n. 1). Possibly d. 1571, when vestry of St Thomas reported the death of a former chantry priest to the authorities

(Taylor, 'Religious Houses of Bristol', 110). Possibly BCL, B.Canon Law, although not so if ages given above are correct (*BRUO 1501–1540*, 255).

LEWYS (LEWES, LEWIS), THOMAS. Franciscan friar, Bristol, at surrender 10 Sept. 1538 (*LP* xiii, pt. 2, 321). Curate, Henbury, Jan. 1541 (H&WRO, 802 BA 2764, fo. 195). Probably priest, Westbury-on-Trym College at surrender 18 Feb. 1544 (to whom living of Henbury appropriated); probably rector, Wraxall, Som., 1560; d. 1562 (Baskerville, 'Dispossessed Religious of Gloucestershire', 96). Vicar, Henbury, 6 Nov. 1556; 4 Oct. 1560 (BAO, EP/J/1/1, pp. 127, 180, 181, 188, 189, 190, 195, 205, transcribed *Hockaday Abstracts*, under Henbury and year; BAO, EP/J/1/2, pp. 61, 71, 83; EP/J/1/5, p. 100). Dispensation granted by Archbp. Parker to hold two benefices 7 Feb. 1561 (PRO, SP 12/76, transcribed in *Hockaday Abstracts* under Henbury and year). Possibly same as stipendiary (one of ministers), St Mary Redcliffe, 1556, 1557, part of 1559 (St Mary Redcliffe Parish Archive, ChW Accts., under dates). Possibly Oxford, B. Canon Law adm. 4 July 1524 (*BRUO 1501–1540*, 255–6).

LONGE, EDMUNDE. Curate, Temple, 1531 (Weaver (ed.), *Wells Wills*, 22). Possibly Oxford, B. Canon Law sup. Jan. 1531) (Foster, iii. 936; *BRUO 1501–1540*, 361).

LONGE (LOVE), THOMAS. Exhibited letters of ordination, Bristol Consistory Court, 1567; ordained 28 May 1567 by Hugo Bp. of Landaven in the parish church of Tredenoge, of Bristol diocese (*Hockaday Collection*, 9(4), transcription of Bristol Cathedral Library, fo. 101, paginated 236 but not consecutive; the original document has not been traced). Rector, St Michael; rector, St Ewen, instituted to both 15 Apr. 1568 (*Registrum Matthei Parker*, 35(i), 269 and 36(ii), 510). Does not appear in any St Ewen accounts until 1579–80, and held living until 1591 (Masters and Ralph (eds.), *Church Book of St Ewen's*, 180–1, 238, 240, 245, 248, 250). See Chapter 6 n. 7.

MAGNE (MAGUS), SIMON. Stipendiary?, All Saints, 1558 (pd. 20*s*. for each of four quarters) (BAO, ChW/AS/under date).

MALMESBURY, ANTHONY. Ex-monk of Malmesbury; priest, Walter Frampton's Chantry, St John the Baptist, at dissolution 1548 (age 52); still receiving pension 1552 (appeared before pension commission); 1555 (Maclean (ed.), 'Chantry Certificates', 237; Baskerville, 'Dispossessed Religious of Gloucestershire, 105; Taylor, 'Religious Houses of Bristol', 122).

MARSHALL, HENRY. Clerk, signed certificate of preaching of Powell and Hubberdine, Bristol, 1533 (*LP* vi. 596). Probably the Master Marshall, priest, who witnessed the will of David Hutton, a reformer among the secular elite (PRO, PCC, Hogen, 30 (13 March 1536)). A chaplain of Hugh Latimer (*LP* x. 1099). Possibly Oxford, B. Canon Law, adm. 9 Dec. 1532; rector of West Kington, Wilts., vacated by Dec. 1539 (of which Hugh Latimer was incumbent in 1533). See Emden for further details of career, none of which was spent in Bristol (*BRUO 1501–1540*, 380).

MARSHALL (MERSHALL), WILLIAM. Stipendiary?, St John. Confessed in Bristol Consistory Court in 1563 to unlawfully ringing the bells at the burial of John Sanders; ordered public penance; failed to certify having done so and was suspended from entering the church; later he appeared and was enjoined to perform his penance the next day. His executorship of the will of Thomas Tasker, parson of St John, was challenged in Bristol Consistory Court in 1563 by Roger and Henry Marwell, next of kin of Tasker; parties agreed to arbitration of Mr Doctor Cottrell; Marshall apparently was named executor (BAO, EP/J/1/4, p. 693; EP/J/1/4, pp. 495, 498, 500, 509, 523, 528, 545); cf. Venn, iii. 149; Foster, iii. 975).

MARTEN, DAVID. Possibly stipendiary, sexton (Sir Davy), All Saints, 1558 (BAO, P/AS/ChW, 1558). Stipendiary, St Mary Redcliffe, part of 1559 (St Mary Redcliffe Parish Archive, ChW Accts., 1559). Literate; toleration of licence as reader, St Nicholas, on petition of Vicar John Rastell, 28 June 1560: dimissory letters granted in Bristol Consistory Court, 2 Mar. 1562; accused in Bristol Consistory Court of preaching in St Nicholas without a licence; denied; appeared for purgation of Edward Butt, clerk, 23 Oct. 1564 (BAO, EP/J/1/5, pp. 71, 361, 693; EP/J/1/6, p. 65). See Chapter 7, p. 143.

MARTHEN (MERDEN, MERTHEN, MARTYN, MARTIN), JOHN. Franciscan friar at surrender, 1538 (*LP* xv. 321). Stipendiary, St Werberg, 26 Apr. 1540, Jan. 1541 (H&WRO, 802 BA 2764, fos. 129, 270). John Martyn, BA, vicar, Somerton, B&W dioc., inst. 30 May 1554 (*Regs. B&W*, no. 693). John Roulande alias Martin underwent purgation in Bristol Consistory Court, 1566 (BAO, EP/J/1/3, fo. 15). Possibly Oxford graduate (*BRUO, 1501–1540*, 383; Foster, iii. 978).

MARTIN (MARTYN, MARTEN, MARTINE), RICHARD. Vicar, Temple, 1598 (McGrath and Williams (eds.), *Bristol Wills*, ii. 71, 74, 104). The will of Richard Smith, shearman of Temple, (p. 104) refers to 'my good friend Richard Martin vicar', and bequeaths 20s. to him, but also gives 6s. 8d to 'the preacher that shall preach my funeral'; this suggests that RM was not a preacher. *Same name*, appointed asst. teacher (*hypodidasculus*) in cathedral grammar school with stipend £2. 8s. 4d., 1572 (E. T. Morgan, *A History of the Bristol Cathedral School* (Bristol: J. Arrowsmith, 1913), 22). Possibly Oxford, scholar of Trinity College in and before 1564 (Foster, iii. 979).

MASDAY (MASSYE, MASTE), JOHN. Prior, Carmelite friars, 17 Aug. 1529 (PRO, PCC, Jankyn, 15 (Roger Davys; 9 July 1530). Priest, Chepe's Chantry, St Thomas, vacated by 3 Sept. 1524 (*Regs. B&W*, no. 192). Chantry priest, St John the Baptist, three quarters of a year 1533, 1534, 1535, 1536, three quarters of a year 1539 (BAO, P/StJB/ChW, under year). Possibly Cambridge, B. Canon Law (Venn, iii. 158).

MASON, JOHN. Clerk, Temple, 28 Dec. 1533 (Weaver (ed.), *Wells Wills*, 23). Possibly took an Oxford degree (Foster, iii. 983; *BRUO, 1501–1540*, 388).

MASON, THOMAS. Office case in Bristol Consistory Court, 1564, against Alice

Mason, calling herself the sister of Thomas Mason, clerk. Asserted that she was his sister; ordered not to frequent his company or unlawfully consort with him until she brought testimonial letters concerning her relationship to him (BAO, EP/J/1/5, p. 699).

MAWDLEY (MAUDELEY, MAWDLYN, MAWDLEN, MAWDELEN, MAIRDLEY), JOHN. Dominican, prior Bristol convent, 1523; B.Th. 22 May 1514; D.Th. 27 July 1523 (Foster, iii. 992). Still in Bristol, 1534 (*Valor ecclesiasticus*, ii. 434). *Same name*, received 40s., 1561, 1570, from cathedral chapter 'Pro consilio in legie' (BAO, DC/A/9/1/2 Computa, under year).

MAXWELL (MASFIELD, MAFFILD, MAYFIELD), THOMAS. Priest, Frampton's Chantry, St John the Baptist, composition for first fruits 4 July 1545; at dissolution 1548 (age 40) (PRO, E 334/3, fo. 60; Maclean, 'Chantry Certificates', 237). Still receiving pension, 1552 (of London), 1555 (Baskerville, 'Dispossessed Religious of Gloucestershire', 117; Taylor, 'Religious Houses of Bristol', 121).

MAYO, WILLIAM. Stipendiary?, All Saints, paid 8s. Christmas quarter, 1558; 1561 (four quarters at 10s. each) (BAO, AS/ChW, under dates; cf. *same name*, *BRUO 1501–1540*, 393).

MEKENS, JOHN. Clerk, 1556. Office case in Bristol Consistory Court against Margaret Mekens. She confessed to being with child by JM, clerk; ordered penance to be performed at St Thomas (BAO, EP/J/1/2, p. 37).

MERYFILD (MIRYFELD, MERYFELD), THOMAS. Priest, Kalendars' Guild, All Saints, instituted 22 June 1493, 1498, resigned Aug. 1501; reinstituted 20 Nov. 1510, 1534, until death between 8 June 1539 and Sept. 1539 (Orme, 'Guild of Kalendars', 47–8; H&WRO, 716–093 BA 2764, fo. 99). John Flooke of Kalendars Guild, beneficiary and executor of his will (Lambeth Reg. Morton, fo. 177ᵛ, transcribed in *Hockaday Abstracts*, vol. 442, under All Saints and date; H&WRO, 802 BA 2764, fo. 99 and BA 3538/3b 1538 (1539), no. 377). Priest, Canynges' Chantry, St Mary Redcliffe, at least by 1496, perhaps as early as 1486, 1505–6, 1507–8 (Williams, *Canynges Chantries*, 26, 116, 117, 167, 168, 169, 170, 171, 172, 233).

MOGLEWIKE, GEORGE. Curate, St Mary Redcliffe, March 1560; asked by court to show proof of admission to ministry; claimed admission seven years before by John Hooper, Bishop of Gloucester, and exhibited letters of institution to the parish church of St Michael in Bedwarden, made for him by John Barlow, the vicar delegate in Worcester diocese, dated 16 Feb. 1552; he was dismissed (BAO, EP/J/1/5, p. 35).

MOLENCE (MOLLEYNES, MOLENSE, MOLYNS, MULLYNS), THOMAS. Ordained subdeacon in St Thomas, Bristol, 24 Sept. 1524; deacon at Glastonbury, 17 Dec. 1524, to title in Winchester College, Oxford (SRO, D/D/B Reg. 12, fo. 9). Ordained priest 7 Mar. 1528 to title of fellowship; of Bristol; Winchester College, Oxford, scholar, admitted 1511, age 13; New College, scholar, admitted 20 Mar. 1517; fellow, 1519, vacated 1529; BA, admitted 8 July 1521, determined 1522; MA, incept 17 July 1525; B.Th. admitted 6 Nov. 1533; chaplain of Holy Trinity chantry, All Saints, Oxford, presented by New College, 20 Oct. 1529 (*BRUO, 1501–1540*, 408). Vicar, All Saints, instituted 9 or 11 Dec. 1533; 1534 (H&WRO, 716–093 BA 2648, Reg. Ghinucci, fos. 28, 63; 802 BA 2764, fo. 99); vacated by 1539 (BAO, P/AS/ChW, 1539). Rector, Heddington, Wilts., admitted 10 Jan. 1542; vacated by Oct 1543 (*BRUO, 1501–1540*, 408). (See also JOHN FYSSHE and JOHN WILLIAMS.)

MORGAN, LEWES (LEWYS). Priest, St Mary Redcliffe, 4 May 1530; 10 Feb. 1535; 25 Sept. 1547; priest, Eborard le French's Chantry, at dissolution 1548 (age 60) (Weaver (ed.), *Wells Wills*, 18, 21; PRO, PCC, Alen, 46 (Agnes Wynysmore; 14 Oct. 1547); Maclean (ed.), 'Chantry Certificates', 237–8). No longer receiving pension, 1552 (Baskerville, 'Dispossessed Religious of Gloucestershire', 104–8, 116–18).

MORICE, WALTER. Stipendiary, St James, 1534 (H&WRO, 802 BA 2764, fo. 100).

MORRE, JOHN. Stipendiary?, St John, paid 10s., Christmas quarter 1533 (BAO, P/StJ/ChW/under date).

MORRELL, JOHN. Clerk, All Saints, 1532 (paid 20s for one quarter; paid for a reward before he came to Bristol, 12d.) (BAO, P/AS/ChW/1532, p. 7).

MORYS (MORSE?), JOHN. Rector, St Michael, admitted 3 Apr. 1523, with pension to predecessor Thomas Hall (H&WRO, 716–093 2648, fo. 116). Cf. *same name*, reader, Mangotsfield, Bristol Deanery, toleration, 28 Feb. 1560 (BAO, EP/J/1/5, p. 36). Possibly graduate of Oxford (Foster, iii. 1035).

MOSELEY, WILLIAM. Priest, Canynges' (St George's) Chantry, St Mary Redcliffe, paid proctors first fruits of £4. 19s. 3d., 18 Mar. 1545; composition for first fruits 24 Mar. 1546; at dissolution 1548 (age 40) (Williams (ed.), *Canynges Chantries*, 37, 122, 234; PRO, E 334/3, fo. 84; Maclean (ed.), 'Chantry Certificates', 245). Still collecting pension (of Roode, Som.; did not appear before the pension commission), 1552, 1555 (Baskerville, 'Dispossessed Religious of Gloucestershire', 117; Taylor, 'Religious Houses of Bristol', 125). Composition for first fruits, Bitton, Glos., Bristol diocese, 8 July 1555; resigned by 12 June 1561; became incumbent, Donhead St Andrew, Wilts., 1564 (Field, *Province of Canterbury*, 28).

MOSLEY, HUMPHREY. Curate, St Ewen, 1567/68–1572/73 (Masters and Ralph (eds.), *Church Book of St Ewen's*, 34, 37, 40, 41, 44, 45). Rector, St Peter, 1583, 1584 (Wadley, *Notes*, 231, 236, 237).

MOULDER (MOLDER?), RADULPHI. Priest, Kalendars' Guild, instituted 7 Oct. 1503, d. by May 1527 (Orme, 'Guild of Kalendars', 48; H&WRO, 716–093 BA 2648, Reg. Ghinucci, fo. 30ʳ). Possibly Raphael Molder (Ralph Mader), Oxford, BA, admitted 31 Jan. 1513, determined Lent 1513 (*BRUO, 1501–1540*, 397).

MOULDER, WILLIAM. Rector, St Peter, res. 27 May 1533 (H&WRO, 716–093 BA 2648, Reg. Ghinucci, fo. 59).

MYLLET, JOHN. Stipendiary, St Lawrence, 26 Apr. 1540; Jan. 1541 (H&WRO, 802 BA 2764, fos. 194, 272).

MYLLS (MYLES), EDWARD. Clerk of St James, 1566–70 (paid 19s. 6d. for three quarters wages, 1566; 20s., 1567; 26s., 1568; 4d. for warning them that were behind at Easter, 1569; £1. 6s. for one year's wage, 1570) (BAO, P/StJ/ChW, under dates).

NEWPORTE, THOMAS. Apparently monk of St James shortly before dissolution; testified in 1556 that he was one of the house of St James and for two yrs. received all tithes unto the house. Born at Presberry, Glos., age 60, rector of Doddington, Glos. diocese (BAO, EP/J/1/1, p. 256, transcribed in *Hockaday Abstracts*, vol. 438, under St James and date).

NICHOLAS. Sexton, stipendiary?, All Saints, 1518 (paid 3s. 4d.), 1528 (paid a quarter's wages, 31s. 4d.), and 1539 (paid for his labour in going to Wells, 2s. 4d.). Stipendiary?, St Mary Redcliffe, 1552 (paid £6) (BAO, P/ChW/AS/ under dates; St Mary Redcliffe Parish Archive, ChW Accts., under date).

NORTHBROOKE (NORBROOKE), JOHN. Preacher, curate, St Mary Redcliffe, 1567 (PRO, E 179/6/23); 1568 (*CSPD* (Elizabeth), vol. xlviii, nos. 11 and 16); 1571 (*CPR* (13 Elizabeth), pt. I, no. 1344); 1574 (McGrath and Williams (ed.), *Bristol Wills*, i. 10 and 19). Exhibited to Bristol ecclesiastical authorities on 27 Nov. 1568, licence (preaching?) given by Matthew Archbishop of Canterbury, dated 27 Oct. 1568 (*Hockaday Collection*, 9(4) (231), transcription of Bristol Cathedral Library MS, fo. 95a). Ministered communion in St Ewen, 1567–8, 1568–9, 1570, 1571 (Masters and Ralph (eds.), *Church Book of St Ewen's*, 207, 211, 214, 217). Proctor for clergy of Bristol diocese in Convocation, 1571, 1572, 1585, 1586, 1589 (Boswell, *Ecclesiastical Division of the Diocese of Bristol*, 7). To receive 20s. (with John Jacobs) from the parish of St John the Baptist, which Master Chester had willed delivered for the poor of St James parish (BAO, P/StJB/ChW 1, 1575). Vicar, Henbury, deanery of Bristol, composition for first fruits 27 Nov. 1576, where apparently residing in 1579 (Thompson, 'Henbury', 165). Possibly presented to vicarage Berkeley, Glos., 1575 and presented to Walton, Wells diocese, 1570, vacated 1577; wrote three works (see Bibliography); born Devonshire and one of first ministers ordained by Gilbert Berkeley, Elizabeth's Bp. of B&W diocese (*DNB*, under Northbrooke). Adams describes him as 'a learned preacher who did much good in this city', but is mistaken in saying that he died of plague in 1574 (*Adams's Chronicle*, 114).

OKES, RICAS. See RICHARD ORIELL.

OLON (OLAN), JOHN. Priest, Spicers Chantry, St Nicholas, instituted 24 May 1528, vacated by 5 Dec. 1533 (H&WRO, 716–093 BA 2648, Reg. Ghinucci, fos. 5, 36, 62).

OLYVER (OLIVER), WILLIAM. Prior, Dominican friars, 7 May 1537; preaching in Bristol, brought before commission (*LP* xii. 1147). Said to have a degree from Cambridge; prior Dominicans, Cambridge, *c.*1533 (Venn, iii. 280);

1534–5 (Walter Gumbley, *Cambridge Dominicans* (Oxford: Oxford University Press, 1938), 42). June 1534, Cranmer protested to Cromwell about WO, OP, lately appointed prior of Dominicans, Cambridge; the man lacked the necessary qualifications, being of 'very small learning, sinister behaviour, ill qualities and of suspected conversation of living'; was also notorious as one who 'most indiscreetly preached against the King's grace's great cause and most defended the authority of the Bishop of Rome'. Cranmer had already sent a note of one of Oliver's sermons, 'which bill, if you had remembered, I doubt not but that ye would have provided for the said friar afore this time'(*LP* vii. 807, cited in Elton, *Policy and Police*, 14).

ORIELL (ORELL), RICHARD. Monk, St Augustine, at dissolution, 1539; chantry priest, Bedminster, 1548 (Baskerville, 'Dispossessed Religious of Gloucestershire', 95, 99; Weaver (ed.), *Wells Wills*, 97). Vicar, Bedminster (and thus, possibly curate St Mary Redcliffe), inst. 5 Nov. 1554, until 1592? (*Regs. B&W*, no. 777; Baskerville, 'Dispossessed Religious', 95). Appeared personally before pension commission, 1552; still receiving pension, 1555 (Baskerville, 'Dispossessed Religious', 99; Taylor, 'Religious Houses of Bristol', 119). Possibly Ricas Okes, curate of Redcliffe, owing for the clerical subsidy in 1556 (PRO, E 179/6/12). See also RICHARD HILL.

PACKEMAN, ROBERT. Stipendiary, Sts Philip and Jacob, Jan. 1541 (H&WRO, 802 BA 2764, fos. 193–4). Administration of his goods, 29 Apr. 1564; of Sts Philip and Jacob; died intestate and goods granted to Joan Warren, his natural sister, wife of John Warren; whole entry scored through (BAO, EP/J/1/5, p. 694).

PACY, CHRISTOPHER. Rector, St Werberg, composition for first fruits 15 Sept. 1544; sureties Walter Campyon of the parish of St Mary-le-Bow, London, grocer, and William Campyon of the parish of St Mary Aldermary, London, merchant tailor; both these parishes had reformist clergy in the 1530s (PRO, E 334/3, fo. 28); Brigden, *London and the Reformation*, 222, 262–3, 307, 384, 399, 402, 450–1; 1552 (PRO, PCC, Powell, 4) (William Shipman; 16 July 1551; 5 Feb. 1552); resigned or deprived *c.*1554, as authorities were seeking him (Seyer, *Memoirs of Bristol*, i. 234–5). Returned to St Werberg (paid £2 per year by parish), 1558; referred to as 'vicar' (of the rectory), 1562 (BAO, P/StW/ChW/3(a), fos. 21, 22, 23, 26, 35). Prebendary and canon, Bristol, instituted 8 Feb. 1560 until d. 1590 (BAO, EP/A/10/1, p. 85). Rector Olveston, Bristol Deanery, 1562 (BAO, EP/J/1/5, p. 420). See Giles Painter. See Chapter 7, n. 84, on the committed Protestants among the city's secular élite who were leaders in the parish of St Werberg.

PAINTER, GILES. Reader, St Nicholas, 2 Dec. 1564; complained of hearing Christopher Pacy preach a heretical doctrine in the cathedral 2 Aug. 1563 (BAO, EP/J/1/6, p. 93 and EP/J/1/5, p. 559; see Chapter 7, pp. 137–8).

PARKER, THOMAS (see next entry). Prior, Dominican friars, Bristol, at surrender, 10 Sept. 1538 (*LP* xiii, pt. 2, 320). Dispensed to hold a benefice with complete change of habit, 1 Dec. 1538 (Chambers, *Faculty Office Registers*, 166).

PARKER, THOMAS (see entry above). Austin friar, at surrender 10 Sept. 1538 (*LP* xiii, pt. 2, 320). Stipendiary, Temple, Jan. 1541 (H&WRO, 802 BA 2764, fo. 194). Baskerville lists as John Parker, in error ('Dispossessed Religious of Gloucestershire', 97). Perhaps the 'Parker' who appears to have been sexton of St Ewen, 1514–15 and 1517–18 (Masters and Ralph (eds.), *Church Book of St. Ewen's*, 153, 164). *Same name*, incumbent Saltford, B&W diocese, 5 Oct. 1539–54, restored at accession of Elizabeth (Field, *Province of Canterbury*, 11).

PATENSON, WILLIAM. Chantry priest, Sts Philip and Jacob, 1534 (H&WRO, 802 BA 2764, fo. 100). Possibly attended Oxford; possibly Cambridge, MA (Foster, iii. 1127; Venn, iii. 320).

PAVYE, BASTIAN. Clerk, underwent purgation in Bristol Consistory Court, 1556 (BAO, EP/J/1/2, p. 15).

PAVYE, HENRY. Monk, St Augustine, 1498, 1503–4, 1506–7, 1511–12, at dissolution 1539 (Sabin, 'Compotus Rolls of St. Augustine's Abbey', 200; Baskerville, 'Dispossessed Religious of Gloucestershire', 95). Curate, Horfield, Bristol deanery, 26 Apr. 1540 (H&WRO, 802 BA 2764, fo. 274).

PAYTWYN, WILLIAM. Stipendiary, Sts Philip and Jacob, 1534 (H&WRO, 802 BA 2764, fo. 100).

PEREPYN, THOMAS. Priest, Alleff and Leches Chantry, Christ Church (Holy Trinity), at dissolution 1548 (age 56) (Maclean, 'Chantry Certificates', 241). Appeared before pension committee, 1552; still receiving pension, 1555 (Baskerville, 'Dispossessed Religious of Gloucestershire', 108; Taylor, 'Religious Houses of Bristol', 126—listed as chantry of St Margarete in parish church of Bristol). Instituted Saltford, B&W diocese, 16 Sept. 1556, ejected at accession of Elizabeth (Field, *Province of Canterbury*, 11). Perpetual curate of Cirencester, 1558–? (Baskerville, 'Dispossessed Religious', 108). Possibly Thomas Peryn, Dominican friar, London Convent, 1508; Oxford Convent 1511; ordained subdeacon 17 June 1508; deacon 22 Dec. 1508; priest 5 Apr. 1511 (*BRUO, 1501–1540*, 444).

PHILIP. 'Sir Philip', priest of Corporation's St George's Chapel; beneficiary of will of Roger Hughes, prebendary of Bristol, 1545 (PRO, PCC, Alen, 5 (14 Dec. 1545; 2 Mar. 1546)). Received annual payments of 8 marks (£5. 6s. 8d.) by bailiff (*Mayor's Kalendar*, 82).

PHILLIPPES (PHYLLIPPES), WILLIAM (WATER). Parish priest (curate), St Thomas 1528, 1531, 1532, 1533, 1534 (PRO, PCC, Jankyn, 18 (William Rycart; 13 Sept. 1528; 18 June 1530; PCC, Hogen, 7 (Thomas Jubbes; 3 July 1533; and 17 Oct. 1533; Weaver (ed.), *Wells Wills*, 20, 25, 26). Stipendiary for one mass, All Saints, 1537 (BAO, P/AS/ChW, 1537, fo. 7). Stipendiary, Christ Church, 1556, 1559 (BAO, P/XCh/ChW/1(3), 1559).

PHILLIPS, BARTHOLOMEW. Curate, St James, 1564, 1565, 1566 (BAO, EP/J/1/5, p. 704, EP/J/1/6, pp. 20, 65, 93; BAO, P/StJ/ChW 1566, fo. 2).

PHILLIPS, JOHN. Possibly stipendiary, St Thomas, 1535 (Weaver (ed.), *Wells Wills*, 29). Office in Bristol cathedral, 1554 (BAO, DC/A/9/1/1 Computa 1554, fo. 41ᵛ). Perhaps instituted to church of Norton Mallewarde, B&W diocese, 1554 (*Regs. B&W*, no. 743).

PICKERING (PYKERYNS, PYKERYNM), ROGER. Sexton, All Saints, 1521, 1522, 1528, 1538, 1541, 1558 (does not appear in next account of 1560) (BAO, P/AS/ChW/under dates).

PINCHYN (PYNCHIN, PINCHIN), THOMAS (Robert Pinxton). Priest, Hospital of St Mark (Gaunts); letter dimissory, 1534 (H&WRO, 716–093 BA 2648, Reg. Ghinucci, fo. 34ᵛ); signed acknowledgement of royal supremacy, 10 Sept. 1534 (*LP* vii. 1216); at surrender, 1539 (*LP* xv. 139). Stipendiary, St John the Baptist, 26 Apr. 1540; Jan. 1541 (H&WRO, 802 BA 2764, fos. 194, 271). Priest, Balls Chantry, Christ Church (Holy Trinity), composition for first fruits 27 June 1544; at dissolution 1548 (age 36) (PRO, E 334/3, fo. 30; Maclean, 'Chantry Certificates', 242). Appeared before pension committee, 1552; still receiving pension, 1555 (Baskerville, 'Dispossessed Religious of Gloucestershire', 104, where in error says Pinchyn former Augustinian friar; Taylor, 'Religious Houses of Bristol', 121). Minor canon (as Richard Pinxton), Bristol Cathedral, 1550 (BAO, DC/A/9/1/1, Computa, 1550). Curate, Christ Church (Holy Trinity), 1555, 1556 (as Richard Pinchin), 1559, 1560 (PRO, PCC, More, 35 (Richard Watleye; 13 July 1555); PRO, E 179/6/12, 6/6, 6/8). Served one Easter, St Ewen, 1559–61 (Masters and Ralph (eds.), *Church Book of St. Ewen's*, 175). Curate, Eastchurch, 1560 (BAO, EP/J/1/5, p. 154). *Hockaday Abstracts* give as curate, St Mark, 11 Sept. 1563, without reference. Latimer, also without reference, says he was reader of St Mark, at £2 per year and resided in an adjoining tenement until he died about forty-five years later (Latimer, *The Annals of Bristol in the Sixteenth Century* (Bristol: J. Arrowsmith, 1908; repr. London: Redwood Press, 1970), 98–9).

POLLARD, FRANCISCUS. Prior, Kalendars' Guild, instituted 15 Apr. 1528 (H&WRO, 716–093 BA 2648, Reg. Ghinucci, fos. 5, 36). Oxford, Magdalen College, demonstrator, admitted 1505–6; fellow, 1507; still in 1512–13; supplicated with regard to proceeding BA, 14 and 16 Apr. and 15 June 1510; BA by 1512 (*BRUO 1501–1540*, 455). Son of John Pollard, mercer, and his wife Maud of St Nicholas, Bristol; in priest's orders by 1521 (Orme, 'Guild of Kalendars', 47).

POPLEY, JOHN. Of Bristol, 1528, when Crown ordered Mayor to attach him (*Mayor's Kalendar*, 51). Priest, Frampton's Chantry, St John the Baptist, Dean of Rural Deanery of Bristol, instituted to both 20 May 1531 (H&WRO, 716–093 BA 2648, Reg. Ghinucci, fos. 16, 47ᵛ). Priest, free chapel of Knowle, Bedminster, with chapel of Leigh annexed; farmed Portebury and Clareham, 1535 (*Valor ecclesiasticus*, i. 183, 187). Chancellor, St David diocese, *c.*1540, owing money to John Smith, merchant of Bristol (Vanes (ed.), *Ledger of John Smythe*, 36, 37). Oxford, B. Canon Law (*BRUO 1501–1540*, 696).

POPYNGAYE, STEPHEN. Ex-Franciscan friar, Dorchester (Baskerville, 'Dispossessed Religious', 464). Curate, Clifton, Bristol deanery, 1556, 1557 (PRO, E 179/6/12, 6/10). Rector, St Werberg, presented 30 Apr. 1557 (*CPR* 4 Philip & Mary). Curate, St James, 1560, 1561 (PRO, E 179/6/8; BAO, EP/J/1/4, pp. 230, 232). Served, probably once, St Ewen, 1559–61 (Masters and Ralph (eds.), *Church Book of St. Ewen's*, 176). Rector, St Martin, Warham, Dorset, 9 Oct. 1562; to marry Margaret Pope of St Werberg (BAO, EP/J/1/5, p. 445). Rector, Knowle, 1573; held for six years (Baskerville, 'Dispossessed Religious', 464).

POWELL, JOHN. Cleric. Will proved in Bristol Consistory Court and administration granted to Mr. David Harris, alderman, 26 Mar. 1563 (BAO, EP/J/1/5, p. 507).

PYEN, JOHN. Carmelite friar, Bristol, dispensed to change his habit, 27 May 1538 (Chambers (ed.), *Faculty Officer Registers*, 135).

PYLLE, JOHN. Instituted to church of Lamyet, B&W diocese, 27 Aug. 1530 (*Regs. B&W*, no. 380). Curate, Charde, Som., 15 Feb. 1542 (Weaver (ed.), *Somerset Medieval Wills*, 72–3). Rector, St Peter, composition for first fruits 27 Feb. 1542 (PRO, E 334/4, fo. 5). Vicar, Temple, 1559 (BAO, EP/J/1/4, p. 12; *Hockaday Abstracts*, vol. 453, under date); vacated by 19 Dec. 1560 (BAO, EP/J/1/5, p. 141). In 1560 he was the surrogate or deputy of Mr John Cotterell (Vicar General of the diocese) for the proving of a will of a parishioner in St Werberg (BAO, EP/J/1/5, p. 9).

PYNDER (PENDARE), JOHN. Austin friar, Bristol, at surrender, 10 Sept. 1538 (*LP* xiii. 319). Stipendiary, St Thomas, Jan. 1541 (H&WRO, 802 BA 2764, fo. 194). Priest, Welles Chantry, St Thomas, 1543–4 (BAO, P/StTh/ChW/1, under date). Priest, Williams Chantry, St Peter, at dissolution 1548 (age 60) (Maclean, 'Chantry Certificates', 240). Possibly appeared before pension commission, 1552; no longer receiving pension, 1555 (Baskerville, 'Dispossessed Religious of Gloucestershire', 107; Taylor, 'Religious Houses of Bristol', 120–6). Became deputy of John Cotterell (Vicar General of Bristol diocese), 8 Jan. 1560 (BAO, EP/J/1/5, p. 7). Perhaps the one instituted to living of Charleton, Devon., Exeter diocese, 29 Dec. 1561 (Field, *Province of Canterbury*, 110).

PYNNOCKE, JOHN. Prior, Kalendars' Guild, instituted 10 Jan. 1529; 1534 (styled 'mr.'); vacated by 24 Mar. 1535 (H&WRO, 716–093 BA 2648, Reg. Ghinucci, fos. 39ᵛ, 36, 73ᵛ; 802 BA 2764, fo. 99). A Bonhomme of Edington, Wilts.; Bishop of Syene, 1518; acted as a suffragan bishop, Salisbury diocese 1518–35. Instituted Prebendary, Durnford, Salisbury cathedral, 15 Sept. 1519, exchanged 24 Aug. 1520; instituted prebendary Chardstock, Salisbury cathedral, 20 Feb. 1524, until death; master of hospital of St John the Baptist, Wells, 1535 (Orme, 'Guild of Kalendars', 47). Orme contends Pynnocke appears not to have been a Master of Arts and represented a decline in qualifications of prior. He contends that because of his position as a master of a hospital in Wells he 'can hardly have been very active in Bristol during his five years as prior, which he terminated by resignation in 1535, shortly before his death' (p. 44). On the contrary, masters of hospitals were often not resident (cf. GEORGE CROFT, herein).

RASTELL (RASTALL, RESTALL, RASTLE), JOHN. Born at Bristol, *c.*1507 (BAO, EP/J/1/1, p. 220, transcribed in *Hockaday Abstracts*, vols. 445–56, under St Nicholas, 1557). Monk (student), St Augustine, at dissolution, 1539. Claimant to chantry in Winterbourne Church, was in 1540 arraigned before the Consistory Court of Worcester on various charges, among others that he 'was a public player of dice and other unlawful games'. Carried his claim to the chantry to the Court of Chancery, before which appeared as witness Nicholas Corbet, also an ex-monk of St Augustine, who testified that when they were monks there he knew JR to be a great dicer and carder and had heard that 'he had got at dice and cards of divers men in his chamber at the late monastery £10, £5 and 5 marks, especially the year before the dissolution of the monastery' (see NICHOLAS CORBETT). Priest, Bradston's Chantry, Winterbourne, 1542–8; appeared before pension commission, 1552; still receiving pension, 1555 (*Hockaday Abstracts*, vol. 'Winterbourne', under date; Baskerville, 'Dispossessed Religious', 454 and 'Dispossessed Religious of Gloucestershire', 95; Taylor, 'Religious Houses of Bristol', 120). Curate, Sts Philip and Jacob, 1541 (PRO, PCC, Alenger, 21 (John White the elder; 21 Jan 1541). Vicar, St Nicholas, presentation 1546; until death; will proved 1 Oct. 1563 (BAO, EP/A/3/69; EP/J/1/5, p. 571). Charged 15 May 1560 (with Thomas Tewe, curate of St Thomas) with permitting an unlicensed preacher to preach in his church (John Figge, vicar of Calne) (BAO, EP/J/1/5, p. 58). Probably became ill or non-resident by 28 June 1560, when he successfully petitioned the Consistory Court to allow David Martin to become reader of the parish during his absence (BAO, EP/J/1/5, p. 71). Not to be confused with the John Rastell of Gloucestershire who was expelled from New College, Oxford, for 'popery', went abroad, and supported the Catholic faith with his publications (McGrath, 'Gloucestershire and the Counter-Reformation', 11 and K. G. Powell, 'The Social Background to the Reformation in Gloucestershire', *Trans. B&GAS* 92 (1973), 116).

RAWLYNS (alias CARTELAGE), JOHN. Chaplain, White's Chantry, St Stephen, instituted 20 May 1527; stipendiary, All Saints, 1534; rector, St Ewen, instituted 15 Aug. 1535, until d. 1555 or 1556 (H&WRO, 802 BA 2764, fos. 99, 272; 716–093 BA 2648, Reg. Ghinucci, fo. 40; Masters and Ralph (eds.), *Church Book of St. Ewen's*, pp. xxxiv, 174). *Same name*, master of the boys, St Augustine's Abbey, 1503–4, who probably taught singing, besides doubling as grammar master to the canons (Orme, *Education in the West of England*, 202–3).

READE (READ, REDE), THOMAS. Monk of Hailes (Cistercian) at dissolution, 1539; still receiving pension, 1552 (of Oxenford; did not appear); 1555 (pension still payable) (Baskerville, 'Dispossessed Religious of Gloucestershire',

90, 113; Taylor, 'Religious Houses of Bristol', 110, 120). *Same name* (Thomas Rede), stipendiary, St Mary Redcliffe, 1557 (St Mary Redcliffe Parish Archive, ChW Accts., under date). Mr Read, stipendiary (minister), St Ewen, 1579–80 (Masters and Ralph (eds.), *Church Book of St. Ewen's*, 63). A Cistercian of same name in Marshalsea prison, 1579 (Baskerville, 'Dispossessed Religious of Gloucestershire', 90). (See also THOMAS BEDE and THOMAS GREADE.)

RISE (RICE, RYCE), ROGER. One of ministers (stipendiary), St Mary Redcliffe, 1554–7 (St Mary Redcliffe Parish Archive, ChW Accts., under year). Stipendiary, All Saints, 1558, 1560 (BAO, P/AS/ChW, 1558, 1560). Curate, St Ewen, probably mid-1562–Dec. 1567 (BAO, EP/J/1/6, p. 93; Masters and Ralph (eds.), *Church Book of St. Ewen's*, 207). Curate, Clifton, Bristol deanery, 1564 (BAO, EP/J/1/5, p. 93). Rector, St John the Baptist, composition for first fruits 8 July 1568 (PRO, E 334/8, fo. 149).

ROBERT. Clerk, St Nicholas, 1543; beneficiary, received 'my black gown that I wear every day lined with satin of "Sypers"' (PRO, PCC, Spert, 25 (Henry White, haberdasher; 20 Apr. 1533; 8 Oct. 1543).

ROCHE, CHRISTOPHER. Dominican friar, recently of Bristol; of B&W diocese, dispensed to change his habit for that of a secular priest, 8 May 1537 (Chambers (ed.), *Faculty Office Registers*, 97).

ROLLES, THOMAS. Stipendiary, St Mary Redcliffe, 1553 (one-quarter year) and 1554 (St Mary Redcliffe Parish Archive, ChW Accts., under year).

ROOST, ROBERT. Vicar, St Leonard, composition for first fruits 28 June 1547 (PRO, E 334, Indexes, set 3; the page in Comp. Bk., vol. 4, which should contain details, is missing). Possibly same as Robert Rowe (see below).

ROWE (ROE), ROBERT. Vicar, All Saints, probably by 1556 when Giles Roe's brother was described as 'curate' and still 5 Feb. 1565, when he was called 'rector'. He had, however, been in poor health since 1561, when his illness had cancelled services in the parish and Richard Houseman had been hired as reader to substitute for him on condition that the reader not preach or minister the sacraments. In 1564 Houseman was ordered to procure letters of ordination, which suggests the possibility that his responsibilities were growing. In Feb. 1565 Rowe's bodily infirmity forced officials of the Consistory Court to take his evidence in a case at his house (BAO, EP/J/1/1, p. 117, transcribed in *Hockaday Abstracts*, vol. 432, All Saints, 1556; EP/J/1/5, pp. 180, 266, 93; EP/J/1/6, p. 125). (See also ROBERT ROOST.)

RYMAR, ROGER. Stipendiary, St Mary Redcliffe, part-time 1559 and 1560 (St Mary Redcliffe Parish Archive, ChW Accts., under year).

SALWEY, THOMAS. Stipendiary, St Leonard, 26 Apr. 1540; Jan. 1541 (H&WRO, 802 BA 2764, fos. 193, 270).

SANDERSON, ROBERT. Franciscan prior, Richmond, at surrender 19 Jan. 1539; possibly prior of Bristol house, 1538 (Taylor, 'Religious Houses of Bristol, 198).

SANDFORD (SAMPFORD), NICHOLAS. Born at Thorpe Salvyn, Yorks. Prior, Austin friars, Bristol, by 1536; at surrender, 1538 (PRO, C1 894; *LP* xiii, pt. 2, 319). Sometime between 1533 and 1538 involved in Chancery case; charged with repaying to John Browne what one of his friars, John Clerke, had stolen from Browne's house (PRO, C1 894). Vicar, Bedminster (and curate, St Mary Redcliffe), 23 Mar. 1540, 1541, 1543; vacated well before 5 Nov. 1554, when successor being replaced (*Regs. B&W*, nos. 777, 946; Baskerville, 'Dispossessed Religious of Gloucestershire', 97; Weaver (ed.), *Wells Wills*, 46). In Sept. and Oct. 1543, testified in probate case, concerning will of John Browne, in which bequests to former Austin friars, including NS, were in dispute; NS was '50 years and more' in age (Weaver (ed.), *Somerset Medieval Wills*, 46).

SAXCTHEGR, JOHN. Priest, Richard White's Chantry, St Stephen, 1527 (BAO, St Stephen's Inventory, p. 33).

SHAYNSHUM (STREINSHAM), WILLIAM. Stipendiary, St Mary-le-Porte, Jan. 1541 (H&WRO, 802 BA 2764, fo. 194). Ex-religious; at Tewkesbury at dissolution, Jan. 1540; St Anne priest in St John the Baptist, Gloucester, 1548, 1552, 1558; appeared personally before pension commission, 1552; pension list, 1555 (Baskerville, 'Dispossessed Religious of Gloucestershire', 85, 107; Taylor, 'Religious Houses of Bristol', 117).

SHEPERDE, RICHARD. Stipendiary, St Ewen, 1534 (H&WRO, 802 BA 2764, fo. 100).

SHEREMAN (SHERMAN, SHARMAN), JOHN. Stipendiary, Temple, 1531, 1535, 1540 (Weaver (ed.), *Wells Wills*, 22, 23; H&WRO, 802 BA 2764, fo. 194). Priest, Frauncis Chantry, Temple, at dissolution 1548 (age 76) (Maclean (ed.), 'Chantry Certificates', 247); still receiving pension, 1555 (Taylor, 'Religious Houses of Bristol, 122). Witness for purgation of John Roulande alias Martin and Bastian Pavye, clerk, 1556 (BAO, EP/J/1/2, p. 15). Curate, St Ewen, 1557 (PRO, E 179/6/10 (not listed 1556)).

SHILBAN, THOMAS. Stipendiary, St Mary Redcliffe, Jan. 1541 (H&WRO, 802 BA 2764, fo. 194).

SHOLD, RICHARD. Clerk, St Nicholas, 1531; received 33*s*. 4*d*. 'for keeping of the crowd [the crypt]' (Nicholls and Taylor, *Bristol, Past and Present*, ii. 163 (from MS accts.).

SIMONDES (SIMONS, SYMONDES, SYMONS, SMYTH?), RICHARD. Curate, St Peter, 18 Dec. 1562; exhibited orders 24 May 1563, granted by Edward Bishop of London, dated 25 July 1560; admonished henceforth not to hold two cures together; curate, Sts Philip and Jacob, made one of sequestrators of tithes, 11 Oct. 1563; 3 Nov. 1564 (BAO, EP/J/1/5, pp. 481, 529, 580; EP/J/1/6, p. 69). Probably identical with Richard Smyth, who compounded for vicarage of Sts Philip and Jacob, 15 Mar. 1566 and whose sureties were of London (PRO, E 334/8, fo. 74). Parish served by curate, Roger Chaloner, 1567; John Tewe presented to living, 1568, but apparently not instituted (PRO, E 179/6/23; BAO, EP/A/3/69(14) 6 June 1568).

SMYTH (-E), JOHN. Probably more than one man. Prior, Austin friars, Bristol, 22 Jan. 1533 (*LP* vi. 66). Possibly son of Johan Vaughan of St Nicholas, Bristol, Dec. 1529 (PRO, PCC, Jankyn (22 Oct. 1530)). Deputy to John Cotterell, B&W diocese by 28 Jan. 1558 and in Bristol diocese by 1570 (*Regs. B&W*, no. 881; BAO, DC/A/9/1/2, Computa, 1570). Vicar, Barow, B&W diocese, instituted 5 May 1546; parson, Weston in Gordano, deprived by 18 Aug. 1554; canon and prebendary of Combe I, B&W diocese, instituted 15 Feb. 1557; vicar, Northpetherton, 6 Jan. 1558; rector, Hunspell, B&W diocese, instituted 3 Mar. 1558 (*Regs. B&W*, nos. 631, 672, 744, 864, 876, 884). BA and BCL *Regs. B&W*, nos. 884, 864).

SMYTH, RICHARD. See RICHARD SIMONDES.

SMYTHYMAN, WILLIAM. Priest, Evorarde le Frenches Chantry, St Nicholas, 1534, 1540, at dissolution 1548 (age 42) (H&WRO, 802 BA 2764, fos. 99, 269; Maclean (ed.), 'Chantry Certificates', 237). Still receiving pension, 1552 (appeared before pension commission); 1555 (Baskerville, 'Dispossessed Religious of Gloucestershire', 105; Taylor, 'Religious Houses of Bristol', 122). Stipendiary, St Nicholas, 1552, 1557 (Wadley, *Notes*, 193; PRO, PCC, Wrastley, 8 (Thomas Johns; 23 Mar. 1556)).

SOWTHALL, RALPH. Chantry priest, St Nicholas, 1534 (H&WRO, 802 BA 2764, fo. 99).

SPENDALLE (SPENDLOVE?), HENRIE. Priest, Forthies Chantry, Sts Philip and Jacob, at dissolution 1548 (age 40) (Maclean (ed.), 'Chantry Certificates', 236). Still receiving pension, 1552 (appeared before pension commission); 1555 (Baskerville, 'Dispossessed Religious of Gloucestershire', 122). Possibly Henry Spendlove, curate, Marshfield, 1551 (Baskerville, 'Dispossessed Religious', 105).

SPRINT, THOMAS. Chantry priest, Holy Trinity (Christ Church), 1534 (H&WRO, 802 BA 2764, fo. 99). Stipendiary, St Ewen, one service?, 1547–8 (Masters and Ralph (eds.), *Church Book of St. Ewen's*, 183). Vicar, Paulett, B&W diocese by 21 May 1537; resigned by 27 Aug. 1542 (*Regs. B&W*, nos. 526, 943). D. about Christmas 1551 (Baskerville, 'Dispossessed Religious of Gloucestershire', 118). Oxford, St Mary Hall, probably scholar in 1532; BA, admitted 21 Feb. 1530, determined Lent 1530; supplicated as *pharmacopola* for leave to practise medicine, Apr. 1548 (*BRUO 1501–1540*, 531). John Sprint, a prominent parishioner of St Ewen, was an apothecary (Masters and Ralph (eds.), *Church Book of St. Ewen's*, p. xxii). John Sprint, son of John Sprint, apothecary, of Gloucester, became dean of Bristol cathedral, 1580. His son became vicar, Thornbury, Glos., 1602; and his grandson John, same name as held the cure of Hampstead, Middlesex from 1633 until ejected, 1662, when settled at Andover, Hants, where was pastor to a dissenting congregation until his death (Foster, iv. 1402). See Appendix 2.

STANDLEY, WALTER. Priest of Anthony Kingston, the original lessee of the property of the priory of St James (PRO, C1 1213).

STAUNTON, THOMAS. Rector, St Lawrence, composition for first fruits 27 May 1550 (PRO, E 334/4, fo. 52).

STERE (STORR), JOHN. Augustinian friar, Bristol, at surrender 10 Sept. 1538 (*LP* xiii, pt. 2, 319; Baskerville, 'Dispossessed Religious of Gloucestershire', 97).

STURGES (TURGES), ROGER. Priest, apparently of Burton's Chantry, St Thomas; d. between 6 Oct. 1535 and 3 Feb. 1536 (Weaver (ed.), *Wells Wills*, 25; PRO, E 334/9, fo. 99; Wadley, *Notes*, 236, 277; McGrath and Williams, *Bristol Wills*, ii. 100).

STYLMPES, JOHN. Cleric, beneficiary, will of Roger Sturges, priest of St Thomas, 6 Oct. 1535 (Weaver (ed.), *Wells Wills*, 28).

SWADALL, WILLIAM. Signed certificate of preaching of Powell and Hubberdine, 5 June 1533 (*LP* vi. 596). Probably Dominican friar; Oxford Convent, 1516; London Convent, 1519; Oxford Convent, 1524, 1526; London Convent at dissolution, 12 Nov. 1538. After twelve yrs. study in logic, philosophy and theology, B.Th. supplicated 19 Mar. 1524, admitted 17 Apr. 1526. Ordained subdeacon 17 May 1516; deacon 17 Dec. 1519; priest 21 Sept. 1521. Licensed to preach in Hereford diocese, 6 Oct. 1529 (*BRUO, 1501–1540*, 549).

SYLKE (SILKE), THOMAS. Of Worcester diocese (almost certainly Bristol). Ordained subdeacon and deacon 28 Oct. 1525, B&W diocese, with dispensation from Archbishop of York, papal legate de latere, for ordination at an irregular season (*Regs. B&W*, no. 480; SRO, D/D/B, Reg. 12, fo. 17). In priest's orders by Jan. 1526. Vicar, St Leonard, by 1529 (PRO, PCC, Jankyn 15 (Roger Davis; 17 Aug. 1529)), 1534, 1540, 1541 (H&WRO, 802 BA 2764, fos. 100, 193, 271); resigned by 23 June 1547 (PRO, E 334, Indexes, set 3 under Robert Roost). Prior, priest of first chantry Kalendars' Guild, instituted 8 Oct 1540 (H&WRO, 716–093 BA 2648, Reg. Bell, fo. 12); at dissolution 1548 (age not given) (Maclean, 'Chantry Certificates', 246). Rector, Spetisbury, Dorset, admitted 1545; vacated by 1574; canon and 5th prebendary of Bristol, admitted 4 June 1546; until death. Rector, Frampton Cotterell, Glos., composition for first fruits 9 Oct. 1553. Vicar, Banwell, Som., 1554; rector, Cheriton, Devon, presented 6 Mar. 1558; Vicar, Marston St Laurence, Northants., 1560. BA, admitted 31 Mar. 1522, determined 1523), MA (incept 2 July 1526) (*BRUO, 1501–1540*, 552; Foster, iv. 1356). D. between 30 June 1571 and 14 Sept. 1575 (*CPR* (13 Elizabeth), pt. 1, C.66/1071, no. 1344; Lambeth Reg. Parker II, fo. 127, transcribed in *Hockaday Abstracts*, vol. 433 (Bristol Cathedral), under 1575).

SYSSELL (SYSELL), JOHN. Asst. teacher (*hipodidascul*) of cathedral grammar school, 1550, 1554 (BAO, DC/A/9/1/1 Computa, under dates).

TASKER, THOMAS. Born at Worcester, *c*.1484 (BAO, EP/J/1/1, p. 193, transcribed in *Hockaday Abstracts*, vols. 445–6, under St Nicholas, 1556; probably should be under 1554). Rector, St John the Baptist, instituted 6 May

1531, until death; Rural Dean of Bristol, collated 11 Dec. 1533 (H&WRO, 802 BA 2764, fos. 100, 271, 272; 716–093 BA 2648, Reg. Ghinucci, fos. 14ᵛ, 28ᵛ). Rector, Wearcon, 1551 (BAO, DC/A/9/1/1 Computa, 1551). D. after 1556; probably shortly before will proved, Jan.–July 1563; inventory of goods worth £7. 2*s*. 6*d*. (PRO, PCC, Wrastley, 5 (William Jaye; 16 Feb. 1556); BAO, EP/J/1/5, p. 545). Possibly Cambridge, BCL (Venn, iv. 200).

TEW (TEWE, CHEW), THOMAS. Curate, St Thomas, 1558, 1559, 1560, 1561, 1563, 1567, 1574, 1583 (PRO, E 179/6/6, 6/8; BAO, EP/J/1/5, pp. 58, 212; McGrath and Williams (eds.), *Bristol Wills*, i. 14; Wadley, *Notes*, 238, 244). Presented to vicarage, Sts Philip and Jacob, but apparently not instituted (BAO, EP/A/3/69(14); see ROGER CHALONER and THOMAS COLMAN). Perhaps the same as incumbent East Buckland, Devon., Exeter diocese, composition for first fruits 23 Dec. 1546–54, restored at accession of Elizabeth (Field, *Province of Canterbury*, 110).

THOMAS, DAVID. Possibly stipendiary, St Mary Redcliffe, 1533 (Weaver (ed.), *Wells Wills*, 19). Priest, Knape Chapel (Chapel of St John the Evangelist), St Nicholas parish, at dissolution 1548 (age 51) (Maclean (ed.), 'Chantry Certificates', 238). Still receiving pension 1552 (appeared before pension commission), 1555 (Baskerville, 'Dispossessed Religious of Gloucestershire', 104; Taylor, 'Religious Houses of Bristol', 121). Rector, Brockly, Som., 1558; d. 1578 (Baskerville, 'Dispossessed Religious', 104).

THOMAS, JOHN. Curate, St Peter, 1564 (BAO, EP/J/1/5, p. 626; EP/J/1/6, p. 65; PRO, E 179/6/18). *Same name*, vicar All Saints, 'master', 1498 (Reg. Archbp. Morton, fo. 177, cited in *Hockaday Abstracts*, vol. 432, under date); instituted St George, Dunster, B&W diocese, 27 Jan. 1529; inst. Camerton, B&W diocese, 16 June 1554 (*Regs. B&W*, nos. 325, 704).

TOGOOD (TOOGOOD), EDWARD. Vicar, Temple, Mar. 1538, deprived by 16 Feb. 1555 (PRO, PCC, Crumwell, 20 (Edward Cowrtelove; 10 Mar. 1538; 10 Apr. 1538); *Regs. B&W*, no. 944). Vicar, Hungerford, Berks., composition for first fruits 24 Sept. 1550 (PRO, E 334/4, fo. 60). Rector, Wraxall, Som., inst. 21 Sept. 1554 (Robert Cheltenham was deprived of this living for marriage). Restored vicar of Temple by 19 Dec. 1560 (BAO, EP/J/1/5, p. 141). Togood may have been married at the accession of Mary and allowed to take another living after giving up his wife. He probably took her back again at the accession of Elizabeth when he returned to Temple; less than a month after his will was proved in Bristol Consistory Court (30 Oct. 1563), another cleric, William Austen, rector of Staunton Quinton, sought the required testimonial letters for his marriage to one Joan Togood of Bristol, widow (20 Nov. 1563) (BAO, EP/J/1/5, pp. 585, 601). Proctor in Bristol Consistory Court, 1560–3 (BAO, EP/J/1/5, pp. 66, 68, 141, 392, 453, 462, 491, 531). Probably d. 1563. Emden mistakenly says he died by Dec. 1560, and does not note his return to Bristol. BA; MA, probably Oxford (*BRUO, 1501–1540*, 570; *Regs. B&W*, no. 758). Of interest: 6 Aug. 1619, Mary Toogood born to Mr Richard Toogood, minister, and Christian his wife (Sabin, *Registers of the Church of St Augustine-the-Less*, 46). Richard Toogood, B.Th., became a canon and prebendary of Bristol's Holy Trinity Cathedral in 1660 and dean of the chapter in 1667 (E. Boswell, *The Ecclesiastical Division of the Diocese of Bristol* (Sherborne: J. Penny, 1827)).

TOSTE (TOFFIT), JOHN. Rector, St John the Baptist, 1510 (witness to will of Robert Fychett, clerk priest of Eborard le Frensch's chantry, St Mary Redcliffe), 1512; gave parish 'a new processional of print', 1512 (PRO, PCC, 36, Bennett, cited in E. Williams, *Canynges Chantries*, 26); BAO, P/StJB/ChW1, fos. 8 and 33; Nicholls and Taylor, *Bristol, Past and Present*, ii. 150). Parson [*sic*], St James and Dean of Bristol (rural dean), 1522 (PRO, PCC, Porche, 23 (Henry Kemys; 1 Oct. 1522; 7 Feb. 1529)).

TOWNELY, WILLIAM. Rector, St Michael, 1556 (BAO, EP/J/1/3, p. 40). Possibly attended Cambridge (Venn, iv. 258).

TOWNSHEND, HENRY. Cleric of Redcliffe; involved in dispute with James Hilman, curate of Redcliffe, who promoted an office case against him in Bristol Consistory Court in December 1560 (BAO, EP/J/1/5, pp. 129, 135, 144).

TURGES, ROGER. See STURGES.

TYSON (TYZON), THOMAS. Rector, St Stephen, composition for first fruits 5 May 1580; 1583, 1593, 1597 (PRO, E 334/9, fo. 99; Wadley, *Notes*, 236, 277; McGrath and Williams (eds.), *Bristol Wills*, ii. 100).

UNDERHILL, WILLIAM. Chantry priest, St. James, 1534; 26 Apr. 1540 (H&WRO, 802 BA 2764, fos. 100, 270).

UNDERWOOD, WILLIAM. Ordained deacon to title of regular canon of monastery of St Augustine, 1 Apr. 1525 (SRO, D/D/B, Reg. 12, B&W diocese, Bp. Clerke, fo. 11). Monk, St Augustine at dissolution, 1539 (Baskerville, 'Dispossessed Religious of Gloucestershire', p. 95). Stipendiary, Christ Church (Holy Trinity), 26 Apr. 1540; Jan. 1541 (H&WRO, 802 BA 2764, fos. 193, 269). The pension commissioners' report of 1552 does not list him, but he reappeared on the pension list of 1555 (Baskerville, 'Dispossessed Religious', 86–7; Taylor, 'Religious Houses of Bristol', 119).

VAUGHAN, RICHARD. Curate, St Leonard, 1556; 1557; possibly 1562 (PRO, E 179/6/12, 6/10; BAO, EP/J/1/5, p. 387). *Same name*, ex-monk of Malmesbury; curate of Churcham, Glos., 1549; 1553 (Baskerville, 'Dispossessed Religious of Gloucestershire', 75).

VAUGHAN, SIMON, Carmelite friar, Bristol, at surrender, 28 July 1538 (PRO, E 36/115, p. 19). Dispensed to leave his order and hold a benefice 10 Sept. 1538 (Chambers (ed.), *Faculty Office Registers*, 162).

VINCENT, W. Vicar, Bedminster and Redcliffe, 10 Apr. 1539 (*Regs. B&W*, no. 945).

WALE (WATE, WHALLEY, WHALE, WALL, WARE), RICHARD. Wale or Wate, Priest, Kalendars' Guild, instituted 27 Sept. 1539; 26 Apr. 1540 when also Curate, St Mary-le-Porte (H&WRO, 716-093 2648, Reg. Bell, fo. 1; 802 BA

2764, fo. 272). Wale witnessed will of John Flooke, prior of Kalendars' Guild, 11 Sept. 1540 (H&WRO, BA 3585/4b 1540, no. 61). Whalley, priest, Kalendars' Guild, at dissolution 1548 (age 40) (Maclean, 'Chantry Certificates', 246). Still receiving pension 1552 (appeared before pension commission), 1555 (Baskerville, 'Dispossessed Religious of Gloucestershire', 105; Taylor, 'Religious Houses of Bristol', 122). Ware and Wall, Deacon, Bristol Cathedral, 1550, 1554; perhaps minor canon, 1554 (BAO, DC/9/1/1 Computa 1550, 1554). Wall, letter dimissory, 18 Sept. 1524; stipendiary, Olveston, Bristol Deanery, 1534 (H&WRO, 716–093 BA 2648, Reg. Ghinucci, fo. 7; 802 BA 2764, fo. 100).

WALWORTH, J. Minister, St Werberg, May 1563; apparently judge in Consistory Court, 1564 (BAO, EP/J/1/5, pp. 520, 706).

WARD, HUGH. Minister, St Ewen, 1558, 1559, 1561/62 (Masters and Ralph (eds.), *Church Book of St. Ewen's*, 174, 195).

WATERHOUSE, EDWARD. Rector, St Ewen, 8 Oct. 1515 (Masters and Ralph (eds.), *Church Book of St. Ewen's*, p. xxxiii). Probably Cambridge BA, MA; of York diocese; ordained priest 26 Mar. 1513, Salisbury diocese (*BRUO 1501–1540*, 609).

WAYNE, WILLIAM. Vicar, Temple, instituted 9 Nov. 1523; title 'Master' suggests degree (*Regs. B&W*, no. 160).

WELLYS, ROBERT. Dominican friar, Bristol, at surrender, 10 Sept. 1538 (*LP* xiii, pt. 2, 320).

WHALEY, JOHN. Stipendiary, St James, Jan. 1541 (H&WRO, 802 BA 2764, fo. 194).

WHARTEN (WHARTON, WARTEN, FORTUNE), ROBERT (J.). Curate, St Mary Redcliffe, 5 Dec. 1561; 28 Feb. 1562, licence to preach from John Bp. of Norwich, dated 7 Oct. 1560, exhibited; ordered by the Consistory Court not to preach outside his cure without authority; inhibited from further preaching within the diocese and province of Canterbury (BAO, EP/J/1/5, pp. 239, 324, 338).

WHITE, JOHN. Rector, St Peter, inst. 27 May 1533; 1534; living vacant in 1540 (H&WRO, 716–093 BA 2648, Reg. Ghinucci, fo. 59). Among first six minor canons of Bristol Cathedral, 1542 (Nicholls and Taylor, *Bristol, Past and Present*, ii. 68). Possibly Oxford BA (*BRUO, 1501–1540*, 36–7).

WILKINS (WYLKINS), WILLIAM. Clerk or stipendiary, St Mary Redcliffe, 1552, 1553, 1554, 1556 (St Mary Redcliffe Parish Archive, ChW Accts., under date).

WILLIAMS, DAVY. Curate, St Mary Redcliffe, 1574 (McGrath and Williams (eds.), *Bristol Wills*, ii. 19). Curate, St James, 1577 (Churchwardens' Accts., quoted in Nicholls and Taylor, *Bristol, Past and Present*, ii. 36–7).

WILLIAMS, HENRY. Chantry priest, St Stephen, 1534; 26 Apr. 1540 (H&WRO, 802 BA 2764, fos. 99, 269). Probably not man of *same name*, prebendary of Bedminster and Redcliffe, 1534–54 (see *BRUO, 1501–1540*, 629–30).

WILLIAMS (WYLLYAMS), JOHN. Of Holy Trinity (Christ Church) parish, Bristol. Vicar, St Nicholas, 1534; non-res. 26 Apr. 1540 (H&WRO, 802 BA 2764, fos. 99, 269). Canon and prebendary of Exeter, collated 4 Nov. 1528; until death; vicar, Colebrooke, Devon, admitted 17 June 1533; until death; canon and 5th prebendary, Bristol, admitted 4 Apr. 1544; until death. Son of Oxford tenant; Winchester College, scholar, admitted 1515, age 14; New College, scholar, admitted 31 Jan. 1519; fellow, 1521; vacated 1526. BA, admitted 22 Mar. 1523; MA, incepted 2 July 1526; B.Th., supplicated 11 Oct. 1532. Sued for rent of schools by University College, Feb. 1528. D. by May 1546 (*BRUO 1501–1540*, 630). (See also THOMAS MOLENCE.)

WILLIAMS, THOMAS. Curate, St Peter, 30 July 1532 (Wadley, *Notes*, 183). Priest, St Nicholas, 26 June 1547 (Wadley, *Notes*, 189). Position (minor canon?), Bristol cathedral, 1554 (BAO, DC/A/9/1/1 Computa, 1554). Possibly Oxford, BA, MA (Foster, iv. 1644). *Same name*, instituted Cheriton Fitzpaine, Devonshire, Exeter diocese, 23 Feb. 1560 (Field, *Province of Canterbury*, 110).

WODBYE, WILLIAM. Rector, St Peter, presented 11 Dec. 1561 (BAO, EP/A/3/68).

WOOLFF, WYLLYAM. Curate, St James, 27 Nov. 1574 (McGrath and Williams (eds.), *Bristol Wills*, i. 15).

WRIGHT, THOMAS. Cleric, St Mary Redcliffe, 1560 (St Mary Redcliffe Parish Archive, ChW Accts., under year). Receiver general for cathedral chapter, 1541(*sic*) (see monogram in Nicholls and Taylor, *Bristol, Past and Present*, ii. 68), 1550, 1551, 1553, 1555, but not 1554 (BAO, DC/A/9/1/1, Computa, under year). Possibly Cambridge BA, Oxford MA (Venn, iv. 477; Foster, iv. 1588).

WRINGTON, WILLIAM. Monk, St Augustine at dissolution, 9 Dec. 1539; presumably alias Houlder, chantry priest, Berkeley, 1548; curate, Dowdeswell, 1551 (Baskerville, 'Dispossessed Religious of Gloucestershire', 95).

WROXALL, THOMAS. Carmelite friar, Bristol, at surrender, 28 July 1538 (PRO, E 36/115, p. 19). Dispensed to leave order and hold a benefice (Chambers (ed.), *Faculty Office Registers*, 162).

WYGGE (WYGGEN), JOHN? Prior, Austin friars, Bristol, 13 Apr. 1535 (*LP* viii. 540). 11 May 1528, Thomas Hemsted confessed before Tunstall, Bishop of London, that the Austins of Clare, namely John Wyggen, Thomas Topley, and William Gardyner held the same heretical opinions as he, that pardons are not profitable; the sacrament of the altar not the very body of Christ but done for remembrance of Christ's passion; pilgrimages were of no effect, etc. He said that they had been misled by Richard Fox, curate of Steeple Bumstead, Essex. Another accused friar of Clare, Robert Topley, a brother of Thomas, declared that Miles Coverdale had left the Austin friars of Cambridge in Lent 1528 and wearing the garb of a secular priest, lived with Richard Fox, preaching like him against confession, worship of images, etc. in the villages of Essex. Gardyner recanted in 1528 and Thomas Topley and John Wyggen must have followed suit. JW is no doubt identical with John Wygge who left the Austins of Oxford in 1531 owing 33s. 8d. The monastery kept his mare which was worth, however, only 7s. It would be in conformity with practices of the period if the man also was the Mr Wygge, prior of the Bristol Austins in July 1535 (Roth, *English Austin Friars, 1249–1538*, ii. 433, 449). Oxford, BTh., supplicated 11 Mar. 1530 (Roth, *English Austin Friars*, ii. 451).

YATE, (YALE?, GATE, GALE?), THOMAS. Stipendiary, St Thomas, Jan. 1541 (H&WRO, 802 BA 2764, fo. 194).

YERETH (YEROTH, -E), THOMAS. Vicar, All Saints, 1539; 26 Apr. 1540 (BAO, P/AS/ChW/1539; H&WRO, 802 BA 2764, fo. 271); instituted after 1534 (see THOMAS MOLENCE). Sacrist, college of chapel of Wymborne Myster, Deanery of Pymp're, Archdeaconry of Dorset, 1535; priest of Rodcotts Chantry in same college, 1535 (*Valor ecclesiasticus*, i. 273).

YOKE, JOHN. Clerk, All Saints, 1533; received 23s. 4d. per qtr. (BAO, P/AS/ChW,/under date).

Appendix 2

Deans of Holy Trinity Cathedral 1542–1580

WILLIAM SNOW. 1542–50 (BAO, DC/A/9/1/1, 1550). B.Th., Oxford (Foster, iv. 1388; *BRUO 1501–1540*, 527; Le Neve, *Fasti Ecclesiae Anglicanae*, i. 222).

JOHN WHITEHEARE. 1550–res. 1552 (BAO, DC/A/9/1/1, 1550).

GEORGE CAREWE. Adm. 5 Nov. 1552–dep. 1554. Probably BA, Oxford; MA, D.Th., probably abroad. (Cont. below.)

HENRY JOLIFFE. Granted 22 Aug., installed 9 Sept. 1554–9; may have resigned when Dalby ceded jurisdiction as Chancellor in the diocese in the Consistory Court 9 June 1559; cited on 29 Aug. by Queen's commissioners to appear in Consistory Court on 1 Sept. having 'fled' with Dalby; commissioners did not reach Bristol until 27 Sept. 1559 (*CPR* (2 Philip & Mary, 203; BAO, EP/J/1/4, pp. 20, 27; EP/A/10/1/1, pp. 85, 86). BA, MA, B.Th., Cambridge (Venn, ii. 483).

GEORGE CAREWE. (See above.) Restored 10 Nov. 1559–res. 1580. LeNeve and Emden are mistaken in saying he vacated in 1571. In 1576 he made three canons his proctors for the rule of the cathedral church (Foster, i. 236; *BRUO 1501–1540*, 101–3; Le Neve, *Fasti Ecclesiae Anglicanae*, i. 223; BAO, EP/A/10/1/1, p. 85).

JOHN SPRINT. Installed 1 Mar. 1580–d. 1590. Made a proxy for government of the cathedral church 2 Dec. 1586. Charged with absence 16 Dec. 1589. 'Auditus' 12 Jan. 1590. Anthony Watson instituted dean 22 July 1590 (BAO, EP/10/1/1, p. 85). BA, MA, B.Th., D.Th., Oxford (Foster, iv. 1402).

Appendix 3

Canons/Prebendaries of Bristol Instituted by 1584

STALL I

JOHN GOUGH. 1542–d. by 1544. Probably BA, Cambridge (as Googe, Gugge) (*LP* xvii. 443 (9); Venn, ii. 232).
JOHN BARLOW. Presented 10 Feb. 1544–deprived 1554. BA, MA, Oxford. (*BRUO 1501–1540*, 26–7).
JOHN RYXMAN. Installed 16 June 1554–d. Dec. 1557. BA, MA, B.Th., Oxford. (*BRUO 1501–1540*, 499; Foster, iii. 1260).
WILLIAM DALBY. Presented 21 Dec. 1558. BCL, Oxford. Resigned jurisdiction as Chancellor of diocese, 9 June 1559; said to have 'fled'; cited 29 Aug. 1559 to appear before Queen's commissioners on 1 Sept.; they did not reach Bristol until 27 Sept. 1559 (BAO, EP/J/1/4, pp. 20, 26; BAO, A/10/1/1, pp. 85, 86; *BRUO 1501–1540*, 158–9).
ARTHUR SAULE. Presented 25 Jan., installed 30 Jan. 1560–at least 1580; successor Richard Hackluyt, installed between 24 May 1585 and 1587 (BAO, EP/A/10/1/1, p. 85; E. Boswell, *Ecclesiastical Division of the Diocese of Bristol*, 10). MA, Oxford (Garrett, *Marian Exiles*, 284–5).

STALL II

ROGER EDGEWORTH. 1542–d. after 24 Dec. 1559, by 17 Jan. 1560 (Wilson, 'An Edition of Edgeworth's *Sermons*', 106). BA, MA, D.Th., Oxford (*LP*, xvii. 443(9); *BRUO 1501–1540*, 184–5).
CHRISTOPHER PACY. Presented 2 Feb., installed 8 Feb. 1560–d. between 22 July and 11 Sept. 1590 (BAO, EP/A/10/1/1, p. 85; Boswell, *Ecclesiastical Division of the Diocese of Bristol*, 10). Styled MA. See Appendix 1.

STALL III

HENRY MORGAN. 1542–resigned 1554 (on promotion as Bishop of St David's, consecrated 1 Apr. 1554). B. Canon Law, BCL, DDL, Oxford (*LP* xvii. 443(9); *BRUO 1501–1540*, 401).

RICHARD HUGHES. Presented 16 Sept. 1554–d. by July 1563. BA, MA, Oxford (cf. *BRUO 1501–1540*, 286–7). See Appendix 1.

JOHN BRIDGEWATER. Admitted 1563–1574 or 1576. Foster says he abandoned his preferments, went to Rheims and joined the Jesuits in 1574, but was deprived of his prebend in Bristol in 1576 (i. 182). His successor's record of institution says he resigned (Lambeth Reg. Grindal, fo. 300, transcribed in *Hockaday Abstracts*, vol. 443, under date). BA, Cambridge(?); MA, Oxford (Venn, i. 216; Foster, i. 82).

CLEMENT FORTH. Admitted 23 Sept. 1577–resigned by 6 Feb. 1584 (Lambeth Reg. Grindal, fo. 300; Reg. Whitgift, fo. 278, transcribed in *Hockaday Abstracts*, vol. 443, under dates). Styled MA.

ROBERT TEMPLE. Admitted 6 Feb. 1584–d. 1611 (Lambeth Reg. Whitgift, fo. 278, transcribed in *Hockaday Abstracts*, vol. 443, under date; Boswell, *Ecclesiastical Division of the Diocese of Bristol*, 11). BA, MA, B.Th., Oxford (Foster, iv. 1565; Venn, iv. 213).

STALL IV

ROGER HUGHES. 1542–d. between 24 Dec. 1545, and 2 Mar. 1546. B. Canon Law, Oxford (*LP* xviii. 443(9); *BRUO 1501–1540*, 287).

JOHN COTTERELL. Admitted 31 Dec. 1545–d. between 21 Feb. and 25 May 1572. BCL, DCL, Oxford (*BRUO 1501–1540*, 140).

THOMAS WETHERED. Admitted 27 Apr. 1574–resigned by 13 Mar. 1577 (Lambeth Reg. Parker, II, fo. 44; Reg. Grindal, fo. 279, transcribed in *Hockaday Abstracts*, vol. 443, under date). Styled MA.

JOHN SAUNDERS. Admitted 13 Mar. 1577–d. by 19 May 1596 (Lambeth Reg. Grindal, fo. 279; Reg. Whitgift, II, fo. 219, transcribed in *Hockaday Abstracts*, vol. 443, under dates). Styled MA. (See *BRUO 1501–1540*, 505.)

STALL V

RICHARD BROWNE. 1542–resigned by 13 Mar. 1544. BCL, B Canon Law, Oxford (*LP* viii. 443(9); *BRUO 1501–1540*, 77).

JOHN WILLIAMS. Granted 13 Mar. 1544 (*LP* xix, pt. 1, 278)–d. by May 1546. BA, MA, B.Th., Oxford (*BRUO 1501–1540*, 630). See Appendix 1.

THOMAS SYLKE. Admitted 4 June 1546–d. between 30 June 1571 and 14 Sept. 1575 (*CPR* (13 Elizabeth), pt. 1, no. 1344). BA, MA, Oxford (*BRUO 1501–1540*, 552). See Appendix 1.

FRANCIS WILLIS. Admitted 14 Sept. 1575–resigned by 22 Feb. 1582 (Lambeth Reg. Parker, II, fo. 127; Reg. Grindal, fo. 334^{v}-335^{r}, transcribed in *Hockaday Abstracts*, vol. 443, under date). Styled MA (cf. Foster, iv. 1649).

CHARLES LANGFORD. Admitted 1582–1606 (Lambeth Reg. Grindal, fo. 334ᵛ–
-335ʳ, transcribed in *Hockaday Abstracts*, vol. 443, under date; Boswell,
Ecclesiastical Division of the Diocese of Bristol, 12). Styled BA; probably BA, MA,
B.Th., D.Th., Oxford (Foster, iii. 876).

STALL VI

GEORGE DOGEON. 1542–d. 14 Dec. 1552. MA, Paris. Incorporated as MA,
B.Th., Oxford D.Th., Italy (*LP* xvii. 443(9); *BRUO 1501–1540*, 171). See
Appendix 1.

THOMAS BAYLEY. Presented 3 Jan. 1553–resigned by 21 Mar. 1582 (*BRUO
1501–1540*, 34; Lambeth Reg. Grindal, fo. 336, transcribed in *Hockaday
Abstracts*, vol. 443, under date). BA, MA, B.Th., Oxford (*BRUO 1501–1540*,
34).

EDWARD GRENE. Installed 21 Mar. 1582–d. 1627 (Lambeth Reg. Grindal, fo.
336, transcribed in *Hockaday Abstracts*, vol. 443, under date; Venn, ii. 254). BA,
Cambridge; attended Oxford (Venn, ii. 254; Foster, ii. 597) Styled MA.

Appendix 4

Chronology of the Dissolution of Religious Houses in Bristol

1536	c.20 June–3 Aug.	Priory or Nunnery of St Mary Magdalen (*LP* ii. 307; *VCH Gloucestershire*, ii. 93).
1538	28 July	Carmelite Friary (*LP* xiii, pt. 1, 1485).
	10 Sept.	Augustinian, Dominican, and Franciscan Friaries (*LP* xiii, pt. 2, 319, 320, 321).
1539	[26 Jan.	Priory of St James leased to Anthony Kingston (PRO, E315/214, fo. 106)].
	9 Dec.	Monastery of St Augustine (*VCH Gloucestershire*, ii. 79; *LP* xv. 139 (iii)).
	9 Dec.	Hospital of St Mark (*LP* xv. 139 (iii)).
1540	9 Jan.	Monastery of Tewkesbury, Glos., and thus officially, the Priory of St James (*VCH Gloucestershire*, ii. 74; *LP* xv. 139).
	——	Hospitallers (Temple Fee). Though not part of a monastic order, the Hospitallers were suppressed by an Act of Parliament. The Act declared them an order more loyal to the Pope than the King, existing for the promotion of superstitious ceremonies, and gave their possessions to the Crown (*VCH Gloucestershire*, ii. 146).
1544	4 Mar.	Hospital of St John (*LP* xix, pt. 1, 157).

Notes

Chapter 1. Introduction

1. H. Gareth Owen, 'The London Parish Clergy in the Reign of Elizabeth I' (Univ. of London, Ph.D. thesis, 1957), p. xviii.
2. The population of Norwich has been estimated at 12,000–12,500, and those of Exeter and Salisbury, the third largest provincial cities, at 8,000 each. The population of London was 60,000. In the subsidy authorized in 1523 Norwich and Bristol ranked after London and were followed by Coventry, Exeter, and Salisbury (W. G. Hoskins, 'English Provincial Towns in the Early Sixteenth Century' in Peter Clark (ed.), *The Early Modern Town* (London and New York: Longman, 1976), 92–3; David H. Sacks, *Trade, Society and Politics in Bristol, 1500–1640* (New York and London: Garland, 1985), 204–13; cf. Peter Clark and Paul Slack, *Crisis and Order in English Towns, 1500–1700* (Toronto: University of Toronto Press, 1972), 5).
3. Fanny Street, 'The Relations of the Bishops and Citizens of Salisbury, 1225–1612', *Wiltshire Magazine*, 39, pt. 1 (June 1916), 185–257; pt. 2 (Dec. 1916), 319–66.
4. Wallace T. MacCaffrey, *Exeter, 1500–1640*, 2nd edn. (Cambridge, Mass.: Harvard University Press, 1976), 175, 196–7, 198, 200–1. Also cf. A. P. Dyer, *The City of Worcester in the Sixteenth Century* (Leicester: Leicester University Press, 1973), 235.
5. Barrie Dobson, 'The Residentiary Canons of York in the Fifteenth Century', *JEH* 30 (1979), 145, 164. The primary civic relationship with the minster in York was between municipal officials and the residentiary canons. The latter were conduits to the court and as such were flattered and cultivated by the mayor and aldermen.
6. Ibid. See also R. B. Dobson, 'Cathedral Chapters and Cathedral Cities: York, Durham and Carlisle in the Fifteenth Century', *Northern Hist.*, 19 (1983), 15–44; Claire Cross, *York Clergy Wills 1520–1600* (York: Borthwick Inst. of Hist. Res., 1984 and 1989), introductions; and MacCaffrey, *Exeter*, 174–8.
7. For the possible impact on protestantization see Claire Cross, 'Parochial Structure and the Dissemination of Protestantism in Sixteenth-Century England: A Tale of Two Cities', in Derek Baker (ed.), *The Church in Town and Countryside*, (SCH 16; Oxford: Basil Blackwell for the Ecclesiastical History Society, 1979), 269–78. She concludes that large numbers of ex-

religious in parish livings helped insulate York's inhabitants from Protestant ideas while Hull's two parishes made dissemination more manageable. Bristol's experience is not conclusive, given eighteen parishes and relatively rapid protestantization, but it suggests that numerous parishes with conservative clergy could not insulate parishioners when other forces were at work.

8. Claire Cross, 'The Incomes of Provincial Urban Clergy, 1520–1645' in O'Day and Heal (eds.), *Princes and Paupers*, 65–89, esp. 66–7.

9. D. M. Palliser, *The Reformation in York, 1534–1553* (York: St. Anthony's Press, 1972); Cross, 'Incomes of Provincial Urban Clergy', 66; Norman P. Tanner, *The Church in Late Medieval Norwich, 1370–1532* (Toronto: Pontifical Institute of Medieval Studies, 1984), 11 ff.; MacCaffrey, *Exeter*, 177. See Table 4.

10. Bristol was among only thirteen medieval boroughs to contain convents of all four major orders of friars. There was London, of course, and among the sixteenth-century provincial capitals, Norwich, Newcastle-upon-Tyne, and York. Lesser towns were Boston, Cambridge, King's Lynn, Lincoln, Northampton, Oxford, Stamford, and Winchester (Barrie Dobson, 'Mendicant Ideal and Practice in Late Medieval York', in P. V. Addyman and V. E. Black (eds.), *Archeological Papers from York Presented to M. W. Barley* (York: York Archeological Trust, 1984), 111).

11. See for example Tanner, *The Church in Medieval Norwich*, 141–54; MacCaffrey, *Exeter*, 175–6; Dobson, 'Residentiary Canons', 164; Peter Heath, 'Urban Piety in the Later Middle Ages: The Evidence of Hull Wills', in Dobson (ed.), *The Church, Politics, and Patronage in the Fifteenth Century*, 221; Elaine M. Sheppard, 'The Reformation and the Citizens of Norwich', *Norfolk Archeology*, 38 (1981), 45; Douglas Jones, *The Church in Chester, 1300–1540* (Manchester: Chetham Society, 3rd ser. 7, 1957), 39.

12. Christopher Hill, *The Economic Problems of the Church from Archbishop Whitgift to the Long Parliament* (Oxford: Clarendon Press, 1956), 203–4. W. G. Hoskins, 'The Leicestershire Country Parson in the Sixteenth Century', *Trans. Leicester Arch. and Hist. Soc.* 21 (1940), 90–1.

13. Margaret Bowker has made an important contribution by addressing the impact of the dissolution of religious houses on clerical recruitment in Lincoln diocese, but she does not focus on the urban dimension ('The Henrician Reformation and the Parish Clergy', *BIHR* 40 (May 1977), 30–47).

14. Peter Heath, *The English Parish Clergy on the Eve of the Reformation* (London: Routledge & Kegan Paul; Toronto: University of Toronto Press, 1969); D. M. Barratt, 'The Condition of the Parochial Clergy from the Reformation to 1660, with Special Reference to the Dioceses of Oxford, Worcester and Gloucester' (Univ. of Oxford, D.Phil. thesis, 1950).

15. Margaret Bowker, *The Henrician Reformation: The Diocese of Lincoln under John Longland, 1521–1547* (New York and Cambridge: Cambridge University Press, 1981) and *The Secular Clergy of the Diocese of Lincoln* (New York and Cambridge: Cambridge University Press, 1968).

16. John H. Pruett, *The Parish Clergy under the Later Stuarts: The Leicestershire Experience* (Urbana, Chicago, London: University of Illinois Press, 1978); F. W. Brooks, 'The Social Position of the Parson in the Sixteenth Century', *Journal of the British Archeological Society*, 3rd ser. 10 (1945–7), 23–37. Hoskins, 'The Leicestershire Country Parson'; J. F. Fuggles, 'The Parish Clergy of the Archdeaconry of Leicester, 1520–1540', *Leicestershire Arch. and Hist. Soc. Proc.*, 46 (1970–1).

17. D. M. Owen, *Church and Society in Medieval Lincolnshire* (Lincoln: Lincolnshire Local History Soc., 1971), 84–91, 132–42. She does suggest that friars remained popular because their ministrations were more personal than those of the parish clergy (p. 91).

18. Philip Tyler, 'The Status of the Elizabethan Parochial Clergy', in J. G. Cuming (ed.), *The Province of York* (Leiden: Brill for the Ecclesiastical History Society, 1967), 76–98.

19. Cross, 'Incomes of Provincial Urban Clergy.'

20. Owen, 'London Parish Clergy in the Reign of Elizabeth I'. E. L. C. Mullins used London as a model to compare religious settlements and argued that it might be representative of the nation in 'The Effects of the Marian and Elizabethan Religious Settlements upon the Clergy of London, 1553–1564' (Univ. of London, MA thesis, 1948), 13.

21. Rosemary O'Day, *The English Clergy: The Emergence and Consolidation of a Profession, 1558–1642* (Leicester: Leicester University Press, 1979).

22. Paul S. Seaver, *The Puritan Lectureships: The Politics of Religious Dissent* (Palo Alto, Calif.: Stanford University Press 1972), 22–6, 125–9, 133–42, 143, 91 ff. O'Day, *English Clergy*, 99–104.

23. O'Day, *English Clergy*, 104.

24. Ibid., 239.

25. Michael L. Zell, 'Church and Gentry in Reformation Kent, 1533–53' (Univ. of California at Los Angeles, Ph.D. diss. 1974) and 'The Personnel of the Clergy of Kent in the Reformation', *EHR* 89 (1974), 513–33. Margaret Bowker picked up Zell's emphasis on the unbeneficed clergy to argue that the demonstrable decline of ordinations in Lincoln diocese after 1536 (when frightened and resentful clergy participated in the Pilgrimage of Grace) prevented the development of a clerical proletariat which might further have resisted religious change ('The Henrician Reformation and the Parish Clergy'). Zell in turn argued that while the clerical proletariat of the nation may have declined numerically by 1560, it nevertheless continued to exist ('Economic Problems of the Parochial Clergy in the Sixteenth Century', in O'Day and Heal, *Princes and Paupers*,

19–43). Zell implies, however, that those with poorly endowed benefices became part of the clerical proletariat, which before the Reformation had consisted of the unbeneficed (pp. 32–43).

26. Zell specifically dismisses the urban clergy from consideration because 'most incumbents did not hold urban livings' ('Economic Problems', 38).

27. Cf. D. M. Owen, *The Records of the Established Church of England* (London: British Record Association, 1970).

28. John Carey and Joseph Hunter (eds.), *Valor ecclesiasticus*, 6 vols. (London: Records Commission, 1810–34), ii. 495.

29. H&WRO, 802 BA 2764 (Visitation Act Book of John Bell, Bishop of Worcester, for the year 1540, with other notes and documents *c.*1520–*c.*1541); PRO, E334 (Composition Books).

30. H&WRO, 716–093 BA 2648/8(ii)–9(iii) (Regs. Silvestro de' Gigli, Giulio de' Medici, Geronimo Ghinucci, Hugh Latimer, and John Bell, 1516–1543); 802 BA 2764; SRO, D/D/Ca/3, 4, 7, 8, 9A, 10, 10A, 12A (court records tentatively described as Commissary because in the only instances where a court heading gives any indication of the official involved, nos. 4 and 9, the Commissary General, who also was the Archdeacon of Bath at the time, is mentioned. I am indebted to Derek Shorrocks, former Somerset County Archivist, for help with this identification). *Regs B&W* (Regs. Thomas Wolsey, John Clerke, William Knight, Gilbert Bourne, 1518–59).

31. PRO, E334/2–8; original wills from H&WRO (BA 3585/3b) and probate records in Bristol's Consistory Court, BAO (EP/J/1/2–6). Having examined some wills in the PRO for accuracy, I have relied heavily on transcriptions and translations of wills from the PRO found in the *Hockaday Abstracts*. Thomas P. Wadley, *Notes or Abstracts of the Wills Contained in . . . the Great Orphans' Book and Book of Wills in the Council House at Bristol, 1381–1605* (Bristol: B&GAS, 1886); D. O. Shilton and R. Holworthy (eds.), *Medieval Wills from Wells* (SRS 40 1925); F. W. Weaver (ed.), *Wells Wills* (London: K. Paul, Trench, Trubner, 1890).

32. *Letters and Papers Foreign and Domestic of the Reign of Henry VIII*, ed. J. S. Brewer, James Gairdner, and R. H. Brodie, 36 vols. (London: Longman, Green, Longman & Roberts, 1862–1932); *Calendar of State Papers Domestic*, Elizabeth (London: HMSO, 1900); *Calendar of Patent Rolls*, Henry VIII, 2 vols. (London: HMSO, 1914–16); *Calendar of Patent Rolls*, Edward VI, 5 vols. (London: HMSO, 1924–9); *Calendar of Patent Rolls*, Mary and Philip and Mary, 4 vols. (London: HMSO, 1936–9); J. R. Dasent (ed.), *Calendar of Patent Rolls*, Elizabeth (London: HMSO, 1939–64); *Acts of the Privy Council* (London: HMSO, 1890–1907). Further examination of most calendared documents was made in the PRO as shown by citations. Sir John MacLean (ed.), 'Chantry Certificates, Gloucestershire (Roll 22)', *Trans. B&GAS* 8 (1878–9), 229–51.

33. BAO Parish accounts of All Saints, St Ewen, Christ Church, St James, St Thomas, St Werberg and the Church Book of St John. In respective parish churches: Churchwardens' Account Book of St Mary Redcliffe and Vestry Book of St Michael. (BAO, DC/A/9/1/1,2 (Computa of the Dean and Chapter); 04026 (Mayors' Audits)).

34. BAO, EP/J/1/2–5. The poor condition of vol. 1 renders it unavailable for viewing, but abstracts were available in the *Hockaday Abstracts* in the Gloucester City Library, sectioned and filed by parishes, under date.

Chapter 2. The Late Medieval Church and Clergy

1. See Chapter 5.
2. See Chapter 6.
3. J. W. W. Bund (ed.), *The Register of the Diocese of Worcester during the Vacancy of the See, usually called 'Registrum sede vacante', 1307–1485*, (Oxford: Worcester Historical Society, 1897), 192–8; *VCH Gloucester*, ii. 77–9; Geoffrey Baskerville, 'The Dispossessed Religious of Gloucestershire', *Trans. B&GAS* 49 (1927), 94–5.
4. *VCH Gloucester*, ii. 74; H&WRO, 802 BA 2764, fo. 100.
5. *LP* xiii, pt. 2, 319, 320, 321; PRO, E 36/115, pp. 13, 19, 155; Baskerville, 'Dispossessed Religious', 96–7. Dorothy Owen says that 'no Lincolnshire friary could compare in numbers with those at Bristol or in the university towns' (*Church and Society in Medieval Lincolnshire*, 86).
6. *LP* vii. 1216 and xv. 139.
7. *VCH Gloucester*, ii. 93; Roy M. Haines, *The Administration of the Diocese of Worcester in the First Half of the Fourteenth Century* (London: Society for the Preservation of Christian Knowledge, 1965), 236; SRO, D/D/B, Reg. 11 (Wolsey), fo. 28 and Reg. 12 (Clerke), fos. 8, 9.
8. H&WRO, 802 BA 2764, fos. 99–100, 193–5; Weaver, *Wells Wills*, 19, 21, 23, 24, 25, 26, 28; PRO, PCC, Jankyn, 18 (William Rycart; 13 Sept. 1528; 18 June 1530); PCC, Hogen, 7 (Thomas Jubbes; 3 July 1533; 17 Oct. 1533); John Maclean (ed.), 'Chantry Certificates (Roll 22), Gloucestershire', *Trans. B&GAS* 8 (1878–9), 234–5, 244–5, 247–8. References to wills in the PRO are from the *Hockaday Abstracts*. Comparison of the two have shown the *Abstracts* to be reliable for my purposes. The first date refers to the day the will was written, the second to the day it was proved.
9. Knowledge of clergy in minor orders generally only remains in court records and we know them only when they are in trouble. These records are not extant for Bristol before 1556. Cf. O'Day, *English Clergy*, 24, 248 and Heath, *English Parish Clergy*, 189.

10. J. F. Nicholls, 'The Free Grammar School of Bristol and the Thorns, its Founders', *TRHS* 1 (1872), 315. Nicholls suggests the hospital was originally a lazar house for lepers, but he may have based this on a faulty assumption (see fn. 11). Although George Croft was the master in 1532, medieval episcopal registers show that in 1340 the institution had a prioress and sisters, having had brothers in the past. In 1344, however, the place was again headed by a prior (Roy M. Haines (ed.), *The Register of Wolstan de Bransford, Bishop of Worcester, 1339–49* (London: Historical Manuscripts Commission, 1966), 68, 105). Rotha Mary Clay points out that it is often difficult to discriminate between hospital and priory and that sometimes they are indistinguishable in aim and scope (*The Medieval Hospitals of England* (London: Methuen & Co., 1909), 205).

11. *VCH Gloucester*, ii. 160. John Latimer assumes that the hospital was founded for lepers because its beneficent purposes were administered by a mixed community of men and women. He also cites evidence, however, which suggests that both men and women were expected to pray for souls ('The Hospital of St. John, Bristol', *Trans. B&GAS* 24 (1901), 172–8). The presence of women, however, did not necessarily dictate the presence of lepers. Furthermore, the hospital of St Mary Magdalen, which did accept lepers, was also close to St Mary Redcliffe church (Clay, *Medieval Hospitals*, 147, 198–9, 206; M. D. Lobel and E. M. Carus-Wilson, *Historic Towns*, *Bristol* (London: Scolar Press, 1975), maps). A chapel attached to the hospital was sometimes called a chantry. The master and brethren of the hospital agreed in 1254 to maintain the chapel of the Holy Spirit in Redcliffe churchyard. A chaplain was to be approved by the archdeacon of Bath and was to officiate no more than two years in succession (Edith Williams, *The Chantries of William Canynges* (Bristol: W. George's Sons, 1950), n. 2, 15–16).

12. Lobel and Carus-Wilson, *Bristol*, maps. In 1560 there were at least five almshouses 'at Lawford's Gate, in the Marsh, in Lewin's Mead, at St. James's Back, in St. Thomas Street' and two other places for the poor 'in Tucker Hall and at Temple Gate' (Wadley, *Notes*, 195).

13. Maclean, 'Chantry Certificates', 239; *The Maire of Bristowe is Kalendar, by Robert Ricart, Town Clerk of Bristol, 18 Edward IV*, ed. Lucy Toulmin Smith (Westminster: Camden Society, 1872), 56–7, hereafter cited as *Mayor's Kalendar*; Lobel and Carus-Wilson, *Bristol*, 14; R. C. Latham (ed.), *Bristol Charters, 1509–1899* (Bristol: BRS, 12, 1949), 29, 30.

14. The Chapel of St George was founded with a fraternity of merchants and mariners attached to it by Richard le Spicer in the fourteenth century (Lobel and Carus-Wilson, *Bristol*, 11). The Corporation paid the chaplain an annual stipend of eight marks (£5. 6s. 8d.) and provided four yards of broadcloth for his gown and hood (*Mayor's Kalendar*, 82). In the late fifteenth century he received 2s. weekly for making a distribution to

the poor in Lewin's Mead almshouse (E. Williams, *Chantries of William Canynges*, 81 n. 3).

15. Maclean, 'Chantry Certificates', 248–9; *GRB* viii. 175–81.
16. J. F. Nicholls and John Taylor, *Bristol, Past and Present*, 3 vols. (Bristol: J. Arrowsmith, 1881–2), i. 200–1; ii. 248; Sacks, *Trade, Society, and Politics in Bristol*, pp. 587–8; Lobel and Carus-Wilson, *Bristol*, 17, maps.
17. Rotha Mary Clay, *The Hermits and Anchorites of England* (London: Methuen & Co., 1914), 70–1, 91–2, 78. In the early sixteenth century there also was a female anchorite at the Dominican friary (PRO, PCC, Holgrave, 4 (Lady Dame Mawde Baker alias Dame Mawde Spicer; 5 Jan. 1504; 26 Mar, 1504)).
18. For a possible reference to a private chaplain in 1402 see Wadley, *Notes*, no. 117 (PRO, PCC, Marche, 53 (Alice Wermystre; Friday after the feast of Apostles Simon and Jude, i.e. 31 Oct. 1421; 22 May 1422); PCC, Bennett, 29 (Thomas Baker alias Spicer; 23 May 1510; 21 June 1510; referring to Sir John Jones, 'late chaplain for my mother')). And see a reference in his mother's will to another, Sir Richard Spinnell, 'my chaplain' (PRO, PCC, Holgrave, 4); PCC, Porche, 39 (Elyn Kemys; 12 Sept. 1528; 29 Oct. 1528); (*LP* xii, pt. 2, 219).
19. For a description of the funeral of William Canynges, one of Bristol's wealthiest merchants in the fifteenth century, see E. Williams, *Chantries of William Canynges*, 78. For employment in anniversaries see p. 22. Williams also points to the opportunities in a city like Bristol for clerks who could keep parish and chantry accounts (p. 86).
20. For commissary Richard Browne, see Chapter 3 and Appendix 1. Also see Wadley, *Notes*, esp. pp. 7, 12, 13, 15, 18, 19, 28, 36, 40, 41, 42, 43, 54, 58, 66, 75, 76, 84, 86, 89, 92, 98, 101, 103, 108, 110, 111, 115, 117, 128, 132, 137, 141, 143, 150 *et passim*.
21. Sacks, *Trade, Society and Politics*, 204–13; Hoskins, 'English Provincial Towns', 92–3. Clerics probably made up between 1 per cent and 4 per cent of the urban population in Europe. One per cent of the total population represented perhaps 1.5 per cent of the total population over the age of fifteen (Carlo M. Cipolla, *Before the Industrial Revolution: European Society and Economy, 1000–1700* (New York: Norton, 1976), 78–81; see also Paul M. Hohenberg and Lynn Hollen Lees, *The Making of Urban Europe, 1000–1950* (Cambridge, Mass.: Harvard University Press, 1985), 43). Josiah Cox Russell has estimated the clerical population of late fourteenth-century England at 3 per cent of the male population, but he suggests that this proportion had lessened considerably by the sixteenth century ('The Clerical Population of Medieval England', *Traditio*, 2 (1944), 177–212). In Coventry in 1523 the clergy were just over 1.5 per cent of the city's total population (Charles Phythian-Adams, *Desolation of a City: Coventry and the Urban Crisis of the Late Middle*

Ages (Cambridge and New York: Cambridge University Press, 1979)). Norman Tanner estimates the clerical population of Norwich at 4 to 6 per cent of the population and a correspondingly greater percentage of adult males (*The Church in Late Medieval Norwich*, 19). The clerical population of York must have been an even greater proportion of the city's inhabitants given its large number of ecclesiastical institutions and its smaller population (Palliser, *The Reformation in York*, 1–4). Unlike Bristol, Norwich and York were cathedral cities; moreover, they each had over forty parish churches in the early sixteenth century while Bristol had only eighteen.

22. For the application of the body as a metaphor for the community, see Mervyn James, 'Ritual, Drama and Social Body in the Late Medieval English town', in James, *Society, Politics and Culture* (Cambridge and London, Cambridge University Press 1986), 16–47.

23. The cache of clerical wills in Norwich might inform us further of the personal relationships among urban clergy (see Sheppard, 'The Reformation and the Citizens of Norwich', 51; Tanner, *The Church in Late Medieval Norwich*, 11–14, 47–51, 140). Claire Cross writes of a 'highly stratified local church', implying rather sharp divisions between the various strata of clergy. She does, however, see a community among the city's chantry priests in the wills she has transcribed. Given the appearance of incumbents in the wills along with the chantry priests, it would seem that this was a broader community than she suggests, although the elite clergy in the minster certainly were set apart from the rest (*York Clergy Wills: 1. Minster clergy*, introduction and *passim*, and *2. Parish clergy*, pp. viii–ix and *passim*). There was not such a strong demarcation in Exeter between the cathedral clergy and the parish priests. (Nicholas Orme, *Exeter Cathedral, as It Was 1050–1550* (Exeter: Devon Books, 1986), 39–41).

24. Wills from the early fifteenth century prove less helpful when they do not identify the institutions to which some clerical beneficiaries belong (see PRO, PCC, March, 3 (William Brunby, vicar of Temple; 20 May 1402; 27 April 1403); and PCC, Marche, 11 (Thomas Zhokfet, vicar of St Nicholas; 10 Feb. 1406; 10 Mar. 1506)).

25. A study of ninety-four clerics' wills from early sixteenth-century London showed that most priests mentioned individual priests as beneficiaries and half named a priest as executor. Eleven preferred fellow priests as executors even though they were survived by a close relation, 'indicating that a professional bond may have superseded a familial one'. The wills none the less revealed close relationships with lay friends and family too (Jacqueline Murray, 'Kinship and Friendship: The Perception of Family by Clergy and Laity in Late Medieval London', *Albion* 20 (1988), 372, 375–6).

26. PRO, PCC, Horne, 16 (23 June 1494; 21 Feb. 1498); E. Williams, *Chantries of William Canynges*, 70.
27. PRO, PCC, Horne, 1 (13 Sept. 1486; 16 Oct. 1496); E. Williams, *Chantries of William Canynges*, 26; Lambeth Reg. Morton, fo. 178.
28. PRO, PCC, Milles, 32 (10 May 1489; 13 Aug. 1489).
29. PRO, PCC Horne, 1 (28 June 1495; 16 October 1496).
30. PRO, PCC, Adane, 19 (27 Nov. 1506; 5 Feb. 1507).
31. In 1402 the vicar of Temple, William of Brunby, also made bequests to the four orders of friars in Bristol (PRO, PCC, March, 3, 20 May 1402; 27 Apr. 1403).
32. T. W. Williams, 'Gloucestershire Medieval Libraries', *Trans. B&GAS* 31 (1908), 85; PRO, PCC, Bennett, 36 (16 Aug. 1510; 10 Feb. 1511).
33. Weaver (ed.), *Wells Wills*, 21.
34. Ibid. 28. See Appendix 1.
35. See Appendix 1 and Chapter 3.
36. Tanner, *The Church in Late Medieval Norwich*, 11–14, 140. The York parish clergy's wills transcribed by Claire Cross range from 1520 to 1600 and so do not cover enough of the pre-Reformation period to give a good sense of relationships among the clergy. There are fourteen wills between 1520 and the dissolution of religious houses in 1539. One testator bequeathed sums for the friars' prayers and presence at burial; another manifested a close relationship with the Grey Friars, whose warden witnessed the will; and another requested burial in a local religious house. Wills made after the dissolution show ex-friars or ex-religious sticking together as well as relating to other secular clergy, but they do not allow judgements on pre-Reformation relationships (*York Clergy Wills: 2. Parish Clergy*, 14, 9, 12, 19, 21, 23, 24, 27, 28, 30, 31, 33, 36, 39, 41, 45, 48, 55, 80, 85, 91, 95; see above).
37. Nicholls and Taylor, *Bristol, Past and Present* ii. 109. Although it did not involve the friars, a similar example of conflict and regulation occurred in Bristol in 1400. The Pope licensed the priest of the chapel of St Mary the Virgin on Bristol Bridge in the parish of St Nicholas to celebrate mass and other divine services and to have a bell rung without permission of the diocesan or the rector of the parish church of St Nicholas, whose hindrance the priest of the chapel feared. The rector of the appropriated living, who undoubtedly was concerned about the drain of resources to the chapel, was the Abbot and Convent of St Augustine.
38. PRO, PCC, Marche, 14 (Thomas Gloucestrer; 5 June 1407; 12 Feb. 1408; burial in Carmelite Friary; legacies to vicar, fabric and crypt of St Nicholas); PCC, Balmyr, 8 (John Herte; 6 Mar. 1502; 10 May 1502; burial in Dominican Friary; legacy to parson and to a chapel within the parish of St Peter); PCC, Stokton, 3 (Thomas Mede of St James; 20 Feb. 1455; 2 Apr. 1455; burial in St Mary Redcliffe; bequests to

parishes of St James and others); Wadley, *Notes*, 262 (Thomas Kempson; 29 Nov. 1475; 16 Jan. 1476; burial St Mary Redcliffe; legacy to vicar of Temple, his curate).

39. Nicholas Orme, 'A Grammatical Miscellany from Bristol and Wiltshire', in N. Orme, *Education and Society in Medieval and Renaissance England* (London: Hambledon Press, 1989), 88, 95.

40. Eighteen volumes of the *VCH* offer information on the friars. These are vols. ii for the counties of Cumberland, Surrey, Warwick, Worcester, Cambridge, Dorset, Durham, Essex, Kent, Leicester, Lincoln, Norfolk, Northampton, Oxford, Somerset, Suffolk, Wiltshire, and Gloucestershire.

41. See also E. B. Poland, *The Friars in Sussex, 1228–1928* (Hove, Sussex: Combridges, 1928), 149 and David Walker, W. J. Shields, and John Kent (eds.), 'A Register of the Churches of the Monastery of St. Peter's Gloucester', in *An Ecclesiastical Miscellany* (Gloucester: B&GAS, 1976), 5–6. The editors conclude on the basis of agreements between ecclesiastical institutions in the register that 'Disputes which led to settlements in the courts of the Church of the crown must have enhanced the routine of many of the abbey's obedientiaries'.

42. A. G. Little and R. C. Easterling, *The Franciscans and Dominicans of Exeter* (Exeter: A. Wheaton & Co.), 40–7; Orme, *Exeter Cathedral*, 25, 41. Wallace MacCaffrey says most of the parish clergy were 'humble men' and that 'Few are shown as having university degrees'. However, that clergy in Bristol were graduates usually was indicated only when they held more than one degree (*Exeter, 1500–1640*, 180). See Chapter 6 for discussion of the parish clergy's standard of education.

43. J. A. F. Thomson, 'Tithe Disputes in Later Medieval London', *EHR* 36 (1963), 1–17; Craig A. Robertson, 'The Tithe-Heresy of Friar William Russell', *Albion*, 8 (1976), 1–16; F. R. H. Du Boulay, 'The Quarrel between the Carmelite Friars and the Secular Clergy of London, 1464–1468', *JEH* 6 (1955), 156–74; Margaret Aston, ' "Caim's Castles": Poverty, Politics and Disendowment', in Dobson (ed.), *The Church, Politics, and Patronage*, 50–9; Poland, *Friars in Sussex*, 152; R. F. Bennett, *The Early Dominicans* (Cambridge: Cambridge University Press, 1937), 115; see also Beryl Fermoy, *The Dominican Order in England before the Reformation* (London: Society for Promoting Christian Knowledge, 1925), 71–3.

44. BAO, P/AS/ChW 1 and 3 under years. It is conceivable that a reference to 'shrine' rather than 'tabernacle' year after year indicated the carriage of the parish's relics rather than the sacrament. The skull of St Thomas of Canterbury and a candlestick belonging to him were given to the parish by its vicar in 1479 (P/AS/ChW 3, p. 78). However the entry for 1499 specifically refers to bearing the sacrament in the Corpus Christi

Day procession and the entry regarding Palm Sunday in 1512 refers to the sacrament in the shrine. Comparable evidence for parish contingents in the Corpus Christi Day procession includes that from St John the Baptist, St Ewen, and a single account from St Nicholas; these contingents did not include friars. This, too, suggests that the friars were carrying the sacrament, the Corpus Christi, for the whole procession, although it is not clear why the parish of All Saints was paying for it (P/StJB/ChW, p. 69; B. R. Masters and Elizabeth Ralph (eds.), *The Church Book of St. Ewen's Bristol, 1454–1584* (B&GAS Records Section, 6, 1967) 136, 139, 142–3, 145, 148, 153; St Nicholas, cited in Nicholls and Taylor, *Bristol, Past and Present,* ii. 158). See pp. 28–32 for further discussion of the Corpus Christi and other processions.

45. See Appendix 1. In 1443 an Austin friar, Thomas Abendon, received a papal dispensation to hold a benefice with cure and received appointments to several churches in the diocese of Baths and Wells (Francix X. Roth, *The English Austin Friars, 1249–1538,* 2 vols. (New York: Augustinian Historical Institute, 1966), i. 247, 497).

46. See Appendix 1.

47. Masters and Ralph (eds.), *Church Book of St. Ewen,* 26; BAO, P/AS/ChW 1 (a) (1525).

48. Wadley, *Notes,* 149–50 and *passim*; PRO, PCC, Wattys, 27 (proved 1 Jan. 1477); PCC, Vox, 7 (20 Oct. 1494; 6 Nov. 1494); PCC, Watkyn, 25 (5 July 1476; 7 May 1476); PCC, Holgrave, 36 (10 June 1505; 28 Aug. 1505); PCC, Fetiplace, 10 (30 Apr. 1512; 22 Jan. 1513).

49. H&WRO, Reg. Gainsborough, fo. 4, cited in *Hockaday Abstracts,* vol. 445, under date. *Calendar of Entries in the Papal Registers relating to Great Britain and Ireland, Letters* (London, HMSO, 1893–), 5. 191.

50. See Chapter 5, pp. 70–1 for a discussion of the patronage of Bristol's parish livings. The abbot and convent also gained the right to have one of their own serve as vicar although there is no evidence of monks serving in local parish churches before the dissolution. This was not uncommon when religious houses were patrons of livings. See for example, Tanner, *The Church in Late Medieval Norwich,* 18, 181–2, 186, 188. See also Heath, *English Parish Clergy,* 175–82; Bowker, *Secular Clergy,* 189–92; and Marjorie Chibnall, 'Monks and Pastoral Work', *JEH* 18 (1967), 165–72.

51. *Hockaday Abstracts,* vol. 432, under date.

52. BAO, P/ChW/StJB 1, p. 9.

53. Bund, (ed.), *Registrum sede vacante,* 192–8.

54. Sabin translates 'conversi' as 'visitor'. It might also have meant one about to take monastic vows or conceivably a lay brother. However, he was termed 'Sir' in a chantry rental, and this indicates he was a secular priest by 1509. Honybrigge does not appear in a 1534 list of clergy for parishes

in Worcester diocese; perhaps he became a stipendiary in one of the parish churches in Bath and Wells (see Appendix 1; Arthur Sabin, 'Compotus Rolls of St. Augustine's Abbey, Bristol', *Trans. B&GAS* 73 (1954), 199; E. Williams, *Chantries of William Canynges*, 111, 231; H&WRO, 802 BA 2764, fos. 99–100). See Chapter 3 for a discussion of Bristol's division into two dioceses.

55. Wadley, *Notes*, 138.

56. BAO, P/AS/ChW 3, 1514–15, 1478–9, 1489–90.

57. While the evidence available for relationships among the clergy in Bristol does not provide a window into their most personal lives, it seems possible, even likely, that interaction among some clergy included sexual activity and that opportunities for relationships that included this element would also have drawn clergy to cities. For the association of homosexuality with the clergy during the Middle Ages see John Boswell, *Christianity, Social Tolerance, and Homosexuality: Gay People in Western Europe from the Beginning of the Christian Era to the Fourteenth Century* (Chicago and London: University of Chicago Press, 1980), 187–93, 198, 207–8, 278; and Brian Patrick McGuire, *Friendship and Community: The Monastic Experience 350–1250* (Kalamazoo, Mich.: Cistercian Publications, 1988), 244–8, 386–7, 419–20. A statute of 1534 against 'buggery or sodomy' may have been aimed at communities of religious, but it may have found a target among other clergy (Stanford Lehmberg, *The Reformation Parliament* (Cambridge, 1970), 185).

58. What Rosemary O'Day says about the seventeenth-century clergy rings true for urban clergy before the Reformation: '. . . because the clergy shared similar interests and similar responsibilities, they developed group identity which was heightened by opportunities for contact. Although the life of a minister is in some ways a solitary, independent one, this fact in itself probably predisposed the cleric to seek out his fellows and identify closely with them' (*English Clergy*, 244). See Patrick Collinson (*The Religion of Protestants: The Church in English Society, 1559–1625* (Oxford: Oxford University Press), 92–140, esp. 97–100) on the use of the term 'professional' for clergy before and after the Reformation and (pp. 14–121) for consideration of the post-Reformation clergy's 'collective self-consciousness' and his comment that 'It would be strange indeed if ecclesiastical life uniquely failed to conform to localized patterns of social existence . . .' (p. 121). He refers, of course, to the conjunction of the market town and the *classis*, but it is an apt expression for my arguments concerning ecclesiastical life in Bristol.

59. See Chapter 3.

60. PRO, PCC, Luffenam, 15 (Margaret Gildeney; 8 Jan. 1431; 28 Jan. 1431); PCC, Wattys, 16 (11 Mar. 1474); no probate recorded; Wadley, *Notes* no. 159 (William Hoton; 3 Sept. 1474; 20 Sept. 1475); PCC,

Ayloffe, 7 (Richard Hoby; 5 May 1516; 12 Apr. 1518); PCC, Bennett, 6 (Thomas Pernant; 16 Aug. 1508; 21 Oct. 1508); PCC, Bennett, 18 (David Philipp; 11 June 1509; 26 June 1509); H&WRO, will (John Flooke; dated 11 Sept. 1540). The only known instance of a bequest of clothing to the friars came in 1413 when the Friars Preachers received the testator's 'best furred gowne wt the hood of scarlet' to pray for his soul as one of their brethren. Friar John Hame received a 'black furred gowne' (PCC, Marche, 28 (John More; 8 Feb. 1413; 8 Nov. 1413)).

61. Wadley, *Notes*, 54 (John Freman, burgess; 14 Nov. 1397; 9 Feb. 1399); 157–8 (Thomas Kempson, 1475); PRO, PCC, Jankyn, 22 (Johan Vaughan; 23 Dec. 1529; 31 Oct. 1530); PCC, Fetiplace, 15 (Davy Leyson; 15 Dec. 1512; 7 May 1513); PCC, Holgrave, 26 (John Esterfeld; 5 Feb. 1505; no date for probate); PCC, Dogett, 27 (Edward Dawes; 21 July 1493; 6 Aug. 1493); PCC, Fetiplace, 6 (Mathew Cotynton; 16 Feb. 1512; 22 Jan. 1513). Freman's son was a friar. Merchant Esterfeld's son was a canon of St George's chapel in Windsor Castle. Cotynton left 6*s.* 8*d.* to Sir William Hopkyn, his sister's son, when he sang his first mass. Leyson left bequests upon condition that his son become a priest.

62. Wadley, *Notes*, 86–7 (Isabel Barstaple, 1412); PRO, PCC, Bodfelde, 8 (Johane Thorne; 10 Apr. 1523; 16 May 1523).

63. PRO, PCC, Marche, 53 (Alice Wermystre; 1421; 22 May 1422); PCC, Wattys, 13 (William Coder, burgess and merchant; 14 Mar. 1474; 2 Apr. 1474); Wadley, *Notes*, no. 279. See also n. 89 below for a brother at the hospital of St Mark on College Green, who also had family in Bristol.

64. Wadley, *Notes*, 17; *Hockaday Abstracts*, vol. 432, under date; Masters and Ralph (eds.), *Church Book of St. Ewen's*, 48.

65. PRO, PCC, Bennett, 6 (16 Aug. 1508; 21 Oct. 1508).

66. PRO, PCC, Fetiplace, 29 (William Muriell; 11 Oct. 1514; 31 Oct. 1514). *Hockaday Abstracts*, vol. 432 (All Saints, 1507).

67. BAO, P/AS/ChW 3.

68. See Appendix 1; PRO, PCC, Powell, 30 (16 July 1552; 15 Nov. 1552).

69. See Table 3, Chapter 6.

70. Alan Kreider, *English Chantries: The Road to Dissolution* (Cambridge, Mass.: Harvard Historical Studies, 97, 1979), 53. Concerning the etiquette required for such intimacy, see Ann Eljenholm Nichols, 'The Etiquette of Pre-Reformation Confession in East Anglia', *Sixteenth Century Journal*, 17 (1986), 145–63.

71. See Chapters 5 and 6.

72. W. K. Jordan, 'Charitable Institutions of England: Bristol and Somerset', *Trans. of the American Philosophical Society*, 50, pt. 8 (1960), 9. For a critique of Jordan's conclusions see Chapter 5.

73. See Chapter 6. In the parish of St Mary Redcliffe both the curate and

the chantry priests had access to a library (E. Williams, *Chantries of William Canynges*, 20, 123 n. 3).

74. Clive Burgess ' "For the Increase of Divine Service": Chantries in the Parish in Late Medieval Bristol', *JEH* 36 (1985), 46–65. See also Kreider, *English Chantries*, 38–70.

75. Richard W. Southern, *Western Society and the Church in the Middle Ages* (Harmondsworth: Penguin, 1970), 242, 244, 249; Heath, *English Parish Clergy*, 175.

76. PRO, SP 1/96, pp. 32–3; BL, Cotton Cleop. E. iv, fos. 21–5, printed in Joyce A. Youings (ed.), *The Dissolution of the Monasteries* (London: George Allen & Unwin; New York: Barnes and Noble, 1971), 149–53. Abbot William Burton was fighting harassment and eventual dissolution by sending Cromwell money. On 21 Feb. 1539, he wrote thanking him for his great goodness to himself and the monastery and sent 20 nobles more than he had before (*LP* xiv, pt. 1, 333).

77. BL, Cotton Cleop. E. iv., fo. 73. See Chapter 3. In 1531 the abbot was on a commission to survey the castle and manor of Thornbury, Gloucs., with a number of illustrious men of the county (*LP* iv. 119 (Grant 61)). He also was on good terms with Thomas Lord Berkeley and Lord Lisle (*LP* vii. 4, 103).

78. BAO, P/AS/ChW 1, p. 81.

79. See Chapter 5.

80. BAO, P/AS/ChW 3, P/StJB/ChW 1, and P/XCh/ChW 1 *passim*. Masters and Ralph (eds.), *Church Book of St. Ewen's, passim*. Payments for bearing banners were made yearly, and occasionally it was specified that they were borne to the monastery of St Augustine (St Austin's). See for example All Saints in 1520 and St Ewen in 1478. By 1544 the monastery had become the Cathedral of the Holy Trinity, but the accounts of the parish of Christ Church (formerly Holy Trinity) register a payment of 4*d.* for bearing the banner to St Austins during Rogation. While we cannot be certain that the processions to the monastery were not exceptions, the character of the accounts suggests otherwise. Entries for most items are rather abbreviated year after year and only occasionally the inclusion of more detail delineates the usual practice further.

81. BAO, 04026 (Mayors' Audits) 1532, 3rd qtr., 1st wk.; 1540 (i.e. 1539), 3rd qtr., 1st wk.).

82. *VCH Gloucester*, ii. 74; *GRB* (BRS 2) 60.

83. Maclean, 'Chantry Certificates', 233.

84. PRO, E 315/214, fo. 106. See Chapter 5 for a discussion of patronage.

85. Nicholls and Taylor, *Bristol, Past and Present*, ii. 109–12, 113–14, 117. Dorothy M. Owen discusses the importance of the friars to town life (*Church and Society*, 85 ff.).

86. *GRB* (BRS 16) 126; Wadley, *Notes*, 9, 34, 39, 40, 42, 54, 59 *et passim*.

87. *Mayor's Kalendar*, 85. See the discussion of the Corpus Christi procession below.

88. Maclean, 'Chantry Certificates', 242–3; *LP* xiii, pt. 2, 327; *GRB* (BRS 8) 178.

89. Richard Fechett (Fletcher), whose sister was married to a local merchant, Charles Hart, was living in Bristol when he made his will in 1546 and may have been a stipendiary at St Ewen (Patrick McGrath and Mary Williams (eds.), *Bristol Wills 1546–1593* (Bristol: University of Bristol, 1975), i. 1–3; see Appendix 1: Thomas Pinchyn, John Elis).

90. PRO, E 315/494, fo. 53.

91. *LP* viii. 289; PRO, E 315/245, fo. 53. The cartulary of the hospital required that the master be accompanied by one or two chaplains whenever he went out either within or without the town. None of the chaplains or brothers were to eat or drink out of the house in the same town unless in the presence of the bishop or prelate or in religious houses, and this only with permission of the master of the house. And they, too, were to travel only in groups lest they should be seen wandering alone in the town (C. D. Ross (ed.), *Cartulary of St. Mark's Hospital, Bristol* (Bristol: Bristol Record Society, 21, 1956), 33–4).

92. Emden, BRUO 1501–1540, 150 (George Croft); *Mayor's Kalendar*, 80.

93. See Appendix 1; BAO, P/AS/ChW 3 (1518); Weaver (ed.), *Wells Wills*, 18; PRO, PCC, Porche, 23 (Henry Kemys; 1 Oct. 1522; 7 Feb. 1529); PCC, Porche, 39 (Elyn Kemys; dated 12 Sept. 1528).

94. See Chapter 3 and Appendix 1: John Flooke and John Goodriche; *LP* ix. 1025.

95. In 1393 the mayor appointed John Seint Powle master 'at the special request of King Richard II' (*GRB* (BRS 2) 55). In 1534 at the request of Anne Boleyn the mayor and corporation granted the right of next presentation to her three nominees (*LP* vii. 89). The *VCH* is mistaken in saying that Bromfield was presented by Anne Boleyn's clients (*VCH Gloucester*, ii. 160; see appendix 1). The master had the patronage of at least two livings in the diocese of Bath and Wells (*Regs. B&W, 1518–1558*, nos. 278 and 506).

96. Apparently in Bristol only the Bakers' Guild participated, probably because of the obvious connection between the host and baking bread (Nicholls and Taylor, *Bristol, Past and Present*, ii. 256–72; James, 'Ritual, Drama and Social body', 41; Miri Rubin, *Corpus Christi: The Eucharist in Late Medieval Culture* (Cambridge: Cambridge University Press, 1991), 238, 275–80; Little and Easterling, *Franciscans and Dominicans*, 26). David Sacks mistakenly accepts an undocumented account of Corpus Christi in Bristol, which assumed Bristol had a civic ceremony as in many other towns '(The Demise of the Martyrs: The Feasts of St. Clement and St. Katherine in Bristol, 1400–1600', *Social History*, 11

(1986), 142). It is difficult to believe that the municipal authorities participated when the procession is not mentioned in the *Mayor's Kalendar* and no payment for it is made in the city's audits, which are extant from 1532. See below for a discussion of civic ceremony.

97. BAO, P/AS/ChW/1466–, *passim*. The friars were paid by the parish. All Saints probably was given the honoured position among the parish contingents because of the communal quality of its dedication, all saints and all souls suggesting the unity and continuity of the Christian community. None of the other parishes record payment for carriage of the sacrament; this is an important fact, for it indicates that the parishes did not have separate processions. The position of monks and friars in the procession is unknown but their presence in groups is suggested by the two friars carrying the host and by the provision of wine to the monks of St Augustine on Corpus Christi day, which paralleled the provision for parish clergy (*Compotus Roll*, 165–6, cited in Rubin, *Corpus Christi*, 164). The order is suggested by that of a similar procession in Exeter (Little and Easterling, *Franciscans and Dominicans*, 26). Further evidence of the participation of the religious and friars in urban processions may be found in Philip Benedict, *Rouen during the Wars of Religion* (Cambridge and New York: Cambridge University Press, 1981), 1–13, esp. 4–5.

98. BAO, P/AS/ChW/1, *passim* and esp. for years 1488–9 and following when the number of priests are specified; P/St.JB/ChW/1, pp. 19, 41, 63, 69, 79, 92, 98; P/XCh/ChW/1, 1544; Masters and Ralph (eds.), *Church Book of St. Ewen's, passim* and esp. pp. 108, 120, 127, and 130.

99. In Exeter the two houses of friars were responsible for the Corpus Christi Day procession (Little and Easterling, *Franciscans and Dominicans*, 26).

100. For discussion of potentially varying symbolism for different groups of participants and non-participants in the Corpus Christi procession, see Rubin, *Corpus Christi*, 265–6, 270–1. On urban ritual see Charles Phythian-Adams, 'Ceremony and the Citizen: The Communal Year at Coventry, 1450–1550', in Peter Clark (ed.), *The Early Modern Town* (London: Longman, 1976), 106–28; Benedict, *Rouen*; and Natalie Zemon Davis, *Society and Culture in Early Modern France* (Palo Alto, Calif.: Stanford University Press, 1985), chs. 4, 5, 6. None of this work focuses on the place of the clergy in late medieval urban life or their relationship to the city, although Benedict deals briefly with their place in the social structure (pp. 1–11). Nevertheless, Phythian-Adams's estimate of the importance of ceremony can certainly be applied to our view of its role in regard to the church in Bristol: 'ceremonial occasions . . . provided at least the opportunities for bringing together in celebratory circumstances those who might otherwise be opposed or separated in their respective spheres. . . . [Ceremony] was a societal mechanism

ensuring continuity within the structure, promoting cohesion and controlling some of its inherent conflicts' (p. 111). 'Ceremony and the attitudes that lay behind its observance lay at the very heart of late medieval urban culture' (p. 179). I would agree with Phythian-Adams's emphasis on ceremony's importance but also with Rubin's view that ritual is open to a variety of meanings among participants and observers.

101. Bernd Moeller has argued that the presence of clergy, who had extra-urban loyalties, created tension in towns and cities, and this tension was more important than anticlericalism to the acceptance of the Reformation on the continent ('Imperial Cities and the Reformation', in B. Moeller, *Imperial Cities and the Reformation* ed. H. C. Erik Midelfort and Mark U. Edwards, Jr. (Philadelphia: Fortress Press, 1972), 41–115; and 'The Town in Church History: General Presuppositions of the Reformation in Germany', in Baker (ed.), *The Church in Town and Countryside*, 257–68). After the Reformation, the clergy of reformed continental cities remained different from other citizens in that, for example, they could not hold office, but they did pledge their loyalty, pay some taxes, and become subject to the civil law-code (Steven E. Ozment, *The Reformation in the Cities* (New Haven, Conn.: Yale University Press, 1975), 85). Clerical citizenship in English cities did not become so much like that of the laity although their national citizenship was certainly clarified by the royal supremacy. English cities still had to deal with ecclesiastical hierarchies and courts, not to mention the Supreme Head or Governor of the Church. A brief perusal of records showing purchases of the freedom of Bristol has not turned up instances of clergy buying the freedom of the city (BAO, 04026 (Mayors' Audits from 1532); Burgess Books (1559–9 and from 1607)). In 1602, however, Robert Fryer, vicar of St Werburgh's was admitted to the Merchant Tailors' Company (Frank H. Rogers, 'The Bristol Craft Gilds during the Sixteenth and Seventeenth Centures' (Bristol Univ., MA thesis, 1949), 21). Peter Heath found examples of clergy admitted to the register of burgesses in Southampton during the reign of Henry VIII and clergy on the roll of the guild merchant of the borough of Preston in 1459 (*English Parish Clergy*, 163). In late fifteenth-century York friars became freemen. David Palliser speculates that the corporation may have mounted a campaign to prevent them and other professional groups from working within the franchise without becoming freemen. It was at the same period that the Textwriters' Guild appealed for protection against part-time competition by the lowly paid city clergy (*Tudor York* (Oxford and New York: Oxford University Press, 1979), 177).

102. The description of civic ceremony is based upon the *Mayor's Kalendar*, 74–81, 85, and Maclean (ed.), 'Chantry Certificates', 229–53, except where noted.

103. David Sacks has attempted to highlight events on St Clement's and St Katharine's days by reading the corporation's processions as attempts to unify the city by proceeding to geographic areas which maintained separate jurisdictions. Unfortunately he incorrectly placed the hospital of St Bartholomew (which housed the chapel of St Clement) on College Green near the abbey of St Augustine. It was located not in this sanctuary whose jurisdiction was so worrisome to the corporation, but in the neighbouring parish of St Michael. If one is looking for symbols of ritual geographic unification here, the better emphasis would be on the crossing of the bridges over the city's two rivers rather than on the entering of two rival jurisdictions. Sacks's reading of the rituals on and around St Katharine's day, however, is extremely insightful ('The Demise of the Martyrs', 148–53).

104. Although Natalie Zemon Davis says that in Lyons this was the one popular rite in which the clergy took the initiative, no clergy were involved in this ceremony in Bristol. If we interpret it as a ceremony of role reversal, it is a reversal of youth and age, obedience and authority. However, in Bristol it also places the secular authorities in the role ordinarily taken by the clergy (at least in Lyons) and the mayor presumably in the real bishop's role. This perhaps reflected the absence of a local bishop in Bristol (*Society and Culture in Early Modern France*, 98).

105. *VCH Gloucestershire*, ii. 78; BAO, Mayor's Audits 1532, 3rd qtr., 1st wk. Given that even the cloistered Benedictines were involved in preaching, it seems almost certain that the more pastorally oriented Augustinians profferred sermons on these occasions (Margaret Jennings, 'Monks and the *Artes praedicandi* in the Time of Ranulph Higden', *Revue Benedictine*, 86 (1976), 119–28). Extant parish accounts record payments before Rogation, that is, about the time of Easter for payment for bearing banners to St Augustine's (BAO, P/AS/ChW, 1455–; P/StJB/ChW, 1469–; Masters and Ralph (eds.), *Church Book of St. Ewen's, passim*).

106. Nicholls and Taylor, *Bristol, Past and Present*, ii. 209; BAO, 04026 (Mayors' Audits), 1532 (3rd qtr. 9th wk.). See note 103.

107. *LP* vii, no. 725.

108. Processions on St George's day are mentioned for 1460–1, 1461–2, 1462–3, and 1464–5 in the parish of St Ewen; 1468–9 in All Saints; 1553–4 in Christ Church.

109. *Mayor's Kalendar*, 81.

110. BAO, Churchwardens' Accounts, under years.

111. Such an extension occurred in 1486 when Henry VII visited the city on Corpus Christi Day and participated in a procession around College Green at St Augustine's. Afterwards the gathered throng, which included the mayor and burgesses, listened to the preaching of the

bishop of Worcester (Leland, *Itinerary*, iv. 185, and another unspecified document, both cited in Nicholls and Taylor, *Bristol, Past and Present*, ii. 83).

112. The mayor was to oversee seven chantries in five parish churches and was to attend services of at least five in four churches (St Mary Redcliffe, All Saints, St James, St Thomas, and perhaps St Stephen). See Chapter 5.

113. See Chapter 3.

114. See the discussion of Lollardy in Chapter 3; and see Burgess, 'Chantries in the Parish', 46–65.

Chapter 3. Community and Conflict: The 1530s

1. Wadley, *Notes, passim*. There are no extant documents from ecclesiastical courts of Worcester diocese in Bristol except wills.

2. Commissary General's (?) Act Books, 1527–34 are extant from Bath and Wells and include records for the deanery of Redcliffe in the archdeaconry of Bath (SRO, D/D/Ca/3, 4, 7, 8, 9A, 10, 11, 12, 12A).

3. A. Hamilton Thompson, 'Diocesan Organization in the Middle Ages: Archdeacons and Rural Deans', *Proc. Brit. Acad.*, 29 (1943), 153–94. R. L. Storey, *Diocesan Administration in the Fifteenth Century* (London and New York: St. Anthony's Hall Publications, 16, 1959), 12. See Appendix 1 for information on four rural deans of Bristol: John Popley (1531, exceptional because he was a chantry priest); John Flooke (1533, possibly 1528); Thomas Tasker (Dec. 1533); John Kene (1539).

4. Bishop Mandel Creighton, 'The Italian Bishops of Worcester', in M. Creighton (ed.), *Historical Essays and Reviews* (London: Longman Green and Co., 1902), 202–34; Phyllis M. Hembry, *The Bishops of Bath and Wells, 1540–1640: Social and Economic Problems* (London: Athlone Press, 1967), 52–3, 59.

5. *LRB*, pp. i, 92–3.

6. See below.

7. *Mayor's Kalendar*, 73.

8. J. A. F. Thomson, *The Later Lollards* (London: Oxford University Press, 1965), 20 and 47.

9. Ibid. 239–53.

10. Margaret Aston, 'Lollard Women Priests?' *JEH* 31 (1980), 441–62.

11. Thomson, *Later Lollards*, 47.

12. See below.

13. J. F. Davis offers a revised view of the men who met at the White Horse tavern in Cambridge, calling them 'evangelicals' rather than Lutherans because of the eclectic nature of their views. He holds they were

Erasmians informed by Lollard views who only superficially and later were influenced by Luther. I persist in calling two of them, Robert Barnes and Thomas Garret, Lutherans, but undoubtedly the flow of ideas was much more complex than this single term indicates (*Heresy and Reformation in the South East of England, 1520–1558* (RHS Studies in History, 34; London, 1983), 65).

14. C. H. Williams, *William Tyndale* (London: Nelson, 1969), 8–11; Samuel Seyer, *Memoirs Historical and Topographical of Bristol* 2 vols. (Bristol: J. M. Gutch, 1821–3), ii. 215; Marshall M. Knappen, *Tudor Puritanism: A Chapter in the History of Idealism* (Chicago and London: University of Chicago Press, 1939; repr. 1970), 7; A. G. Dickens, *The English Reformation* (New York: Schocken Books, 1964), 70.

15. *DNB*, under Robert Barnes; E. Gordon Rupp, *Studies in the Making of the English Protestant Tradition* (Cambridge: Cambridge University Press, 1947), 31–46. Neither Rupp nor the *DNB* mentions Barnes's connection to Bristol, saying only that he was examined in February 1526 for a sermon preached at Cambridge the previous December and was sentenced to carry a faggot in penance at St Paul's. A seventeenth century Bristol chronicler, using local calendars, records that in the civic year 1525–6 'the reverend martyr Doctor Barnes wore a faggot at his back in Bristow'. (William Adams, *Adams's Chronicle of Bristol*, ed. Francis F. Fox (Bristol: J. W. Arrowsmith for Francis F. Fox, 1910), 86. Local antiquarians (perhaps using but failing to reference old calendars) state that Dr Barnes had to do penance for carrying a copy of Tyndale's *New Testament* into the country. He cast faggots into a fire at the east end of St Paul's and repeated the ceremony at Bristol. They add that he had to wear a faggot worked in his gown as a token to all that he had only just escaped burning (Nicholls and Taylor, *Bristol, Past and Present*, 229–30). There is, of course, the possibility that a calendarist's reference to Barnes's penance in London was elaborated to include Bristol. It is difficult to fathom the omission of the incident in other references, particularly Foxe (see 'The Career of Robert Barnes', in *The Yale Edition of the Complete Works of Thomas More* (New Haven, Conn.: Yale University Press, 1973), viii. 1367–1415).

16. *BRUO 1501–1540*, 228–9; *DNB*, under Thomas Gerard; T. S. Holmes (ed.), *Register of Bishop Bubwith of Bath and Wells*, SRS 29 (1914), pp. lxiv–lxv, lxix; Thomson, *Later Lollards*, 34, 37, 47. Rupp, *Studies*, 20–2; see Appendix 1: Roger Lewys.

17. John Davis, 'Joan of Kent, Lollardy, and the English Reformation,' *JEH* 33 (1982), 227–8.

18. Hugh Latimer was living near his cure of West Kingston, Wiltshire, when he preached in Bristol in 1533 (see below).

19. Thomas More, *Confutation of Tyndale's Answer*, ed. J. P. Lusardi, R. L.

Marius, R. J. Schoeck, and L. A. Schuster, *The Yale Edition of the Complete Works of St Thomas More* (New Haven, Conn.: Yale University Press, 1973), viii. 812–6. Janet Wilson suggests that this incident occurred early in More's tenure as chancellor (26 Oct. 1529–16 May 1532) ('Roger Edgeworth's Sermons: Reformation Preaching in Bristol', *Proc. Fourth Harlaxton Conference on Early Tudor England* (1987), 22 n. 39 (typescript)).

20. More, *Confutation*, 812–6. Dickens, *English Reformation*, 29. Three priests named Nicholas have been identified in Bristol in the early 1530s: Corbett, Harris, and Sandford. See Appendix 1. Sandford is the most likely candidate as a purchaser of proscribed books. He was prior of the Austin friars whose house was in Temple parish in the Redcliffe section of the city where Lollards are known to have lived. Robert Barnes also was an Austin friar. After the surrender of his house he became vicar of Bedminster, the mother church of two parish churches in Redcliffe, St Mary Redcliffe, and St Thomas. Other Austins were employed by those two churches.

21. PRO, PCC, Hogen, 30 (27 Oct. 1535; 13 Mar. 1536). See below.

22. Thomson, *Later Lollards*, 46.

23. According to J. F. Davis, 'When the Lollards stem from the middle class there come hints of a bigger organization with the disbursement of money and the publication of books. In 1531 an informer tells of a society of Christian Brethren in London with clerks and auditors to whom the members paid sums of money' *Heresy and Reform*, 27.

24. Dickens, *English Reformation*, 33–7.

25. Latimer preached two sermons on the second Sunday in Lent (9 Mar.) at St Nicholas church in the morning and Black Friars in the afternoon, and at St Thomas church on the following Monday (*LP* vi. 799; BL, Cotton Cleop. E. iv., fo. 73). Latimer's initial invitation to preach at Lent came from the clergy rather than the mayor (*LP* vi. 247; cf. G. R. Elton, *Policy and Police: The Enforcement of the Reformation in the Age of Thomas Cromwell* (Cambridge: Cambridge University Press, 1972), 113.

26. Direct evidence of Latimer's anticlericalism appeared in a letter Latimer wrote during the conflict: 'But I know the wasp that stings them [his clerical opposition in Bristol] & makes them to swell. When purgatory is purged & pilgrimages pillaged from their abuses, profits must needs fall away'. (*LP* vi. 433 (ii); PRO, SP 6/1, no. 19).

27. *LP* vi. 317. The implication of this argument is, of course, that Bristol and its clergy were the focus of a continued national clerical resistance to the anticlericalism manifested by Crown and parliament. Michael Kelly first pointed out the aggressive stance the clergy took before their submission in 1532, but concluded they were overcome when their posture brought an increasingly rigid response from the King. The Latimer affair in

Bristol shows that the submission of the clergy in convocation was followed by yet another round of conflict (Michael J. Kelly, 'The Submission of the Clergy', *TRHS* 5th ser. 15 (1965), 97–119.)

28. Mayor Clement Base was on a commission with two reformists to investigate 'seditious preaching' in 1535. See p. 47.

29. The question of motivation must be dealt with cautiously. K. G. Powell asserts that the visit of the mayor, sheriff, and some aldermen to Thornbury to hear Latimer's chaplain, John Erley, preach is evidence that the 'Henrician Revolution' was accepted. This statement is made in the context of another asserting the influence of Protestant ideas. We do not know why the visit was made; but we must be careful not to assume or to imply that it was for religious reasons. We simply cannot separate the religious from the political, even in a visit to hear a reformist preacher (*LP* vi. 1192; K. G. Powell, 'The Beginnings of Protestantism in Gloucestershire', *Trans. B&GAS* 40 (1971), 143.

30. *LP* vi. 246; BL, Cotton Cleop. E. v., fo. 394. Richard Browne, who wrote to Bagard seeking prohibition of Latimer's preaching, was the commissary of the official principal of Worcester in April 1532 and probably was the 'Brown the learned man of Bristol' with whom Bishop Clerk of Bath and Wells viewed ground in 1535 (*LP* ix. 383). He was prebendary of Gloucester 1541–54, of Bristol, 1542–4, of Worcester 1541–6. Emden makes two men of this name prebendaries of Gloucester and recognizes neither as prebendary of Bristol, but it is likely that the same Richard Browne held all these posts (*BRUO 1501–1540*, 77; see Appendix 3). Two other letters show that John Hilsey, prior of the local Dominicans, also sought prohibition of Latimer's preaching by Bagard (*LP* vi. 433 (iii); BL, Cotton Cleop. E. iv., fo. 140). Since Bishop Ghinucci of Worcester was absent, Bagard was the acting ordinary of the diocese. For more on Hilsey, see Appendix 1.

31. John Foxe, *Acts and Monuments*, 4th edn., 8 vols., ed. J. Pratt (London: Religious Tract Society, 1877), vii. 478; *LP* vi. 799; BL, Cotton Cleop. E. iv., fo. 73, and PRO, SP 2/O, pp. 196–8).

32. *LP* vi. 572 (ii); PRO SP 6/12, p. 113; John LeNeve, *Fasti Ecclesiae Anglicanae, Salisbury*, rev. edn.; (London: Institute of Historical Research, 1962–7); Joseph Foster, *Alumni Oxoniensis*, pt. I, 4 vols. (Oxford and London: Parker and Company, 1888–91), iii, 1190.

33. *LP* vi. 799; BL, Cotton Cleop. E. iv., fo. 73.

34. *LP* vi. 433 (ii and iii); PRO SP 6/1, no. 19.

35. *DNB*, under Edward Powell.

36. *LP* vi. 247.

37. Harold S. Darby, *Hugh Latimer* (London: Epworth Press, 1953), 69–70.

38. Hilsey is said to have entered the Dominican order in Bristol where he had received religious instruction. From Bristol he went to the

Dominican house at Oxford, where he received the BD degree in May 1527 and the DD in 1532. He returned to Bristol where he was prior of the local house in the spring of 1533. In April 1534 Cromwell appointed him provincial of his order and commissioner for visiting friaries throughout England. In the fall of 1535 he became Bishop of Rochester, replacing Fisher, whose refusal to sign the oath of supremacy brought about his condemnation and execution for treason. He continued in Cromwell's favour until his death before the end of 1538 (*DNB*). Thomas Wright (ed.) identifies the letter Hilsey wrote to Bagard as one to Cromwell (*Three Chapters of Letters relating to the Suppression of the Monasteries* (London: Camden Society, 27, 1843), Letters iv and v, p. 37, and the *DNB* mistakenly inferred that Hilsey at this time regarded Cromwell as his patron. There is no evidence to indicate that Hilsey had had any dealings with Cromwell before the Latimer controversy in Bristol. The direction of his career after the controversy suggests that he benefited from his role in it.

39. Cromwell had been party to the original prohibition of Latimer's preaching, but changed his mind at some point. His reversal was made known to Bagard sometime between 2 May (the date of Hilsey's letter) and Rogation week (12–18 May) when Latimer preached. Hilsey's plea alone did not change Bagard's position (*LP* vi. 411).

40. *LP* vi. 572 (iv); PRO, SP 6/3, no. 11, p. 111.

41. BAO, 04026 (Mayors' Audits, 1533, 3rd qtr., 10th wk.). 'For hire of horses and my costs and my servants to Wells at Mr. Mayor's command to get license to the doctor of the black friars to preach 2*s.* 4*d.*' This was the first week of June according to the civic year which began at Michaelmas.

42. In 1494 William Mede, former mayor, endowed an annual sermon on the feast of Pentecost (Whitsunday) before the mayor and commonalty of Bristol and other devout people in St Mary Redcliffe. He gave the corporation a tenement, the rent of which was to support the sermon. The preacher's pay was 6*s.* 8*d.* and the mayor collected 3*s.* 4*d.* for inviting the preacher for dinner. The rest of the rent was for strewing the church with flowers and rushes, ringing the bells and laying formed cushions, presumably for the mayor and corporation. In 1533 the corporation paid for three sermons at St Mary Redcliffe in Whitsun week: 20*s.* for the three sermons, 3*s.* 4*d.* to Mr Mayor for the 'convydyng' of the preachers (convivatio, banquet), and 18*d.* for the laying of formed cushions and ringing the bell (BAO, 04026 (Mayors' Audits, 1533, 3rd qtr., 11th wk.)). Whitsunday in 1533 was 1 June.

43. *LP* vi. 433 (iii) and 411; PRO SP 6/1, no. 19, and SP 1/75, pp. 222–7.

44. Clerke himself was absent at the time of the Corporation's quest for Hilsey's licence, returning to the diocese on 1 July (Hembry, *Bishops of*

Bath and Wells, 52–3, 59; J. J. Scarisbrick, *Henry VIII* (London:
Methuen, 1968), 300, 329, 215, 273–4).

45. Hembry, *Bishops of Bath and Wells*, 69. The earliest extant reference to
Dogeon as vicar of Temple is in the will of Edward Barkehowse, dated
28 Dec. 1533 (Weaver (ed.), *Wells Wills*, 23). The date of his institution
is unknown. The last prior institution extant for the parish is that of
William Wayne on 9 Nov. 1523. (*Regs. B&W*, no. 16). A will of Temple
parish dated 8 March 1531, named John Sharman priest and Edmond
Long 'my curate' (Weaver (ed.), *Wells Wills*, 22).

46. Although Powell preached at least once on St Augustine's Green, in
Worcester diocese, it is possible that he also preached at St Mary
Redcliffe and St Thomas since as prebendary of Bedminster and
Redcliffe he was patron of the two churches. His views, moreover,
coincided with those of Bishop Clerke in whose diocese the churches lay.

47. *LP* vi. 868.

48. *LP* vi. 596; PRO, SP 1/76, p. 183. The book of articles is no longer
attached.

49. *LP* vi. 596; PRO SP 1/76, p. 183; Foxe, *Acts and Monuments*, vii. app.

50. See above for a discussion of Hutton's possible connections with the sale
of proscribed books and to Lollard antecedents (*LP* vi. 1570; Powell,
'Beginnings of Protestantism', 143; *LP* vii. 89). In his will William
Shipman requested at his burial the presence only of those ministers who
belonged to his parish church and disavowed the presence of 'sturdy
beggars' for 'penny dole'. More important, he left four pounds for the
preaching of twelve sermons in his parish church of St Werberg and
showed special concern for reformist cleric Christopher Pacy: 'Always
see that Mr Pacy our parson be rewarded and not fail 40s.' The will of
William's brother John Shipman, written in 1539, also revealed a
convinced Protestant viewpoint. He commended his soul 'unto Christ
Jesu, my maker and redeemer, in whom and by the merits of whose
blessed passion is all my whole trust of clean remission and forgiveness
of all my sins'. His funeral was to be held 'without any pomp or pride of
the folly of this world'. In 1538 Shipman became executor of the will of
David Hutton's mother Alice Hutton, who asked that her executors
'shall distribute the residue of my goods among poor honest householders
in Bristol', as God should put it in their minds, 'and as they would I
should do for them in like case'. (PRO, PCC, Powell, 4 (16 July 1551; 5
Feb. 1552); PRO, PCC, Spert, 21 (3 Aug. 1539; 1 June 1543); PRO,
PCC, Cyngley, 26 (15 Jan. 1537; 26 Apr. 1539)). Cary probably was the
father named William, whose son, Richard Carye the elder, a merchant
with Protestant connections, participated in a reformist attack on Bishop
Cheyney in 1568 (PRO, PCC, Hogen, 30 (27 Oct. 1535; 13 Mar. 1536);
Wadley, *Notes*, 245; *CSPD* (Elizabeth), xlviii. 22; see Chapter 7). William

Kelke was surely related to John and Thomas Kelke (sheriff in 1559 and mayor in 1573). John spent Mary's reign in Frankfort and Thomas was briefly imprisoned late in 1555. Thomas also participated in the reformist attack on Cheyney (Christina H. Garrett, *The Marian Exiles* (Cambridge: Cambridge University Press, 1938), 202; *APC* 1554–6, 191, 208; see Chapter 7, n. 84).

51. *LP* vi. 796; PRO, SP 1/77, p. 208.

52. Foxe puts Hubberdine in jail at Bristol on 4 July 1533. If the Corporation had jailed Hubberdine at that early date, their authority was at stake in the results of the investigation to an even greater degree (*Acts and Monuments*, viii, app., p. 775). G. R. Elton, however, says he was admitted to the Tower that day according to a 1535 list of prisoners (*Policy and Police*, 117).

53. *LP* vi. 799; BL Cotton Cleop. E. iv., fo. 73; the second part of this document is in the PRO, SP 2/O, pp. 196–8; Elton, *Policy and Police*, 116.

54. *LP* vi. 799; BL, Cotton Cleop. E. iv., fo. 73. The three former mayors were John Cable (1509–10), Thomas Broke (1512–13), and Richard Tonnell (1528–9). The conservatism of the group is shown primarily in their report to Cromwell. The only one for whom stronger evidence is available is Thomas Broke, although he and Cable died in the 1530s, precluding further involvement in the religious struggles in the city. Broke's will reveals that his 'ghostly father' or confessor was George Dogeon, vicar of Temple parish and chaplain of the conservative bishop of Bath and Wells, John Clerk. Broke left a gown of 'violet ingrain' and a feather bed to Dogeon, and £13. 6s. 8d. 'to a priest to pray for me and my friends and to help to maintain the honor of God in [Temple] church, by the space of two years' (Weaver (ed.), *Wells Wills*, 28–9 (Cable); PRO, PCC, Hogen, 37 (Broke; 10 Feb. 1536; 24 June 1536)). The only one of the three commission members still alive in 1539, Richard Tonnell, was among the members of the corporation and clergy who received verbal abuse from the supporters of the radical preacher, George Wishart (*LP* xiv (pt. 2), 184 (1); BL, Cotton Cleop. E. v., fos. 390–1; see below).

55. *LP* vi 799; BL, Cotton Cleop. E. iv., fo. 73. Gilbert Cogan was sheriff in 1522–3 and Chamberlain in 1535 (*Adams's Chronicle of Bristol*, 85; John Latimer, 'The Maire of Bristowe is Kalendar: Its List of Civic Officers Collated with Contemporary Legal manuscripts', *Trans. B&GAS* 26, pt. 1 (1903), 135; BAO, 04026 (Mayors' Audits, 1535)). Entrance to the Common Council generally occurred through occupation of the sheriff's office (Sacks, *Trade, Society, and Politics in Bristol*, 63–4). Adams has proven a reliable source for names of mayors and sheriffs, which are named in entries for each civic year. Cogan, for example, is listed as sheriff under 1522.

56. *LP* vi. 799; BL, Cotton Cleop. E. iv., fo. 73; PRO, SP 2/O, pp. 196–8.)
57. Ibid.
58. Ibid.
59. Ibid. The fact that the three former mayors who were commissioners signed this report and that sheriff John Smyth deposed against Latimer suggests some disagreement among the corporate elite. Other evidence confirms, however, that the corporation's *policy* favoured Latimer.
60. *LP* vi. 796; PRO, SP 1/77, p. 208.
61. *LP* vi. 873, 956.
62. *DNB*, under Edward Powell, Robert Barnes, and Thomas Gerard (Garret). Dr Nicholas Wilson of Cambridge also joined the conservative preachers at some point in the fray. He was sent to the Tower in April 1534 when he refused the oath of succession. Unlike More and Fisher, however, he submitted and saved his life (*LP* vi. 433 (vi) and 411; PRO, SP 6/1, no. 19; SP 1/75, pp. 222–7; Foxe, *Acts and Monuments*, vii, app., p. 775; Elton, *Policy and Police*, 113, 225, and 402–3).
63. The involvement of some clergy on both sides undoubtedly is not recorded. John Cardmaker alias Taylor, a Franciscan friar with Protestant convictions, was a member of the Bristol convent in 1533. In September 1533 he was licensed to preach in Worcester diocese. By 1534 he had become warden of the Exeter Franciscans and welcomed Latimer to that city. Becoming a secular priest in 1537, he was burned for heresy in 1555 (*BRUO 1501–1540*, 101; H&WRO, 716–903 BA 2648, fo. 60; *Reg. B&W*, 121). John Rawlyns, stipendiary at All Saints by 1534, may also have been involved. The conservative Floke was vicar of that parish, and in 1537 Rawlyns was jailed for speaking against Latimer (*LP* iv. 1147 (iv); PRO, SP 1/119, pp. 181–97; see below).
64. *LP* vi. 433 (iii); PRO, SP 6/1, no. 19. Robert Circeter was prior of St James in 1535 and 1539. Robert Cheltenham, who was prior in 1523 was still among the monks of Tewkesbury at its surrender, although he was at Deerhurst priory in 1535. Both men had BD degrees from Oxford. Robert Cheltenham had a DD degree and became curate of the parish church of St James in 1540. Both are indicative of the calibre of priors at St James (*Valor ecclesiasticus*, ii. 484, 485; *LP* xv. 49; *VCH Gloucester*, ii. 75; H&WRO, 716–903 BA 2648, fo. 194.; *BRUO 1501–1540*, 668; Foster, *Alumni Oxoniensis*, pt. I, 277).
65. *LP* vi. 411; PRO, SP 1/75, 222–7.
66. *LP* vi. 1133. Flemyng was not among the city's parish clergy in 1540 (H&WRO, 716–903 BA 2648, fos. 193–5, and 269–72).
67. Thomas Smyth, coroner, deposed against the Dean of Bristol, John Floke, for advising against prayer for the King and Queen (*LP* vi. 572 (iii); PRO, SP 6/3, p. 111). Latimer himself asserted that the dean (Floke) was the informer of Powell who was acting on what he was told

(*LP* vi. 433; PRO, SP 6/1, no. 19). Bagard wrote Cromwell that he had not consented to Hubberdine's preaching at Bristol and had told the dean of Bristol so. Bagard also explains the rumour that he had forbidden the dean of Bristol to pray for the King and Queen, saying that there were two or three 'doting deans' who had misheard and misreported him in this and other things (*LP* vi. 433 (v); vii. 722; PRO, SP 6/1, no. 19; SP 2/P (18)).

68. *BRUO 1501–1540*, 289–90 (Hilsey), 207–8 ('Fluke'). Foster, *Alumni Oxonienses*, pt. III, 1190 (Powell) and II, 583 (Goodrich).

69. H&WRO, 716–903 BA 2648, fos. 23ᵛ and 20ʳ.

70. See Appendix 1: John Floke and John Goodriche.

71. *LP* v. 909, grant 20.

72. John Kene was curate of Christ Church from at least September 1536 until he became parson 10 May 1538 (*LP* xii, pt. 1, 1147 (iii); PRO, SP 1/119, pp. 181–97; H&WRO, 716–903 BA 2648, fo. 6ᵛ).

73. New licences for preaching were required by an inhibition promulgated by Archbishop Cranmer in April 1534 (*LP* vii. 463; H&WRO, 716–903 BA 2648, fo. 68ʳ).

74. *Regs. B&W*, no. 581.

75. H&WRO, 716–903 BA 2648, fo. 62ᵛ. *Regs. B&W*, no. 319.

76. H&WRO, 716–903 BA 2648, fo. 71ᵛ.

77. Ibid., fos. 35ᵛ, 73ʳ, 271; H&WRO, BA 3585/4b, 1540, No. 61; *Regs. B&W*, no. 511. Thomas Sylke was admitted as prior of the Kalendars on 8 Oct. 1540 (H&WRO, 716–903 BA 2648, fo. 12).

78. *LP* xiv, pt. 2, 184; BL, Cleop. E. v., fos. 390–1.

79. In 1536 Latimer visited the Worcestershire and Warwickshire portions of his diocese. Most of his time as bishop was divided between his manor at Hartlebury and London (Allan G. Chester, *Hugh Latimer, Apostle to the English* (Philadelphia: University of Pennsylvania Press, 1954), 108–58.

80. Philip Hughes, *The Reformation in England* (New York: Macmillan 1951–4; 5th rev. edn., 1963; 3 vols. in 1), i. 346. Cranmer visited Bristol in 1534 according to local accounts (*Adams's Chronicle*, 88). The Church-wardens' Accounts of Christ Church record an expenditure of 4*d* 'For ringing against the coming of Canterbury to Church' (BAO, P/ChW/CC1, fo. 14ᵛ (1534)). It is possible that he was lending his authority to the requirement that the clergy subscribe to the royal supremacy. The abbot and monks of the abbey of St Augustine signed acknowledgement on 9 Sept. 1534. There also was a visitation of the clergy in 1534 by officials of Worcester diocese (*LP* vii. 1216; H&WRO, 802 BA 2764, fos. 99–100).

81. *LP* ix. 189 and 162; PRO, SP 1/95, pp. 199 and 169. The local authorities undoubtedly were responding to letters Cromwell sent in

April and June to both lay and ecclesiastical authorities throughout the country in efforts to enforce acceptance of the Royal Supremacy (Elton, *Policy and Police*, 231–2).

82. *LP* ix. 163. There is no evidence that Cromwell acted on the request of the humanist schoolmaster of Reading, Leonard Cox, in May 1534, that Cromwell as Bristol's recorder bestow upon him the mastership of the free school there (*LP* vii. 659).

83. Latimer was a suitor to Cromwell for a number of people (Chester, *Hugh Latimer*, 108–58).

84. *LP* ix. 189; PRO, SP 1/95, p. 199. The letter was sent by Clement Base and William Shipman, mayors in 1533 and 1534 respectively, and by David Hutton, sheriff in 1527. Sir Francis Bigod, the well-known Protestant reformer of Yorkshire, who would revolt against the King's handling of the Pilgrimage of Grace, was another intermediary of theirs with Cromwell (ibid.). See above for the reformist views and connections of Shipman and Hutton. They were among those certifying the 'synystrall' preaching of Powell and Hubberdine in 1533. Of Base we only know that he was the mayor who invited Latimer to preach before the corporation at Easter 1533 and that he served on another investigatory commission in 1537 (see text at nn. 25, 28, 29, 60, and 87). It is not unlikely that the conservative preacher Roger Edgeworth was among the preachers this commission considered adversaries of God's word (see Chapter 4).

85. *LP* xi. 778; PRO, SP 1/108, pp. 203–4.

86. The oath for inquiry, issued on February 25, 1537, read as follows, '(1.) First, who made the slanderous Pater Noster, Ave and Crede that was set up at Bristol; (2.) Of the seditious and traitorous preaching in Bristol since Christmas last. (3.) Of all slanderous speakers by the lord bishop of Worcester. (4.) Of such as scornfully & slanderously say that he hath now found our Lady again, as though he had lost and despised her before. (5.) Of one Glaskedian pewterer of Bristol who lately said "A vengeance on him! I would he had never been born, I trust to see him burned ere I die." (6.) To enquire of seditious & slanderous bills [that] have been lately set up or found copied or sent abroad in Bristol & elsewhere more unto the same especially of one bill that was supposed to be set up (by) one belonging to Reynold Pole. (7.) Of all other seditious & slanderous words & bills, etc.' (*LP* xii, pt. 1, 508 (i); PRO, SP 1/116, pp. 119–24).

87. *LP* xii, pt. 1, 1147; PRO, SP 1/119, pp. 184–97. The mayors were John Shipman (1529–30), Thomas White (1530–1), Clement Base (1532–3), William Shipman (1533–4), William Chester (1537–8), Henry White (1543–4), and William Cary (1546–7). Apparently three or four were reformers or sympathizers. For the reformist credentials of William and John Shipman and William Cary see above, n. 50. Clement Base may

have sympathized with Latimer in 1533, and was on the commission investigating conservative preaching in 1535, but we have no other evidence of an association with reform (see above). Thomas White and William Chester were among those verbally attacked by a religious radical in 1539 (*LP* xiv, pt. 2, 184; BL, Cotton Cleop. E. v., fos. 390–1; see nn. 29, 59, and 84). Of Henry White nothing is known. Nor have the views of Abingdon or Appowell been identified.

88. *LP* xii, pt. 1, 1147; PRO, SP 1/119, pp. 184–97. The report states that they examined the witnesses on 7 May. It is doubtful that the investigation was limited to one day's work. In any case, the report came over two months after the inquiry was ordered.

89. *LP* xii, pt. 1, 1147 (ii, 3); PRO, SP 1/119, pp. 184–97.

90. Henry Gee and W. J. Hardy (eds.), *Documents Illustrative of English Church History* (London: Macmillan, 1910), 272; *LP* xii, pt. 1, 1147 (iii); PRO, SP 1/119, pp. 184–97. Elton makes the bills reformist 'parodies' of the *Pater Noster*, *Ave*, and *Creed* (*Policy and Police*, 118).

91. *LP* xii, pt. 1, 1147 (iii, 2); PRO, SP 1/119, pp. 184–97.

92. *LP* xii, pt. 1, 1147 (iii, 6); PRO, SP 1/119, pp. 184–97.

93. Ibid. (iii).

94. Ibid.

95. Ibid.

96. Ibid. The Injunctions of August 1536 required each cleric having cure of souls to preach concerning the abolishment of the Pope's 'usurped power and jurisdiction' every Sunday for one quarter and then twice per quarter (A. G. Dickens and Dorothy Carr (eds.), *The Reformation in England to the Accession of Elizabeth I* (London: Edward Arnold, 1967), 78).

97. *LP* xii, pt. 1, 1147 (iii); PRO, SP 1/119, pp. 184–97.

98. *LP* xii, pt. 1, 1147 (iii, iv, and v); pt. 1, PRO, SP 1/119, pp. 184–97. Kene's remarks may have been particularly abrasive because he had not been in Bristol long. There is no earlier mention of him. John Rawlyns had been in Bristol at least since 1534 when he was a stipendiary at All Saints. He was instituted as rector of St Ewen on 15 Aug. 1535, and remained there until his death sometime between 11 Aug., when he last signed an account, and the end of 1556 (H&WRO, 716–903 BA 2748, fo. 40). Masters and Ralph (eds.) are mistaken in saying he died in 1555 (*Church Book of St. Ewen's*, p. xxxiv; see p. 174). In 1538 Rawlyns was indicted for the rape of an 8-year-old girl, but there is no evidence of conviction (*LP* xiii, pt. 2, 110; PRO, SP 1/135, pp. 102–4). William Glaskeryon, a pewterer and thus a well-to-do craftsman, was a parishioner of Rawlyns at St Ewen and had been proctor of the church some twenty or more years before. He probably kept an account during the years 1502–14 when no accounts were entered in the Church Book

(Masters and Ralph (eds.), *Church Book of St. Ewen*, 161, 163, 164, 165, 152). In addition to facing charges himself, Glaskeryon also signed two charges against Kene.

99. *LP* xii, pt.1, 508 (ii, iii) and 1147 (i, ii); PRO, SP 1/116, pp. 119–24; SP 1/119, pp. 184–97). The conservative Roger Edgeworth linked Luther and Wycliffe in his second sermon at Redcliffe Cross, preached after May 1536 and possibly as late as 1537. He decried their doctrine of evangelical liberty. That Christ sets us to do what we will, he said, was slander of the gospel and false (*Sermons Very Fruitfull, Godly and Learned, Preached and Set Foorthe by Maister Roger Edgeworth* (London, 1557) *STC* 7482; 19/B).

100. *Mayor's Kalendar*, 55.

101. *LP* xiv, pt. 1, 1095; PRO, SP 1/159, pp. 59–60.

102. *LP* xiv, pt. 2, 184; BL, Cotton Cleop. E. v., fos. 390–1. One letter is dated 10 Jan. and another was written by early March. (The four Sundays of Lent in 1539 were 23 Feb. and 2, 9, and 16 March, and the writer threatens the loss of a cleric's ear by 'middle Lent Sunday').

103. Ibid. The following are mentioned in the letter: Thomas White, mayor, 1530–1; Richard Abington, mayor, 1525–6, 1536–7; Thomas Pacy, mayor, 1531–2, 1542–3; John Hutton, mayor, 1524–5, 1535–6; Richard Tonnell, mayor, 1528–9; Roger Coke, mayor, 1534–5, 1541–2, 1551–2; John Smith, mayor, 1547–8, 1554–5 (sheriff, 1532–3); Nicholas Thorne, mayor, 1544–5 (sheriff, 1528–9); Thomas Sylke, sheriff, 1529–30; Robert Elliot, mayor, 1540–1 (sheriff, 1521–2); Thomas Hart, sheriff, 1535–6; Richard Prin, sheriff, 1536–7 (or possibly Edward Prin, sheriff, 1549–50); Robert Addams, mayor, 1545–6, 1558–9 (sheriff, 1530–31); Nicholas Woodhouse, sheriff, 1534–5; Thomas Hanson, rector, St Stephen, 1516–*c*.1556; Thomas Sylke, vicar, St Leonard, *c*.1529–46; Thomas Tasker, rector, St John, 1531–62; John Rawlins, rector, St Ewen, 1535–56; John Floke, prior, Kalendars Gild, 1535–40; Thomas Yereth, vicar, All Saints, 1539–40. Except where specified all of the civic identifications were made from *Adams's Chronicle*. Most of the mayors had previously been sheriff, but shrievalties are noted only when this was the primary identification for the letter writer in 1539. All probably were on the Common Council. For the clergy, see Appendix 1, under names.

104. Ibid.

105. Ibid. See the following note.

106. Ibid. Those others mentioned in this letter are as follows: John Mauncell, sheriff, 1531–2; Current sheriffs David Harris and William Jay; Richard Bromley or Richard Cheltnam, curates of St James, 1534, 1539, respectively; Henry Collins, vicar, St Augustine-the-Less, 1534, 1540; Among the three priests of St Leonard may have been

Thomas Salwey, stipendiary in 1540; David Broke, Deputy Recorder to Cromwell 1533, elected Recorder 1541 (Latham (ed.), *Bristol Charters*).

107. *LP* xiv, pt. 2, 184; BL, Cotton Cleop. E. v., fos. 390–1. Yet others mentioned in the third letter are as follows: John Harris, appointed schoolmaster of Bristol Grammar School, *c*.1542 by Nicholas Thorne; dismissed in 1561, probably for his Catholic views. He went to Douai in 1576 (Patrick McGrath, 'Gloucestershire and the Counter-Reformation in the Reign of Elizabeth I', *Trans. B&GAS* 88 (1969), 5–28); John Jarvis, sheriff, 1525–6; Anthony Paine, sheriff, 1533–4; William Young, mayor, 1555–6 (sheriff, 1539–40).

108. *LP* xiv, pt. 2, 184; BL, Cotton Cleop. E. v., fos. 390–1. William Chester, mayor 1537–8, was himself a pointmaker, a craft of those working in fine leather (the name coming from the points on gloves) and had a special relationship with the Wishart party. It is significant, no doubt, that when a riot broke out over the christening of a child in 1561 or 1562, it was 'pacified by the help of Mr. Chester, a pointmaker, with his company' (*Adams's Chronicle*, 1561).

109. *LP* xiv, pt. 2, 184; BL, Cotton Cleop. E. v., fos. 390–1.

110. A grave shortage of corn may have increased the chances of disorder. On 19 July 1539, Mayor Thomas Jeffrys wrote Cromwell begging for restraint of corn exports because of a daily price rise and the danger of scarcity. Cromwell granted the request (*LP* xiv, pt. 1, 1288).

111. *LP* xiv, pt. 2, 184; BL, Cotton Cleop. E. v., fos. 390–1. The following excerpts from the letters exhibit the writer's confidence. 'I trust you shall all repent of it [accusing Wishart] shortly when my lord Privy Seal hears of it.' 'Yet once again to the enemies of God's word, as the knave the mayor . . . and enemies of my lord Privy Seal.' 'I write charitably that you deliver the reader ere the bishop know it, or he will ruffle among you for it.' 'Commend me to all the knave priests that be the enemies of God's word; for if we live and the bishop together, they shall not trouble this town except the King do fail us . . .' 'You shall know more of my mind when our bishop comes from London.' 'There is another knave Harrys in town, . . . but when the bishop do come he shall handle him in his kind.' 'All these of this diocese that have cure shall go like knaves to sing *Ave Regina* when the bishop come.'

112. Parliament assembled 23 Apr. and at Henry's request sent up a committee consisting of Cromwell and eight bishops equally divided between reformers (including Latimer) and Catholics to create a plan for religious unity. When stalemate resulted, Henry become personally involved, authorizing presentation on 16 May of six articles of Parliament for discussion. The King had his way and the act was passed. Denial of six positions constituted heresy: (1) transubstantiation, (2) communion in

one kind for laymen, (3) celibacy of priesthood, (4) inviolability of vows of chastity, (5) necessity of private masses, (6) necessity of auricular confession (Dickens, *English Reformation*, 176–7).

113. Chester, *Hugh Latimer*, 157–8.
114. *Mayor's Kalendar*, 55.
115. *LP* xv. 183.
116. Bell's visitation occurred on 26 Apr. 1540 (H&WRO, 802 BA 2764).
117. Edgeworth, *Sermons*, 1/A-70/D.

Chapter 4. Religious Conflict: Resistance and Change

1. Edgeworth, *Sermons*, *passim*.
2. Ibid. 169/A.
3. Ibid. 236/D.
4. Ibid. 272/D-273/A, B, C.
5. Ibid. 231/C.
6. Ibid. 273/C, D.
7. Ibid. 276/D.
8. Ibid. 133/A.
9. For discussions of Catholic and reformist views of the sacrament of the altar see Hughes, *Reformation in England*, ii. 39, 49, 101, 108–11, 120–1, 123–4, 131, 136, 143–6; iii. 86–91; William P. Haugaard, *Elizabeth and the English Reformation: The Struggle for a Stable Settlement of Religion* (Cambridge: Cambridge University Press, 1968), 106–7, 108–9, 238–9, 250–1, 252, 254–5, 264, 265–9; Harold J. Grimm, *The Reformation Era* (New York: Macmillan, 1954, 1965; repr. 1966), 127–8, 134–5, 192–7, 313–16, 351–5.
10. Denial of transubstantiation was a hallmark of Lollardy in early sixteenth-century Bristol (Thomson, *Later Lollards*, 47; see Chapter 3).
11. Haugaard discusses changes in England's official view of the sacrament. See n. 9, above.
12. Hughes, *Reformation in England*, ii. 27, 36–7, 49, 108. Grimm, *Reformation Era*, 128, 235, 144.
13. For Luther's theology see Paul Althaus, *The Theology of Martin Luther*, trans. Robert C. Schultz (Philadelphia: Fortress Press, 1966).
14. Lawrence Stone has traced the growth of education in England in the latter sixteenth century 'The Educational Revolution in England, 1560–1640', *P&P*, 28 (1964), 41–80. Elizabeth Russell, however, pointed out that better records from the late sixteenth century may have distorted Stone's view ('The Influx of Commoners into the University of Oxford before 1581: An Optical Illusion?' *EHR* 92 (1977), 721–45. Jo Ann

Hoeppner Moran has pushed the growth of education back into the medieval period and argues that the laity surpassed the clergy in benefiting from what was essentially a church-led effort to better educate the clergy (*The Growth of English Schooling, 1340–1548: Learning, Literacy, and Laicization in Pre-Reformation York Diocese* (Princeton, NJ: Princeton University Press, 1985)). Clerical authority, which depended somewhat upon a monopoly of literacy and education, was under direct attack by this social development. Moreover, the new Protestant emphasis on the lay priesthood and Scriptural authority ratified and encouraged the education of the laity as a moral obligation.

15. See Chapter 3 for the articulation of solefideism and the negation of good works, and see below for the rising interest in Scripture.
16. Grimm, *Reformation Era*, 314–5, 351–5.
17. Hughes, *Reformation in England*, ii. 25–6, 40–1, 99, 101.
18. Edgeworth, *Sermons*, 157/A, C, D; 291–3.
19. Ibid., 282/B, C. He had argued earlier that it was the clergy's duty, rather than the laity's, to labour in Scripture and preach (ibid. 100/A, B).
20. Ibid. 279/A, B, C, D.
21. Ibid. 279/D-280/A.
22. Ibid. 288/B, C. Compare Collinson, *Religion of Protestants*, 100–3.
23. Edgeworth, *Sermons*, 288/D; 289/A. This new brand of clergy which Edgeworth condemns suggests a very early manifestation of 'mechanic' preachers. This pejorative name for self-appointed evangelists of a certain type was associated with the turmoil of the mid-seventeenth century but also was evident by the second decade of Elizabeth's reign. These men were primarily artisans but could also be small farmers or traders, and often were itinerant. They certainly were not the trained clerical specialists Edgeworth lauded, but they were extremely articulate and had an intimate knowledge of the vernacular Bible. With a strong concern for interior religion, they made Scripture the basis both for personal decisions and as the external authority for religious beliefs (J. W. Martin, 'Christopher Vitel: An Elizabethan Mechanik Preacher', *Sixteenth Century Journal*, 10 (1979), 15).
24. In August 1560 Archbishop Parker's concerns reflected those of Edgeworth during Edward's reign. Parker wrote to the bishops advising them to raise the standards of admission to the clergy and not to ordain men of non-clerical background. 'Whereas occasioned by the great want of ministers, we and you both, for tolerable supply thereof, have heretofore admitted unto the ministry sundry artificers and others, not traded and brought up in learning, and, as it happened in a multitude, some that were of base occupations.' This was to cease. Once the major battle between Protestants and Catholics had been decided, it was safe to call for a more able and learned clergy (J. Bruce (ed.), *Correspondence of*

Matthew Parker (Cambridge: Parker Society, 1853), 120–1, cited in O'Day, *English Clergy*, 130).

25. Edgeworth, *Sermons*, 295/A. This criticism came near the end of Edward's reign.

26. Ibid. 93/C. Edgeworth referred to the abandonment of clerical dress in his homily on ceremonies which was preached sometime from *c.*1543 to before 1548.

27. Ibid. 36/B.

28. Ibid. 36/B, C.

29. Ibid. 31/D; 32/A.

30. Ibid. 36/D.

31. Ibid. 160/C; 161/A, D; 162/C.

32. Ibid. 175/C.

33. Ibid. 220/A.

34. H&WRO, 802 BA 2764, fo. 117.

35. Edgeworth, *Sermons*, 34/A.

36. Ibid. 34/B. The criticism of women's role was rendered in his fourth sermon at Redcliffe Cross *c.*1539, soon after the injunction of Sept. 1538 had required an English translation of the Bible in parish churches.

37. Ibid. 34/B, C.

38. Ibid. 33/A.

39. Ibid. 34/A.

40. Ibid. 34/B.

41. Many times women were prosecuted in church courts for defamation, which involved witnesses and often a public statement. Examples from Bristol's Consistory Court may be found in *Hockaday Abstracts*, vols. 434 (Christ Church), 443 (St Mary Redcliffe), 445–6 (St Nicholas), all under year 1556. These are transcriptions from the originals at BAO, EP/J/1/1, which are no longer available.

42. Edgeworth, *Sermons*, 36/A.

43. Ibid. 35/A.

44. Ibid. 165/C. This comment occurred in the seventh sermon in the series preached in Bristol's cathedral sometime from *c.*1543 to before 1548.

45. Ibid. 40/B. These comments were made *c.*1539 in the context of a discussion of the difference between an image and an idol.

46. Ibid. 65/B. It appears Edgeworth is speaking of both clergy and laity in these remarks made *c.*1544.

47. Ibid. 222/A-B. The thirteenth sermon in Bristol's cathedral may have been preached *c.*1552–3.

48. Ibid. Introduction. Although Edgeworth resigned his preferments at Wells and Salisbury, he remained a prebendary and canon at Bristol until his death in late Dec. 1559 or Jan. 1560. See Appendix 1 and Chapter 8.

49. Although Rosemary O'Day attributes declining clerical recruitment

during the Reformation to several causes, she goes on to say that 'the shortage of clergy in the 1560s and 1570s was the result of doubts cast upon the status of the ministry much earlier during the English Reformation when Protestantism had as yet little hold on the minds of the people' (*English Clergy*, 29). This does not hold for Bristol. The drop in the clergy's status came precisely because Protestantism had gained a hold on the minds of a good number of people, for this in turn had caused religious conflict and a breakdown of the consensus on the clergy's role. Asserting that the period 1550–80 was not the nadir of clerical status, she argues that '[f]rom about 1560 onwards the advanced Protestants in England and Wales were working hard to instil in the minds of the people the importance of the pastoral and preaching functions'. They fostered the education of promising youth. Fruition came with the generation born in the 1560s and 1570s and eligible for ordination in the late 1570s and 80s (ibid.). The chronological limits of this book do not allow a detailed assessment of this argument, but it seems not to hold for Bristol either. While there were 'advanced Protestants' in Bristol, even among members of the corporate elite, interest in a pastoral ministry seems to have been very limited through most of Elizabeth's reign (see Chapters 6 and 7). More generally there is no reason to think the clergy's status would not have risen had the outcome of the Reformation been reversed and Catholicism been maintained. The rise in clerical status which O'Day postulates for the nation occurred because a consensus had been renewed, not because the Protestants were successful. The Protestant victory determined only the definition of the clerical role, not its increased status.

Chapter 5. Religious Houses and Chantries: Dissolutions and Surrenders

1. See Appendix 4 for a chronological treatment of local surrenders and dissolutions. While the Carmelites surrendered 28 July 1538, the other three houses were recalcitrant. By August Cromwell's deputy reported that the Dominicans were willing but the Franciscans and the Austins were 'stiff'. Moreover the prior of the Austins had sold the plate and other implements of the house as well as the timber that grew about it for a profit of over 100 marks. He claimed that the King's patent gave him the right to sell the house and all if he wanted. Nevertheless on 10 Sept. the three remaining friaries surrendered (*LP* xiii, pt. 1, 756 and 1485; pt. 2, 200, 319, 320, 321).

2. The description of this dispute depends on *The Great White Book* (Elizabeth Ralph (ed.), Bristol: BRS, 32, 1979), 1–3, 17–67.

3. Tanner, *Notitia monastica* (Bristol) (London: Society for the Encouragement of Learning, 1744), no. 11, cited in *Mayor's Kalendar*, 56; Nicholls and Taylor, *Bristol, Past and Present*, ii. 64–5; *VCH Gloucester*, ii. 78.

4. PRO, STAC 2/6, 3844; Nicholls and Taylor, *Bristol, Past and Present*, i. 239.

5. See Chapter 3.

6. *LP* xii 508; PRO, SP 1/116, pp. 119–24.

7. C. S. Taylor, 'The Chronological Sequence of the Bristol Parish Churches', *Trans. B&GAS* 32, pt. 2 (1909), 211; Haines (ed.), *Register of Wolstan de Bransford*, no. 667; *VCH Gloucester*, ii. 75–6.

8. Taylor, 'Chronological Sequence', 209, 211. Gilbert Burnet, *The History of the Reformation of the Church of England* (London: J. F. Dove for Richard Priestly, 1820), ii. 224.

9. Taylor, 'Chronological Sequence', 211, 212–3; Haines (ed.), *Register of Wolstan de Bransford*, nos. 960, 235, 501, 520, 667, 1285, 795, 966, 968, 975, 983, 987.

10. Taylor, 'Chronological Sequence', 204, 213; *VCH, Gloucestershire*, ii. 147; *Regs. B&W*, 29; George H. Cook, *Medieval Chantries and Chantry Chapels* (London: Phoenix House, 1947), 273.

11. Taylor, 'Chronological Sequence', 212; *LP* xviii, pt. 1, 436.

12. See Chapter 6 for parochial stasis and Chapter 3 for clerical moves. Floke's successor at All Saints was Thomas Molence. See Appendix 1. John Rawlins was a stipendiary at All Saints in 1534 and may very well have worked with Floke there during the Latimer episode of 1533. See Chapter 3 for his later opposition to Latimer and see Appendix 1.

13. See K. L. Wood-Legh, *Perpetual Chantries in Britain* (London and New York: Cambridge University Press, 1965), 65–92, 155–81.

14. Maclean (ed.), 'Chantry Certificates', 229–53; *Mayor's Kalendar*, 76–7; Wood-Legh, *Perpetual Chantries*, 27–8 n., 167, 171, 327 n; PRO, E 334/2, fo. 61; 3, fos. 1 and 84. Lay patronage also extended to the Chapel of the Assumption on Bristol Bridge, Forthey's Chantry in Sts Philip and Jacob, and to some extent the Kalendars Guild. *Regs. B&W*, 35; PRO, PCC, Feliplace, 29 (Robert Forthey, 23 October 1514); Nicholas Orme, 'The Guild of Kalendars, Bristol' *Trans. B&GAS* 96 (1978), 37.

15. *LP* v. 596; PRO, SP 1/32, pp. 34–5; *LP* x. 1099; PRO, SP 1/104, p. 157; H&WRO, 716–903 BA 2648, fo. 62[r]. See Chapter 3.

16. H&WRO, 716–903 BA 2648, fo. 3[r]. The parishioner was Henry Phillippes, about whom nothing is known. That he never served as sheriff makes it unlikely that he was a member of the Common Council.

17. See below.

18. *LP* xii, pt. 1, 508; PRO, SP 1/116, pp. 119–24; George Corrie (ed.), *Latimer's Remains* (Cambridge: Parker Society, 1848).

19. See Chapter 4 for Edgeworth. The only extant parish account for 1538, that of All Saints, reflects the impact of the injunctions. The clerk and sexton of the parish received 2*d*. for taking down the image, the vicar 8*d*. for sending the relic to the Bishop, the Bishop's clerk 2*d*. The parish representatives, who apparently visited a local tavern after receiving the injunctions, received 3*d*. (BAO, P/AS/ChW (a) (1538)).

20. Ralph (ed.), *Great White Book*, 3–4, 72–82. Latham (ed.), *Bristol Charters*, 14–16; Sacks, *Trade, Society and Politics*, i. 11–12, 65–8; ii. 566–611; see Chapter 3 for dissension among the pointmakers.

21. PRO, PCC, Hogen, 11 (Thomas Brown; 31 Mar. 1531); PCC, Powell, 4 (William Shipman; 16 May 1551; 5 Feb. 1552).

22. Wood-Legh, *Perpetual Chantries*, 307–9.

23. Kreider, *English Chantries*, 42–64.

24. Burgess, 'Chantries in the Parish', 46–65. Short term chantry endowments could increase the number of priests in a parish considerably at any one time. There were twelve chaplains celebrating in Christ Church in 1505, at least most of whom were undoubtedly temporary chantry priests (PRO, PCC, Holgrave, 36 (Hugh John; 10 June 1505; 28 Aug. 1505)).

25. Burgess, 'Chantries in the Parish', 60, 65. The proctors of Canynges chantries in St Mary Redcliffe certainly kept a tight reign on the priests there. In 1517–18, 16*d*. was 'abated to the Vicary and two priests because of their absences at an obit'. (E. Williams, *Chantries of William Canynges*, 191).

26. Peter Heath says, 'About this recurring obit with its display and the social awareness of its founders, there was prominent a concern for the esteem of this world, whatever anxieties about the next may have been implied'.

27. Cf. J.J. Scarisbrick, *The Reformation and the English People* (Oxford: Basil Blackwell, 1984), 1–108.

28. See Appendix 1: William Bower.

29. See Chapter 3, nn. 50 and 84 for the Shipman brothers. For the Kelkes see Chapter 3, n. 50 and Chapter 7, nn. 81 and 84. The parson of St Werberg in the 1540s and 1550s up to the accession of Mary was Christopher Pacy (see Chapter 7). The curate of St Mary Redcliffe was John Northbrooke (see Chapter 7). For both see Appendix 1.

30. One of his sureties on the composition for first fruits for the position in St Mary Redcliffe was one Robert Boner, 'innholder', of Bristol (PRO, E 334/2, fo. 80; Christina H. Garrett, *The Marian Exiles* (Cambridge: Cambridge University Press, 1938), 284–5).

31. See Appendix 1: William Bower; Haugaard, *Elizabeth and the English Reformation*, 50, 357, 389.

32. In 1514 Robert Forthey founded a chantry in the parish church of Sts Philip and James, and John Coke, his confessor, was to have it for life,

'sick and whole' (PRO, PCC, Feliplace, 29; 23 Oct. 1514). As a rule, however, chantries did not provide livings for 'super-annuated' priests (Kreider, *English Chantries*, 24–6). Bishop Latimer also sought to utilize chantries in a reformist manner by expanding the priests' duties throughout the diocese to include the education of children (Corrie (ed.), *Latimer's Remains*, 244). While it would be improbable that none of Bristol's chantry priests were involved in education, the evidence is so slight as even to discourage speculation (Nicholas Orme, *Education in the West of England, 1066–1548*, (Exeter: Exeter University Press, 1976), 35–42).

33. In the parish of Christ Church some chantry land had not passed to the Crown as late as 15 Elizabeth, and the income had been used to pay priests, curates, and clerks and for church ornaments. The parish was forced at that time to purchase the lands from the Crown (Nicholls and Taylor, *Bristol, Past and Present*, ii. 174–5). And in the parish of St Thomas the vestry had to pay the Crown 30s. in 1579 to discharge a similar claim (C. S. Taylor, 'Some Old Deeds Belonging to the Church of St Thomas, Bristol', *Proc. of the Clifton Antiquarian Club*, 1 (1888), 153; see C. J. Kitching, 'The Quest for Concealed Lands in the Reign of Elizabeth I', *TRHS* 5th ser. 24 (1974), 63–78). In 1588, however, Queen Elizabeth gave back Church lands previously confiscated from St Mary Redcliffe, 'that the same, the rents, issues and profits thereof, should be employed in maintaining and keeping the said church in its wonted beauty and repair—it being a great ornament to these parts of this kingdom' (E. Williams, *Chantries of William Canynges*, 1).

34. See Chapter 6 for a discussion of the parish clergy's decline and the laity's response to it.

35. Maclean, 'Chantry Certificates', 232, 234, 235, 238. The chantry certificates indicate that some endowments in rents were no longer supporting the number of priests intended. Edith Williams discusses the decline in rental income to support Canynges' chantries in St Mary Redcliffe and in the Abbey of St Augustine in the first two decades of the sixteenth century (*Chantries of William Canynges*, 107). See Chapter 6, especially Table 5, for a discussion of inflation and its effects on parish livings. Kreider relates the 'drastic decline in urban rents' to 'chantry pluralism'. The only known case of pluralism on chantry positions in Bristol is that of Walter or William Bower, who was incumbent of two chantries in 1548. See above and Appendix 1.

36. Jordan, 'Charitable Institutions of England', 3–94.

37. Cf. Scarisbrick, *The Reformation*, 187, who points out that there was a shift in favour of the Church in the laity's philanthropy early in the seventeenth century.

38. John Latimer says that local parish churches gave plate worth £523 to the

corporation, which additionally gave about £480 more to acquire lands of dissolved religious houses (*The History of the Society of Merchant Venturers of the City of Bristol* (Bristol: J. W. Arrowsmith, 1903), 36–7). Direct evidence from the parishes of St Stephen and All Saints, however, indicates that the parishes loaned, rather than gave, plate and cash to the corporation worth £60 and £41. 12*s*. 10*d*., respectively (BAO, P/AS/ChW/1539 (-40); P/StS/Inventories, 1539).

39. PRO, E 117/2/66, pp. 1–20, transcribed in Hockaday Abstracts, vols. 432–453, each bill placed by parish and year (1553). See Dickens, *English Reformation*, 254–5. Latimer, says that plate worth upwards of £1,000 apparently was confiscated (*Merchant Venturers*, 37–8).

40. The Mayors' Audit shows payments in late Feb. 1540 for the washing, accounting, packing, and carriage to London of the church plate (BAO, 04026 (1540, 2nd qtr., 3rd and 4th wks.))

41. *LP* xiii, pt. 2, 322; PRO, SP 1/136, pp. 124–5.

42. *LP* xvi. 878 (10).

43. See above.

44. *LP* xix, pt. 1, 1035 (79); xviii, pt. 1, 436. The outspoken and conservative John Kene had added the living of St Lawrence to his living at Christ Church in 1548. Perhaps this motivated the corporation to get their hands on the advowson for the future. See Appendix 1.

45. Latham, *Bristol Charters*, 112, 29–30.

46. PRO, E 315/ 214, fo. 106.

47. Ibid.

48. PRO, E 318/164 and 165, transcribed in *Hockaday Abstracts*, vol. 426 (Bristol City, 1543).

49. Ibid.

50. Jean Vanes (ed.), *The Ledger of John Smythe, 1538–1550*, (Bristol: Bristol Record Society and Historical Manuscripts Commission, 28, 1974), 25–6.

51. *LP* xviii, pt. 2, 231 (p. 119); xvii. 699 (fo. 20b); *GRB* i. 162–4.

52. *GRB* iv. esp. pp. 31–5, 108–21.

53. *CPR* Edward VI (1548–9), pp. 102–12.

54. On 6 Sept. 1535 Lady Jane Guildford wrote to Cromwell requesting exemptions to the late injunctions for the hospital of St Mark or Gaunts, where she lodged, concerning women in the precincts and the freedom of the Master and a chaplain to go out of the house (*LP* ix. 289). It is not clear how long Lady Guildford remained at the Hospital of St Mark, but after the dissolution of the priory of St Mary Magdalen the following July, she sought lease of that house. Sir Richard Ryche wrote to Cromwell on 15 Aug. that he had leased the house to 'Wykes' but would do his best to get it back for Lady Guildford (*LP* xi. 307). Apparently he was successful for she leased the house 10 Mar. 1537 (*LP* xiii, pt. 1,

1520). On 30 Aug. 1538, however, Lady Guildford made her will, and she must have died soon after (*LP* xiii, pt. 2, 219). Leland, visiting the city around 1542, mentions Wykes as dwelling in the house, and in 1545 it went to Brayne (Leland, *Itinerary*, vi. 89; PRO, E 318/164, transcribed in Hockaday Abstracts, vol. 426 (Bristol City, 1545)).

55. Leland, *Itinerary*, vi. 88.

56. British Museum print in 'A Brief Guide to the Priory Church of St James, Haymarket, Bristol', pamphlet available in parish church.

57. By the early 1540s the chapel on Brandon Hill was also defaced, and the town clerk had secured the site for a windmill (Clay, *Hermits and Anchorites*, 191).

58. *LP* xiii, pt. 2, 325; PRO, SP 1/136, pp. 128–9; *LP* xix, pt. 1, pp. 174, 178 and no. 1035 (159); *CPR* (Edward VI), vol. iii (1549–51), p. 319; pt. x, p. 211; *CPR* (Elizabeth), iii. 266.

59. The site had previously been granted to David Hobbys (*LP* xv. 1032 (p. 565)). Three drafts of free stone were hauled from the friars at 2*s.* per draft for repairs at St Thomas made on the right side of the high altar, at St Nicholas altar, at St James altar, and on the buttress of the tower. Tile stones were bought from Thomas Harrys and Johnson Mic . . . at 8*d.* per 100 at a cost of 2*s.* 8*d.*, and 4*d.* was paid for hauling them from the White Friars (*LP* xvi. 878 (10); BAO, P/StT/ChW/1 (1543–4)).

60. *CPR* (4 Edward VI), pt. iv, p. 267; Vanes (ed.), *Ledger of John Smythe*, 229.

61. BAO, P/AS/ChW/1554–8, *passim*.

62. Nicholls and Taylor, *Bristol, Past and Present*, i. 259; ii. 113; George H. Cook, *Letters to Cromwell on the Suppression of the Monasteries* (London: John Baker, 1965), 175; *Mayor's Kalendar*, 55.

63. *LP* xiii, pt. 2, 322.

64. BAO, 04026 (Mayors Audits), 1541. The gaol privy was the 'jakes' at 'Newgate'.

65. Wadley, *Notes*, 190.

66. *LP* xv. 831 (67).

67. BAO, P/ChW/StW/1553–6.

68. Wadley, *Notes*, 195.

69. Ibid. 227; Nicholls and Taylor, *Bristol Past and Present*, ii, 111.

70. See Chapter 7.

71. Bowker, 'Henrician Reformation', 46. P. Hughes, *Reformation in England*, iii. 53 n. 1; Christopher Haigh, *Reformation and Resistance in Tudor Lancashire* (Cambridge: Cambridge University Press, 1975), 73–4.

72. Zell, 'Economic Problems', 19–43.

73. See Chapter 2.

74. *LP* xiii, pt. 1, 1485; pt. 2, 319, 320, 321; PRO, E 36/115, pp. 7, 13, 19, 51, 115, 153, 161; *LP* xiii, pt. 2, 200.

75. D. S. Chambers (ed.), *Faculty Office Registers, 1534–49* (Oxford: Clarendon Press, 1966), 97, 115, 135. See Appendix 1: Christopher Roche, William Collys, and John Pyen.

76. See Chapter 3 and Appendix 1. Hilsey replaced Bishop Fisher at Rochester in 1535 (*DNB*, under John Hilsey). John Cardmaker was in the Bristol Franciscan house in 1533 and was licensed to preach in Sept. of that year. As warden of the Exeter house, he welcomed Latimer to that city in 1534. He left the order in 1537 and went to London, after which he may have gone to Louvain. During the reign of Edward VI he became canon and chancellor at Wells. At the accession of Mary he was deprived of his livings for marriage. He tried to escape to the continent with his bishop, William Barlow. He was caught, convicted, and burned at Smithfield, London, 30 May 1555 (Emden, *BRUO 1501–1540*, 101; MacCaffrey, *Exeter, 1540–1640*, 176, 187; *LP* xiii, pt. 2, 217).

77. *LP* xii, pt. 2, 508 (ii, iii); PRO, SP 1/116, pp. 119–24 (ii, iii).

78. Chambers (ed.), *Faculty Office Registers*, 162, 166, 135.

79. Stipendiaries John Merden (Marthen), St Werberg; Thomas Lee (Thomas or John Lye), St Lawrence; Henry Lawnne (Hugh Lawe or Lane), St Peter; and Thomas Lewys, curate of Henbury (H&WRO, 802 BA 2764, fos. 193, 194, 195 (26 Apr. 1540)).

80. Nicholas Sandeford, ex-prior, vicar of Bedminster and curate of St Mary Redcliffe, 1540–3; John Yngman, curate of St Thomas, 1540; John Pindar, stipendiary of St Thomas and curate of St Mary Redcliffe, 1540; Thomas Parker, stipendiary of Temple, 1540. See Appendix 1.

81. Abbot Morgan Guilliam, Prior Humphrey Hyman, student John Rastell, John Carye, Henry Pavye, William Wrington, William Underwood, Richard Hill, Richard Oriell, Richard Carsy (Kersey), and Richard Hughes (Baskerville, 'Dispossessed Religious of Gloucestershire', 94–5; *VCH Gloucester*, ii. 78–9; see Appendix 1).

82. Prior John Colman, Richard Fetchett (Fletcher), Thomas Pynchyn, John Eles (Helys, Ellys). Robert Benet left the house before the surrender (*LP* vii. 1216; xv. 139; see Appendix 1).

83. St Augustine: Humphrey Hyman, vicar, All Saints, 1542–*c.*1555; John Rastell, vicar, St Nicholas, 1546–63; William Underwood, stipendiary, Christ Church, 1540; Richard Oriell, chantry priest, Bedminster (near Bristol, mother church of St Mary Redcliffe and St Thomas), 1548 and vicar, Bedminster, 1554–92?; Nicholas Corbett (not present at surrender), curate, St Peter, 1540–2 and vicar, Sts Philip and James, 1544–? (gone by 1547). Tewkesbury: Alexander Beley (Bulle), stipendiary, St Nicholas, 1540–1 and stipendiary, St Leonard 1541; William Shaynshum (Streinsham), stipendiary, St Mary le Porte, 1541; Roger Compton, chantry priest, St James, 1548; Thomas Bristowe, fraternity priest, St John the Baptist, 1548; Robert Cheltenham (alias Netheway?), curate, St

James, 1541–2, 1545. Cheltenham was prior of St James (a cell of Tewkesbury) in 1523. Thomas Bristowe's name is suggestive of connection to Bristol, and it is quite possible that he and the other monks who took jobs in Bristol had previously served there as religious.

84. Monks of St Augustine: John Carye, curate, Olveston, 1540; Henry Pavye, curate, Horfield, 1540; William Wrington alias Houlder, chantry priest, Berkeley, 1548. Abbot Morgan Guilliam and Richard Carsy had gone to the Isle of Wight. Richard Hughes became prebendary in Bristol cathedral (1554–63) after a stint in Norfolk. There is no further evidence of Richard Hill, and it is possible that he and Richard Oriell were the same man. See Appendix 1.

85. See Appendix 1. 1540: Thomas Bede, St Philip, ex-monk, Hailes; Roger Hawerding, St Philip, ex-religious; William Carre, St Werberg; ex-religious. 1541–8: Thomas Griffith, priest, Burton's Chantry, St Thomas, possibly ex-friar (Austin) or ex-religious. 1542–54: Bishop Paul Bush, provincial of the 'Bonhommes', a reformed order of the Austin friars, and last Provost of their house of Edington, Wilts. 1542–50: Dean John Snow, last prior of Braden-Stoke priory, Wilts. (*BRUO 1501–1540*, 89, 527). 1544–8: David Dowell, priest, Holwaye's Chantry, All Saints, ex-monk (Cleeve). 1546: John Boroughes, sexton, Bristol cathedral, possibly ex-friar (Franciscan). 1548: Thomas Bristow, priest, Fraternity of St John the Baptist, St Ewen, ex-monk (Tewkesbury); Roger Compton, priest, Ponam's Chantry, St James; ex-monk (Tewkesbury) (Bristow and Compton may have served in Tewkesbury's Bristol priory, St James); Anthony Malmesbury, priest, Frampton's Chantry, St John the Baptist, ex-monk (Malmesbury). 1556, 1557: Richard Vaughn, curate, St Leonard, ex-monk (Malmesbury); Stephen Popingaye, curate, Clifton, Bristol deanery; 1557, rector, St Werberg, ex-friar (Franciscan).

86. H&WRO, 802 BA 2764, fos. 193–5, 269–72. The inclusion of St Mary Redcliffe, St Thomas, and Temple in a Worcester diocesan document was unusual and doubtless related to plans to incorporate them into the deanery of Bristol in a new diocese. They were taken from Bath and Wells and included in the diocese of Gloucester established in Sept. 1541 and then in the diocese of Bristol founded in June 1542.

87. Baskerville, 'Dispossessed Religious of Gloucestershire', 104–8.

88. Thomas Sylke, Prebendary of Bristol cathedral; Richard Wale, deacon in cathedral 1550, 1554; William Hunt, precentor, sacristan, minor canon in Bristol cathedral 1554, 1561, 1570; Roger Lewys, chantry priest of St Thomas, became vicar of Bedminster, the mother church, and was deprived in 1554; Thomas Pinchin, curate, Christ Church 1556, 1559, 1560; William Smythyman, stipendiary, St Nicholas, 1552. David Thomas, rector, Brockely, Somerset; John Collyer, vicar, Olveston, 1546–61; Henry Spendalle, curate, Marshfield; David Dowell, curate,

Stapleton, 1557. Nothing known: Lewis Morgan, Roger Capes, Roger Compton, Thomas Kynge, John Pendar, Robert Foster, Philip Barrey. See Appendix 1.

89. See Appendix 1: John Shereman, curate St Ewen, 1557.

90. Franciscans Thomas Lewys, John Duke, John Marthen (Merden), Thomas Lee. Friars who left in the 1530s before the surrenders of the houses: Dominicans, prior John Hilsey and prior William Oliver (certain); William Collys (possible); Franciscan John Cardmaker (certain); Carmelite prior John Masday (possible) (fled at surrender). Hospital of St Mark: Prior John Colman, Richard Fletcher (Fetchett). See Appendix 1 for all, esp. Guilliam and Rastell. Others may have had degrees; there are many gaps in the universities' registers.

91. Certain: John Popley, St John, 1531; William Bower, St Mary Redcliffe, 1543, 1548, St Werberg, 1548; Thomas Sprint, Christ Church, 1534. Probable: William Benet, St Nicholas, 1533–9. Possible: John Masday, St Thomas, 1524; John Coke, All Saints, 1534; Thomas (Richard) Griffith, St Thomas, 1541, 1548; Nicholas Harris, St Stephen, 1534, Kalendars Guild in All Saints, 1548; Thomas King, Our Lady of the Assumption Chapel on Bristol Bridge, 1548; Roger Lewys, St Mary Redcliffe, 1545; William Patenson, St Philip, 1534; Thomas Perepyn, Christ Church, 1548. See Appendix 1.

92. Burgess, 'Chantries in the Parish', 54–9.

93. Knappen, *Tudor Puritanism*, 433.

94. John Northbrooke, *A Treatise against Dicing, Dancing, Plays and Interludes with Other Idle Pastimes* (London, 1577; repr. London: F. Soherl, jun., for the Shakespeare Society, 1843), 113–14.

95. Kreider, *English Chantries* 26–8.

96. Burgess, 'Chantries in the Parish', 59, 50.

97. See Table 3. The median of the fourteen figures would be either £7 or £7. 4s. 2d.

98. Maclean, 'Chantry Certificates', *passim*.

99. Kreider, *English Chantries*, 19–21, 50–4, 57–9.

100. Burgess, 'Chantries in the Parish', 59. Arthur Sabin concludes that in early sixteenth-century Bristol, 'There must have been a small floating population of such choirmasters' as those in the monastery of St Augustine, who seemed to come and go so frequently 'Compotus Rolls of St Augustine's Abbey', 196.

101. Roger Edgeworth, *Sermons*, 289D–290A.

102. Extant wills began to reflect sermon endowments in the early 1550s (PRO, PCC, Powell, 4 (William Shipman; 16 May 1551; 5 Feb. 1552; left £4 for twelve sermons); PCC, Coode, 29 (Roger Wygmaure, gent.; 3 July 1550; 16 Dec. 1550; left money for twenty sermons)). In the 1530s, however, wills began to reflect a change in funeral practices, by

requesting that burial be without 'pomp or pride' and by specifying that only the clergy of the parish church be present. Some requested that no poor be present at the funeral, preferring to leave alms to bedridden rather than sturdy poor (PRO, PCC, Hogen, 11 (Thomas Brown; 31 Mar. 1531); PCC, Spert, 21 (John Shipman; 3 Aug. 1539); 1 June 1543); PCC, Dyngley, 29 (John Hewes; 29 July 1539; 14 Aug. 1539); William Shipman, see above; PCC, Wrastley, 41 (Francis Codrington; 10 Aug. 1557; 29 Oct. 1557; F. W. Weaver (ed.), *Somerset Medieval Wills, 1383–1558*, 3 vols. (Somerset Record Society, 16, 19, 21, 1901–5), 44–7 (John Browne, 20 Aug. 1538; 8 Feb. 1543)).

103. Maclean, 'Chantry Certificates', *passim*. Alan Kreider found that in six shires he investigated the average age for chantry priests at the dissolution ranged from 47 to 55. He found 'astonishingly few' who were younger than 30 at the dissolution. The tendency towards age rather than youth he attributes to the entry of ex-religious into chantry livings (*English Chantries*, 24–7).

104. Geoffrey Baskerville, *English Monks and the Suppression of the Monasteries* (New Haven, Conn.: Yale University Press, 1937), 239–40; Mullins, 'Effects of the Marian and Elizabethan Religious Settlements', 55.

105. Baskerville, 'Dispossessed Religious of Gloucestershire', 94.

106. *LP* xv. 49; PRO, E 315/245, fo. 159.

107. *LP* xv. 139 (iii); PRO, SP 1/157, fo. 119.

108. John Masday received £6 per year as a stipendiary priest in the parish church of St John, 1533–9 (BAO, P/StJ/ChW 1 Minute and Account Book, under year). At the visitation of 1534 Masday paid 8s. 9d., apparently to the subsidy. By comparing his payment to that of others we have arrived at the ranges of stipends paid in Bristol's Worcester parishes at that time (H&WRO, 716 903 BA 2648/8(ii)–9(iii), fos. 98-100). This stipend range rose a pound or so for parish curates in the 1550s. See Chapter 6.

109. Maclean, 'Chantry Certificates', *passim*. See Chapter 6.

110. See Chapter 6, esp. Table 5.

111. Religious houses throughout England made a large number of grants of first and next presentation in the period prior to 1539 (O'Day, *English Clergy*, 82–3).

112. Baskerville, 'Dispossessed Religious of Gloucestershire', 94.

113. PRO, E 334/3, fo. 104 and E 334/2, fo. 58.

114. BAO, DC/A/9/1/1 Computa, 1550; Maclean, 'Chantry Certificates', 246.

115. *Regs. B&W* no. 526. See Appendix 1.

116. Nicholas Sandeford, former prior of the Austins, became vicar of Bedminster in 1540, a living which had the 'chapel' of St Mary Redcliffe attached. He sometimes was referred to as vicar of Redcliffe although

this was officially only a curacy or chaplainage. He no doubt was collecting income from the parish, may have acted as curate, and may have been paying one or more of his former friars to fill in for him there when necessary. Baskerville says John Ingman and John Pindar, both former Augustinian friars in Bristol, were curates of St Mary Redcliffe in 1540, but the Worcester episcopal list shows Ingman as curate of St Mary Redcliffe and Pindar as stipendiary of St Thomas, also a 'chapel' of Bedminster (PRO, PCC, Pynnyng, 2 (John Browne, gent.; Aug. 1538; 8 Feb. 1543)). Bequests were made to Sandeford and four friars including Pindar (*LP* xiii pt. 2, 319; *Registers B&W*, no. 946; Weaver (ed.), *Somerset Wills*, 46. Baskerville, 'Dispossessed Religious of Gloucestershire', 97; H&WRO, 802 BA 2764, fo. 194). It is worth keeping in mind that Redcliffe was the area in which Lollards had usually lived and that the reformer Robert Barnes, who apparently visited Bristol in the 1520s, was an Austin friar. Moreover the churchwardens of St Mary Redcliffe were cited in the local ecclesiastical court in the 1560s for allowing unlicensed preaching. By the late 1560s the puritan John Northbrooke was curate of the church. See Chapter 7 and Appendix 1.

117. Maclean, 'Chantry Certificates', 247. PRO, E 336/10 (Clerical Subsidy); C. S. Taylor, 'The Religious Houses of Bristol and their Dissolution', *Trans. B&GAS* 29, pt. 1 (1906), 122. See Appendix 1. Alan Kreider's research in six shires showed 7.6 per cent of chantry priests at the dissolution over 70 years old. Three claimed to be 86, 87 and 90, respectively (*English Chantries*, 24).

118. *LP* xv; PRO, SP 1/157, fo. 119; PRO, E 315/245, fo. 7; H&WRO, 802 BA 2764, fo. 271; PRO, E 334/3, fo. 20; BAO, DC/A/9/1/1 Computa, 1550 (Robert Pinxton); PRO, PCC, More, 35 (Richard Watleye; 13 July 1555; bequest to Thomas Pynchyn 'my curate'); PRO, E 336/12 (Clerical Subsidy. Richard Pynchin, curate, Holy Trinity (Christ Church)); BAO, EP/J/1/5, p. 154; *Hockaday Abstracts*, Newnham, Gloucestershire, 1563.

119. BAO, DC/A/9/1/2 Computa 1561, 1570. Bower apparently was involved with reformer Arthur Saule at Oxford in 1553. In Jan. 1561 Saule became a prebendary of Bristol, and in 1563 both Bower and Saule were supporters of the puritanical party in the Lower House of Commons (see Appendix 1: William Bower; Appendix 3: Arthur Saule; and see n. 31 above).

120. Dickens, *English Reformation*, 278–9; Mullins, 'Effects of the Marian and Elizabethan Religious Settlements', 109–33. One can only wonder if urban clergy were slower than their rural counterparts to marry because of their worsening economic condition in the face of inflation. See Chapter 6.

121. See Appendix 1.

Chapter 6. The Decline of the Parish Clergy

1. John Bossy argues that the church and the rural parish were not representative of a unified community; rather parish activities were carried on in an effort to achieve some sense of community where it did not come naturally. The role of the priest was to aid in peacemaking among hostile parishioners. This also holds for urban parishes and for the urban civic community. This view, however, does not preclude the fact that an institution which responds to a societal need can also reshape that society. Thus the parson served as an arbitrator of disputes and also as a symbol for the unity of the parish community ('Blood and Baptism: Kinship, Community, and Christianity in Western Europe from the Fourteenth to the Seventeenth Century', in Derek Baker (ed.), *Sanctity and Secularity: The Church and the World* (Studies in Church History, 10; Oxford: Basil Blackwell for the Ecclesiastical History Society, 1973), 129–43; cf. also *Lyndwood's Provinciale*, ed. J. V. Bullard and H. Chalmers Bell (London: The Faith Press, 1929), 28).

2. In very few cases has it been possible to determine the social or geographic origins of clerics. See Appendix 1.

3. Among the responsibilities of the vicar of All Saints in 1525 was delivering copies of writings concerning lands in which the parish had an interest, probably by virtue of a bequest. He and another were paid 23*d*. 'for wine and other pleasures' when they rode to deliver the writings. The vicar also was repaid for a fine he had paid in connection with the affair, again probably to gain access to a bequest. In that same year the parish also paid him 3*s*. 4*d*. towards the cost of buying two antiphonaries, for which the parish paid £11. The parish also paid for the carriage of the two books. It appears the vicar had been on a shopping trip (BAO, AS/ ChW 3 (1525)). Adding to the parson's power as well as his responsibilities was the duty, at least on occasion, of choosing the priests who were to celebrate in chantries. This may also have been done by executors of wills, but undoubtedly the incumbents would have been consulted, given that all the parish priests worked in close proximity. In 1415 a parishioner in the parish of St Werberg specifically designated his rector to choose the chaplain to celebrate for twenty years in the parish church (PRO, PCC, Marche, 30 (Henry Lokke; Morrow of Ascension 1414; 8 Nov. 1415)).

4. Both vicars John Williams of St Nicholas and John Collys of St Philip were non-resident in 1540. Neither were listed in a subsidy list of 1534 as non-resident, but they were two of only three who had curates (assistants) and this suggests the possibility that they already were non-resident. Thomas Sylke, vicar of St Leonard, also had a curate, but he

made his career in Bristol (H&WRO, 802 BA 2764, fos. 269, 270, 99, 100). John Goodriche, rector of Christ Church (Holy Trinity), and John Flooke, vicar of All Saints were pluralists. See Appendix 1.

5. *CSPD* (Elizabeth), xii. 108; PRO, SP 15/12, no. 108. The evidence for dating the survey does not allow certainty, but places it sometime between the summer of 1564 and late 1565. Late 1565 is the most likely date and the date I have used in my calculations. The evidence for the later dating comes from the parishes of St John and St Werberg. The will of Thomas Tasker, former parson of St John was in probate between Jan. and July 1563. This suggests Tasker had died late in 1562. The survey reported a vacancy of three years; thus it would appear that it was made late in 1565. It is possible, of course, that Tasker died earlier and that the survey, then, was made earlier. At St Werberg, Stephen Popingaye was presented to the living 30 Apr. 1557. The accounts of 1558 show that former parson Christopher Pacy, who apparently had left at the accession of Mary, had returned to the parish (he soon became a prebendary and canon in the cathedral). It would seem that Pacy's return (and presumably Popingaye's ouster) should be dated after Elizabeth's accession 17 November 1558. The survey reports a vacancy of seven years; this would date the report in late 1565. The primary evidence which would date the report in the summer of 1564 is the institution of Richard Simondes (Smyth) to the vicarage of St Philip on 9 June 1564. Since the survey reported a vacancy in the living of seven years, this suggests it was written before Simondes's institution. Since Simondes's composition for first fruits, however, was not made until 15 Mar. 1566, it is possible that the surveyors were not aware that the living had been filled. This suggests, of course, that the survey was made in the records rather than on the ground and that it was, indeed, made in late 1565. See Appendix 1.

6. See Appendix 1: Roger Rise, Richard Simondes, John Tewe, and Thomas Colman. In 1576 Thomas Colman was commissioned to sequester the living, which was vacant on the death of the last incumbent. However, John Tewe, *presented* to the living in 1568, was still alive.

7. Archbishop Parker instituted Thomas Love to the Bristol livings of St Ewen and St Michael on 15 Apr. 1568 (*Registrum Matthei Parker Diocesesis Cantuariensis A.D. 1559–1575*, transcribed by Margaret Thompson, ed. W. H. Frere (Oxford: Canterbury and York Society, 35–6, 39, 1928–33), 35(i), 269 and 36(ii), 510). Love had exhibited his letters of ordination in Bristol Consistory Court in 1567. Both livings were in the patronage of Robert Brayne, but since they had been vacant for years, the right of presentation *pro hac vice* had fallen to the Crown, and it is likely that the livings were filled without reference to the parishioners at all (cf. O'Day, *English Clergy*, 76). It also seems likely that

Love never claimed his living at St Ewen since on 4 Apr. 1579, Richard
Arthur was admitted to the living by Archbishop Grindal on presentation
by Brayne's heirs and it was vacant because of the death of John Rawlins,
'last incumbent', who died in 1556 (Lambeth Reg. Grindal, fo. 309ʳ
(transcribed in *Hockaday Abstracts*, vol. 437, St Ewen, 1579)) *The Church
Book of St. Ewen* shows Arthur was already serving as minister (untenured
curate) in 1577–8 (Masters and Ralph (eds.), *Church Book of St. Ewen*,
59). There is no extant account for the following year, but the account of
1579–80 revealed a legal dispute between Arthur and the parish (p. 62),
and in Oct. 1579, Arthur signed a release and quitclaim of the rectory
and made a bond for £100, pledging not to revoke his resignation or
attempt to procure the rectory in the future (pp. 258–9). On 4 Apr.
1579, the same day that Arthur was instituted to the living, the parish
paid 'Mr. Long' 9s. 4d. 'more . . . for a months service', and Thomas
Longe signed the parish account as parson for the year 1579–80 and
held the living until 1591 (pp. xxxiv, 180–1). It seems likely that Thomas
Longe was the Thomas Love or Lone instituted in 1568 and that he
appeared eleven years later in 1579 to claim the living, putting the
parishioners who had sequestered the tithes in a bind. Arthur, the
untenured curate, may have responded by seeking institution himself.
The legal implications are not clear and probably were not clear to the
parishioners, who took the course of removing the second rector from
the position and taking care that he should make no claim in the future.
The parishioners may have feared a suit from Longe in regard to the
tithes they had sequestered and their payments of various curates since
1568. In 1580–1 they 'lent' Mr Longe £1. In 1583 they gave him an
advance on his salary. Where Longe had been and why he turned up in
1579 is a mystery. It is possible that he was content to leave sequestration
and payment of a curate to the parish since the living was so poor, but
decided to fight the institution of another parson whereby he would lose
any claim to the living. If he had been resident in the parish of St
Michael, he would have been aware of Arthur's institution and may have
decided to serve the second parish rather than lose it; a worsening
economic situation may have been a factor. It is hard, however, to
reconcile his presence in the city and the parish's seeming ignorance of
his legal position as their rector. It is also possible that his attempt to take
up his cures prompted Arthur to seek institution. In any case, Longe's
story in some form seems a likely explanation for the dispute between
Arthur and the parish, which the editors of the church book were at a
loss to explain. See Appendix 1.

8. See Appendix 1: John Gregory and Richard Arthur for St Mary-le-
   Porte; John Knight, Thomas Caverly, and Thomas Tyson for St
   Stephen. There is no evidence of incumbents before 1570 in St

Augustine-the-Less, St Leonard, St Werberg, St Peter, or Christ Church. Christopher Devereaux was curate of St Peter in 1575 and Humphrey Mosley was parson in 1583. John Eaton (Hayton) was curate of Christ Church in the 1560s and Richard Houseman in 1575 (Nicholls and Taylor, *Bristol Past and Present*, ii. 15).

9. In 1561 as many as 10 per cent of the nation's livings were vacant although the proportion varied from place to place. It was more serious in populous areas such as Canterbury and London than in the dioceses of Oxford and Gloucester (O'Day, *English Clergy*, 31). O'Day notes the 'curious anomaly' that just at the time of greater emphasis on pastoral care, it was being withdrawn from many congregations. This chapter discusses that anomaly in Bristol and attempts to explain the reasons for it.

10. 'Educational Revolution in England', 41–80. Elizabeth Russell challenged Stone's interpretation on the grounds that earlier records for Oxford were incomplete ('Influx of Commoners into the University of Oxford', 721–45). Jo Ann Hoeppner Moran pushes the beginnings of the growth of lay education back to the mid-fourteenth century, putting sixteenth-century changes in the context of evolution rather than revolution. She credits the Church's pursuit of clerical education with greater opportunities for the laity, which allowed them to surpass the clergy (*Growth of English Schooling*, *passim*, esp. 224–5). Margaret Aston carries the evolutionary scheme even further, pushing the beginnings of the growth of lay literacy back to 'an acquaintance with letters that penetrated the whole of English society' and markedly accelerated during the thirteenth century. She credits this primarily to the growth of royal administration rather than the church ('Devotional Literacy', in *Lollards and Reformers: Images and Literacy in Late Medieval Religion* (London: Hambledon, 1984), 101–33).

11. *BRUC, BRUO, BRUO 1501–1540*, Foster, and Venn.

12. See E. Russell, 'Influx of Commoners into the University of Oxford', 725, for the ways in which a student could fail to leave any trace in the records.

13. See Appendix 1. The clergy of Surrey also experienced a decline in education during the Reformation. Between 1520 and 1530, 34.1 per cent of the identified incumbents possessed degrees: under Edward VI, 14.3 per cent; in 1562, 22.62 per cent; and in 1581, 29.5 per cent (R. Christophers, 'Social and Educational Background of the Surrey Clergy, 1520–1620' (Univ. of London, Ph.D. diss., 1975), 50). Rosemary O'Day asserts that clerical education was on the increase in the fifteenth and early sixteenth centuries. About one-third of those beneficed or vacating benefices in London between 1522 and 1530 were graduates, about a sixth of the beneficed in Norwich between 1503 and 1528, and about a

fifth of the beneficed in Canterbury and Durham. Staffordshire archdeaconry in 1531, however, contained no graduate clergy (*English Clergy*, 77–8). According to Susan Brigden, the beneficed clergy of London were the country's best educated and their educational level was rising before the Reformation. She does not make clear the effect of the Reformation (*London and the Reformation* (Oxford: Oxford University Press, 1989), 57–61). In the diocese of Canterbury there were significantly fewer graduates among the clergy in the 1550s than earlier in the century under Archbishop Warham (Zell, 'Personnel of the Clergy of Kent', 525). Between 1504 and 1532, 39 per cent of the Canterbury institutions (including those in archiepiscopal peculiars outside Kent) were graduates (Michael J. Kelly, 'Canterbury Jurisdiction and Influence during the Episcopate of William Warham' (Univ. of Cambridge, Ph.D. thesis, 1963), 14–17, cited in Zell, 'Personnel of the Clergy of Kent', 525). In the diocese of Canterbury under Bourgchier's tenure (1454–86) about one-fifth of those instituted or already beneficed were graduates (Heath, *English Parish Clergy*, 81). These figures suggest that the number of graduates grew in the diocese in the early sixteenth century and declined during the Reformation. In Lincoln diocese between 1495 and 1520 only 11 per cent of those presented to livings were graduates, but this was an increase over the period 1421–31 when only 3.5 per cent were graduates (Bowker, *Secular Clergy*, 45).

14. When the vicar of Temple John Mason died in 1489, he left 'a book of sermons of St. Magdalene' to the church of Egmond and three books to his own parish church (PRO, PCC, Milles, 32 (10 May 1489; 13 Aug. 1489)). The early sixteenth-century parson of St Ewen John Colman gave two books of 'sermon matters' and 'a little portas' to his parish, where they were tied with a chain in the chapel of St John (Masters and Ralph (eds.), *Church Book of St. Ewen's*, pp. xxxiii, 10; cf. Roy M. Haines, '"Wild Wittes and Wilfulness"; John Swetstock's Attack on those "Poysunmongeres", the Lollards', in G. Cuming and D. Baker (eds.), *Popular Belief and Practice* (Studies in Church History, 8; Cambridge: Cambridge University Press, 1972), 152–3).

15. Bowker, 'Henrician Reformation and the Parish Clergy', 30–47; D. M. Barratt, 'The Condition of the Parochial Clergy from the Reformation to 1660', 5, 55; Michael Zell, 'Economic Problems of the Parochial Clergy', 19–43; O'Day, *English Clergy*, 127–9.

16. O'Day, *English Clergy*, 127–8.

17. *CSPD* (Elizabeth), xii. 108; PRO, SP 15/12, no. 108.

18. Bowker and Zell, by taking into account the third tier of clergy, the unbeneficed proletariat, argue that the large majority of clergy saw the acquisition of a benefice as the goal of the clerical career (Bowker, Henrician Reformation and the Parish Clergy'; Zell, 'Economic

Problems of the Parochial Clergy' and 'Personnel of the Clergy of Kent'). R. N. Swanson agrees. (*Church and Society in Late Medieval England* (Oxford and New York: Basil Blackwell, 1989), 27–8, 43–50). O'Day, on the other hand, asserts that the goal of the pre-Reformation clerical career was to rise above a parochial benefice to a position in the secular government or in the higher echelons of the church. The 'ultimate ambition' was to relinquish responsibility for the cure of souls. Only after the Reformation was the idea of a cleric's having a parish cure idealized and the pastoral role also posited for the archdeacon, the dean, and the bishop. O'Day does recognize that the pastoral ideal was limited by institutional realities and by the practice of rewarding servants of state and Church with cathedral prebends and wealthy benefices (*English Clergy*, 232). In Bristol the large number of educated incumbents before the Reformation suggests that indeed a benefice was a goal of a respectable clerical career. The longevity of many of the beneficed as well as their educational status, however, suggests that most local clergy would not have expected to have gained a benefice. Clergy who were drawn there temporarily or who made their lives there did so because of the other kinds of opportunities available, such as chantry positions, both tenured and untenured, which involved teaching or singing (cf. Burgess, 'Chantries in the Parish', 46–65). The possibility of gaining a benefice increased as the livings became impoverished, but of course the livings were less desirable. By the beginning of Elizabeth's reign none of the models of a clerical career were functioning. There was no bishop, nor promise of one. Chantries no longer existed. Parish curates were not seeking benefices, lay readers were not seeking ordination. The poverty of the livings, moreover, meant that a benefice in Bristol would not be the ultimate ambition during the later Elizabethan period. The preacher rather than the parish parson or the episcopal shepherd would be idealized and rewarded. The only exception lay with the prebendaries of the cathedral. They seem to have been divided between professionals of the sort O'Day refers to and puritans who seem to have been preachers rather than pastors. See below and Chapter 7.

19. Christopher Hill, *Economic Problems*, 107, 117, 118, 203, 204; Hoskins, 'Leicestershire Country Parson', 90, 91; MacCaffrey, *Exeter*, 178–9; Palliser, *Reformation in York*, 3. Livings in London were unusually wealthy with almost half worth more than £20 and less than one-third worth less than £15 in 1535 (Brigden, *London and the Reformation*, 49). Claire Cross asserts that the view of urban parishes as the impoverished small inner-city livings of the ancient towns is simply a conventional stereotype which originated in the sixteenth century and belies the variety of urban parish structures (Cross, 'Incomes of Provincial Urban Clergy', 65–89). This is a significant step forward in understanding the

sixteenth-century church in urban settings, but we should be cautious about discarding a generalization (or stereotype) which sixteenth-century writers found so useful. Perhaps in order to retain this useful analytical tool we could make it more precise by distinguishing 'inner-city' livings (primarily dependent on personal tithes and oblations) from 'single-city' livings (which had boundaries coinciding with the township's) and 'outer-city' livings (on the edges of towns and cities), both of which had greater sources of income. This terminology reflects the more precise understanding of the sixteenth-century complaints concerning poor town livings which Cross has given us and provides some necessary shorthand for communications among twentieth-century scholars.

20. John Caley and Joseph Hunter (eds.), *Valor ecclesiasticus*.
21. Ibid. ii. 495. It appears that city authorities conducted the survey of livings themselves, for the accounts of 1535 show 10s. paid to the town clerk for 'the making of the king's book' and 3d. ob. for the box and the carriage of the king's 'books' to London (BAO, 04026 (Mayors' Audits, fos. 53 and 55; 2nd qtr., 6th and 8th wks.)).
22. PRO, E 334; H&WRO, 802 BA 2764, fos. 99–100.
23. Christopher Hill, *Economic Problems*, 110, 190; J. J. Scarisbrick, 'Clerical Taxation in England 1485 to 1547', *JEH* 11 (1960), 53.
24. Felicity Heal, 'Economic Problems of the Clergy', in Heal and O'Day (eds.), *Church and Society in England*, 103. Heal says, 'there seems little warrant for the assumption made by Christopher Hill that the vicarage figures are distorted by the inclusion of great tithes paid to the appropriator. The *Valor* may have underestimated the potential income to be derived from glebe and tithes, but it remains the best available survey of income actually obtainable in the 1530s'. Rosemary O'Day notes that the base for the valuation of livings varied. Although this can make the *Valor* 'exceedingly difficult to use', she concludes that it does allow a rough estimation of the incumbent's income (*English Clergy*, 172).
25. BAO, AP/V/5/A.
26. Tithes are discussed below.
27. Heath, *English Parish Clergy*, 173.
28. Christopher Hill, *Economic Problems*, 202.
29. *Valor ecclesiasticus*, ii. 316–7, 495, 498; v. 21–5. See Zell, 'Economic Problems of the Parochial Clergy', 34–5, for comparisons with other counties, towns and dioceses. The contrast in median income of clergy in the city of York and in the Ridings is substantial. Incomes for rectors in the Ridings was over £13; in York, £4. 7s. 8d. For vicars in the Ridings median incomes ranged from £7. 8s. 0d. to £9. 8s. 10d.; in York the figure was £4 (Kreider, *English Chantries*, 22).
30. Palliser, *Reformation in York*, 3.
31. Heath, *English Parish Clergy*, 173.

32. Kreider, *English Chantries*, 23–5. Heal, 'Economic Problems of the Clergy', 104. In Elizabeth's reign £30 became accepted as the minimum competence for a minister (Christopher Hill, *Economic Problems*, 205).

33. Only one useful glebe terrier is extant for the city's livings, an eighteenth-century document of the parish of Sts Philip and James (BAO, EP/V/5/A).

34. Taylor, 'Religious Houses of Bristol', 81.

35. Lobel and Carus-Wilson, *Bristol*, 18.

36. Tewkesbury Abbey was the appropriator and the monks of St James probably collected the tithes of that parish. The Brayne family became impropriator after the dissolution and brought a number of tithe suits to the local consistory court. In 1556 John Northall attempted to get a commutation of the great tithe of hay (BAO, EP/J/1/1, p. 206).

37. BAO EP/V/5/A.

38. A print of Millerd's map is available in the Bristol Archives Office.

39. BAO 04026 (Mayors' Audits, 1532). In 1532 the vicar of All Saints held a shop built on to the church in Corn Street for which land he paid a rent of 10*d.* to the corporation.

40. St Nicholas: BAO, EP/J/1/2, pp. 2, 22, 45, 51, 57, 64, 73, 79, 193, 194; EP/J/1/5, pp. 337, 340. St Michael: EP/J/1/6, pp. 52, 62, 64, 67, 74, 75. Temple: EP/J/1/5, pp. 69, 113, 254. St Philip: EP/J/1/5, pp. 611, 646, 627, 632, 638, 597, 599; EP/J/1/6, p. 63.

41. BAO, EP/J/1/1, pp. 196, 203, 207, 208, 209, 218, 256, 257, 267, 174, 175, 206; EP/J/1/2, pp. 55, 59, 69, 82; EP/J/1/5, pp. 297, 304, 311, 327.

42. In the urban parishes of Leicester practically all tithes were converted to a fixed money payment before or during the great inflation (Pruett, *Parish Clergy under the Later Stuarts*, 99).

43. BAO, EP/V/5/A.

44. A drift contained 16 horses.

45. BAO, EP/J/1/6, p. 69.

46. BAO, EP/V/5/A.

47. BAO, EP/J/1/2, pp. 55, 59, 69, 82; EP/J/1/1, 174, 175, 206.

48. Copies of the accounts of the churchwardens of St Mary-le-Porte, Bristol, survive only in the *Hockaday Abstracts*, vol. 442 (entered chronologically under the parish name.)

49. Maclean, 'Chantry Certificates', 237, 244. See Table 6 for parish populations in 1548. It appears that retention of torches used in burials also was a source of income for incumbents (PRO, PCC, Logge, 13 (Henry Merimen; 31 May 1479; 7 Aug. 1481); PCC, Vox, 17 (William Spenser; 20 Oct. 1494; 6 Nov. 1494)).

50. Wadley, *Notes, passim*; Maclean, 'Chantry Certificates', 233, 236, 237, 244, 248, 249, 250.

51. Edgeworth, *Sermons Very Fruitfull, Godly and Learned*, 289/D. See Chapter 4, *passim* and Chapter 5 n. 102.
52. Wadley, *Notes, passim*.
53. Masters and Ralph (eds.), *Church Book of St Ewen's*, p. xxiii. A. G. Little, 'Personal Tithes', *EHR* 60 (1945), 76–7.
54. 27 Henry VIII, c. 12; 2 & 3 Edward VI, c. 13; A. G. Little, 'Personal Tithes', 76–7; Christopher Hill, *Economic Problems*, 91; O'Day, *English Clergy*, 174–5.
55. BAO, EP/J/1/1, pp. 193–4; EP/J/1/1/2, pp. 22, 45, 51, 57, 64, 73, 79 (*Hockaday Abstracts*, vols. 445–6, St Nicholas, 1556). This issue had arisen as early as 1396 when the rector of St Stephen sued two parishioners of the parish of St John for such tithes (A. G. Little, 'Personal Tithes', 78).
56. BAO, EP/J/1/1, p. 194.
57. H. G. Owen, 'London Parish Clergy', 205.
58. Compare accounts of St Ewen parish 1562–84 in Masters and Ralph (eds.), *Church Book of St. Ewen's*, 195–251.
59. BAO, EP/J/1/5, pp. 580, 584.
60. Masters and Ralph (eds). *Church Book of St. Ewen's*, 200, 199.
61. Ibid. 195–251.
62. BAO, P/StJ/ChW, 1572 (extant from 1566).
63. *Hockaday Abstracts*, vol. 442.
64. H. G. Owen, 'London Parish Clergy', 308–9.
65. In 1546 John Smythe, a prominent merchant of St Werberg's parish, paid 13*d.* per week in 'allmes' and 20*d.* per quarter for the clerk's wages. The notation of 'alms' instead of tithe suggests that Smythe regarded his payments as free offerings rather than legally required tithes (Vanes (ed.), *Ledger of John Smythe*, 75).
66. See J. A. F. Thompson, 'Tithe Disputes in Late Medieval London', 1–17.
67. Vanes (ed.), *Ledger of John Smythe*, 26. A. G. Dickens mentions disastrous slumps in urban rent endowments for chantries (*English Reformation*, 211) and D. M. Palliser notes that in the 1560s the corporation of York was desperately selling houses to tenants because repair costs were exceeding rents (*Reformation in York*, 25).
68. In 1577–8 and 1579–80 the rates in St Ewen parish ranged from 2*s.* to 13*s.* In 1581–82, from 1*s.* to 10*s.* Six of the parishioners were paying lower rates. Among them was the 'elder statesman' of the parish, John Sprint, whose rate was reduced from 13*s.* 4*d.* to 10*s.* The total collection dropped 12*s.* 10*d.* Perhaps parishioners took advantage of the Arthur confusion to alter their rates downward (Masters and Ralph (eds.), *Church Book at St. Ewen's*, 235, 239, 243–4; see above).
69. E. H. Phelps Brown and Sheila V. Hopkins, 'Seven Centuries of the

Price of Consumables, Compared with Builders' Wage Rates', *Economica*, 2nd ser. 23 (1956); repr. in E. M. Carus-Wilson (ed.), *Essays in Economic History*, 2 (London: E. Arnold, 1962), 168–96, esp. p. 194. There are only a few clues concerning inflation in Bristol specifically. Between 1539 and 1550 the price of a tun of oil sold by merchant John Smythe rose from £15 to £23, a rise of 53 per cent. The price of iron rose almost 100 per cent, from £6. 4s. 11d. to £12; Andalusian wine 43 per cent, from £7 to £10; and Gascon wine 55 per cent, from £4. 10s. to £7. Grain prices fluctuated wildly in Bristol depending upon the harvest, but the notations of a local chronicler suggest a changing notion of an unusually high price. In 1534 wheat rose from 8d. and 9d. to 2s. 4d. a bushel. In 1550 when wheat sold for 4s. 8d. a bushel and the people 'could scant get bread for money', the mayor and commonalty provided that every baker should bake bread for the commons. In 1552, however, there was a plentiful harvest and wheat sold for 12d. a bushel. Wheat sold for 5s. a bushel in 1556, falling to 22d. towards the end of the year, and in 1557 it was selling at 12d. a bushel. In 1534 the chronicler noted a low price of 8d. and 9d., while eighteen years later in 1552, a 'plentiful harvest' brought a low price of 12d. per bushel. The high prices which he deemed worthy of notice were 2s. 4d. in 1534, 4s. 8d. in 1550, and 5s. in 1556 (*Adams's Chronicle, passim*, under year).

70. In 1549 Hugh Latimer asserted that no priest with a benefice less than 12 to 14 marks [£8 to £9. 6s. 8d.] would be able to 'buy him books nor give his neighbor drink' (H. Latimer, *Seven Sermons before Edward VI*, ed. Edward Arber (London, 1869), 40, cited in Kreider, *English Chantries*, 23). For most urban incumbents the figures undoubtedly should be higher.

71. Sacks, *Trade, Society, and Politics*, 10–11.

72. 26 Henry VIII, c. iii; Scarisbrick, 'Clerical Taxation in England', 41–54; Lehmberg, *Reformation Parliament*, 207. It appears that in 1544 the living of St Mary-le-Porte was temporarily reassessed and excluded from payment of the tax. See Table 3.

73. Christopher Hill, *Economic Problems*, 192–3; Heal, 'Economic Problems', 111–12; *LP* vii. 1355.

74. Scarisbrick, 'Clerical Taxation in England', 53.

75. Christopher Hill, *Economic Problems*, 188. See Table 7.

76. Scarisbrick, 'Clerical Taxation in England', 53. Heal, 'Clerical Tax Collection under the Tudors: The Influence of the Reformation', in O'Day and Heal, *Continuity and Change*, 113.

77. PRO, E 179/6/10.

78. Masters and Ralph (eds.), *Church Book of St. Ewen's*, *196*, *198*, 203, 204, 208, 211, 214, *219*, 224, 227, 230, *231*, 234. The italic page numbers reflect the use of the term 'subsidy'; both terms were used on p. 244.

79. Ibid. 196–244.
80. *CSPD* (Elizabeth), xii. 108.
81. PRO, E 179/6/3 (1557): St Stephen, St Peter, St Augustine; E 179/6/11 (1558): Same; E 179/6/13 (1558): St Stephen, St Peter, St Augustine, St Leonard, St Mary-le-Porte; E 179/6/4 (1559): Same; E 179/6/9 (1560): Christ Church (Holy Trinity), St Leonard, St Stephen; E 179/7/49 (1560): St Stephen, St Nicholas, St Mary-le-Porte.
82. PRO, E 179/6/12 and E 179/6/10 (1556, 1557): Thomas Pinchyn, Christ Church (Holy Trinity); Dns Bacheller, All Saints; Ric Vaughan, St Leonard; Thomas Carleton, St James; Richard Okes, Redcliffe; Stephen Popingaye, Clifton (Bristol Deanery); John Sherman, St Ewen (1557 only). E 179/6/6 (1559): Thomas Pinchyn, Christ Church (Holy Trinity); John Tewe, St Thomas (also E 179/9/13, no date). E 179/6/8 (1560): Thomas Pinchyn, Christ Church (Holy Trinity); Stephen Popingaye, St James. E 179/6/9 (1561): Thomas Pinchyn, Christ Church (Holy Trinity); Stephen Popingaye, St James; John Tewe, St James [i.e. St Thomas]. E 179/18 (1564): John Hayton, Christ Church (Holy Trinity); John Thomas, St Peter; John Gregory, St Mary-le-Porte. E 179/6/20 (1565?): John ——, St Mary Redcliffe. E 179/6/21 (1565?): John Gregory, St Mary-le-Porte. E 179/6/23 (1567): John Eaton (Hayton), Christ Church (Holy Trinity); John Lynche, St John the Baptist; Robert Cheltenham, Sts Philip and James; John Gregory, St Mary-le-Porte; John Norbrooke, St Mary Redcliffe.
83. Heal, 'Clerical Tax Collection', 117.
84. BAO, P/AS/ChW/1539.
85. Ibid. 1563.
86. BAO, St Stephen's Inventory, fo. 54^r. An interesting example of clerical borrowing occurs in John Smythe's ledger. John Popley, 'priest chancellor of Saynt Davis' (St David's diocese, Wales) owed £3. 13s. 4d. in Aug. 1540. He apparently owed that sum to Thomas Whaley, a Bristol surgeon, who in turn had owed Smythe, and Popley's debt to Whaley was transferred to Smythe. Popley was a resident cleric in Bristol in the late 1520s and early 1530s and perhaps later. (Vanes (ed.), *Ledger of John Smythe*, 36–7). See Appendix 1.
87. Even before the Reformation various parishioners in St Mary Redcliffe had co-signed a loan of 75s. to their 'vicar' John Vaughn from the coffer of Canynges Chantries. By 1519 Vaughn had become vicar of Keynsham and still owed his former parish 17s. 6d. (E. Williams, *Chantries of William Canynges*, 180–98, esp. 180, 189, 198).
88. Masters and Ralph (eds.), *Church Book of St. Ewen's*, 184, 185, 187, 189, 192, 193. This is quite different from an undoubtedly loyal parishioner's purchase of lands and tenements to the use of the ageing 'vicar' Nicholas Pittes, who left them in his will to the parish's wardens on condition they

hold an annual obit. They very likely were meant to aid him in retirement (PRO, PCC, Horne, 16 (Nicholas Pittes; 23 June 1494; Feb. 21, 1498)).

89. *CSPD* (Elizabeth), xii. 108.

90. Thomas Tasker, St John the Baptist, 6 May 1531–*c.*1562 (died); Thomas Hanson, St Stephen, by 1517–*c.*1555 (died); John Fysshe, St Michael, 4 Sept. 1528–*c.*1555; John Rawlins, St Ewen, 15 Aug. 1535–*c.*1556 (died); John Kene, Christ Church, 10 May 1535–*c.*1555 (resigned); Edward Togood, Temple, 1538–*c.*1554 (resigned); Humphrey Hyman, All Saints, 27 July 1541–*c.*1555; David Condon, Sts Philip and Jacob, 1547–*c.*1558; Christopher Pacy, St Werberg, 1544–*c.*1554 (resigned) (his predecessor was Edward Gayner, by 1517–1547); Robert Roost, St Leonard, 1547–*c.*1558. In the fifteenth century Nicholas Pyttes was 'vicar' of St Mary Redcliffe for at least thirty years (E. Williams, *Chantries of William Canynges*, 67, 68, 70, 74, 78, 123, 223).

91. George Harris became vicar of St Nicholas in 1564 and remained until his death in 1593. In the mid-1550s Robert Rowe became vicar of All Saints where he remained for at least ten years. In the thirteen years after the departure of John Fysshe, rector of St Michael, in 1555, the parish had three different rectors (William Townely, John Gregory, Thomas Love). In the parish of Temple the situation was similar. After the resignation of Edward Togood *c.*1554–5, five vicars served in the following fifteen to sixteen years, including Togood's renewed service between 1560 and 1563 (Walter Jaye, John Pyll, Togood, Richard Deane, Richard Barwicke). See Appendix 1.

92. St Peter: Richard Simondes, 1562; John Thomas, 1564; Christopher Devereaux, 1570. St Mary Redcliffe: Roger Lewys, *c.*1553; Richard Oriell, 1554; James Hylman, 1560; Robert Wharten, 1561, 1562; John Northbrooke, 1567 (1564?); Davy Williams, 1574.

93. St James: Thomas Carleton, 1556, 1557, 1558; Stephen Popingaye, 1560; Bartholomew Phillips, 1564, 1566. St Philip: John Edwards, 1562; Thomas Dobins, 1563; Richard Simondes, 1563, 1564 (vicar, 1564–?1567); Roger Chaloner, 1567 (1572?).

94. St Ewen: John Shereman, 1557; Hugh Warde, 1558, 1559, 1561–2; Roger Rise, *c.*1561–7; Humphrey Mosley, 1567–73; Morice Durante, 1574; Richard Arthur, 1577, 1578. Occasional Service: Thomas Pinchyn, 1559; Bastion Pavy, 1566; John Northbrooke, 1567; Mr —— and Mr Haulton, 1576; Stephen Popingaye, 1559–61.

95. The rectory of St Mary-le-Porte was vacant in 1540 (H&WRO, 802 BA 2764, fo. 272). Compositions for first fruits of the rectory were made by Bartholomew Cowde, Thomas Reade, and John Carlyne in 1542, 1543, and 1544 respectively. In 1544 the first fruits were reduced from £7 to £5. 5s. 9d. See Appendix 1.

96. See Appendix 1: Richard Arthur, John Tewe, John Blake.

97. See Appendix 1: Roger Rise, Thomas Pinchyn.
98. H&WRO, 802 BA 2764, fos. 99–100; Maclean, 'Chantry Certificates', *passim*. St Mary Redcliffe, St Thomas, and Temple were not in the Worcester list of 1534 and their clergy has been estimated on the basis of chantry positions and information from documents such as wills and accounts. A will of 1505 left 8*d.* to each of the twelve chaplains celebrating at that time in the parish of Christ Church to be present at the burial. This suggests that short-term chantry endowments could increase the number of priests in a parish considerably at any one time (PRO, PCC, Holgrave, 36 (Hugh John; 10 June 1505; 28 Aug. 1505)).
99. Alan Kreider has suggested that slightly less than one-quarter of the chantry priests in the four shires he studied were involved in the cure of souls (*English Chantries*, 50–9). Also see Clive Burgess, 'Chantries in the Parish', 50–9 for a discussion of the contributions of chantry priests to the parish.
100. Reports of arrears in the clerical subsidy show the following stipends in a number of parishes: Christ Church (Holy Trinity), £7 and £6. 13*s.* 4*d.*; All Saints, £6. 13*s.* 4*d.*; St Leonard, £6. 13*s.* 4*d.* and £7; St James, £6. 13*s.* 4*d.*; St Mary Redcliffe, £6. 13*s.* 4*d.* (PRO, E 179/6/12 and E/179/6/10 (1556)). Christ Church, £6. 13*s.* 4*d.*; St Thomas, £6. 13*s.* 4*d.* (E 179/6/6 (1559)). In clerical subsidies 1560–7 all owed 6*s.* 8*d.* (stipends not given), which indicates the stipends were £8 or below (PRO, E 179/6/8, 9, 18, 21, 23).
101. H. G. Owen, 'London Parish Clergy', 69.
102. 21 Henry VIII, c. 13.
103. John Fontayne (probably BA), rector of St Lawrence, was classified as non-resident by 1540, possibly holding another position without cure. John Williams (BD), vicar of St Nicholas, was also non-resident in 1540, holding the living of Colebrook, Devon (*BRUO 1501–1540*, 630). John Collys (MA, possibly BD), vicar of St Philip, may have been curate of Mangotsfield in 1534; in 1540 he was non-resident in Bristol and may have been vicar of the rural living of Letylton, Glouc., worth £11 in 1535 and rector of Pryston worth £13. 6*s.* 4*d.* John Floke (MA) vicar of All Saints 1517–33 and vicar of Bedminster (and thus possibly curate of St Mary Redcliffe) 1533–4, was also the vicar of Portebury 1529–40, a living worth £10. 11*s.* 1*d. ob.* He was resident, however, in Bristol. While at All Saints his combined living would have been £14. 14*s.* 5*d. ob.* At Bedminster his combined income would have been £14. 13*s.* 4*d.*, if he did not serve St Mary Redcliffe and paid a chaplain for the chapel of Leigh. If, however, he also collected income from and served St Mary Redcliffe, the total would have been more than £12 greater, less funds paid out for stipends to assistants. In 1535 Floke, still vicar of Portebury, became prior of the Kalendars' Guild in Bristol and received a

dispensation from Worcester diocesan authorities to hold a second living. Far from impoverished, he left £4 to his scholar when he died in 1540. Another resident Bristol parson, John Goodriche (DD), rector of Christ Church, 1524–38, worth £11, was also vicar of Clevedon, worth £15. 14s. 4d., in 1535. In that year he also farmed four rectories from Deerhurst Priory, Glouc., for which he paid £33 (*Valor ecclesiasticus*, ii. 484). Thus his total income must have exceeded £26. 14s. 4d. by a significant amount, out of which he paid at least one curate. See Appendix 1, under names.

104. John Pylle combined the livings of St Mary-le-Porte and St Peter, 1548–53. John Kene combined Christ Church and St Lawrence, 1543–53. Nicholas Corbet, vicar of Sts Philip and Jacob in 1544, was vicar of Pawlett, 1542–5. Thomas Sylke, vicar of St Leonard, 1529–47, was prior of the Kalendars' Guild in All Saints, 1540–8. See Appendix 1, under names.

105. Cf. Bowker, *Secular Clergy*, 89–109, for the extent and consequences of non-residence in Lincoln diocese before the Reformation.

106. Thomas Tasker was rector of St John from 1531 until his death in 1563 when he left an inventory of goods worth the substantial amount of £7. 2s. 6d. (BAO, EP/J/1/5, p. 545). There is no evidence that he held more than these two livings; the local dean and chapter were patrons of the living of Wearcon. Edward Togood, vicar of Temple 1538–c.1554–5 and 1560–3, also appeared in the consistory court as a proctor during the latter period. See Appendix 1, under names.

107. Richard Simondes: curate, St Peter, 1563; curate Sts Philip and Jacob, 1563. John Gregory: rector, St Michael, 1564–c.1568; curate, St Mary-le-Porte, by 1564–79. Thomas Longe (Love): rector, St Michael, 15 Apr. 1568–? rector, St Ewen, 15 Apr. 1568–91. Roger Rise: curate, Clifton, near Bristol, 1564; curate, St Ewen, probably mid-1562–Dec. 1567. John Rastell: vicar, St Nicholas, by 19 Nov. 1546–by 1 Oct. 1563. Apparently became non-resident in 1560. See Appendix 1, under names.

108. Richard Simondes, curate of St Peter and Sts Philip and Jacob was ordered not to hold two cures together on 24 May 1563. Roger Rise was permitted to hold two cures for a very short time (BAO, EP/J/1/5, p. 529). John Gregory was for a time rector of St Michael and curate of St Mary-le-Porte. John Tewe was perpetual curate of St Thomas and was presented to the vicarage of Sts Philip and Jacob in 1568 but apparently was not instituted to the living. See Appendix 1, under names.

109. See Chapter 7.

110. PRO, E 334/2, fo. 72; BAO, DC/A/9/1/1, 1551 and 1553; EP/J/1/1, p. 117 and EP/J/1/6, p. 125. It appears that Robert Rowe was vicar by 1556 (Baskerville, 'Dispossessed Religious of Gloucestershire', 95).

111. Baskerville, 'Dispossessed Religious of Gloucestershire', 95.
112. BAO, DC/A/9/1/1 Computa, *passim*.
113. Christopher Hill, *Economic Problems*, 202, 208. Hoskins asserts that 'the economic position of the parson had been radically altered for the worse by a new burden, and that was the freedom to marry and to have children' ('Leicestershire Country Parson', 108–9). F. W. Brooks, however, says that 'The probability seems to be that the marriage of the clergy may have conduced to their increased prosperity. In a peasant economy a wife and family are assets'. 'Social Position of the Parson', 37. A. G. Dickens remarks that the country parson's lack of a family 'may have proved on balance an economic disadvantage' (*English Reformation*, 47, 244–6). Only Hill considers the urban clergy.
114. Roger Lewis was deprived of the vicarage of Bedminster in 1554 and may have been curate at St Mary Redcliffe, a chapel of Bedminster. He had married a widow named Catherine Weaver (*Regs. B&W* (Bourne), fo. 16). Edward Togood may also have resigned his living for marriage. See Appendix 1.
115. Dickens, *The English Reformation*, 246. See Chapter 4.
116. Cf. Rosemary O'Day's argument that clerical marriage, which led in the seventeenth century to direct clerical dynasties and marriage between clerical families, contributed to the consolidation of the clerical profession through social and kin ties. This, she says, engendered a sense of community among the clergy (*English Clergy*, 161–6, 244). There is some evidence of multi-generational families of clergy in Bristol in the seventeenth century. John Sprint, dean of Bristol Cathedral in 1580, had a son and a grandson who were clerics. The son of Edward Chetwynd, corporation lecturer in 1606 and dean of Bristol Cathedral from 1617 until his death in 1639, also was a minister; John Chetwynd was vicar of Temple and canon in Bristol Cathedral when he died in 1692. Richard Toogood, MA, became vicar of All Saints in 1619 and St Nicholas in 1626, a canon in Bristol Cathedral in 1660 and Dean of the chapter from 1667 until his death in 1683. He may have been related to Edward Toogood, vicar of Temple in the mid-sixteenth century (d. 1563). Richard's son and grandson also were ministers. James Brent, parson of St Michael in 1616, was father of clerics Humfrey and James, whose son Charles also was a cleric. In the later seventeenth century Charles was incumbent at St Werberg and at Christ Church, where he was buried in 1729. Richard Standfast, who became parson of Christ Church in 1634 and canon in Bristol Cathedral in 1660, fathered a cleric, John, and perhaps also was related to William, son of Nicholas of Bristol, who also became a cleric (*Hockaday Abstracts*, vols. 425–7, 432–4, 444–6, 452–3 under city, cathedral, parish, and date; Venn and Foster, under name).

117. In addition to those discussed in the text, Bartholomew Phillips, curate of St James, may have been married. In 1564 he was ordered to prove his marriage to a woman he apparently was living with (BAO, EP/J/1/5, p. 704).
118. See Appendix 1, under name. The living of St Michael was worth £6 (Table 3). It appears that in 1564 the stipend at St Mary-le-Porte was no more than £8 because Gregory owed 6s. 8d. to the subsidy (PRO, E 179/6/18). The following year, however, he owed 10s. and the church-wardens' accounts show his stipend as £11. In 1568 his stipend was £10 (PRO, E 179/6/20; *Hockaday Abstracts*, vol. 442). His stipend as subdeacon was £5 (BAO, DC/A/9/1/2, 1561).
119. BAO, EP/J/1/6, pp. 52, 75. Suits against Nicholas Thorne (son of mayor, 1544–5) and Edmund Jones (sheriff 1564–5). Gregory appears to have won both cases.
120. In 1556 diocesan officials ordered new parson William Townely to repair the rectory of St Michael under pain of the law. He had replaced John Fysshe who had farmed out the tithes. We do not know the state of the rectory in 1564 when Gregory became parson, but its upkeep was a drain on the living's resources (BAO, EP/J/1/1, p. 149; EP/J/1/2, p. 40).
121. Hockaday Abstracts, vol. 442, St Mary-le-Porte, 1568. The Church-wardens' Accounts report 'For mending of the side of the chancel next to the curate's house & making clean of the gutter at times 2s.'
122. Ibid. 1565–6 and 1568; BAO, DC/A/9/1/2, 1570.
123. Wadley, *Notes*, p. 211.
124. Churchwardens' Accounts of St Mary Redcliffe, 1554, 1556 and 1557, located in the archive of the parish church; BAO, P/AS/ChW/1558 and 1560; EP/J/1/6, p. 93; Masters and Ralph (eds.), *Church Book of St. Ewen's*, 34.
125. Masters and Ralph (eds.), *Church Book of St. Ewen's*, pp. xxxiv–xxxv.
126. Ibid. 194–207.
127. BAO, EP/J/1/5, p. 589.
128. Ibid. 93; PRO, E 179/6/12; E 179/6/10.
129. See Table 3.
130. Ibid.
131. PRO, E 179/6/12; E 179/6/10; *CPR* IV Philip and Mary, 30 Apr. 1557 (presentation of Stephen Popingaye to the rectory of St Werberg).
132. See Chapter 7 and Appendix 1.
133. PRO, E 179/6/8; BAO, EP/J/1/5, p. 230.
134. Masters and Ralph (eds.), *Church Book of St. Ewen's*, 176.
135. BAO, EP/J/1/5, p. 445. He was rector of St Martin, Warham, Dorset, a living not listed in the *Valor ecclesiasticus*.
136. Cf. O'Day, *English Clergy*, 16.
137. PRO, E 179/6/12, 10, 6, 8, 9, 18, 20, 21, 23.

138. Thomas Cowper, St Leonard, 2 Mar. 1560; David Martin, St Nicholas, 28 June 1560; John Blake, St Thomas, 29 May 1561; Richard Houseman, All Saints, 3 Sept. 1561 and 2 Dec. 1564; John Lee (Lyll), St John the Baptist, 1564 and 18 Apr. 1566. David Martin received letters dimissory to receive all sacred orders from some bishop on 2 Mar. 1562. He was called 'curate' on 22 Apr. 1564. On 2 Dec. 1564, Richard Houseman was given a few months to procure letters of ordination. John Blake, Giles Painter, and William —— appeared on the same day, while John Lee was suspended from his office for not appearing (BAO, EP/J/1/5, pp. 36, 65, 71, 212, 226, 361; EP/J/1/6, p. 93). See Appendix 1 for John Lee's (Lyll's) unusual circumstances. The apparent pressure on the readers to seek ordination and their low income suggest that they worked part time as readers and had other jobs. They may have resisted ordination to protect their other jobs, to avoid becoming full-time curates, or for religious reasons (BAO, P/AS/ChW/1560–1 and 1562–3). Other evidence of the ecclesiastical authorities' concern lies in the request that George Moglewike, curate of St Mary Redcliffe in 1560, present proof of his admission to the ministry to the court (BAO, EP/J/1/5, p. 35; see Appendix 1). See Rosemary O'Day ('The Reformation of the Ministry, 1558–1642', in O'Day and Heal (eds.)., *Continuity and Change*, 55–76) for a discussion of Archbishop Parker's scheme for readers. Also cf. O'Day (*English Clergy*, 12–13) on evidence from Chester of readers serving 'apprenticeships' of five or six years before ordination, and on the clergy's means of supplementing their resources, 'trading or practicing a craft being the most common' (p. 127). She notes, however, that rules restricting the clergy's occupational activity as well as taxation were real barriers to recruitment.

139. *CSPD* (Elizabeth), xii. 108; PRO, SP 15/12, no. 108; *CPR* c.66/1091; 14 Eliz. I, pt. X, 3195. The granddaughters of Henry Brayne and their husbands were licensed to alienate the advowsons 23 Jan. 1572. They included the livings of St James, Sts Philip and James, St Michael, St John, St Ewen, Christ Church (Holy Trinity), and St Peter from Tewkesbury Abbey; St Mary-le-Porte, which passed from Keynsham Priory to the Crown; and St Lawrence, which passed from Lord Lisle to the Crown (*LP* xviii, pt. 1, 436; Nicholls and Taylor, *Bristol, Past and Present*, 157). The dean and chapter were patrons of St Augustine-the-Less, St Leonard, St Nicholas, and All Saints (*CSPD* (Elizabeth), xii. 108).

140. The corporation purchased the lands of the Hospitallers (Templars) in Temple Fee in 1544. It also should be noted that the hospital of St Mark had become parochial by the time of its dissolution in Dec., 1539, and the corporation became patron with the purchase of the hospital's lands in 1544. The parish was served by a perpetual (stipendiary) curate. The crown retained the advowson of St Stephen. See Chapter 5.

141. St John and St Lawrence. (*CSPD* (Elizabeth), xii. 108).
142. BAO, EP/J/1/6, pp. 39–41.
143. *Brayne* v. *Walter Grene*, St James (BAO, EP/J/1/1, pp. 293, 294, 296); v. *John Northall* (EP/J/1/2, pp. 55, 59, 62, 82); v. *William Tyndall* (EP/J/1/1, pp. 174, 175, 206); v. *William Ball*, St James (EP/J/1/2, pp. 55, 60, 70, 76); v. *John Harrys and John Jenkyns*, St James (EP/J/1/4, p. 39); v. *John Northall, William Ball, William Coxe* (EP/J/1/4, pp. 34, 37); v. *Nicholas Shethe*, St James (EP/J/1/4, p. 43); v. *John Northall* (EP/J/1/5, pp. 276, 286, 293, 300, 309, 327); v. *Walter Smithe*, St Philip (EP/J/1/5, pp. 297, 304, 311); v. *William Auste*, St Peter (EP/J/1/5, pp. 297, 304, 312, 317, 326; v. *Anthony Philips*, St Mary-le-Porte (EP/J/1/5, pp. 297, 304); v. *Mr Jaye*, St John (EP/J/1/5, p. 297); v. John Ryder, St Philip (EP/J/1/5, pp. 298, 305, 312, 328); v. *George Higgins*, St Werberg (EP/J/1/5, pp. 298, 295); v. *John Pruet, Robert Risby*, and *William Grene*, St James (EP/J/1/5, pp. 639, 645, 649, 650, 656, 688, 694, 695, 701 and /6, pp. 3, 11, 18, 25, 29, 30, 32, 39, 50, 63, 66, 57, 61, 69, 72); v. *Philip Langley*, St James (EP/J/1/5, pp. 288, 294, 302, 310, 316); v. *John Pruet*, St James (EP/J/1/6, pp. 33, 51, 61, 66, 76, 81, 88, 96, 112, 125, 129, 131, 136, 142, 150, 152, 155). The parish names often reflect the parish of residence of the defendant who was renting pasture in St James or another parish where Brayne was impropriator. Which parish the suit regards is not often clear since in most of the cases only the court actions are recorded. In 1552 Henry Brayne's suit against John Northall went to Chancery (PRO, C/1289 and 1105, 44–49). His son Robert's suit against Dominick Chester for a tax on imports during Whitsun Week, formerly due to the abbot of Tewkesbury, also ended up in Chancery in 1561 (PRO, C 3/15, 46).
144. Heal, 'Economic Problems', 115.
145. See Chapters 3 and 4 concerning preaching and religious divisions.
146. BAO, EP/J/1/4, pp. 187, 503. H. G. Owen, 'London Parish Clergy', 67; Heath, *English Parish Clergy*, 31.
147. Cf. Rosemary O'Day's discussion of the effects of congregationalist forms of ecclesiastical organization. Among them was an emphasis on the relationship between the minister and his congregation at the expense of his relationships with other clergy. This acted against the development of a clerical profession. Although Bristol's parish churches were still firmly within the organization of the state Church and under the discipline of the ecclesiastical hierarchy, the effects of the situation were similar to that of independent congregations (except that Bristol's curates undoubtedly merited less respect than congregationalist ministers). It also can hardly be doubted that the parish laity's experience in employing curates contributed to the development of Nonconformist congregations in Bristol by the early seventeenth century

(*English Clergy*, 239–41; Nicholls and Taylor, *Bristol, Past and Present*, ii. 21, 285–94).

148. See Chapter 7.

149. *LP* xii, pt. 2, 184 (2); BL Cleop. E.V., fos. 390–1. Thomas Sylke, 'priest of St Leonard', who became a prebendary and canon in the cathedral. See Chapter 3 and Appendix 1.

150. *LP* xii, pt. 2, 1147 (iii, 1); PRO, SP 1/119, pp. 184–197.

151. Edgeworth, *Sermons*, 26; 279/D-280/A; 288/B, C; 288/D; 289/A; 170/A, C, D; 291-293; 273/D.

152. The first graduate clergy in each parish were Samuel Davys, St Mary Redcliffe, 1592; probably William Robinson, St Nicholas, 1595; Francis Arnold, All Saints, 1597; William Yeman, Sts Philip and Jacob, 1603; probably Mr William Davills, St John the Baptist, 1605; Richard Collins, St Werberg, 1606; probably Simon Mace, St Stephen, 1610; Robert Prichard, St Peter, 1622; John Norton, St Leonard, 1626; Jacob Brent, St Michael, 1636 (possibly Thomas Newton, 1597); and Abel Soveringe, Temple, 1639 (*Hockaday Abstracts*, vols. 432, 439–40, 443–4, 447–50, 452–3, under parish and date; Venn and Foster, under name).

Chapter 7. The New Diocese and its Clerical Élite

1. David Marcombe, 'The Durham Dean and Chapter: Old Abbey Writ Large', in O'Day and Heal (eds.), *Continuity and Change*, 125; BL Cotton Cleop. E. iv., fo. 305, transcribed in Hockaday Abstracts, vol. 27 (1539).

2. Suffragan bishops were assistants to other bishops in diocesan administration, and they were not intended to reside in the places from which they took their names. The institution of Henry Holbeach as suffragan bishop of Bristol in March 1538 did not alter Bristol's position within the diocese of Worcester (Geoffrey Hill, *English Dioceses: A History of their Limits from the Earliest Time to the Present Day* (London: Elliot Stock, 1900), 382–4, 388; *LP* xiii, pt. 1, 401 and 648 (2).

3. *VCH Gloucester*, ii. 26.

4. *The Statutes of Bristol Cathedral* (Bristol: I. E. Chillcott for the Dean and Chapter, 1870), pp. iv–v; Isabel M. Kirby (comp.), *A Catalogue of the Records of the Bishop and Archdeacons and of the Dean and Chapter of Bristol Diocese* (Bristol: City Corporation, 1970), pp. ix, xvi. Although the bulk of Dorset was in Bristol diocese, thirty parishes remained in the dean of Salisbury's peculiar. In addition, six Dorset towns were royal peculiars. This put about a quarter of the county outside the ordinary's jurisdiction (Rachel Lloyd, *Dorset Elizabethans at Home and Abroad* (London: John Murray, 1967), 67).

5. R. C. Latham says that it is 'perhaps remarkable' that the town was raised to the dignity of city in the same charter which created the bishopric rather than obtaining a second one. He suggests that Chancery may have been too busy or that economy dictated a single charter. It is possible that the creation was too hurried to allow for a second charter (Latham (ed.), *Bristol Charters*, 5).

6. See Chapter 3.

7. Hembry, *Bishops of Bath and Wells*, 59, 61–6.

8. Heal, 'Economic Problems', 113–14.

9. Dickens, *The English Reformation*, 193; Brigden, *London and the Reformation* 321–40.

10. *LP* xv. 183.

11. H&WRO, 802 BA 2764, fo. 269.

12. The Catholic Edward Powell and the Lutheran Thomas Garrett were bound to the same hurdle, which carried them from the Tower to Smithfield. Powell, long an opponent of Lutheran teaching, had preached in Bristol against the King's divorce and against Latimer in 1533. In 1534 he was committed to the Tower for refusing to take the oath of supremacy, where he remained until his execution as a traitor. Garrett, who was a sometime chaplain of Latimer, was arrested in Bedminster, Somerset, in 1528 and his arrest was reported to the commissary by the dean in neighbouring Bristol. Robert Barnes, another Lutheran, had also been associated with Bristol. See Chapter 3.

13. In 1522 the King gave permission for the Corporation of Bristol to purchase grain from Worcestershire or thereabout in order to lower prices for the inhabitants of the city. Ten years later, in 1532, the sheriffs of Gloucester confiscated grain which had been sold to the corporation of Bristol and sold it by commandment of the mayor of Gloucester. The Bristol authorities took the matter to the Star Chamber where the Gloucester offenders were ordered to make restitution and pay court costs (*Mayor's Kalendar*, 49, 51–2).

14. Sir F. Maurice Powicke and E. B. Fryde (eds.), *Handbook of British Chronology*, 2nd edn. (London: RHS, 1961) 227. The prior of St James, Tewkesbury's Bristol cell, probably would not have preached against Latimer without the support of his abbot. See Chapter 3.

15. *Hockaday Abstracts*, vol. 433 (1542); Taylor, 'Religious Houses of Bristol', 99.

16. Christopher Haigh, 'Finance and Administration in a New Diocese: Chester, 1541–1641', 145 and William J. Sheils, 'Some Problems of Government in a New Diocese: The Bishop and the Puritans in the Diocese of Peterborough, 1560–1630', 168, both in O'Day and Heal (eds.), *Continuity and Change*. Taylor gives £414 for Peterborough, but this is for 1575 ('Religious Houses of Bristol', 99–100); cf. Sheils, 168.

Felicity Heal gives figures for 1553: Chester, £495; Peterborough, £380; Oxford, £340; Bristol, £311 (*Of Prelates and Princes: A Study of the Economic and Social Position of the Tudor Episcopate* (Cambridge: Cambridge University Press, 1980), 182).

17. *Hockaday Abstracts*, vol. 433 (1542).
18. Taylor, 'Religious Houses', 99–100; *LP* xvii. 1154 (60); BAO, DC/A/9/ 1/1–2, *passim.* The £20 included a dividend of £17. 16s. 8d. and 8d. per day for residence or licensed absence (*Statutes of Bristol Cathedral*, 14–15).
19. PRO, PR 34 Henry VIII, p. 6, m. 4 (License to Paul Bush), transcribed in *Hockaday Abstracts*, vol. 433 (Bristol Cathdral, 1542). See Appendix 3 for a list of prebendaries. Information on these men may be found under names in *BRUO 1501–1540*, Venn, and Foster.
20. Foster, i. 220, ii. 738; *BRUO 1501–1540*, 89, 295.
21. See below. Ernst Messenger classified Bush as an 'Anglo-Catholic' in spite of Bush's votes in favour of both the Edwardian Prayer Books and his vote for the communion in both kinds. He attributes the votes to Bush's married state (rather than perhaps the other way around). His only evidence for his designation as an 'Anglo-Catholic' is the bishop's answer to Cranmer's question concerning the oblation and sacrifice of Christ in the mass, that it was a giving thanks to the Father and a presentation of 'the very body and blood of Christ unto God the Father' (*The Reformation, the Mass, and the Priesthood*, 2 vols. (London: Longmans, Green and Co., 1936–7), i. 331, 335, 351, 358, 359, 409, 520). Bishop Bush, an ex-religious, was allowed to resign rather than be deprived for marriage at the accession of Mary. His wife, Edith Ashley, however, had died shortly before Mary's accession, leaving a son. At his death on 11 Oct. 1558, Bush was rector of Winterbourne, Glouc. He was the author of six works on various topics, one as early as 1525 and another as late as 1554 (*BRUO 1501–1540*, 89).
22. *APC*, 3, pp. 186, 210; *CPR 1551* (5 Edward VI), pt. V, transcribed in *Hockaday Collection*, 9(4), p. 161 (not numbered sequentially).
23. PRO, Req 2/340 (1559, 1561).
24. The stone may have related to the building activity undertaken by Abbot Newland in the late fifteenth and early sixteenth centuries. Numerous loads of freestone and ragstone were brought from the quarry at Dundry and from Felton (Sabin, 'Compotus Rolls of St. Augustine's Abbey', 198).
25. *BRUO 1501–1540*, 140–1; PRO, E 179/6/1; BAO, EP/J/1/5, pp. 1–5, 7, 392, 462, 531; EP/J/1/4, p. 54; Lambeth Reg. Parker, II, fos. 32^v and 27^v, transc. in *Hockaday Abstracts*, vol. 433 (Bristol Cathedral, 1563).
26. *BRUO 1501–1540*, 140–1; W. H. Frere, *The Marian Reaction in its Relation to the English Clergy* (London: Church Historical Society, 18, 1896), 69–70, 173–4.

27. *BRUO 1501–1540*, 140–1; K. G. Powell, *The Marian Martyrs and the Reformation in Bristol* (Bristol: Bristol Historical Association, 1972), 13–15.

28. Margaret Bowker points out the power of a bishop in contrast to his deputies (*Secular Clergy*, 19–23, 179).

29. *Handbook of British Chronology*, 208. The measure primarily served to create adequate episcopal income, although it still was far below average.

30. *CSPD* (Elizabeth, 1547–80), xxii, nos. 11, 16, 22. See below.

31. Lambeth Palace Archives, MSS. 934, no. 74, cited in Lloyd, *Dorset Elizabethans*, 69, 298.

32. Ibid.

33. *APC* 3, pp. 186, 210; *Hockaday Collection*, 9(4), p. 161, (not paginated sequentially).

34. Transcribed in *Hockaday Abstracts*, Gloucester Diocese, 1563 (said to be similar to others in Christ Church College, Cambridge, Parker MSS., cxxii, art. 9, 287).

35. *BRUO 1501–1540*, 140–1; PRO, PCC, Draper, 13 (12 Feb. 1572; 25 May 1572); Lloyd, *Dorset Elizabethans*, 68–9.

36. *Handbook of British Chronology*, 252. Cheyney remained Bishop of Gloucester and held the see of Bristol *in commendam* until his death 25 Apr. 1579. (ibid. 208, 227).

37. *Hockaday Collection*, 9 (4), p. 191 (not paginated sequentially).

38. Lloyd, *Dorset Elizabethans*, 69, 297.

39. F. Douglas Price, 'The Commissioners for Ecclesiastical Causes for the Dioceses of Bristol and Gloucester, 1574', *Trans. B&GAS*, 59 (1938), 84.

40. Lloyd, *Dorset Elizabethans*, 69–70, 298. Partly as a result of the confusion over jurisdiction, Catholics were able to flourish in Dorset (ibid. 67).

41. *CSPD* (Elizabeth, 1547–80), xxii, p. 196; PRO, SP 12/22, fo. 8 (cited in Lloyd, *Dorset Elizabethans*, 68).

42. Natives of Bristol were Arthur Saule (Garrett, *Marian Exiles*, 284–5), John Sprint (Foster, iv. 1402), Thomas Sylke (Appendix 1), and John Williams (*BRUO 1501–1540*, 630). Christopher Pacy may also have been a native. The name was that of a prominent family, and his career in Bristol spanned some forty-six years (see Appendix 1). Sylke was the former vicar of St Leonard and prior of the Kalendars' Guild. Williams held the vicarage of St Nicholas. Pacy had been vicar of St Werberg. Roger Edgeworth was prior of the Kalendars' Guild, c.1526–8 (see Appendix 1). Richard Browne was a commissary in the diocese of Worcester, resident in Bristol in 1533 (see Chapter 2). George Dogeon was vicar of Temple parish in Bristol and chaplain of Bishop Clerke of Bath and Wells in the 1530s (see Appendix 1). Richard Hughes was a former monk of St Augustine's Abbey (Taylor, 'Religious Houses', 119;

Baskerville, 'Dispossessed Religious of Gloucestershire', 95). John Barlowe had been dean of nearby Westbury College for over thirteen years (*BRUO 1501–1540*, 26–7).

43. See below.
44. See Appendix 1, Appendix 3, and Chapter 4.
45. See Chapter 3, Appendix 1, and Appendix 3.
46. See above and below.
47. See Appendix 3.
48. *LP* x. 19, 1041, 1182; see below. Elton says Barlowe was 'a close ally of Cromwell', and that he found himself in Wales at the time of the fall of Anne Boleyn. These connections would have been less important by the time he became a prebendary in 1545. In fact, he was a chaplain of the King when the Crown presented him to the canonry (*Policy and Police*, 363–4. *LP* xix, pt. 1, 141 (21)).
49. *BRUO 1501–1540*, 552. The register of Oxford University indicates Sylke was from Worcester diocese, in which diocese, of course, most of Bristol was in 1522. In 1525 he was ordained in the diocese of Bath and Wells, Bristol's other diocese (SRO, D/D/B Reg. 12, fo. 17). He probably was related to Thomas Sylke, cardmaker, who was sheriff of Bristol in 1529–30, and thus, a member of the Common Council. Thomas and John Sylke, merchants of Bristol, lost a grant of presentation outside the city in 1541 (*LP* xvi. 1226 (15)).
50. *BRUO 1501–1540*, 552; PRO, PCC, Janker, 22 (Johan Baughan; 23 Dec. 1529; 31 Oct. 1530).
51. H&WRO, 716 093 BA 2648, fo. 12ᵛ. Sylke was instituted prior 8 Oct. 1540 (Maclean, 'Chantry Certificates', 246). This post was ultimately in the Mayor's patronage and required annual sermons. By 1548 these had been allocated to a paid deputy, possibly because Sylke was busy with chapter affairs and preached in the cathedral (Orme, 'Guild of Kalendars', 45 and *passim*).
52. BAO, DC/A/9/1/1–2, *passim*; PRO, C 1/1199 (1547–51); Req. 2/340 (1559, 1561).
53. *Ledger of John Smythe*, 39, 269. It is possible that this is not our man. It is not unlikely, however, that Thomas Sylke visited Roger Edgeworth, who was in Wells from *c.*1535. The date is from Janet Wilson, 'An Edition of *Sermons very fruitful, godly and learned* by Roger Edgeworth, from the Text of 1557' (Univ. of Cambridge Ph.D. thesis, 1985), 67 (Roger Edgeworth, *Sermons Very Fruitfull Godly and Learned: Preaching in the Reformation c.1535 to c.1553*, ed. Janet Wilson (Boydell and Brewer, 1992), forthcoming).
54. *CPR* (13 Elizabeth), pt. I, 1344.
55. Lambeth Reg. Parker, II, fo. 127, transc. in *Hockaday Abstracts*, vol. 433 (Bristol Cathedral, 1575).

56. *BRUO 1501–1540*, 630. One John Williams was Mayor in 1519–20 and still an alderman and prominent parishioner of St John in 1533 (BAO, P/StJ/C/1 (1533)).

57. H&WRO, 802 BA 2764, fos. 99, 269. A search of episcopal registers from 1516 does not reveal the date of his institution.

58. Williams died by May 1546 (*BRUO 1501–1540*, 630). John Rastell was compounded for first fruits of the vicarage of St Nicholas on 19 Nov. 1546 (PRO, E 334/3, fo. 104).

59. PRO, C 1/1100 (1547–51). Emden's biographical information on two men appears to include information which should be combined for this Richard Brown, who also was prebendary at Worcester and Gloucester (*BRUO 1501–1540*, 77). He undoubtedly was the commissary of the official principal of Worcester in Apr. 1532 and was living in Bristol in Mar. 1533 and Sept. 1535 (*LP* vi. 246 and ix. 383 (SP 1/96, pp. 183–4)). He assumed some office in Gloucester's Consistory Court in 1541, but not knowing what the office was, Hockaday could only say that he did not show up as chancellor or judge in any of the court's documents (Frank S. Hockaday, 'The Consistory Court of the Diocese of Gloucester', *Trans. B&GAS* 46 (1924), 195–287). I would hazard the guess that he continued his post as commissary in Bristol when it was transferred to the new diocese of Gloucester. In 1554 Browne was deprived of his preferment at Gloucester for marriage (*BRUO 1501–1540*, 77).

60. *BRUO 1501–1540*, 26–7.

61. PRO, PCC, Alen, 18 (4 Aug. 1546; Oct. 1546); *Hockaday Collection*, 9(4), 184.

62. *BRUO 1501–1540*, 26–7. Emden is mistaken in saying that Barlow was deprived of his Bristol preferment in 1553. He was still in the chapter in 1554 (*Hockaday Collection*, 9 (4), 195; BAO, DC/A/9/1/1 (1554); see Appendix 1, George Moglewike).

63. *BRUO 1501–1540*, 287.

64. PRO, PCC, Alen, 5 (24 Dec. 1545; 2 Mar. 1546.)

65. Jordan, 'Charitable Institutions', 40.

66. The first dean of Bristol, William Snowe, had been the last prior of Bradenstoke. Nothing is known of his tenure. A letter of 1534 suggests that he knew Lady Lisle; this may have been the key to his preferment. His successor in 1550 was John Whiteheare. Other than his involvement with Sylke, Edgeworth, and Cotterell in selling stone from the cathedral, the only evidence of his activities in the chapter is his signature on the chapter's accounts. George Carewe, who collected preferments under four Tudors, was dean from 1552 until 1554. He had been licensed for non-residence from a benefice in 1547 to study overseas and apparently came to Bristol from abroad. Although deprived of a number of

preferments at the accession of Mary, some were restored during her reign and others gained. He was restored as dean of Bristol upon the accession of Elizabeth (*CPR* (Philip and Mary II), 22 Aug. 1554; McGrath, 'Gloucestershire and the Counter-Reformation, 9; *LP* vii. 723; BAO, DC/A/9/1/1 (1550); *BRUO 1501–1540*, 101–2; see Appendix 3).

67. *BRUO 1501–1540*, 158; BAO, EP/J/1/2, pp. 4, 6–7, 8, 11, 42–3, 66.

68. *APC* vi. 158.

69. K. G. Powell discusses the evidence for the number and identities of those who burned for heresy from various sources and concludes that while no definite conclusions can be drawn, there were probably at least four. While Foxe gives six, only two are given in the two extant Consistory Court cause books (1556, 1557–8). Local calendars and secondary works are references for the others (*Marian Martyrs*, 9–15 and appendix.

70. Foxe, *Acts and Monuments*, appendix, 503–4, 737.

71. Dalby ceded his jurisdiction of the city and diocese in the Consistory Court on 9 June 1559. Then a commission for the jurisdiction from the dean and chapter of Canterbury was presented to Hugh Jones, LLB. (BAO, EP/J/1/4, p. 20). Not until 27 Sept. 1559, did the Queen's visitors reach Bristol (ibid. 27). Cotterell did not take over until 8 Jan. 1560, when the Archbishop's commission of 22 Dec. 1559, was read in the consistory court of Bristol (EP/J/1//5, pp. 1–5, 7).

72. See Appendix 3: Pacy and Saule. By 1561 both the teacher and assistant teacher in the cathedral's grammar school also were reformers. See Appendix 1: William Eydon and Walter Bower.

73. *CPR* (Elizabeth I), p. 256; PRO, E 334/3, fo. 28. See Appendix 1. He was a beneficiary of the will of William Shipman of the parish of St Werberg (PRO, Powell, 4, 16 July 1551; 5 Feb. 1552). (See Chapter 3.)

74. PRO, E 334/3, fo. 28; Dickens, *The English Reformation*, 28.

75. Seyer, *Memoirs of Bristol*, i. 234–5.

76. See Appendix 1.

77. BAO, P/StW/ChW/3(a), fos. 21, 22, 23, 26, 35 (1558–62); EP/J/1/5, p. 420.

78. BAO, EP/A/10/1/1, p. 85; Edward Boswell, *The Ecclesiastical Division of the Diocese of Bristol, Methodically Digested and Arranged, containing Lists of the Dignitaries, and Officers of the Cathedral, the Parish Churches, or Benefices, and the Patrons, and Incumbents within the Diocese* (Sherborne, Dorset: J. Penny, 1827), 10; Garrett, *Marian Exiles*, 284–5; Haugaard, *Elizabeth and the English Reformation*, 24, 50, 64–5, 72, 357, 359, 378; John Strype, *Annals of the Reformation and the Establishment of Religion, and Other Various Occurrences in the Church of England, during Queen Elizabeth's Happy Reign*, 4 vols. in 7 (Oxford: Clarendon, 1824), i. pt. 1, 500–6.

79. *CSPD* (Elizabeth, 1547–80), xlviii. 11, 16, 22; Haugaard, *Elizabeth and the English Reformation*, 356, 357, 358, 375. See *DNB*, under James Calfhill. Calfhill and Northbrooke are traditionally referred to as puritans, largely because of the former's Calvinism and the latter's writing against popular amusements. The term is used here with the understanding that they were not outside the Protestant mainstream. Cheyney, on the other hand, retained a Lutheran view of the eucharist and supported the doctrine of free will. By 1581 Thomas Norton, Cranmer's son-in-law and normally a moderate critic of the Church, remembered Cheyney as a heretic beause he was a Lutheran and a free-will man (*DNB*, under Richard Cheyney; Patrick Collinson, *The Elizabethan Puritan Movement* (Berkeley: University of California Press, 1967), 206).

80. The various responses of Protestants on issues of free will and predestination have received attention from historians (see n. 85 for Collinson; see also O. T. Hargrave, 'The Predestinarian Controversy among the Marian Protestant Prisoners', *Historical Magazine of the Protestant Episcopal Church*, 47 (1978), 131–51; and David W. Atkinson, 'Devotional Responses to Doctrinal Dilemmas: Piety in the English Reformation', *Historical Magazine of the Protestant Episcopal Church*, 52 (1983), 167–79; also cf. Peter White, 'The Rise of Arminianism Reconsidered', *P&P* 101 (1983), 34–54 and William Lamont, 'The Rise of Arminianism Reconsidered', *P&P* 107 (1985), 225–31.

81. The following corporation members signed the complaint (merchants are marked with *M*, retailers with *R*; those marked with *MR* were retailers who probably voted with the merchants in a dispute of 1571): Aldermen Robert Saxey (MR) and Roger Jones (R); sheriffs Thomas Kyrkland (R) and Robert Smythe (M); future mayors Thomas Kelke (sheriff, 1559–60, M), Thomas Aldworth (sheriff, 1566–7, M), Richard Cole (sheriff, 1569–70) (MR), John Browne (sheriff, 1558–9; M), Thomas Yonge (sheriff, 1562–3, R), Thomas Rowland (sheriff, 1569–70, M) and Walter Stanfast (sheriff 1577–8); and past or future sheriffs Randall Hassall (1571–2, R), Ralph Dole (1578–9), George Higgins (1560–1, M), and Robert Halton (1574–5), who at the time was Chamberlain. Schoolmaster Thomas Turner also signed along with John White (M), Robert Pressty (M), John Carry (M), Thomas Symons (M), Thomas Deconson, Richard Cary, Thomas Wade, William Pill (R), John Boydell (R), and Philip Scapulis. Robert Saxey was a draper closely connected to merchant interests (Sacks, *Trade, Society, and Politics*, 607). Richard Cole was a retailer, but he was related to merchants and probably allied with them. The merchant Robert Smythe called him 'brother' in his will, and he was son-in-law of the merchant William Carr (Wadley, *Notes*, 200–1 and 208). Junior members of the Common

Council usually became sheriff (Sacks, *Trade, Society, and Politics*, 694). The Corporation included forty-two members plus the Recorder; even with some absences more than fourteen votes would have been needed to have engaged the Corporation in an official complaint against Cheyney.

82. The merchants had formed the Merchant Venturers in 1552 to exclude the retailers from long-distance trade, but the formation of the monopoly undoubtedly had been a matter of discussion for some time. Around 1539 Roger Edgeworth preached that men should not meddle 'too much with other mens occupations that you cannot skill on . . . For when a taylor forsakynge his own occupation will be a merchaunt venterer . . . God send him well to prove'. (Edgeworth, of course, was explaining how the untrained, that is, the laity, should not study 'divinity'.) (*Sermons Very Fruitfull, Godly and Learned*, 43/C; see Patrick McGrath (ed.), *Records Relating to the Society of Merchant Venturers of the City of Bristol in the Seventeenth Century* (Bristol: BRS, 17, 1952), pp. ix–xx, and *Merchants and Merchandise in Seventeenth Century Bristol* (Bristol: BRS, 19, 1955), pp. xxv–xxvi). David Sacks sees the rivalry between retailers and merchants as the emergence of two rival concepts of the urban community, the merchants supporting a hierarchical arrangement of specialized economic functions, the retailers an arrangement wherein members of 'undifferentiated' legal and economic groups possessed equal rights to trade abroad. The retailers felt that the merchants had 'violated the very bonds of community' (*Trade, Society, and Politics*, 588–611). The merchants did support hierarchy, but they also supported the creation of a central economic force, as Sacks says himself, 'a fulcrum' (p. 911), around which other economic activities revolved. This trend in the city's economic life paralleled changes in the city's ecclesiastical life wherein a diverse church and clerical community were replaced by a centralized entity at the cathedral surrounded by untenured clerical atoms in parochial service. This steep hierarchy is only a bit less so when the lay elite are placed at the top and the parish lay elite sandwiched between the two clerical elements.

83. The twelve men signing the articles were as follows: Robert Alflate (R), Philip Jamkyns, John Alkin (R), William Zale, Thomas Wisshe, John Busshe, Thomas Debne, William Lile, William Cowper, Thomas Warrent (M), Edmond Smythe (M), William Gyttynes (MR). Edmond Smythe was the brother of sheriff Robert Smythe, whose signature appeared on the letter, and had married a sister of the Chester brothers, one of whom was sheriff in 1567–8 and another, mayor in 1569–70. Philip Jamkyns was listed among members of the elite who owed money to a local tucker in 1567, while Robert Alflate and John Alkin were soapmakers, belonging to one of the few crafts which could bring great

wealth (Wadley, *Notes*, 195, 199–202; for designations *M* and *R* see n. 81).

84. Prominent among them was Thomas Kelke, a merchant who was sheriff in 1559–60, master of the Merchant Venturers in 1566, and mayor in 1573–4. He and his brother John were among the hotter sort of Protestants visible early in Mary's reign. John, possibly a merchant, and his wife were among the English exiles in Frankfurt at least between 27 Aug. 1555 and June 1557. Thomas was a prisoner in the Tower on 10 Nov. 1555, and apparently had just been released on 23 Dec. when the Council ordered the mayor and sheriff of Bristol to deliver his goods to him. Reform may have been a tradition in the family. One of the men who certified the preaching of conservatives Powell and Hubberdine as 'synystral' in 1533 was William Kelke, who had been sheriff in 1529–30. Thomas was brother-in-law to John Cutt, who was sheriff in 1554–5 and mayor in 1566–7, and witness and overseer of his will. By the mid-1560s he lived in fashionable St Werberg's parish, where he was a church proctor (warden) and joined other committed Protestants, Thomas Aldworth, Robert Pressy, and Robert Halton, in the vestry. Thomas Kelke's will of 1583 indicated his committed Protestantism. It said 'Oh Lord into thy hands I do commit | my soul which is thy due | for why thou has redeemed it | my Lord and God most true.' By the time of Thomas's death, John was already dead, his wife residing in London (Latimer, *Merchant Venturers*, 326; Garrett, *Marian Exiles*, 202; *APC* 1554–6, pp. 191 and 208; *LP* vi. 596; PRO, SP 1/76, p. 83; see n. 81 above; BAO, P/StW/ChW/3(a) 1565; Wadley, *Notes*, 210 and 230). Garrett also lists a Roger Kelke, student and gentleman of Lincolnshire, who is not identified with Bristol. He was a rigid nonconformist (*Marian Exiles*, 202–3).

85. *Elizabethan Puritan Movement*, esp. 159–67; *Archbishop Grindal, 1519–1583: The Struggle for a Reformed Church* (Berkeley and Los Angeles: University of California Press, 1979), esp. 289–90; and *Religion of Protestants*, esp. 84–91.

86. BAO, EP/J/1/6, p. 270. See above.

87. *DNB*, under name; A. Hamilton Thompson, 'Notes on the Ecclesiastical History of the Parish of Henbury', *Trans. B&GAS* 38 (1915), 145, 165; *CPR* (13 Elizabeth), pt. I, no. 1344; Knappen, *Tudor Puritanism*, 225, 432, 440.

88. BAO, EP/J/1/5, p. 559 and EP/J/1/6, p. 93. For a complete discussion of the sixteenth- and seventeenth-century dispute over this doctrine and its meaning see Dewey D. Wallace, jun., 'Puritan and Anglican: The Interpretation of Christ's Descent into Hell in Elizabethan Theology', *Archiv für Reformationsgeschichte*, 69 (1978), 248–87. See also Haugaard, *Elizabeth and the English Reformation*, 252, 56–7, 344. Of particular

interest for the Bristol context is the connection between this doctrine and that of purgatory. That those who had lived before Christ had been rescued by him from hell suggested the existence of purgatory to some. It also challenged the puritans' emphasis on grace and predestination which precluded the elects' having spent any time anywhere but in heaven. Public debate on purgatory began in Bristol with Latimer's sermons in 1533 and continued in the heresy of 'soul sleep' evident in 1564, which we discuss below.

89. John Northbrooke (Norbrooke), *Spiritus est Vicarius Christi in Terra: A Breefe and Pithie Summe of the Christian Faith, Made in Fourme of Confession, with a Confutation of the Papistes Objections and Argumentes in Sundry Pointes of Religion, Repugnant to the Christian Faith* (London, 1571, 1582), preface 'To the Reader' (*STC* 18664). This was a serious accusation since it involved heresy, and Northbrooke added a preface 'To the Reader' to answer the charge. He carefully asserted his orthodoxy while positing a Calvinist view of the doctrine, that is, belief in the spiritual rather than the literal descent of Christ into hell. The bald statement of the doctrine opened the door to misinterpretation, he claimed. 'We must not gather, or descant upon bare words and take them literally as we lilt.'

90. E. Boswell, *Ecclesiastical Division*, 7. Thompson, 'Notes on the Ecclesiastical History of the Parish of Henbury', 165.

91. Compare Collinson, *Religion of Protestants*, 141–88, esp. 147–9.

92. Garrett, *Marian Exiles*, 284–5.

93. BAO, EP/A/10/1, p. 85. Nothing is known of Bayley's religious views. Colin W. Field apparently has confused Bayley with an Elizabethan Catholic who went abroad (*The Province of Canterbury and the Elizabethan Settlement of Religion* (Robertsbridge, Sussex: C. W. Field, 1973), 5, 7, 17, 26, 29). Thomas Bayley held his prebend in Bristol until he resigned sometime between 24 Sept. 1576 and 21 Mar. 1582, when Edward Grene took his stall (Lambeth Reg. Grindal, fo. 336^b, transcribed in *Hockaday Abstracts*, vol. 433 (Bristol Cathedral, 1582); see Appendix 3).

94. BAO, EP/A/10/1, p. 85. See Appendix 1, Thomas Sprint.

95. See Appendix 3.

96. *Adams's Chronicle*, under 1588. BAO, 04264(1) Common Council Proceedings, p. 125.

97. *Statutes of Bristol Cathedral*, 13.

98. See below.

99. Joan Simon, *Education and Society in Tudor England* (London and New York: Cambridge University Press, 1966), 186–7.

100. BAO, EP/J/1/5, p. 706. See below.

101. BAO, EP/J/1/5, pp. 381, 388, 394, 402, 406; 187, 224, 503, 580, 646; 71, 114, 140, 36, 212, 266; 324, 529, 619, 704; EP/J/1/6, p. 93; EP/J/1/2, pp. 62, 466.

102. BAO, EP/J/1/5, *passim*. In at least one instance the court commissioned a member of the parish clergy, the perpetual curate of St James, to prove a will (BRO, EP/J/1/6, p. 20).

103. BAO, EP/J/1/5 (1562). Only those probate cases which were other than routine were counted.

104. BAO, EP/J/1/5, pp. 223, 262.

105. Ibid. pp. 222, 577.

106. Ibid. pp. 246, 686, 693, 699.

107. Ibid. p. 706.

108. For an extensive discussion of Christian mortalism see Norman T. Burns, *Christian Mortalism from Tyndale to Milton* (Cambridge, Mass.: Harvard University Press, 1972), esp. 8–15, 19–34, 113–19.

109. Burns, *Christian Mortalism*, 8. It is well to keep in mind that the inability to write did not preclude the ability to read; reading and writing were and are separate arts. Between the fourteenth and seventeenth centuries many readers, well-educated and otherwise, considered writing an expertise best left to the experts. Moreover, books were to be heard as well as seen (Aston, 'Lollards and Literacy', in *Lollards and Reformers*, 195). Guillam was ordered to do penance in the cathedral and a parish church, probably either St Mary Redcliffe or Temple. Only the letters 'Re' for the parish are readable in the document, and he was apprehended at Redcliffe gate. However, he was identified as 'of the hospice without the gate of Temple.' These parishes across the Avon had been associated with Lollardy before the Reformation. See Chapter 3.

110. Lutheran reformers in England who followed Luther in his adherence to soul sleeping failed to support it vigorously, and soon it became identified solely with the Anabaptists, that catch-all for English religious radicals. Calvin attacked soul sleepers on scriptural grounds, and the doctrine was explicitly denied in the fortieth of the Edwardian Articles of 1553. Along with other Articles against Anabaptists, however, it was removed from the Articles in 1563. Burns nevertheless cites publications in 1565, 1576, 1581, and 1587 attacking soul sleep and a dispute over it in 1597 to suggest that the matter was not completely settled (Burns, *Christian Mortalism*, 117–19). The Forty-two Articles of 1553 also condemned the doctrine that a regenerate man lives without sinning (Article 14) and that Christians are freed from the moral as well as the ceremonial law of Moses (Article 19) (pp. 59–60). The sectarian view that the Old Testament was invalid was refuted by Article 7 of the Thirty-nine Articles, which asserted its value and insisted that Christians were bound by its moral commandments (pp. 27–8, 32–4, 19, 25; Haugaard, *Elizabeth and the English Reformation*, 251–2, 259).

111. Nicholls and Taylor, *Bristol, Past and Present*, i. 252; *Adams's Chronicle*, under 1561. In 1539, when the preaching of George Wishart had

prompted conflict, Chester and the pointmakers were prominent. One of Wishart's supporters had warned the authorities to discharge Wishart's sureties, 'for if the pointmakers do rise some of you will lose your ears, and that shortly'. Chester was described as 'a double knave . . . for sometimes he is with us and sometimes he is with the knaves'. His wife was a 'foolish drab . . . the enemy of God's word' (*LP* xiv, pt. 2, 184 (3); BL Cleop. E. v, fos. 390–1). The difficulties of the pointmaking trade apparently had created divisions between established masters such as Chester and the apprentices. Although the precise elements in the decline of the trade are not known, a contemporary discourse on the decay of the towns attributed it to rising imports, for 'now the poorest young man must have gear from London and overseas'. Claiming that pointmaking was once the 'chiefest mystery' in Bristol and a great provider of work, he compared it to the decline of Coventry's industry in blue thread, which had been followed by the city's decay (Anon. (J. Hales or Sir T. Smith?), *A Discourse of the Common Weal* (1549), 125–31, cited in A. L. Rowse, *The England of Elizabeth* (Madison: University of Wisconsin Press, 1950), 163, and Whitney R. D. Jones, *The Tudor Commonwealth 1529–1559* (London: Macmillan, 1970)). In Gloucester by 1574 the authority of both local ecclesiastical and local secular institutions had failed, and the Crown established an Ecclesiastical Commission for the Dioceses of Gloucester and Bristol. Although the mayor of Bristol was a member, he never sat at the commission's proceedings and no case involving Bristol is noted in the extant record. The most difficult cases before the commission involved nonconformists, including those who refused to allow the christening of their children (Price, 'Commissioners for Ecclesiastical Causes', 69, 86).

112. BAO, EP/J/1/5, pp. 21, 31, 34, 37, 38, 439, 444.
113. Ibid., pp. 476, 477.
114. BAO, EP/J/1/6, p. 65.
115. BAO, EP/J/1/5, p. 704.
116. Ibid., p. 130.
117. Ibid., p. 619.
118. Ibid., p. 58.
119. Ibid., pp. 239, 324, 338.
120. BAO, EP/J/1/6, p. 93.
121. BAO, EP/J/1/5, pp. 693, 699. Richard Taverner was an early English Protestant translator (William A. Clebsch, *England's Earliest Protestants* (New Haven, Conn.: Yale University Press, 1964, 256; see also J. K. Yost, 'German Protestant Humanism and the Early English Reformation: Richard Taverner and Official Translation', *Bibliotheque d'Humanisme et Renaissance*, 32 (1970), 613–25; James H. Pragman, 'The Augsburg Confession in the English Reformation: Richard Taverner's Contribution', *Sixteenth Century Journal*, 11 (1980), 75–85.

122. See Appendix 3.
123. See Appendix 2.
124. BAO, 04272 (Old Ordinance Book), fos. 54[r], 57[v], 58[v]. The first evidence of a rate for a lecturer is a list of 27 May 1585. There is also a list for 19 July 1586. The first evidence of a lecturer, however, is an ordinance for a stipend for Mr Temple on 10 Sept. 1586. For a discussion of the conjunction of magistracy and ministry in many English towns of the period see Collinson, *Religion of Protestants*, 141–88, esp. 170–7 on town lecturers.
125. BAO, 04272, fos. 54[r], 57[v], 66[r]; 04264 (1), p. 30. Christenings, burials, and weddings in various canon's families appear in the parish register of St Augustine-the-Less (Arthur Sabin (ed.), *The Registers of the Church of St. Augustine-the-Less, Bristol, 1577–1700* (Gloucester: B&GAS Records Section, 1958)). See Saule (pp. 1, 6), Grene (pp. 8, 9, 11, 48; Gulliforde (p. 35); and Dean Simon Robson (p. 44).
126. BAO, 04264(1), pp. 108, 126, 127, 178, 129, 130. Edward Chetwynd must have come from Oxford sometime around 8 Jan. 1607, when the council approved his moving allowance. He completed the DD degree on 15 Dec. 1606, and was the lecturer of Abingdon, Berks., in that same year. Foster, however, also describes him as public lecturer of Bristol in 1606 (pp. 268–9).
127. *Adams's Chronicle*, 183–4. A similar situation arose in a parish church in Norwich where civic officials worshipped (Collinson, *Religion of Protestants*, 141–5).
128. Foster, 268–9.
129. Historical Manuscripts Commission, *Appendix to the Fourth Report*, 144.
130. BAO, 04026. Payment of Mr Yemans occurs in the Audits every year from 1616 to 1631. His will was proved in 1633 (E. George and S. George, *Guide to the Probate Inventories of the Bristol Deanery of the Diocese of Bristol (1542–1804)* (Gloucester: BRS, 1988), 262). There are no Corporation accounts for 1632 and 1633 and thereafter the lecturer's name is omitted through 1649, with reference simply to 'the Lecturer of St Walburge [Werberg]' (PRO E 334/12, fo. 214). His successor at Sts Philip and Jacob was John Pearse or Pierce, whose composition for first fruits was dated 22 Nov. 1633 (*Hockaday Abstracts*, vol. 448 under parish and date).
131. BAO, 04026. The entry is in the section of 'Officers' Fees' paid at 'Our Lady Even' and Michaelmas in each account, 1613–31 (see above). He may have given only one lecture per week, which would have meant an increase in stipend per sermon over that of Temple in 1586; nevertheless, this was a substantial savings for the Corporation.
132. BAO, 04272, fo. 58[v].
133. BAO, 04264(1), pp. 54, 82. Some or all of Gulliford's stipend may have come from the vicarage of Congresbury to which the Mayor and

Common Council, as governors of Queen Elizabeth's Hospital, presented him in 1604.

134. BAO, 04264 (1), p. 108.
135. The living of Sts Philip and Jacob was valued at £15 in 1535 and £35 in 1698, and still taxed at the lower value during Yemans tenure (PRO, E 334/12, fo. 214; Lambeth Archbishop Act Books 4, fo. 579, transcribed in *Hockaday Abstracts*, vol. 448 (Sts Philip and Jacob, 1698)).
136. See above.
137. BAO, 04272, fo. 58^v; 04026, 1616–31. The proctors of St Nicholas were to keep account of any failure of Mr Temple to preach as required. Many entries of payments to Mr Yeamans were for the lectures at 'St Walburges [Werburg]'.
138. BAO, 04272, fos. 54^r, 57^v, 66^r; 04264(1), p. 30.
139. See Appendix 1.
140. Seaver, *Puritan Lectureships*, 77, 99-100, 321. Seaver says that a few years later the assessment provided only £44 for eighteen parishes while three lecturers were receiving £30 each. The list of 1599 entitled 'A Rate for the Preachers' Stipend yearly' shows parishes and sums adding up to £44. 6s. 8d. (BAO, 04264(1), p. 30). It seems most likely, however, that this was to pay the stipend of the Corporation's preacher, not those of the parishes. Although the Council's letter said they had been informed that the Corporation was sponsoring three preachers, the only evidence found of more than one Corporation preacher is for 1601. (ibid. 54).

Bibliography

MANUSCRIPT MATERIALS

BRISTOL, BRISTOL ARCHIVES OFFICE

EP/A/3	Presentation Deeds
EP/A/10/1/1	Catalogue of Deans, *c.*1639
EP/J/1/1	(See *Hockaday Collection* below)
EP/J/1/2–6	Cause Books, Bristol Consistory Court
EP/J/10	Fees Table, Consistory Court Officers
EP/V15/A	Glebe Terrier, Sts Philip and Jacob, eighteenth century
DC/A/9/1–4	Computa, Dean and Chapter
DC/A/8/1	Chapter Minutes (extracts)
P/AS/ChW 1(a)	Churchwardens' Accounts, All Saints, 1466–
P/XCh/ChW 1(a)	Churchwardens' Accounts, Christ Church, 1531–
P/StE/ChW 1(a)	Churchwardens' Accounts, St Ewen, 1547–
P/StJ/ChW 1	Churchwardens' Accounts, St James, 1566–
P/StP&J/ChW 3(a)	Churchwardens' Accounts, Sts Philip and Jacob, 1562–
P/StT/ChW 1–	Churchwardens' Accounts, St Thomas, 1543–
P/StW/ChW 3(a)	Churchwardens' Accounts, St Werberg, 1548–
P/AS/ChW 3	Minute Book, All Saints (Edward IV)
P/AS/ChW 6	Easter Books, All Saints, 1575–
P/XCh/ChW 6	Easter Books, Christ Church, 1570–
P/StE/ChW 3	Church Book, St Ewen, 1455–1583
P/StE/V.1	Vestry Book, St Ewen, 1596
P/StJB/ChW 1	Minute and Account Book, St John, 1469–1581
P/AS/C 1&2	Chantry Accounts and Rent Rolls, All Saints
P/StT/Ch 2	Rental Rolls, St Thomas, 15th–17th centuries (5)
P/StJB/Misc.	Documents, St John, 15th Century–1800
P/StS/ChW	Inventories, St Stephen, 1494–1550
P/StS/I(1–3)	Receipts, St Stephen, 1562-1578
04026	Mayors' Audits, 1532–
04272	Old Book of Ordinances, 1506–
08154	Tolzey Court Cause or Action Book, 1476–
04264	Council Proceedings, 1598–
04046	Audit of Corporation Lands of St John of Jerusalem
04490	Survey of Gaunts Hospital, 1542–7

BRISTOL, PARISH CHURCHES' ARCHIVES

Churchwardens' Accounts, St Mary Redcliffe, 1548–
Vestry Book, St Michael, 1575–

GLOUCESTER, HOCKADAY COLLECTION AND ABSTRACTS,
GLOUCESTER CITY LIBRARY

Abstracts and transcriptions of documents from the BAO, H&WRO, PRO, Lambeth Palace Library, British Library, and Dr Williams' Library, London. This material has been microfilmed by the Church of the Latter Day Saints and may be used in their reading rooms in most major cities (0423/345–362). Especially important are transcriptions of documents no longer extant (e.g. St Nicholas and St Mary-le-Porte) or producible (BAO, EP/J/1/1). This was also my source for transcriptions and translations of wills in the PRO, (PCC).

LONDON, BRITISH LIBRARY

Cotton Cleop. E. iv., fo. 73 and v., fos. 390–1 and 394.

LONDON, LAMBETH PALACE LIBRARY (Transcribed in *Hockaday Abstracts* under parish and date) Archiepiscopal Registers: Parker, Grindal, Whitgift.

LONDON, PUBLIC RECORD OFFICE

E 25	Acknowledgements of Supremacy
E 36	Exchequer Miscellaneous Books
E 117	Church Goods
E 179	Subsidy Rolls
E 301	Certificates of Colleges and Chantries
E 315	Augmentations Miscellaneous Books
E 318	Particulars for Grants
E 323	Treasurer's Accounts of Augmentations
E 331	Institutions Books
E 334	Composition Books
E 336	Miscellaneous Books, First Fruits and Tenths
C 1	Early Chancery Proceedings
C 47	Chancery Miscellanea
C 85	Significations for Excommunications

PROB   Prerogative Court of Canterbury Administrations and Registers of Wills
Sta Cha   Star Chamber Proceedings
Req 1   Court of Requests, Misc. Bks.
Req 2   Court of Requests, Proceedings
SP 1   State Papers, Henry VIII
SP 2   State Papers, Henry VIII
SP 6   State Papers, Theological Tracts
SP 10   State Papers, Edward VI
SP 12   State Papers, Domestic, Elizabeth I
SP 15   State Papers, Domestic, Addenda

WORCESTER, HEREFORD AND WORCESTER RECORD OFFICE

716–093 BA 2648/8(ii)--9(iii)   Registers of Bishops Silvestro de' Gigli (1512–21), Medici (1521–2), Geronimo Ghinucci (1522–5), Hugh Latimer (1535–9), John Bell (1539–43)

802 BA 2764   Visitation Act Book of John Bell, Bishop of Worcester for the year 1540, with other notes and documents *c.*1520–*c.*41

BA 3585/3b & 4b   Wills

TAUNTON, SOMERSET RECORD OFFICE

D/D/Ca/3, 4, 7, 8, 9A, 10, 10A, 11, 12, 12A Commissary General's (?) Act Books, 1527–34
D/D/B/Reg. 11 & 12 (Wolsey and Clerke) Unprinted Ordination Lists

PRINTED PRIMARY MATERIALS

ADAMS, WILLIAM, *Adams's Chronicle of Bristol*, ed. F. F. Fox (Bristol: J. W. Arrowsmith for Francis F. Fox, 1910).

ATCHLEY, CUTHBERT, 'Extracts from an Ancient Vestry Book at St Nicholas's Church, Bristol'. *All Saints, Clifton, Parish Magazine*, 11 (1889–90), 335–40.

BATESON, MARY (ed.), *A Collection of original Letters from the Bishops to the Privy Council* (Camden Society Miscellany, 9, 1893).

BICKLEY, F. B. (ed.), *The Little Red Book of Bristol* (Bristol: W. C. Hemmons, 1900).

BUND, J. W. W. (ed.), *Register of Godfrey Giffard, Bishop of Worcester, 1268–1301* (Oxford: Worcester Historical Society, 1900).

—— *Register of William Ginsborough, Bishop of Worcester, 1303–7* (Oxford: Worcester Historical Society, 1907).

—— *The Register of the Diocese of Worcester during the Vacancy of the See, usually called 'Registrum sede vacante', 1307–1435* (Oxford: Worcester Historical Society, 1897).

BURNET, GILBERT, *The History of the Reformation of the Church of England*, 6 vols. (London: J. F. Dove for Richard Priestly, 1820).

Calendar of Entries in the Papal Registers relating to Great Britain and Ireland (London: HMSO, 1893–).

Calendar of Patent Rolls, Henry VIII, Edward VI, Mary and Philip and Mary, Elizabeth (London: HMSO, 2 vols. (1914–16) 5 vols. (1924–9); 4 vols. (1936–9); 4 vols. (1939–64)).

Calendars of the Proceedings in Chancery, in the Reign of Queen Elizabeth, 3 vols. (London: Record Commission, 1827).

Calendar of State Papers Domestic, Elizabeth (London: HMSO, 1900).

CALEY, JOHN, and HUNTER, JOSEPH, (eds.), *Valor ecclesiasticus*, 6 vols. (London: Records Commission, 1810–34).

CARDWELL, EDWARD (ed.), *Documentary Annals of the Reformed Church of England, 1546–1716*, 2 vols. (Oxford: Oxford University Press, 1839–44).

CHAMBERS, D. S. (ed.), *Faculty Office Registers, 1534–49.* (Oxford: Clarendon Press, 1966).

CHURCHILL, IRENE J. *Canterbury Administration . . . Illustrated from Original Records* (London and New York: Society for Promoting Christian Knowledge, 1933).

CORRIE, GEORGE, (ed.), *Latimer's Remains* (Cambridge: Parker Society, 1848).

COX, JOHN E. (ed.), *Miscellaneous Writings and Letters of Thomas Cranmer* (Cambridge: Parker Society, 1844–6).

DASENT, J. R., (ed.), *Acts of the Privy Council of England*, new series. 32 vols. (London: HMSO, 1890–3).

DICKENS, A. G., and CARR, DOROTHY (eds.), *The Reformation in England to the Accession of Elizabeth I* (London: Edward Arnold, 1967).

DUNCAN, LELAND L., *Index of Wills Proved in the Prerogative Court of Canterbury, 1558–83* (British Record Society, Index Library, 18, 1898).

EDGEWORTH, ROGER, *Sermons Very Fruitfull, Godly and Learned, Preached and Set Foorthe by Maister Roger Edgeworth* (London: R. Caly, 1557). *STC* 7482.

ELLIS, HENRY, (ed.), *Original Letters Illustrative of English History* (London: Dawsons of Pall Mall, 1969).

FOXE, F. F., 'Regulations of the Vestry of St Stephen's', *Proc. of the Clifton Antiquarian Club*, 1 (1888), 199–206.

FOXE, JOHN, *Acts and Monuments*, 4th edn., 8 vols. ed. Josiah Pratt, (London: Religious Tract Society, 1870).

FRERE, WALTER H., and KENNEDY, WILLIAM, (eds.), *Visitation Articles and Injunctions of the Period of the Reformation*, 3 vols. (London: Alcuin Club Collections, 1910).

FRY, EDWARD A., (ed.), *A Calendar of Wills and Administrations proved in the Consistory Court of the Bishop of Worcester, 1451–1652*, 2 vols. (London: British Record Society, 1904–10).

—— *Calendar of Wills Contained in the Great Orphans' Books Now Preserved in the Council House in Bristol, 1379–1674* (London: British Record Society, 1897).

—— and PHILLIMORE, W. P. W. (eds.), *A Calendar of Wills Proved in the Consistory Court of the Bishop of Gloucester, 1541–1800* (London: British Record Society, 1907).

GEE, HENRY, and HARDY, W. JOHN, (eds.), *Documents Illustrative of English Church History* (London: Macmillan, 1910).

GREEN, EMANUEL (ed.), *The Survey and Rental of the Chantries, Colleges and Free Chapels, Guilds, Fraternities, Lampes, Lights, and Obits in the County of Somerset* (SRS, 2; London: Somerset Record Society, 1888).

HAINES, ROY M. (ed.), *The Register of Wolstan de Bransford, Bishop of Worcester, 1339–49* (London: Historical Manuscripts Commission, 1966).

Historical Manuscripts Commission, *Reports*.

HOLMES, THOMAS SCOTT (ed.), *Register of Bishop Bubwith of Bath and Wells, 1407–1424* (SRS, 29; London: Somerset Record Society, 1914).

HUGHES, PAUL, and LARKIN, JAMES, (eds.), *Tudor Royal Proclamations*, 3 vols. (New Haven, Conn.: Yale University Press, 1964).

KNOX, T. F. *The First and Second Diaries of the English College, Douay* (London: D. Nutt, 1878).

LATHAM, R. C. (ed.), *Bristol Charters, 1509–1899* (BRS, 12; Bristol: Bristol Record Society, 1947).

LELAND, JOHN, *Leland's Itinerary in England & Wales*, vol. 5. ed. L. Toulmin Smith (Carbondale, Ill.: Southern Illinois University Press, 1964).

LENEVE, JOHN, *Fasti Ecclesiae Anglicanae*, rev. edn. (London: Institute of Historical Research, 1962–7).

Letters and Papers Foreign and Domestic of the Reign of Henry VIII, ed. J. S. Brewer, James Gairdner, and R. H. Brodie, 36 vols. (London: Longman, Green, Longman, & Roberts, 1862–1932).

Lyndwood's Provinciale, ed. J. V. Bullard and H. Chalmers Bell (London: Faith Press, 1929).

MACLEAN, JOHN, (ed.), 'Chantry Certificates, Gloucestershire', *Trans. B&GAS* 8 (1878–9), 229–53.

—— 'Inventories of, and Receipts for, Church Goods in the County of Gloucester and Cities of Gloucester and Bristol', *Trans. B&GAS* 12 (1888), 70–113.

McGrath, Patrick, (ed.), *Merchants and Merchandise in Seventeenth Century Bristol*. (BRS, 19; Bristol: Bristol Record Society, 1955).

—— *Records relating to the Society of Merchant Venturers of the City of Bristol in the Seventeenth Century* (BRS 17; Bristol: Bristol Record Society, 1952).

—— and Williams, Mary (eds.), *Bristol Wills 1546–1593* (Bristol: University of Bristol Dept. of Extra-Mural Studies, 1975).

—— *Bristol Wills 1597–1598* (Bristol: University of Bristol Dept. of Extra-Mural Studies, 1978).

The Maire of Bristowe is Kalendar, by Robert Ricart, Town Clerk of Bristol, 18 Edward IV, ed. Lucy Toulmin Smith (Westminster: Camden Society, 1872).

Masters, B. R., and Ralph, Elizabeth (eds.), *The Church Book of St. Ewen's Bristol, 1454–1584* (Gloucester: B&GAS, Records Section, 1967).

Maxwell-Lyte, Henry, (ed.), *Registers of the Bishops of Bath and Wells, 1518–1559* (SRS, 55; London: Somerset Record Society, 1940).

—— *The Registers of Oliver King, Bishop of Bath and Wells, 1496–1503, and Hadrian de Castello, Bishop of Bath and Wells, 1503–1518* (SRS, 54; London: Somerset Record Society, 1939).

More, Thomas, *Confutation of Tyndale's Answer*, ed. J. P. Lusardi, R. L. Marius, R. J. Schoeck, and L. A. Schuster, *The Yale Edition of the Complete Works of St Thomas More* (New Haven, Conn.: Yale University Press, 1973), viii. 812–16.

Nichols, J. G., *Narratives of the Days of the Reformation* (London: Camden Society, 77, 1859).

Northbrooke, John, *Spiritus est Vicarius Christi in Terra: A Breefe and Pithie Summe of the Christian Faith, Made in Fourme of Confession, with a Confutation of the Papistes Objections and Arguments in Sundry Pointes of Religion, Repugnant to the Christian Faith* (London, 1571). *STC* 18664.

—— *Spiritus est Vicarius Christi in Terra: The Poore Mans Garden, Wherein are Flowers of the Scriptures, and Doctours, Very Necessary and Profitable for the Simple and Ignoraunt People to Read: Truely Collected and Diligently Gathered Together* (London, 1573). *STC* 18668.

Peacock, E. (ed.), *Instructions for Parish Priests by John Myrc* (Early English Text Society, 31, rev. edn., 1902).

Phillimore, W. P. W., and Duncan, Leland L. (eds.), *A Calendar of Wills Proved in the Consistory Court of the Bishop of Gloucester, 1541–1560* (London: British Record Society, 1895; Kraus Reprint, 1968).

Public Record Office, *Lists and Indexes*.

Ralph, Elizabeth (ed.), *The Great White Book of Bristol* (BRS, 32; Bristol: Bristol Record Society, 1979).

Registrum Matthei Parker Diocesesis Cantuariensis A.D. 1559–1575, transcribed by E. Margaret Thompson, ed. W. H. Frere (Oxford: Canterbury and York Society, 35, 36, 39, 1928–33).

Registrum: sive, Liber irrotularius [Register of the Prior of St. Mary, Worcester], ed. William H. Hale (London: Camden Society, 1865).

Ross, C. D. (ed.), *The Cartulary of St. Mark's Hospital, Bristol* (BRS 21; Bristol: Bristol Record Society, 1956).

Sabin, Arthur, (ed.), *The Registers of the Church of St Augustine-the-Less, Bristol, 1577–1700* (Gloucester: B&GAS, Records Section, 1958).

—— *Some Manorial Accounts of St. Augustine's Abbey Bristol* (BRS 22; Bristol: Bristol Record Society, 1960).

—— and Beachcroft, Gwen (eds.), *Two Compotus Rolls of St. Augustine's Abbey, Bristol* (BRS, 9; Bristol: Bristol Record Society, 1938).

Shilton, D. O., and Holworthy, R. (eds.), *Medieval Wills from Wells* (SRS, 40; London: Somerset Record Society, 1925).

Smith, J. C. C., *Index of Wills Proved in the Prerogative Court of Canterbury, 1383–1558* (London: British Record Society, 1893–5).

The Statutes of Bristol Cathedral (Bristol: E. Chillcott for the Dean and Chapter, 1870).

Statutes of the Realm, ed. A. Luders *et al.*, 11 vols. (London: Dawson's of Pall Mall, 1810–28).

Strype, John., *Annals of the Reformation and the Establishment of Religion, and Other Various Occurrences in the Church of England, during Queen Elizabeth's Happy Reign*, 4 vols. in 7 (Oxford: Clarendon, 1824).

—— *Ecclesiastical Memorials Relating Chiefly to Religion and the Reformation of It, and the Emergencies of the Church of England, under King Henry VIII, King Edward VI, and Queen Mary I*, 3 vols. in 6 (Oxford: Clarendon, 1822).

Taylor, C. S, 'Regulations of the Vestry of St Thomas in 1563', *Proc. of the Clifton Antiquarian Club*, 1 (1888), 193–8.

Vanes, Jean (ed.), *The Ledger of John Smythe, 1538–1550* (BRS, 28; Bristol: Bristol Record Society and Historical Manuscripts Commission, 1974).

Veale, E. W. W. (ed.), *The Great Red Book of Bristol* (BRS, 2, 4, 8, 16; Bristol: Bristol Record Society, 1933–53).

Wadley, Thomas P., *Notes or Abstracts of the Wills Contained in . . . the Great Orphans' Book and Book of Wills in the Council House at Bristol, 1381–1605* (Gloucester: B&GAS, 1886).

Weaver, F. W. (ed.), *Somerset Medieval Wills, 1383–1558*, 3 vols. (SRS, 16, 19, 21; London: Somerset Record Society, 1901–5).

—— *Wells Wills* (London: K. Paul, Trench, Trubner, 1890).

Wilkins, David (ed.), *Concilia Magnae Britanniae et Hiberniae . . . 446–1718*, 4 vols. (London: R. Gosling, 1737).

Wright, Thomas (ed.), *Three Chapters of Letters relating to the Suppression of the Monasteries* (Camden Society, 27, 1843).

SECONDARY SOURCES

ADAMS, NORMA, 'The Judicial Conflict over Tithes', *EHR* 52 (1937), 1–22.

AINSLIE, J. L. *The Doctrine of Ministerial Order in the Reformed Churches of the Sixteenth and Seventeenth Centuries*. (Edinburgh: T. & T. Clark, 1940).

ALTHAUS, PAUL, *The Theology of Martin Luther*, trans. Robert C. Schultz (Philadelphia: Fortress Press, 1966).

ARCHBOLD, WILLIAM A. J. *The Somerset Religious Houses* (Cambridge: Cambridge University Press, 1892).

ASTON, MARGARET, ' "Caim's Castles": Poverty, Politics and Disendowment', in Dobson (ed.), *The Church, Politics, and Patronage*, 45–81.

—— 'Lollard Women Priests?' *JEH* 31 (1980), 441–62.

—— *Lollards and Reformers: Images and Literacy in Late Medieval Religion* (London: Hambledon, 1984).

—— 'Lollardy and the Reformation: Survival or Revival?' *History*, 49 (1964), 149–70.

ATKINSON, DAVID W., 'Devotional Responses to Doctrinal Dilemmas: Piety in the English Reformation', *Historical Magazine of the Protestant Episcopal Church*, 52 (1983), 167–79.

BAKER, DEREK (ed.), *The Church in Town and Countryside* (Studies in Church History, 16; Oxford: Basil Blackwell for the Ecclesiastical History Society, 1979).

—— *Materials, Sources, and Methods* (Studies in Church History, 11; New York: Barnes and Noble for the Ecclesiastical History Society, 1975).

—— *Reform and Reformation: England and the Continent c.1500–c.1750* (Studies in Church History, 2, Subsidia; Oxford: Basil Blackwell for the Ecclesiastical History Society, 1979).

—— *Sanctity and Secularity: The Church and the World* (Studies in Church History, 10; Oxford: Basil Blackwell for the Ecclesiastical History Society, 1973).

—— *Schism, Heresy, and Religious Protest* (Studies in Church History, 9; Cambridge: Cambridge University Press for the Ecclesiastical History Society, 1972).

BARKER, W. R., *St. Mark's or the Mayor's Chapel Bristol* (Bristol: W. C. Hemmons, 1892).

BARRAT, D. M., 'The Condition of the Parochial Clergy from the Reformation to 1660, with Special Reference to the Dioceses of Oxford, Worcester and Gloucester' (Univ. of Oxford, D.Phil. thesis, 1950).

BARRETT, WILLIAM, *The History and Antiquities of the City of Bristol, Compiled from Original Records and Authentic Manuscripts in the Public Record Office or Private Hands* (Bristol: W. Pine, 1789).

BARRON, CAROLINE M., 'The parish fraternities of medieval London', in Barron and Harper-Bill (eds.), *The Church in Pre-Reformation Society*, 13–37.

—— and CHRISTOPHER HARPER-BILL (eds.), *The Church in Pre-Reformation Society: Essays in Honour of F. R. H. du Boulay* (Woodbridge: Boydell Press, 1985).

BARRY, JONATHAN, 'The Parish in Civic Life: Bristol and its Churches 1640–1750', in S. J. Wright (ed.), *Parish Church and People: Local Studies in Lay Religion 1350–1750* (London: Hutchinson, 1988), 152–78.

BASKERVILLE, GEOFFREY, 'The Dispossessed Religious of Gloucestershire', *Trans. B&GAS* 49 (1927), 63–122.

—— 'The Dispossessed Religious', in G. Baskerville (ed.), *Essays in History Presented to R. Lane Poole* (Oxford: Clarendon Press, 1927), 436–65.

—— 'Elections to Convocation in the Diocese of Gloucester under Bishop Hooper', *EHR* 44 (1928), 1–32.

—— *English Monks and the Suppression of the Monasteries* (New Haven, Conn.: Yale University Press, 1937).

—— 'Some Ecclesiastical Wills', *Trans. B&GAS* 52 (1930), 281–93.

BAYNE, C. G., 'Visitation of the Province of Canterbury, 1559', *EHR* 28 (1913), 637–77.

BENEDICT, PHILIP, *Rouen during the Wars of Religion* (Cambridge and New York: Cambridge University Press, 1981).

BENNETT, R. F., *The Early Dominicans* (Cambridge: Cambridge University Press, 1937).

BETTEY, J. H., *Bristol Parish Churches during the Reformation, c.1530–1560* (Bristol: Bristol Branch of the Historical Association, 1979).

—— *The Suppression of the Monasteries in the West Country* (Gloucester: Alan Sutton, 1989).

BINDON, JOHN, 'Desecrated and Destroyed Churches of Bristol', *Proc. Arch. Inst., Bristol* (1851), 127–33.

BLACK, THOMAS, 'Thomas Cromwell's Patronage of Preaching', *Sixteenth-Century Journal*, 8 (1977), 37–50.

BLENCH, J. W., 'John Longland and Roger Edgeworth, Two Forgotten Preachers of the Early Sixteenth Century', *Review of English Studies*, NS 5 (1954), 123–43.

—— *Preaching in England in the Fifteenth and Sixteenth Centuries* (Oxford: Basil Blackwell, 1964).

BOSSY, JOHN, 'Blood and Baptism: Kinship, Community, and Christianity in Western Europe from the Fourteenth to the Seventeenth Centuries', in Baker (ed.), *Sanctity and Secularity*, 129–43.

—— 'The Mass as a Social Institution 1200–1700', *P&P* 100 (1983), 29–61.

BOSWELL, EDWARD, *The Ecclesiastical Division of the Diocese of Bristol, Methodically Digested and Arranged, containing Lists of the Dignitaries, and Officers of the Cathedral, the Parish Churches, or Benefices, and the Patrons, and Incumbents within the Diocese* (Sherborne: J. Penny, 1827).

BOSWELL, JOHN, *Christianity, Social Tolerance, and Homosexuality: Gay People in*

Western Europe from the Beginning of the Christian Era to the Fourteenth Century (Chicago and London: University of Chicago Press, 1980).

BOWKER, MARGARET, 'The Henrician Reformation and the Parish Clergy', *BIHR* (May 1977), 30–47.

—— *The Henrician Reformation: The Diocese of Lincoln under John Longland, 1521–1547* (New York and Cambridge: Cambridge University Press, 1981).

—— *The Secular Clergy of the Diocese of Lincoln* (New York and Cambridge: Cambridge University Press, 1968).

—— 'The Supremacy and the Episcopate: The Struggle for Control, 1534–1540', *Historical Journal*, 18 (1975), 227–43.

BRADY, THOMAS A., *Ruling Class, Regime and Reformation at Strasbourg, 1520–1555* (Leiden: Brill, 1978).

BRAMBLE, J. R., 'Ancient Bristol Documents from the Records of St Nicholas Church, "How the Clerke and the Suffragan of Seynt Nicholas Church Ought to do"', *Proc. Clifton Antiq. Club*, 1 (1888), 142–150.

BRIDGETT, T. E., 'The Bristol Pulpit in the Days of Henry VIII', *Dublin Review.*, 3rd. ser. 1 (1879), 73–95.

BRIGDEN, SUSAN, *London and the Reformation* (Oxford: Oxford University Press, 1989).

—— 'Religion and Social Obligation in Early Sixteenth-Century London', *P&P* 103 (1984), 67–112.

—— 'Tithe Controversy in Reformation London', *JEH* 32 (1981), 285–307.

—— 'Youth and the English Reformation', *P&P* 95 (1982), 37–67.

BRITTON, J., *History and Antiquities of the Abbey & Cathedral of Bristol* (Bristol, 1836).

BROOKS, F. W., 'The Social Position of the Parson in the Sixteenth Century', *Journal of the British Archeological Society*, 3rd ser. 10 (1945–7), 23–37.

BURGESS, CLIVE, 'A Service for the Dead: The Form and Function of the Anniversary in Late Medieval Bristol', *Trans. B&GAS* 105 (1987), 183–211.

—— '"By quick and by dead": Wills and Pious Provision in Late Medieval Bristol', *EHR* 102 (1987), 837–58.

—— 'Chantries in Fifteenth-Century Bristol' (Univ. of Oxford D.Phil. thesis, 1981).

—— '"For the Increase of Divine Service": Chantries in the Parish in Late Medieval Bristol', *JEH* 36 (1985), 46–65.

BURNS, NORMAN T., *Christian Mortalism from Tyndale to Milton* (Cambridge, Mass.: Harvard University Press, 1972).

BURRAGE, CHAMPLIN, *The Early English Dissenters* (Cambridge: Cambridge University Press, 1912).

CARLYLE, R. M., and CARLYLE, A. J., *Hugh Latimer* (Boston: Houghton Mifflin, 1899).

CARSON, T. E., 'The Problem of Clerical Irregularities in the Late Medieval Church: An Example from Norwich', *Cath. Hist. Rev.*, 72 (1986), 185–200.

CHECKLAND, S. G., 'English Provincial Cities', *EHR* NS 6 (1953), 195–203.

CHESTER, ALLAN G., *Hugh Latimer, Apostle to the English* (Philadelphia: University of Pennsylvania Press, 1954).

CHEYNEY, C. R., 'William Lyndwood's Provinciale', *Medieval Texts and Studies* (Oxford: Clarendon Press, 1973), 158–84.

CHIBNALL, MARJORIE, 'Monks and Pastoral Work', *JEH* 18 (1967), 165–171.

CHRISMAN, MIRIAM U. *Strasbourg and the Reform: A Study in the Process of Change* (New Haven, Conn.: Yale University Press, 1967).

CHRISTIANSON, P., 'Reformers and the Church of England under Elizabeth and the Stuarts', *JEH* 31 (1980), 463–82.

CHRISTOPHERS, R., 'Social and Educational Background of the Surrey Clergy, 1520–1620' (Univ. of London, Ph.D. thesis, 1975).

CIPOLLA, CARLO M., *Before the Industrial Revolution: European Society and Economy, 1000–1700* (New York: Norton, 1976).

CLARK, PETER, *English Provincial Society: Religion, Politics, and Society in Kent, 1500–1640* (Hassocks: Harvester Press, 1976).

—— 'Reformation and Radicalism in Kentish Towns, *c.*1500–1553', in W. J. Mommsen (ed.), *Stadtburgertum und Adel in der Reformation* (London: German Hist. Institute, 5 (1979), 107–127.

—— (ed.), *The Early Modern Town* (London and New York: Longman, 1976).

—— (ed.), *The Transformation of English Provincial Towns* (London: Hutchinson & Co. Ltd., 1984).

—— and PAUL SLACK (eds.), *Crisis and Order in English Towns, 1500–1700* (Toronto: University of Toronto Press, 1972).

—— *English Towns in Transition, 1500–1700* (Oxford and New York: Oxford University Press, 1976).

CLAY, ROTHA MARY, *The Hermits and Anchorites of England* (London: Methuen & Co., 1914; repr., Detroit: Singing Tree Press, 1968).

—— *The Medieval Hospitals of England* (London: Methuen & Co., 1909).

CLEBSCH, WILLIAM A., *England's Earliest Protestants* (New Haven, Conn.: Yale University Press, 1964).

CLUTTERBUCK, R., 'Bishop Cheyney and the Recusants of the Diocese of Gloucester', *Trans. B&GAS* 5 (1875), 222–37.

COLE, H. *King Henry the Eighth's Scheme of Bishopricks* (London: Charles Knightis & Co., 1838).

COLLINSON, PATRICK, *Archbishop Grindal 1519–1583: The Struggle for a Reformed Church* (Berkeley and Los Angeles: University of California Press, 1979).

—— *The Birthpangs of Protestant England: Religious and Cultural Change in the Sixteenth and Seventeenth Centuries* (New York: St. Martin's Press, 1988).

—— 'A Comment: Concerning the Name Puritan', *JEH* 31 (1980), 483–8.

—— *The Elizabethan Puritan Movement* (Berkeley: University of California Press, 1967).

COLLINSON, PATRICK, *The Religion of Protestants: The Church in English Society, 1559–1625* (Oxford: Oxford University Press, 1982).

—— 'Toward a Broader Understanding of the Early Dissenting Tradition', in C. R. Cole and M. E. Moody (eds.), *The Dissenting Tradition* (Athens: Ohio University Press, 1975).

CONSTABLE, G., 'Resistance to Tithes in the Middle Ages', *JEH* 13 (1962), 172–85.

COOK, GEORGE H., *The English Mediaeval Parish Church* (London: Phoenix House Ltd., 1955).

—— *Letters to Cromwell on the Suppression of the Monasteries* (London: John Baker, 1965).

—— *Medieval Chantries and Chantry Chapels* (London: Phoenix House, 1947).

CREIGHTON, BISHOP MANDEL, 'The Italian Bishops of Worcester', in M. Creighton (ed.), *Historical Essays and Reviews* (London: Longman Green and Co., 1902), 202–34.

CROSS, CLAIRE, *Church and People, 1450–1660: Triumph of the Laity in the English Church* (Hassocks: Harvester Press, 1976).

—— '"Dens of loitering lubbers": Protestant Protest against Cathedral Foundations, 1540–1640', in Baker (ed.), *Schism, Heresy, and Religious Protest*, 231–8.

—— 'The Development of Protestantism in Leeds and Hull, 1520–1640: The Evidence from Wills', *Northern Hist.*, 18 (1982), 230–8.

—— 'From Estate to Profession: The Transformation of the English Clergy in the 16th and Early 17th Centuries', in P. Butel (ed.), *Sociétés et groupes sociaux en Aquitaine et en Angleterre* (Bordeaux: Fédération Historique du Sud-Ouest, 1979), 85–93.

—— 'The Incomes of Provincial Urban Clergy, 1520–1645' in O'Day and Heal (eds.), *Princes and Paupers in the English Church*, 65–89.

—— 'Parochial Structure and the Dissemination of Protestantism in Sixteenth-Century England: A Tale of Two Cities', in Baker (ed.), *The Church in Town and Countryside*, 269–78.

—— 'Priests into Ministers: The Establishment of Protestant Practice in the City of York, 1530–1630', in Peter N. Brooks (ed.), *Reformation Principle and Practice: Essays in Honor of A. G. Dickens* (London: Scolar Press, 1980), 205–25.

—— *York Clergy Wills 1520–1600: 1. Minster clergy* (York: Borthwick Inst. of Hist. Res.), 1984.

—— *York Clergy Wills 1520–1600: 2. Parish clergy* (York: Borthwick Inst. of Hist. Res., 1989).

CUMING, G. H. (ed.), *The Mission of the Church and the Propagation of the Faith* (Studies in Church History, 6; Cambridge: Cambridge University Press for the Ecclesiastical History Society, 1970).

—— *The Province of York*, Studies in Church History, 4 (1967).

—— and BAKER, DEREK (eds.), *Popular Belief and Practice* (Studies in Church History, 8; Cambridge: Cambridge University Press for the Ecclesiastical History Society, 1972).

DAELY, J. I., 'Pluralism in the Diocese of Canterbury during the Administration of Matthew Parker, 1559–1575', *JEH* 18 (1967), 33–49.

DARBY, HAROLD S., *Hugh Latimer* (London: Epworth Press, 1953).

DAVIES, HORTON, *Worship and Theology in England from Cranmer to Hooker, 1534–1603*, vol. 1 of 2 vols. (Princeton, NJ: Princeton University Press, 1970).

DAVIS, J. F., *Heresy and Reformation in the South East of England 1520–1558* (RHS Studies in History, 34; London, 1983).

—— 'Lollardy and the Reformation in England.' *Archiv für Reformationsgeschichte*, 73 (1982), 217–37.

DAVIS, JOHN, 'Joan of Kent, Lollardy, and the English Reformation', *JEH* 33 (1982), 225–33.

DAVIS, NATALIE ZEMON, *Society and Culture in Early Modern France* (Palo Alto, Calif.: Stanford University Press, 1985).

DEMAUS, ROBERT, *Hugh Latimer* (London: Religious Tract Society, 1904).

DICKENS, A. G., 'Aspects of Intellectual Transition among the English Parish Clergy of the Reformation Period', *Archiv für Reformationsgeschichte*, 43 (1952), 51–70.

—— 'Early Protestantism and the Church in Northamptonshire', *Northamptonshire P&P* 7 (1983), 27–39.

—— 'The Edwardian Arrears in Augmentations Payments and the Problem of the Ex-religious', *EHR* 55 (1940), 384–418.

—— *The English Reformation* (New York: Schocken Books, 1964; London: Batsford, 1989).

—— 'Heresy and the Origins of English Protestantism', in J. S. Bromley and E. H. Kossman (eds.), *Britain and the Netherlands* (London: Chatto & Windus, 1960), ii. 47–66.

—— *Lollards and Protestants in the Diocese of York, 1509–1555*, 2nd edn. (Oxford: Oxford University Press, 1982).

—— *The Marian Reaction in the Diocese of York*, part I, 'The Clergy'; part II, 'The Laity' (York: St Anthony's Hall Publications, 11 and 12, 1957).

—— 'A Municipal Dissolution of Chantries at York, 1536', *York Arch. Journal*, 36 (1944–7), 164–73.

—— 'The Shape of Anticlericalism and the English Reformation', in E. I. Kouri and T. Scott (eds.), *Politics and Society in Reformation Europe: Essays for Sir Geoffrey Elton on his Sixty-Fifth Birthday* (Basingstoke and London: Macmillan, 1987), 379–411.

The Dictionary of National Biography, ed. Leslie Stephen and Sidney Lee, 63 vols. (London and New York: Oxford University Press, 1885–1900).

DOBSON, BARRIE (ed.), *The Church, Politics, and Patronage in the Fifteenth Century* (Gloucester: Allan Sutton, and New York: St Martins, 1984).

—— 'Mendicant Ideal and Practice and Late Medieval York', in P. V. Addyman and V. E. Black (eds.), *Archeological Papers from York Presented to M. W. Barley* (York: York Archeological Trust, 1984).

—— 'The Residentiary Canons of York in the Fifteenth Century', *JEH* 30 (1979), 145–74.

DOBSON, R. B., 'Cathedral Chapters and Cathedral Cities: York, Durham and Carlisle in the Fifteenth Century', *Northern Hist.*, 19 (1983), 15–44.

—— *Durham Priory, 1400–1450* (Cambridge: Cambridge University Press, 1973).

—— 'The Foundation of Perpetual Chantries by the Citizens of Medieval York', in Cuming (ed.), *Province of York*, 22–38.

DOLAN, CLAIRE, 'L'Image du protestant et le conseil municipal d'Aix au Sules', *Renaissance and Reformation*, NS 4 (1980), 152–64.

DuBOULAY, F. R. H., 'The Quarrel between the Carmelite Friars and the Secular Clergy of London, 1464–68', *JEH* 6 (1955), 156–74.

DYER, A. P., *The City of Worcester in the Sixteenth Century* (Leicester: Leicester University Press, 1973).

ELLIS, HENRY, *Original Letters, Illustrative of English History*. 3rd ser., 4 vols. London, 1846.

ELTON, G. R., *Policy and Police: The Enforcement of the Reformation in the Age of Thomas Cromwell* (Cambridge: Cambridge University Press, 1972).

EMDEN, A. B., *A Biographical Register of the University of Cambridge to 1500* (Cambridge: Cambridge University Press, 1963).

—— *A Biographical Register of the University of Oxford, to A.D. 1500* (Oxford: Oxford University Press, 1957–9).

—— *A Biographical Register of the University of Oxford, A.D. 1501–1540* (Oxford: Clarendon Press, 1974).

—— *A Survey of Dominicans in England, 1268–1538* (Rome: Istituto Storico Domenicano, Santa Sabina, Dissertationes Historicae, 1967).

EVANS, JOHN, *Chronological Outline of the History of Bristol* (Bristol: J. Arrowsmith, 1900).

EVANS, JOHN T., *Seventeenth Century Norwich: Politics, Religion, and Government, 1620–1690* (Oxford: Oxford University Press, 1979).

EVERITT, ALAN (ed.), *Perspectives in English Urban History* (London: Macmillan, 1973).

FERMOY, BERYL, *The Dominican Order in England before the Reformation* (London: Society for Promoting Christian Knowledge, 1925).

FIELD, COLIN W., *The Province of Canterbury and the Elizabethan Settlement of Religion* (Robertsbridge, Sussex: C. W. Field, 1973).

FINES, JOHN, 'Heresy trials in the Diocese of Coventry and Lichfield, 1511–12', *JEH* 14 (1963), 160–74.

FLETCHER, J. M., and UPTON, C. A. 'Expenses at *Admission* and *Determination* in Fifteenth-Century Oxford: New Evidence', *EHR* 100 (1985), 331–7.

FOSTER, ANDREW, 'The Function of a Bishop: The Career of Richard Neile, 1562–1604', in O'Day and Heal (eds.), *Continuity and Change* 33–54.

FOSTER, JOSEPH, *Alumni Oxonienses*, pt. I, 4 vols. (Oxford and London: Parker and Company, 1888–91).

FRASER, DEREK, 'The Pied Piper and the Magpie: Current Work in Urban History', *JBS* 25 (1986), 227–33.

FRERE, WALTER H., *The English Church in the Reigns of Elizabeth and James I* (New York: Macmillan, 1904).

—— *The Marian Reaction in its Relation to the English Clergy* (London: Church Historical Society, 18, 1896).

GAIRDNER, J., *The English Church in the Sixteenth Century from the Accession of Henry VIII to the Death of Mary* (London: Macmillan, 1904).

GARRETT, CHRISTINA H., *The Marian Exiles* (Cambridge: Cambridge University Press, 1938).

GEE, HENRY, *The Elizabethan Clergy and the Settlement of Religion, 1558–1576* (Oxford: Clarendon Press, 1898).

GEORGE, E. and GEORGE, S., *Guide to the Probate Inventories of the Diocese of Bristol (1542–1804)* (Gloucester: Bristol Record Society and B&GAS, 1988).

GORING, JEREMY, 'The Reformation of the Ministry in Elizabethan Sussex', *JEH* 34 (1983), 345–66.

GOTTFRIED, ROBERT S., *Bury St. Edmunds and the Urban Crisis, 1290–1539* (Princeton, NJ: Princeton University Press, 1982).

GRAY, IRVINE, and RALPH, ELIZABETH (eds.), *Guide to the Parish Records of the City of Bristol and the County of Gloucester* (Gloucester: B&GAS Records Section, 1963).

GRIM, HAROLD, J., *The Reformation Era 1500–1650* (New York: Macmillan, 1954, 1965; repr. 1966).

GROVE, HENRY, *Alienated Tithes in Impropriated Parishes, Commuted or Merged under Local Statutes and the Tithe Acts: Together with all Crown Grants of Tithes, Henry VIII to William III* (London: printed by author, 1896).

GUMBLEY, WALTER, *The Cambridge Dominicans* (Oxford: Oxford University Press, 1938).

HAIGH, CHRISTOPHER, 'Anticlericalism and the English Reformation', *History*, 68 (1983), 391–407.

—— 'Finance and Administration in a New Diocese: Chester, 1541–1641', in O'Day and Heal (eds.), *Continuity and Change* 145–66.

—— 'From Monopoly to Minority: Catholicism in Early Modern England', *TRHS* 5th ser. 31 (1981), 129–47.

—— 'Puritan Evangelism in the Reign of Elizabeth I', *EHR* 92 (1977), 30–58.

HAIGH, CHRISTOPHER, 'The Recent Historiography of the English Reformation', *HJ* 25 (1982), 995–1007.

—— *Reformation and Resistance in Tudor Lancashire* (Cambridge: Cambridge University Press, 1975).

—— 'Revisionism, the Reformation and the History of English Catholicism' (with a reply by Patrick McGrath), *JEH* 36 (1985), 394–406.

—— 'Some Aspects of the Recent Historiography of the English Reformation', in Mommsen (ed.), *Stadtburgertum und Adel in der Reformation*, 88–106.

—— (ed.), *The English Reformation Revised* (Cambridge: Cambridge University Press, 1987).

HAINES, ROY M., *The Administration of the Diocese of Worcester in the First Half of the Fourteenth Century* (London: Society for the Preservation of Christian Knowledge, 1965).

—— ' "Wild Wittes and Wilfulnes": John Swetstock's Attack on Those "Poysunmongeres", the Lollards', in Cuming and Baker (eds.), *Popular Belief and Practice*, 143–53.

HALL, BASIL, 'The Early Rise and Gradual Decline of Lutheranism in England (1520–1600)', in Baker (ed.), *Reform and Reformation*, 103–33.

HANAWALT, BARBARA A., 'Keepers of the Lights: Late Medieval English Parish Gilds', *Journal of Medieval and Renaissance Studies*, 14 (1984), 21–37.

HARGRAVE, O. T., 'The Predestinarian Controversy among the Marian Protestant Prisioners', *Historical Magazine of the Protestant Episcopal Church*, 47 (1978), 131–51.

HARPER-BILL, CHRISTOPHER, 'Archbishop John Morton and Canterbury, 1486–1500', *JEH* 29 (1978), 1–21.

HART, A. TINDALL, *The Country Clergy, 1558–1660* (London: Phoenix House Ltd., 1958).

HARTRIDGE, R. A. R., *A History of Vicarages in the Middle Ages* (Cambridge: Cambridge University Press, 1930).

HAUGAARD, WILLIAM P., *Elizabeth and the English Reformation: The Struggle for a Stable Settlement of Religion* (Cambridge: Cambridge University Press, 1968).

HEAL, FELICITY, 'Clerical Tax Collection under the Tudors: The Influence of the Reformation', in O'Day and Heal (eds.), *Continuity and Change*, 97–124.

—— 'Economic Problems of the Clergy', Heal and O'Day (eds.), *Church and Society in England*, 1976.

—— *Of Prelates and Princes: A Study of the Economic and Social Position of the Tudor Episcopate* (Cambridge: Cambridge University Press, 1980).

—— and O'DAY, ROSEMARY (eds.), *Church and Society in England: Henry VIII to James I* (Hamden, Conn.: Archon Books, 1977).

HEATH, PETER, *The English Parish Clergy on the Eve of the Reformation* (London: Routledge & Kegan Paul; Toronto: University of Toronto Press, 1969).

—— 'Urban Piety in the Later Middle Ages: The Evidence of Hull Wills', in Dobson, (ed.), *The Church, Politics, and Patronage in the Fifteenth Century*, 209–34.

HEMBRY, PHYLLIS M., *The Bishops of Bath and Wells, 1540–1640: Social and Economic Problems* (London: Athlone Press, 1967).

HILL, CHARLES P., *The History of Bristol Grammar School* (London: Pitman, 1951).

HILL, CHRISTOPHER, *Economic Problems of the Church from Archbishop Whitgift to the Long Parliament* (Oxford: Clarendon Press, 1958).

—— 'From Lollards to Levellers', in Maurice Cornforth (ed.), *Rebels and their Causes: Essays in Honour of A. L. Morton* (London: Lawrence and Wishardt, 1978, 49–68).

HILL, GEOFFREY, *English Dioceses: A History of their Limits from the Earliest Time to the Present Day* (London: Elliot Stock, 1900).

HILL, J. W. F., *Tudor and Stuart Lincoln* (Cambridge: Cambridge University Press, 1956).

HINNEBUSCH, WILLIAM, *The History of the Dominican Order*, 2 vols. (Staten Island, NY: Alba House, 1965, 1973).

HOCKADAY, FRANK S., 'The Consistory Court of the Diocese of Gloucester', *Trans. B&GAS* 46 (1924), 195–287.

HODGETT, G. A. J., 'The Unpensioned Ex-Religious in Tudor England', *JEH*, 13 (1962), 195–202.

HOHENBERG, PAUL M., and LEES, LYNN HOLLEN, *The Making of Urban Europe, 1000–1950* (Cambridge, Mass.: Harvard University Press, 1985).

HOLDERNESS, B. P., 'The Clergy as Money-Lenders in England, 1550–1700', O'Day and Heal (eds.), *Princes and Paupers*, 195–210.

HOSKINS, W. G., *The Age of Plunder: King Henry's England, 1500–1546* (London and New York: Longman, 1976).

—— 'English Provincial Towns in the Early Sixteenth Century', in Peter Clark (ed.), *The Early Modern Town* (London and New York: Longman, 1976), 91–105.

—— 'The Leicester Country Parson in the Sixteenth Century', *Trans. Leicester Arch. Soc.*, 21 (1940), 90–114.

—— *Provincial England: Essays in Social and Economic History* (London: Macmillan; New York: St Martins Press, 1963).

HOULBROOKE, RALPH, *Church Courts and the People during the English Reformation, 1520–1570* (Oxford and New York: Oxford University Press, 1979).

—— 'The Decline of Ecclesiastical Jurisdiction under the Tudors', in O'Day and Heal (eds.), *Continuity and Change*, 239–58.

—— 'The Protestant Episcopate, 1547–1603: The Pastoral Contribution', in Heal and O'Day (eds.), *Church and Society*, 78–98.

HUDD, A. E., 'The Chapel of the Assumption on Old Bristol Bridge', *Proc. Clifton Antiq. Club*, 4 (1897–9), 1–11.

—— 'Two Bristol Calendars, Fox MS.', *Trans. B&GAS*, 19 (1895), 85–141.

HUDSON, ANNE, 'The Examination of Lollards', *BIHR* 46 (1973), 145–59.

—— *Lollards and their Books* (London: Hambledon Press, 1985).

—— 'Some Aspects of Lollard Book Production', in D. Baker (ed.), *Schism, Heresy and Religious Protest*, 147–57.

HUGHES, PHILIP, *The Reformation in England* (New York: Macmillan, 1951–4; 5th rev. edn., 1963; 3 vols. in 1).

HUGHES, PHILIP EDGCUMBE, *Theology of the English Reformers* (London: Hodder & Stoughton, 1965).

HUTTON, EDWARD, *The Franciscans in England 1224–1538* (London: Constable & Company Ltd., 1926).

HUTTON, RONALD, 'The Local Impact of the Tudor Reformations', in Haigh (ed.), *The English Reformation Revised*, 114–38.

HYETT, FRANCIS A., *The Bibliographer's Manual of Gloucestershire Literature*, 3 vols. (Gloucester: J. Bellows, 1895–7).

—— 'Catalogue of Mss. in the British Museum relating to the County of Gloucester and the City of Bristol', *Trans. B&GAS* 20 (1897), 161–221.

—— and AUSTIN, R., *Supplement to the Bibliographer's Manual of Gloucestershire Literature*, 2 vols. (Gloucester, 1915–16).

JACK, SYBIL, 'The Last Days of the Smaller Monasteries in England', *JEH* 21 (1970), 97–124.

JACKSON, W. A., FERGUSON, F. J., and PANTZER, K. F. (eds.), *A Short-Title Catalogue of Books Printed in England, Scotland, and Ireland and of the English Books Printed Abroad 1475–1640* (London: Bibliographical Society, 1976, 1986).

JAMES, MERVYN, 'Ritual, Drama and Social Body in the Late Medieval English Town', *P&P* 98 (1983), 3–29.

JARRET, BEDE, *The London Dominicans* (London: Burns, Oates and Washbourne Ltd., 1921).

JENNINGS, MARGARET, 'Monks and the *Artes praedicandi* in the Time of Ranulph Higden', *Revue Benedictine*, 86 (1976), 119–28.

JOHNSON, ANNE MIDDLEMAS, 'The Reformation Clergy of Derbyshire, 1536–1559', *Derbyshire Arch. Journal* 100 (1980), 49–63.

JOHNSTON, A. F., 'The Guild of Corpus Christi and the Procession of Corpus Christi in York', *Medieval Studies.*, 38 (1976), 372–84.

JONES, DOUGLAS, *The Church in Chester, 1300–1540* (Manchester: Chetham Society, 3rd. ser., 7, 1957).

JONES, NORMAN, *Faith by Statute/Parliament and the Settlement of Religion 1559* (Cambridge: Cambridge University Press, 1982).

JORDAN, W. K., 'Charitable Institutions of England: Bristol and Somerset', *Trans. of the American Philosophical Society*, 50, pt. 8 (1960), 3–94.

KELLY, MICHAEL J., 'The Submission of the Clergy', *TRHS* 5th ser. 15 (1965), 97–119.

KENNEDY, W. P. M., *Elizabethan Episcopal Administration* (Alcuin Club Collections, 27, 1924).

KIRBY, ISABEL M. (comp.), *A Catalogue of the Records of the Bishop and Archdeacons of Gloucester* (Gloucester: City Corporation, 1968).

—— *A Catalogue of the Records of the Dean and Chapter of Gloucester* (Gloucester: City Corporation, 1968).

—— *A Catalogue of the Records of the Bishop and Archdeacons and of the Dean and Chapter of Bristol Diocese* (Bristol: City Corporation, 1970).

KITCHING, C. J., 'The Quest for Concealed Lands in the Reign of Elizabeth I', *TRHS* 5th ser. 24 (1974), 63–78.

KNAPPEN, MARSHALL M., *Tudor Puritanism: A Chapter in the History of Idealism* (Chicago and London: University of Chicago Press, 1939; repr. 1970).

KNOWLES, DAVID, *The Religious Orders in England*, vol. 3, *The Tudors* (Cambridge: Cambridge University Press, 1959).

—— and HADDOCK, R. NEVILLE, *Medieval Religious Houses* (London and New York: Longmans, Green & Co., 1953).

KREIDER, ALAN, *English Chantries: The Road to Dissolution* (Cambridge, Mass.: Harvard Historical Studies, 97, 1979).

LAMONT, WILLIAM, 'The Rise of Arminianism Reconsidered', *P&P* 107 (1985), 225–331.

LANDER, STEPHEN, 'Church Courts and the Reformation in the Diocese of Chichester, 1500–58', in O'Day and Heal (eds.), *Continuity and Change*, 215–37.

LATIMER, JOHN, *The Annals of Bristol in the Seventeenth Century* (Bristol: W. George, 1900).

—— *The Annals of Bristol in the Sixteenth-Century* (Bristol: J. Arrowsmith, 1908; repr. London: Redwood Press, 1970).

—— *The History of the Society of Merchant Venturers of the City of Bristol, with Some Account of the Anterior Merchants' Guilds* (Bristol: Arrowsmith, 1903).

—— 'The Hospital of St. John, Bristol', *Trans. B&GAS* 24 (1901), 72–8.

—— 'The Maire of Bristowe is Kalendar: Its List of Civic Officers Collated with Contemporary Legal Manuscripts', *Trans. B&GAS* 26, pt. 1 (1903), 108–37.

LAWRENCE, CLIFFORD H., *Medieval Monasticism: Forms of Religious Life in Western Europe in the Middle Ages* (London and New York: Longman, 1984).

LEADAM, I. S. (ed.), *Select Cases in the Star Chamber* (London: Selden Society, 1910).

LEHMBERG, STANFORD, *The Later Parliaments of Henry VIII, 1536–1547* (Cambridge: Cambridge University Press, 1977).

—— *The Reformation of Cathedrals: Cathedrals in English Society, 1485–1603* (Princeton, NJ: Princeton University Press, 1988).

LEHMBERG, STANFORD, *The Reformation Parliament* (Cambridge: Cambridge University Press, 1970).

LEIGHTON, WILFRID, 'Endowed Charity in Bristol and Gloucester', *Trans. B&GAS* 67 (1948) 1–24.

LITTLE, A. G., 'Educational Organisation of the Mendicant Friars in England (Dominicans and Franciscans)', *TRHS*, NS 8 (1894), 49–70.

—— 'Personal Tithes', *EHR* 60 (1945), 67–88.

—— and EASTERLING, R. C., *The Franciscans and Dominicans of Exeter* (Exeter: A. Wheaton & Co., 1927).

LITTLE, L. K., *Religious Poverty and the Profit Economy in Medieval Europe* (Ithaca, NY: Cornell University Press, 1978).

LLOYD, RACHEL, *Dorset Elizabethans at Home and Abroad* (London: John Murray, 1967).

LOACH, JENNIFER, 'The Marian Establishment and the Printing Press', *EHR* 101 (1986), 135–48.

—— 'Protestant Sectarianism in England', in *The Church in a Changing Society* (Uppsala: Swedish Society of Church History, NS 30, 1978).

LOBEL, M. D., and CARUS-WILSON, E. M., *Historic Towns, Bristol* (London: Scolar Press, 1975).

LUSARDI, J. P., 'The Career of Robert Barnes', in L. A. Schuster *et al.* (eds.), *The Complete Works of St Thomas More*, vol. 8., *1365–1415* (New Haven, Conn., and London: Yale University Press, 1973).

LYNCH, MICHAEL, 'From Privy Kirk to Burgh Church: An Alternative View of the Process of Protestantization', in Norman MacDougall (ed.), *Church, Politics and Society: Scotland 1408–1929* (Edinburgh: John Donald Publishers Ltd., 1983), 85–96.

MACCAFFREY, WALLACE T., *Exeter, 1540–1640*, 2nd. edn. (Cambridge, Mass.: Harvard University Press, 1976).

MCGRATH, PATRICK, 'Elizabethan Catholicism: A Reconsideration', *JEH* 35 (1984), 414–28.

—— 'Gloucestershire and the Counter-Reformation in the Reign of Elizabeth I', *Trans. B&GAS* 88 (1969), 5–28.

—— (ed.), *Merchants and Merchandise in Seventeenth-Century Bristol* (BRS, 19; Bristol Record Society, 1955).

—— 'The Wills of Bristol Merchants in the Great Orphan Books', *Trans. B&GAS* 68 (1949), 91–109.

—— and ROWE, JOY, 'Anstruther Analysed: The Elizabethan Seminary Priests', *Recusant Hist.* 18 (1986), 1–13.

—— 'The Marian Priests under Elizabeth I', *Recusant Hist.* 17 (1984), 103–21.

MCGUIRE, BRIAN PATRICK, *Friendship and Community: The Monastic Experience 350–1250* (Kalamazoo, Mich.: Cistercian Publications, 1988).

MCHARDY, A. K., 'Clerical Taxation in Fifteenth-Century England: The

Clergy as Agents of the Crown', in Dobson (ed.), *The Church, Politics, and Patronage in the Fifteenth Century*, 168–92.

McNAB, B., 'Obligations of the Church in English Society: Military Arrays of the Clergy, 1369–1418', in W. C. Jordan, *et al.* (eds.), *Order and Innovation in the Middle Ages* (Princeton, NJ: Princeton University Press, 1976), 293–314 and 516–22.

MALDEN, H. E., 'Notes on the Local Progress of Protestantism in England in the Sixteenth and Seventeenth Centuries', *TRHS* 2nd. ser. 2 (1885), 61–76.

MANNING, ROGER B., *Religion and Society in Elizabethan Sussex: A Study of the Enforcement of the Religious Settlement* (Leicester: Leicester University Press, 1969).

MARCHANT, RONALD A., *The Church Under the Law: Justice, Administration and Discipline in the Diocese of York, 1560–1640* (London: Cambridge University Press, 1969).

—— *The Puritans and the Church Courts in the Diocese of York, 1560–1642* (London: Longmans, 1960).

MARCOMBE, DAVID, 'The Durham Dean and Chapter: Old Abbey Writ Large?', in O'Day and Heal, (eds.), *Continuity and Change*, 125–44.

MARTIN, G. H., 'Church Life in Medieval Leicester', in A. E. Brown (ed.), *The Growth of Leicester* (Leicester: Leicester University Press, 1970).

MARTIN, J. W., 'Christopher Vitel: An Elizabethan Mechanik Preacher', *Sixteenth Century Journal.*, 10 (1979), 15–22.

—— 'The Protestant Underground Congregations of Mary's Reign', *JEH* 35 (1984), 519–38.

MASON, EMMA, 'The Role of the English Parishioner, 1100–1500', *JEH* 27 (1976), 17–29.

MAYHEW, G. J., 'The Progress of the Reformation in East Sussex 1530–1559: The Evidence from Wills', *Southern History*, 5 (1983), 38–67.

MESSENGER, ERNST, *The Reformation, the Mass, and the Priesthood*, 2 vols. (London: Longmans, Green and Co., 1936–7).

MINCHONTON, W. E., 'Bristol—Metropolis of the West in the Eighteenth Century', in Clark (ed.), *The Early Modern Town* 297–313.

MOELLER, BERND, 'Imperial Cities and the Reformation', in B. Moeller, *Imperial Cities and the Reformation*, ed. H. C. Erik Midelfort; trans. Mark U. Edwards, Jr. (Philadelphia: Fortress Press, 1972), 41–115.

—— 'The Town in Church History: General Presuppositions of the Reformation in Germany', in Baker (ed.), *The Church in Town and Countryside*, 257–68.

MOMMSEN, W. J., (ed.), *Stadtburgertum und Adel in der Reformation/The Urban Classes, the Nobility and the Reformation* (German Hist. Institute, London, 5, 1979).

MOORMAN, J. R. H., 'The Foreign Element among the English Franciscans', *EHR* 62 (1947), 289–303.

MOORMAN, J. R. H., *The Grey Friars in Cambridge 1225–1538* (Cambridge: Cambridge University Press, 1952).

MORAN, JO ANN HOEPPNER, 'Clerical Recruitment in the Diocese of York, 1340–1530: Data and Commentary', *JEH* 34 (1983), 19–54.

—— *The Growth of English Schooling, 1340–1548: Learning, Literacy, and Laicization in Pre-Reformation York Diocese* (Princeton, NJ: Princeton University Press, 1985).

MORGAN, E. T., *A History of the Bristol Cathedral School* (Bristol: J. Arrowsmith, 1913).

MULLINS, E. L. C., 'The Effects of the Marian and Elizabethan Religious Settlements upon the Clergy of London, 1553–1564', (Univ. of London, MA thesis, 1948).

MURRAY, JAQUELINE, 'Kinship and Friendship: The Perception of Family by Clergy and Laity in Late Medieval London', *Albion*, 20 (1988), 369–85.

NEALE, JOHN, *Elizabeth and her Parliaments* (London: Jonathan Cape, 1953).

NICHOLLS, J. F., 'The Free Grammar School of Bristol and the Thornes, its Founders', *TRHS* 8 (1872), 311–23.

—— and TAYLOR, JOHN, *Bristol, Past and Present*, 3 vols. (Bristol: J. Arrowsmith, 1881–2).

NICHOLS, ANN ELJENHOLM, 'The Etiquette of Pre-Reformation Confession in East Anglia', *Sixteenth Century Journal*, 17 (1986), 145–63.

O'DAY, ROSEMARY, *The Debate on the English Reformation* (London and New York: Methuen, 1986).

—— *The English Clergy: The Emergence and Consolidation of a Profession, 1558–1642* (Leicester: Leicester University Press, 1979).

—— 'The Reformation of the Ministry, 1558–1642', in O'Day and Heal (eds.), *Continuity and Change*, 55–76.

—— 'The Role of the Registrar in Diocesan Administration', in O'Day and Heal (eds.), *Continuity and Change*, 77–96.

—— and HEAL, FELICITY, (eds.), *Continuity and Change* (Leicester: Leicester University Press, 1976).

——*Princes and Paupers in the English Church, 1500–1800* (Totowa, NJ: Barnes and Noble, 1981).

ORME, NICHOLAS, 'Education at a Medieval Cathedral: Exeter', *JEH*, 32 (1981), 265–83.

—— *Education in the West of England, 1066–1548* (Exeter: Exeter University Press, 1976).

—— *Exeter Cathedral as it Was 1050–1550* (Exeter: Devon Books, 1986).

—— 'A Grammatical Miscellany from Bristol and Wiltshire', in N. Orme, *Education and Society in Medieval and Renaissance England* (London: Hambledon Press, 1989).

—— 'The Guild of Kalendars, Bristol', *Trans. B&GAS*, 96 (1978), 35–52.

OWEN, DOROTHY M., *Church and Society in Medieval Lincolnshire* (Lincoln: Lincolnshire Local History Soc., 1971).

—— *The Records of the Established Church of England* (Archives and the User, 1; London: British Record Association, 1970).

OWEN, H. GARETH, 'The Episcopal Visitation: Its Limits and Limitation in Elizabethan London', *JEH* 11 (1960), 179–85.

—— 'The London Parish Clergy in the Reign of Elizabeth I', (Univ. of London, Ph.D. thesis, 1957).

—— 'Parochial Curates in Elizabethan London', *JEH* 10 (1959), 66–73.

OWST, G. R., *Preaching in Medieval England* (Cambridge: Cambridge University Press, 1926).

OXLEY, J. E., *The Reformation in Essex to the Death of Mary* (Manchester: Manchester University Press, 1965).

OZMENT, STEVEN E., *The Reformation in the Cities* (New Haven, Conn.: Yale University Press, 1975).

PALLISER, DAVID M., 'Civic Mentality and the Environment in Tudor York', *Northern Hist.*, 18 (1982), 78–115.

—— 'Popular Reactions to the Reformation during the Years of Uncertainty, 1530–70', in Heal and O'Day (eds.), *Church and Society* (Hamden, Conn., 1977), 35–56.

—— *The Reformation in York, 1534–1553* (York: St Anthony's Press, 1971).

—— *Tudor York* (Oxford and New York: Oxford University Press, 1979).

PANTIN, W. A., 'Chantry Priests' Houses and Other Medieval Lodgings', *Medieval Archeology*, 3 (1959), 216–58.

—— 'Medieval Priests' Houses in South-West England', *Medieval Archeology*, 1 (1957), 118–46.

PHELPS BROWN, E. H., and HOPKINS, SHEILA V., 'Seven Centuries of the Price of Consumables, Compared with Builders' Wages Rates', *Economica*, 2nd ser. 23 (1956) 179–96; repr. in E. M. Carus-Wilson (ed.), *Essays in Economic History*, 2 (London: E. Arnold, 1962), 168–96.

PHYTHIAN-ADAMS, CHARLES, 'Ceremony and the Citizen: The Communal Year at Coventry, 1450–1550', in Clark (ed.), *Early Modern Town*, 106–28.

—— *Desolation of a City: Coventry and the Urban Crisis of the Late Middle Ages* (Cambridge and New York: Cambridge University Press, 1979).

PLATT, COLIN, *The English Medieval Town* (London: Secker & Warburg, 1976).

POGSON, R. H., 'The Legacy of the Schism: Confusion, Continuity, and Change in the Marian Clergy', in J. Loach and R. Tittler (eds.), *The Mid-Tudor Polity, c.1540–1560* (Totawa, NJ: Rowman & Littlefield, 1980), 116–36.

—— 'Revival and Reform in Mary Tudor's Church: A Question of Money', *JEH* 25 (1974), 249–65.

POLAND, E. B., *The Friars in Sussex, 1228–1928* (Hove, Sussex: Combridges, 1928).

POUND, JOHN, 'Clerical Poverty in Early Sixteenth-Century England: Some East Anglian Evidence', *JEH*, 37 (1986), 389–96.

POWELL, K. G., 'The Beginnings of Protestantism in Gloucestershire', *Trans. B&GAS* 90 (1971), 141–57.

—— *The Marian Martyrs and the Reformation in Bristol* (Bristol: Bristol Historical Association, 1972).

—— 'The Social Background to the Reformation in Gloucestershire', *Trans. B&GAS* 92 (1973), 96–120.

POWICKE, SIR F. MAURICE, and FRYDE, E. B. (eds.), *Handbook of British Chronology*, 2nd edn. (London: Royal Historical Society, 1961).

PRICE, F. DOUGLAS, 'The Abuse of Excommunication and the Decline of Ecclesiastical Discipline under Queen Elizabeth', *EHR* 57 (1942), 106–15.

—— *The Commission for Ecclesiastical Causes within the Diocese of Bristol and Gloucester, 1574* (Gloucester: B&GAS Records Section, 10, 1972).

—— 'The Elizabethan Apparitors in the Diocese of Gloucester', *Church Quarterly Rev.*, 134 (1942), 37–55.

—— (ed.), 'The Commissioners for Ecclesiastical Causes for the Dioceses of Bristol and Gloucester, 1574', *Trans. B&GAS* 59, (1938), 61–184.

PRUETT, JOHN H., *The Parish Clergy under the Later Stuarts: The Leicestershire Experience* (Urbana, Chicago, London: University of Illinois Press, 1978).

REYNOLDS, SUSAN, *An Introduction to the History of English Medieval Towns* (Oxford: Clarendon Press, 1977).

RICHARDSON, H. G., 'The Parish Clergy of the Thirteenth and Fourteenth Centuries', *TRHS* 3rd ser. 6 (1912), 89–128.

ROBERTSON, CRAIG A., 'The Tithe-Heresy of Friar William Russell', *Albion*, 8 (1976), 1–16.

ROGERS, FRANK H., 'The Bristol Craft Gilds during the Sixteenth and Seventeenth Centuries' (Bristol Univ., MA thesis, 1949).

ROTH, FRANCIS X., *The English Austin Friars, 1249–1538*, 2 vols. (New York: Augustinian Historical Institute, 1961–6).

ROWSE, A. L., *The England of Elizabeth* (Madison: University of Wisconsin Press, 1950).

RUBIN, MIRI, *Corpus Christi: The Eucharist in Late Medieval Culture* (Cambridge: Cambridge University Press, 1991).

RUPP, E. GORDON, *Studies in the Making of the English Protestant Tradition* (Cambridge: Cambridge University Press, 1947).

RUSSELL, ELIZABETH, 'The Influx of Commoners into the University of Oxford before 1581: An Optical Illusion?' *EHR* 92 (1977), 721–45.

RUSSELL, JOSIAH COX, 'The Clerical Population of Medieval England', *Traditio*, 2 (1944), 177–212.

SABIN, ARTHUR, 'Compotus Rolls of St Augustine's Abbey, Bristol', *Trans. B&GAS*, 73 (1954), 192–207.

SACKS, DAVID HARRIS, 'The Demise of the Martyrs: The Feasts of St. Clement and St. Katherine in Bristol, 1400–1600', *Social History*, 11 (1986), 141–69.

—— *Trade, Society, and Politics in Bristol, 1500–1640* (New York and London: Garland, 1985).

—— *The Widening Gate: Bristol and the Atlantic Economy, 1450–1700* (Berkeley: University of California Press, 1991).

SAUL, NIGEL, 'The Religious Sympathies of the Gentry in Gloucestershire, 1200–1500', *Trans. B&GAS* 98 (1980), 99–112.

SCARISBRICK, J. J., 'Clerical Taxation in England, 1485–1547', *JEH* 11 (1960), 41–54.

—— *Henry VIII* (London: Methuen, 1968).

—— *The Reformation and the English People* (Oxford: Basil Blackwell, 1984).

SCHILLING, HEINZ, 'The Reformation and the Hanseatic Cities', *Sixteenth Century Journal*, 14 (1983), 443–56.

SEAVER, PAUL S., *The Puritan Lectureships: The Politics of Religious Dissent, 1560–1662* (Palo Alto, Calif.: Stanford University Press, 1970).

SEYER, SAMUEL, *Memoirs Historical and Topographical of Bristol*, 2 vols. (Bristol: J. M. Gutch, 1821–3).

SHEILS, WILLIAM J., 'Religion in Provincial Towns: Innovation and Tradition', in Heal and O'Day (eds.), *Church and Society in England*, 156–76.

—— 'Some Problems of Government in a New Diocese: The Bishop and the Puritans in the Diocese of Peterborough, 1560–1630', in O'Day and Heal (eds.), *Continuity and Change*, 167–90.

SHEPPARD, ELAINE M., 'The Reformation and the Citizens of Norwich', *Norfolk Archeology*, 38 (1981), 44–58.

SKEETERS, MARTHA C., 'The Creation of the Diocese of Bristol', *Trans. B&GAS* 103 (1985), 175–8.

SIMON, JOAN, *Education and Society in Tudor England* (London and New York: Cambridge University Press, 1966).

SIMPSON, J. J., 'St. Peter's Hospital', *Trans. B&GAS* 48 (1926), 193–226.

SLACK, PAUL. 'Poverty and Politics in Salisbury, 1597–1666', in Clark and Slack, (eds.), *Crisis and Order in English Towns, 1500–1700*, 164–203.

—— 'Religious Protest and Urban Authority: The Case of Henry Sherfield, Iconoclast, 1633', in Baker (ed.), *Schism, Heresy, and Religious Protest*, 295–302.

SMITH, ALBERT E. (ed.), *Wills Proved in Gloucestershire Peculiar Courts* (Gloucester: City Libraries, Local History Pamphlet, 2, 1960).

SMITH, DAVID M., *Guide to Bishops' Registers of England and Wales: A Survey from the Middle Ages to the Abolition of Episcopacy in 1646* (London: RHS, 1981).

SOUTHERN, RICHARD W., *Western Society and the Church in the Middle Ages* (Harmondsworth: Penguin, 1970).

STEIG, MARGARET, 'The Parochial Clergy in the Diocese of Bath and Wells, 1625–1685' (Univ. of California at Berkeley Ph.D. diss., 1970).

—— 'Some Economic Aspects of Parochial Churches in the Diocese of Bath and Wells in the Seventeenth Century', *Albion*, 2 (1971), 212–22.

STONE, LAWRENCE, 'The Educational Revolution in England, 1560–1640', *P&P* 28 (1964), 41–80.

STOREY, R. L., *Diocesan Administration in the Fifteenth Century* (London and York: St Anthony's Hall Publications, 16, 1959).

STOWE, A. MONROE, *English Grammar Schools in the Reign of Queen Elizabeth* (New York: Columbia University Press, 1908).

STREET, FANNY, 'The Relations of the Bishops and Citizens of Salisbury, 1225–1612', *Wiltshire Magazine*, 39 (1916), 185–257, 319–66.

SWANSON, R. N., *Church and Society in Late Medieval England* (Oxford and New York: Basil Blackwell, 1989).

——'Problems of the Priesthood in Pre-Reformation England', *EHR* 105 (1990), 845–69.

—— 'Titles to Orders in Medieval English Episcopal Registers', in H. Mayr-Harting and R. I. Moore (eds.), *Studies in Medieval History Presented to R. H. C. Davis* (London: Hambledon Press, 1985).

—— 'Universities, Graduates, and Benefices in Late Medieval England', *P&P* 106 (1985), 28–61.

TANNER, NORMAN P., *The Church in Late Medieval Norwich 1370–1532* (Toronto: Pontifical Institute of Medieval Studies, 1984).

TAYLOR, C. S., 'The Chronological Sequence of the Bristol Parish Churches', *Trans. B&GAS* 32, pt. 2 (1909), 202–18.

—— 'The Religious Houses of Bristol and their Dissolution', *Trans. B&GAS* 29, pt. 1 (1906), 81–126.

—— 'Some Old Deeds belonging to the Church of St. Thomas, Bristol', *Proc. of the Clifton Antiquarian Club*, 1 (1888), 151–5.

THOMPSON, A. HAMILTON, 'Diocesan Organization in the Middle Ages: Archdeacons and Rural Deans', *Proc. Brit. Acad.*, 29 (1943), 153–94.

—— *The English Clergy and their Organization in the Later Middle Ages* (London: Clarendon Press, 1947).

—— 'Notes on the Ecclesiastical History of the Parish of Henbury', *Trans. B&GAS* 38 (1915), 99–186.

THOMSON, J. A. F., *The Later Lollards* (Oxford: Oxford University Press, 1965).

—— 'Piety and Charity in Late Medieval London', *JEH* 16 (1965), 178–95.

—— 'Tithe Disputes in Late Medieval London', *EHR* 78 (1963), 1–17.

THRUPP, SYLVIA, *The Merchant Class of Medieval London* (Chicago: University of Chicago Press, 1948).

TITTLER, ROBERT, 'The End of the Middle Ages in the English Country Town', *Sixteenth Century Journal*, 18 (1987), 471–87.

—— and BATTLEY, SUSAN, 'The Local Community and the Crown in 1553: The Accession of Mary Tudor Revisited', *BIHR* 67 (1984), 131–9.

TYLER, PHILIP, 'The Status of the Elizabethan Parochial Clergy', in Cuming (ed.), *Province of York*, 76–98.

VENN, J., and VENN, J. A., *Alumni Cantabrigenses*, pt. 1, 4 vols. (Cambridge: Cambridge University Press, 1922–7).

The Victoria History of the County of Cambridge and the Isle of Ely, ii (London, 1948).

—— *Cumberland*, ii (London, 1905).

—— *Dorset*, ii (London, 1908).

—— *Durham*, ii (London, 1907).

—— *Essex*, ii (London, 1907).

—— *Gloucester*, ii (London, 1972).

—— *Kent*, ii (London, 1926).

—— *Leicester*, ii (London, 1954).

—— *Lincoln*, ii (London, 1906).

—— *Norfolk*, ii (London, 1906).

—— *Northampton*, ii (London, 1906).

—— *Oxford*, ii (London, 1907).

—— *Somerset*, ii (London, 1969).

—— *Suffolk*, ii (London, 1907).

—— *Surrey*, ii (London, 1905).

—— *Warwick*, ii (London, 1965).

—— *Wiltshire*, iii (London, 1956).

WALKER, DAVID, SHIELDS, W. J., and KENT, JOHN (eds.), 'A Register of the Churches of the Monastery of St. Peter's Gloucester', in *An Ecclesiastical Miscellany* (Gloucester: B&GAS Records Section, 1976).

WALLACE, DEWEY D., jun., 'Puritan and Anglican: The Interpretation of Christ's Descent into Hell in Elizabethan Theology', *Archiv für Reformationsgeschichte*, 69 (1978), 248–87.

WARE, SEDLEY L., *The Elizabethan Parish in its Ecclesiastical and Financial Aspects* (Baltimore: Johns Hopkins Press, 1908).

WARREN, ANN K., *Anchorites and their Patrons in Medieval England* (Berkeley, Los Angeles, and London: University of California Press, 1985).

WARREN, R. H., 'The Medieval Chapels of Bristol', *Trans. B&GAS*, 30 (1907), 182–211.

WATT, MARGARET H., *The History of the Parson's Wife* (London: Faber & Faber, 1946).

WEAVER, F. W. (ed.), *Somerset Incumbents* (Bristol: C. T. Jeffries and Sons, 1889).

WHITE, PETER, 'The Rise of Arminianism Reconsidered', *P&P* 101 (1983), 34–54.

WILLIAMS, C. H., *William Tyndale* (London: Nelson, 1969).

WILLIAMS, EDITH, *The Chantries of William Canynges* (Bristol: W. George's Sons, 1950).

WILLIAMS, T. W., 'Gloucestershire Medieval Libraries', *Trans. B&GAS*, 31 (1908), 76–91.

WILSON, JANET M., 'An Edition of Roger Edgeworth's *Sermons very fruitfull, godly and learned*' (Univ. of Oxford, D.Phil. thesis, 1985).

—— 'Roger Edgeworth's Sermons: Reformation Preaching in Bristol', Proc. 4th Harlaxton Conference on Early Tudor England (1987), typescript.

WOODCOCK, BRIAN, *Medieval Ecclesiastical Courts in the Diocese of Canterbury* (Oxford: Oxford University Press, 1951).

WOOD-LEGH, K. L., *Perpetual Chantries in Britain* (London and New York: Cambridge University Press, 1965).

WOODWARD, G. W. O., *The Dissolution of the Monasteries* (London: Blandford Press, 1966, 1969).

YOUINGS, JOYCE A. (ed.), *The Dissolution of the Monasteries* (London: George Allen & Unwin; New York: Barnes and Noble 1971).

YOUNGS, F. J., 'The Tudor Government and Dissident Religious Books', in C. R. Cole and M. E. Moody (eds.), *The Dissenting Tradition* (Athens: Ohio University Press, 1975).

ZELL, MICHAEL L., 'Church and Gentry in Reformation Kent, 1533–53' (Univ. of California at Los Angeles, Ph. D. diss., 1974).

—— 'Economic Problems of the Parochial Clergy', in O'Day and Heal (eds.), *Princes and Paupers*, 19–43.

—— 'The Personnel of the Clergy of Kent in the Reformation Period', *EHR* 89 (1974), 513–33.

Index